Gypsies, Tinkers and Other Travellers

Gypsies, Tinkers and other Travellers

Edited by

Farnham Rehfisch,

Department of Sociology and Social Anthropology,
University of Hull, England

1975

Academic Press

London   New York   San Francisco
A Subsidiary of Harcourt Brace Jovanovich, Publishers

ACADEMIC PRESS INC., LONDON, LTD.
24–28 Oval Road
London NW1

United States Edition published by
ACADEMIC PRESS INC.
111 Fifth Avenue
New York, New York 10003

Library of Congress Catalog Card Number: 18503
ISBN 0 12 585850 7

PRINTED IN GREAT BRITAIN BY
WILLIAM CLOWES & SONS, LIMITED,
LONDON, BECCLES AND COLCHESTER

Preface

For some time I have been anxious to edit a book of this kind. This is not because literature dealing with Gypsies and Travellers (Tinkers) is not available in large quantities. For over two centuries books and articles have purported to record the life, history and culture of these people. Valuable studies are available primarily on their language history and folklore. Unfortunately, reliable studies on their social structure and social organization are few and far between. This is not surprising, since it is now widely recognized that to achieve this, requires long-term contact and intimate interaction with the groups concerned, or what social anthropologists usually term "participant observation". This requires long-term observation, gaining the confidence of informants and some training to "sort the wheat from the chaff". An example of how writers have been misled when such research is not done follows.

One evening I was sitting with some informants, and the conversation turned to Traveller marriage. Informants argued that the usual practice was that there was no particular ceremony. The young couple set up their own tent, caravan or whatever and were considered as "married". The literature is replete with tales of ceremonies of the couples jumping over bonfires, besoms, etc. Simson states that the Tinker priest collects earth in a bowl, mixes samples of the bride's and groom's wine with this and then hands the bowl to the two and states that unless they can separate the two samples, they must remain together.[1] When I repeated this to informants they roared with laughter and one very old man said this tale had been told by members of his family for many years. The explanation that he gave was that often they were asked about marriage customs by outsiders and if they gave a straightforward answer they would receive a small gift, or nothing at all. If the tale were embroidered, they would then receive a more generous donation. I attribute many of the more fantastic

---

1. Simson, W. (1865). *A History of the Gipsies*, pp. 260–261, London.

descriptions of their social institutions to this cause. A number of my fellow contributors writing on Gypsies agree with me on this point. The only means whereby one can learn about a society's customs is by gaining their real friendship and by observation.

It is only now that a volume of this kind can be produced, since it is only in the last few years that trained social anthropologists and sociologists have turned their attention to these groups. All contributors to this volume are trained researchers and have done intensive studies of the people of whom they have been writing. These two criteria were primordial in their selection. The fact that so few references are made to previous studies indicates that in other areas as well as Scotland these have proved unreliable.

It is welcome indeed, that at a time when these minority groups are being so severely pressurized by the growth of industrial society, the attention of scholars is being attracted by them. Hopefully this will lead to an amelioration of their plight. Perhaps empirical knowledge of their problems will lead to realistic schemes to help them maintain their liberty of action and human dignity.

I should like to thank the School of Scottish Studies in Edinburgh for financing the research my wife and I carried out on the Scots Travellers, and I am certain that my colleagues would join me in thanking those institutions which financed their own work where such help was granted.

FARNHAM REHFISCH

Contents

Contributors . . . . *v*

Preface . . . . *vii*

Chapter One
The American Rom: A Case of Economic Adaptation
ANNE SUTHERLAND 1

Chapter Two
American Rom and the Ideology of Defilement
CAROL MILLER 41

Chapter Three
Gypsies Travelling in Southern England
JUDITH OKELY 55

Chapter Four
Some Notes on Gypsies in North Britain
ANONYMOUS 85

Chapter Five
Boyash Gypsies: Shantytown Ethnicity
WILLIAM KORNBLUM 123

Chapter Six
Some Mānuš Conceptions and Attitudes
APARNA RAO 139

Chapter Seven
Kinship, Marriage, Law and Leadership in Two Urban Gypsy
Settlements in Spain
TERESA SAN ROMÁN 169

Chapter Eight
Ways of Looking at Roms: The Case of Czechoslovakia
WILLY GUY 201

Chapter Nine
Irish Travelling People
BETTINA BARNES 231

Chapter Ten
The Effects of Economic Change on Irish Traveller Sex Roles
and Marriage Patterns
GEORGE GMELCH 257

Chapter Eleven
Scottish Travellers or Tinkers
A. and F. REHFISCH 271

Chapter Twelve
The Social Organization of a Pariah Group in Norway
FREDRIK BARTH 285

Glossary and Index 301

CHAPTER ONE

The American Rom:
A Case of Economic Adaptation

Anne Sutherland

This essay is not a study of Gypsies, a term which includes numerous culturally diverse groups of persons who speak a variety of languages including many dialects of Romany; it is a description of the economic adaptability of one specific group of Rom who immigrated to America via South America some three generations past. Every statement about Gypsies, in this case those particular Gypsies who call themselves Rom,[1] must be clarified and supported as much as possible. This may seem obvious, but the problems and limitations of information gathered by non-gypsies (*gaje*) about Gypsies are very real indeed. Misleading the *gaje* is one and only one technique of survival. Add to this the fanciful inclinations of the writer, and the result is the present situation in Gypsy studies—a surfeit of wild generalizations and a paucity of solid reliable information. Consequently, I shall begin by qualifying immediately a previous statement.

A "group of Rom" refers to the economic and spacial grouping which the Rom call a *kumpania*. *Kumpania* should not be confused with *wortacha* or "partners" (Lee)[2] which refers to an alliance of men or women for a specific job such as fixing fenders. I believe Cotten has made this mistake when she defines *kumpania* as a "temporary

---

1. *Me sam Rom* (I am a Rom); capitalized to distinguish it from *rom*, meaning husband; adult (Gypsy) male.
2. Lee, Ronald (1967). "The Gypsies in Canada" *J.G.L.S.*, Vol. XLVI, p. 42.

grouping of people for the specific and exclusive purpose of accomplishing a given job, after which its members break up, returning to their individual *tserhas* and going their own separate ways."[3] The *kumpania* does not exist for the purpose of executing one job, but is a social, political and ceremonial unit of much more duration. What she means by "returning to one's *tserha*," (or *vitsa* as other Rom call it), I cannot say, since the *vitsa* is a category of kin and not a spacial grouping. This kind of confusion of terms is very common among Gypsiologists and is not entirely absent among Gypsies themselves.

To understand better what a *kumpania* is, let us consider what it was like in the recent past. According to Yoors,[4] who travelled with the Lowara as a boy in pre-Second World War Europe, a *kumpania* referred to a group of Rom who travelled together in wagons or with tents, who may or may not be related, but who joined together temporarily for economic reasons and for security. As Yoors describes it, the *kumpania* is an extremely flexible unit, but even though individual members, relationships, and leaders may change in a particular *kumpania*, the *kumpania* keeps its form and its rules of organization. One of the rules is that newcomers to the territory of a *kumpania* must get permission to work in that area and perhaps pay something in compensation since they will be exploiting the economic resources, the *gaje* (non-gypsies). In exchange, the *kumpania* will help acquaint the newcomer with local conditions, laws and authorities. A newcomer who does not respect the territory of a *kumpania* may find himself in trouble with non-gypsy authorities (Yoors). We can conclude therefore, that the European *kumpania* was, before the war, a travelling group which moved within a certain area and protected its right to exploit the economic resources of that area.

In America the *kumpania* has become more bound to a territory and less fluid in composition than among pre-Second World War Lowara. The most important change is not that it is connected to a territory but that the territory is almost entirely urban rather than primarily rural. Ronald Lee, a Canadian Gypsy, points to a "Gypsy Map" of North America:

The Gypsies of each town and city of the U.S.A. and Canada are organised into what we call *kumpaniyi* or 'unions'. Each *kumpania* is composed of all the male members of the community inhabiting that particular town or city, and they, together with their families, are under the supreme authority of the *Kris Romani* (tribunal of Gypsy

3. Cotten, Gropper, Rena M. (1955). *J.G.L.S.*, Vol. XXXIV, p. 22.
4. Yoors, Jan (1967). *The Gypsies*, pp. 121–123, 135, Allen and Unwin, London.

elders) which is their only authority in matters of Gypsy law and ceremonial behaviour. (*Romania*).[5]

Though Lee emphasizes the males of the community, most Rom described the *kumpania* as composed of so many *tsera* (tents) or households. As among the Lowara, the *kumpania* maintains a monopoly, or tries to establish a monopoly, on the economic resources of the area (fortune-telling licences, welfare, etc.), and the families in a *kumpania* co-operate with each other as *wortacha* (partners) in exploiting these resources and protecting them from other Rom.

More important, the *kumpania* is the basic unit of public, moral, social and political behaviour which comes under the authority of the *kris romani*. Individual families, extended families (*familiyi*), and even the *vitsa*,[6] do not have the authority to make public verdicts and decisions on questions of law and social behaviour (*romania*). Since these are units of kin they are expected to support their relatives. As Yoors has emphasized, the *kumpania* is not a kin group; it contains a cross-section of various kin groups. Important questions of morality, and trials (*kris romani*) on these questions, will usually involve several *kumpaniyi*. For example, two *familiyi* may arrange a marriage, but it is not a binding contract until it is sealed in the presence of the *kumpania*. If, however, a *kumpania* in fact only contains one extended family (*familia*), as some small and tightly controlled *kumpaniyi* do, then it is not a sufficiently broad cross-section of persons to hold a *kris* by itself or make decisions beyond those which are family matters.

The members of a *kumpania* often celebrate life cycle rituals and other feasts together. They solve personal conflicts and problems, disagreements over economic matters, and questions of morality. To solve these problems they hold discussions (*diwano*), and if the issue is important enough or if a breach of *romania* has occurred, they may call a trial (*kris romani*) for a final decision. They take up collections to help needy families, to pay fines, bail or funeral costs, or to contribute to a newly married couple. Thus the *kumpania* is not only the largest economic group occupying a specific territory, it is the largest viable social and ceremonial group.

Kumpaniyi on the West Coast of America generally take one of three forms. These forms are more points on a continuum rather than

5. Lee, Ronald (1967). "The Gypsies in Canada", *J.G.L.S.*, Vol. XLVI, pp. 1–2, 38–51.

6. The *vitsa* (pl. *vitsi*) is a large unit of cognatic kin composed of several branches headed by siblings or first cousins called *familiyi* (sing. *familia*). Each *vitsa* has a name and identifies itself with one or another *natsia* (*natsiyi*) which can be translated loosely as nation or tribe. See Sutherland, Anne (1975). *Gypsies: The Hidden Americans*, London, for a complete description and analysis of these categories.

separate types. At one end of the continuum there is strict control of
the economic resources such as a monopoly on fortune-telling licences.
In this case the *kumpania* is usually small and consists of one *familia* (in
several households) who allow only their close relatives to join the
kumpania. The leader of the *kumpania* will be the head of the *familia*
and there is no one in the *kumpania* who can challenge his or her position.
In the middle of the continuum is a fairly open *kumpania* which contains
several *vitsi* although it is dominated by one. It fails to have a strict
monopoly of the economic resources, for these are often areas where
welfare is the main source of income. Welfare, theoretically, is available
to anyone whereas a fortune-telling licence is more difficult to obtain.
Where a licence is not required to tell fortunes, such as in Hawaii or
Texas, again it is very difficult to have a strictly controlled *kumpania*.
In this kind of *kumpania*, families of different *vitsa* and *natsia* co-reside
more or less peacefully under the leadership of the *rom baro* who is a
liaison with the authorities and arbitrator for any problems that arise.
The *rom baro*, who is most likely from the largest *vitsa* in the *kumpania*,
will have challengers for his position, but if he is an effective and just
leader, he will keep the support of the *kumpania*.

At the end of the continuum of least control is open territory, both
in terms of who can live there, and what they can do for a living.
Strictly speaking it is not a *kumpania* for there is very little sense of a
united community. Each group of extended families will have their
own patriarch or matriarch to whom they look for leadership, but there
is no generally recognized leader for the whole *kumpania* (although
there may be contenders for leadership). This is a very unstable situation, and the current tendency is for the open territories eventually to
become dominated by a leader of a large *vitsa* and develop into the
second type of *kumpania*.

An example of a very strictly controlled *kumpania* is the Los Angeles
kumpania as it was under the leadership of the late Big George Adams
(*Joji Baro*) who monopolized fortune-telling establishments in Southern
California until his death in 1964. He controlled entry into his area
through force and with the help of the police, and his monopoly of
fortune-telling establishments made him very wealthy and powerful.
He shared his wealth with his relatives and friends by setting them up
in fortune-telling, and they in turn gave him a certain cut for his protection from outside competition. The same situation existed in San
Francisco under the rule of Barbara Miller prior to 1966. When these
two leaders were gone, both *kumpaniyi* became open territory and until
now no one has been able to establish the kind of control that existed
formerly.

It is the *kumpania* of the middle of the continuum, a group unable to enforce an economic monopoly, organized under one leader who has only limited control, which is probably the most common on the West Coast of America. The specific *kumpania* which I shall examine here, falls into this area. Within it, the Kashtare *vitsa* has the largest number of people and most influence. One Kashtare family elder is the acknowledged leader of the *kumpania*, but he has several rivals for his position and he lacks a great deal of control over families outside his *vitsa*. A history of the development of this *kumpania* will illustrate the nature of the group and its composition.

THE BARVALE KUMPANIA

Barvale is a depressed town of substandard housing in a large metropolitan area, its most noticeable feature being the maze of railway tracks that form natural boundaries for the various ethnic groups, Blacks, Mexican-Americans, Indians and poor Whites, most of whom subsist on welfare.

Before 1964, there were only a few isolated Rom families in Barvale and several Boyash families who had managed to obtain fortune-telling licences before the illegalization of fortune telling by the Town Council.[7] In 1964, several events changed this situation and brought about a sudden influx of Rom families. First, Big George Adams, the powerful leader of the Machwaya in California, died in August. His death was a great blow to his people because none was strong enough to take control of his empire and maintain the monopoly the Machwaya had enjoyed until then. This meant that, apart from San Francisco, which was still run by Barbara Miller, California had become open territory. Besides, Big George's funeral attracted thousands of Rom from all over the country, and many of these people drifted up to Barvale.

The second change was that in February, 1964, when the welfare programme expanded to include employable fathers. Before 1964, an employable father living with his family was required to have or be looking for a job. For most Rom families, welfare support had been difficult to obtain unless they could prove that one or the other parent was incapacitated. One Rom family managed to do this for several years by disguising their identity, the mother claiming to be insane. It took two years for the welfare department to realize they were a "Gypsy" family and not "suffering from wanderlust" and "schizophrenia".

---

7. Ayers, Gene (1966). "Seers Confirm it—He's Fouled Up", *Oakland Tribune*, Metropolitan News Section, pp. 11 and 15, August 21.

A third factor which changed the ethnic composition of Barvale was the increasing amount of automation in farm labour, a major source of income for most Rom families in California. This meant that families who depended on summer farm work to tide them over the winter were forced to look for other alternatives such as welfare.

A fourth factor which made Barvale more appealing than other towns in California, was the availability of cheap housing. Before urban renewal in Barvale, there were a large number of houses doomed to be torn down within months. The landlords of the houses wanted to get some rent from them, and they did not care who rented them or what they did to them. This was ideal housing for the Rom since it was cheap, they could knock out all the walls to make it into one big room, and they were not likely to get evicted for violating garbage regulations. When one house was torn down they were quite happy to move to another condemned one. Some of them even took advantage of a fund for re-locating families forced to move by the renewal project. Each family got $500 for "moving expenses".

Finally, the Rom who came to Barvale after 1964 immediately began cultivating good relations with the police. They invited the police to their feasts and weddings, and the heads of family agreed to keep their people from stealing and committing petty crimes. Of course, they could not be responsible for the "riff-raff" who come to town (i.e., families not of the leaders' *vitsa*), and these the police were encouraged to move on. The police responded favourably to this cultivation of good relations since in general they face extremely hostile ethnic groups who feel mistrust and contempt towards them. The Gypsies were the first and only group in Barvale who actually made friendly overtures to the police, and the police were both flattered and sympathetic to the Gypsies' problems. They consider the Gypsies their biggest success story.

Apart from the isolated families prior to 1967, the first big families to come to Barvale were the Mikailesti[8] headed by "Big Mick" who soon emerged as the leader. After testing out the welfare and police departments, and establishing an informer relationship with them, Big Mick began bringing in relatives and establishing his own power over the area. He immediately gathered information on how he could manipulate the welfare department. His social worker described one interview in this way:

> "Big Mick" is now recognized as the leader of the Gypsies in this area, and they both respect and fear him. We suspect that it is "Big

8. There is insufficient information on these families to give a statistically significant influx–outflux figure.

Mick" who is encouraging and assisting Gypsy families to settle in this community. His motives are not known, but it is possible that he has a desire for power and is empire-building in his own small way. ... (he) has close contact with the police and I suspect that he is an informer on occasions when he wishes to punish someone. He as much as told me this during the interview.

... During the home visit, I had the feeling that (he) was interviewing me just as much as I was interviewing him ... and I had the feeling that he was "playing dumb" on many occasions to find out how much I knew about the Gypsies. He also asked many policy questions. One of the questions he asked was, "if more Gypsy families come here, will it spoil it for the rest of us?"

Then, in the beginning of 1965, there arrived a large number of Kuneshti families led by five siblings and their spouses, and at the end of the summer of 1965, six or seven families of Gurkwe arrived (Fig. 1). By December, 1965, the welfare office had approximately 65 Gypsy cases numbering about 455 people.

To handle the sudden influx of Gypsy families coming in under Big Mick's encouragement, the welfare department put all Gypsies under one social worker, and formed a Gypsy team composed of an intake worker, a field worker, a public health nurse, a medical social worker, a school guidance worker and a fraud investigator. The Gypsies also had their own team to handle the welfare department, composed of Big Mick, the leader of the Gurkwe, and three or four Kuneshti leaders (Tompkins).[9]

Then in February, 1966, Big Mick's wife died. Since she had been a powerful force in his leadership, there was a struggle for power among the various leaders, including the leaders of the new Kashtare families, Stevan and Spiro. Big Mick kept control, but not for long, because:

A most devastating thing occurred in the Spring of 1966, ... Big Mick (our local "king") ran off with another man's wife! What made this doubly shocking was that Mick's late wife was barely in her grave three months when he did this shameful deed. I have never seen such outrage among any group of people. His closest friends and even his relatives joined in the chorus of vilification. They swore that if he ever returned they would black both his eyes, force him to return the wife, and pay the husband damages. One woman exclaimed: "He has disgraced his family and has brought shame to all of us!" (Tomkins).[10]

With Big Mick gone and disgraced, a bitter struggle for control ensued for three months. Each of the major patriarchs approached the

9. Tompkins, Janet (1965b). *Gypsies in Barvale*. Report to the Welfare Department, Barvale, California, Part II, pp. 1–11.
10. Tompkins, Janet (1967). Op cit., Part III, pp. 1–16.

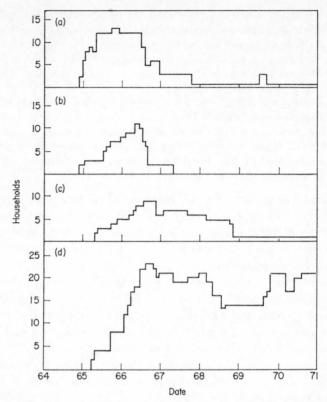

FIG. 1   Number of (a) Kuneshti, (b) Gurkwe, (c) Machwaya and (d) Kashtare
households in Barvale, 1964–1970.

welfare and police departments requesting that they appoint him "king".

Meanwhile, the Kashtare *vitsa* who had recently lost a family elder nearby, had swelled their ranks with relatives attending the *pomana* feasts (Fig. 1). Their family head, an impressive 350 pound man named Stevan, emerged as leader. When this happened in the autumn of 1966, the Gurkwe and Kuneshti families began to leave (Fig. 1), their leaders disgruntled.

During 1965 and 1966, several Machwaya families had also come to Barvale, but some were only distantly related to each other, and they had no strong leader. Mostly they represented the replacement of Machwaya throughout California since the death of Big George. In 1966, Machwaya families began gathering awaiting the death of an old Machwano patriarch named Budo who at 85 could no longer travel. Approximately ten families gathered around Budo: when he died in November, 1966, they drifted off, the largest exodus being in the autumn of 1968 during civil disturbances. There are still a few Machwaya families in Barvale of which only one is not closely intermarried with Kashtare.

Since 1968, the largest and most powerful *vitsa* in Barvale has been the Kashtare *vitsa*. There are five distinct Kashtare *familiyi* in Barvale and though they do not always agree about everything, they generally accept Stevan's leadership. Many of the families are more or less permanently based in Barvale, but others frequently travel back and forth to Oregon, Alaska, Los Angeles and Texas. Besides the Kashtare, there are a few Machwaya and Kuneshti families, but they do not form a large, cohesive group.

The present composition of the *kumpania* is very difficult to determine since it is in a constant state of flux. Since I finished field work there have been a number of changes. For example, one Kuneshti family has been thrown out and returned several times. During these periods of absence, Stevan ordered all the Kuneshti to stay in their own Kuneshti dominated *kumpania*.

But Stevan sees the Machwaya as his main rivals. "The Machwaya don't like us to have Barvale. They always run people out of town. This isn't right. Now we run them out of town and they don't like us." He has been at loggerheads with an educated Machwano for a long time, and before that he threw out another Machwano who tried to move in from Santa Rosa. At the same time it seems that Stevan is bringing more families of his own *vitsa* and that Barvale is more and more becoming an exclusively Kashtare town.

Ignoring the movement of families to and from the *kumpania*, Table 1 gives an indication of the number of households and people in each *familia* during one period of time as a sample of the composition of the *kumpania*.

As can be seen from Table 1, apart from the large majority of Kashtare *familiyi* (1–5) and the three Machwaya *familiyi* (6–8), there are only various isolated *familiyi* in Barvale consisting of an extended family occupying one household each. These isolated families have no other relatives in the *kumpania* to turn to for support and aid. The only exceptions are families 12 and 13 who say they are "cousins" and who have arranged a marriage between two of their children. The Kuneshti head of family also has a weak link with Kashtare *familia* 2 whose matriarch is his sister, and he is trying to arrange a marriage with *familia* number 3 to establish affinal ties there.

The Kashtare *vitsa* on the other hand is represented by five large *familiyi* and is closely intermarried with Machwaya *familia* 6. The heads of *familiyi* 1 and 2 are half-brothers so that their descendants are half-

TABLE 1   Population and households—spring 1970

Vitsa	Familia	Head	Households	No. of persons
Kashtare	1	"Stevan"	6	44
Kashtare	2	"Spiro"	5	44
Kashtare	3	"Sonia"	5	38
Kashtare	4	"Mary"	2	19
Kashtare	5	"Rosie"	1	12
Machwaya/Kashtare	6	"Ruby"	4	33
Machwaya	7		3	26
Machwaya	8		1	5
Romanitchal	9		1	6
Gurkwe	10		1	3
Lameshti	11		1	8
Micheleshti	12		1	11
Mineshti	13		1	11
Kuneshti	14		1	6
		TOTAL	33	266

Average household size: 8 persons

Kashtare and Machwaya/ Kashtare			23	190
Machwaya			4	31
Kuneshti			1	6
Miscellaneous families			5	39
			33	266

first cousins. The heads of *familiyi* 4 and 5 are both the widows of first cousins (FBS) to the heads of *familiyi* 1 and 2 so their descendants are also cousins. The head of *familia* 3 is aunt (FBW) to the head of family 1; therefore her descendants are cousins both to him and his *familia* (Fig. 2).

Furthermore there are marriages between the *familiyi*. Two second generation members of *familia* 2 are married to two second generation members of *familia* 4 (Fig. 3). The Machwaya Kashtare *familia* 6 is headed by an old matriarch who is the elder sister of Stevan's wife. Her elder brother was at one time married to Stevan's sister and a younger brother is married to Stevan's first cousin (FBD) and she herself was once married to a Kashtare. As a result of these four marriages, these two groups of families are very closely linked and have arranged marriages in the next generation as well (see Fig. 4).

Data such as contained in Table 1 represent only a short moment in the history of the *kumpania*; however, they serve to exemplify its

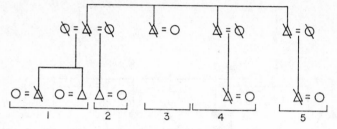

Only the heads of *familia* are shown here. Each *familia* includes two to three generations of descendants

FIG. 2   The five Kashtare *familiyi*

composition. For, although the *kumpania* occupies a specific territory and residents generally live in houses, these households are very mobile. Since there has been much speculation on just how mobile American Rom are, it would be useful to determine more precisely the amount of travelling undertaken by families in the *kumpania*.

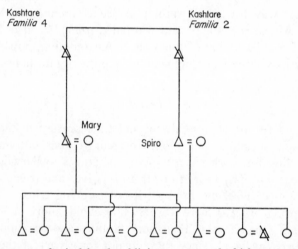

There are four genealogical levels of living persons of which two are not shown here

FIG. 3   Marriages between two Kashtare *familiyi* in one *kumpania*

Travelling is undoubtedly extremely important for the Rom for a large number of reasons. However, because they no longer travel in groups of caravans or pitch their tents in the fields of America, many Rom claim that they are no longer nomadic, and they speak with nostalgia about the "good old days" when they were "on the road." They have been supported in this conclusion by non-gypsies who feel they

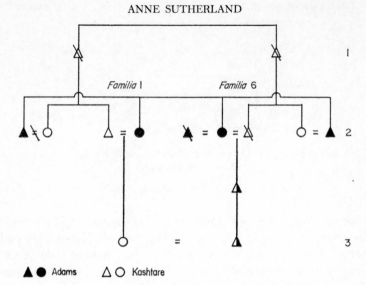

▲● Adams   △ ○ Kashtare

FIG. 4   Kashtare and Machwaya intermarriage

are on their way towards assimilation (see for example, Weybright (1938),[11] Murin (1949)[12] and Cotten (1955)[13]; also Sutherland (1975)[14] for a discussion of this issue). Assimilation, however, is not necessarily inevitable when nomadic people move into houses.

Travel

Figure 5 is a record of time absent and time present in the *kumpania* by household during a nine month period. It does not include, (a) daily travelling for work when the person returns to Barvale the same night or next day, (b) visits to or from relatives and friends in nearby *kumpaniyi*, or (c) weekend fishing trips or camping trips.

In the spring of 1970 there were 33 households more or less permanently residing in Barvale. Transitory families and occasional visitors have not been included, since they do not form part of the *kumpania* proper. From Fig. 5 it can be calculated that on average households were travelling outside the *kumpania* 42 per cent of the time.

Figure 6 gives the fluctuation in the amount of travelling by months. April and June were peak travelling months because of the special events at those times. In March, many families left for a time because of a big fight which occurred at Easter. In April, a *pomana* (death feast)

11. Weybright (1938). "Who Can Tell the Gypsie's Fortune?" Survey Graphic, March.
12. Murin, Stephen (1949). "Hawaii's Gypsies", *Social Progress in Hawaii*, **14**, pp. 14–37.
13. Cotten Gropper, Rena M. (1955). See footnote 3, p. 2 op. cit.
14. Sutherland, Anne (1975) op. cit.

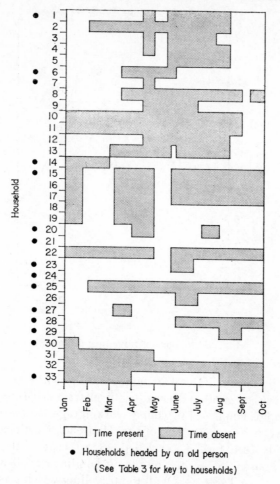

Fig. 5   Time absent from the Barvale *kumpania*

was held in Oregon and most Kashtare relatives from Barvale attended, returning at the end of April.

At the end of May, the Romany School ended, and Stevan, along with the welfare authorities, gave the families a free hand to leave and work during the summer months. By September most families had returned since the summer harvest was over, and this month showed the least absentee households. It is possible that this range of fluctuation in periods of two to three months occurs year-round as this seemed to be the usual time families would stay in one place before they became restless and wanted to travel.

Certain households travelled more than others. A breakdown of

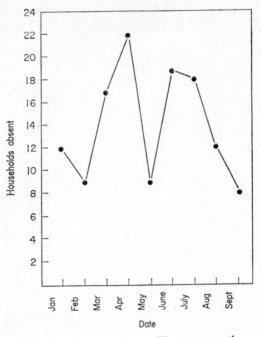

Fɪɢ. 6   Amount of travelling per month

households by age indicates that households which were headed by an elder who was over 50 and usually infirm travelled considerably less than households composed of young working age families headed by a person between 30 and 40 years of age. Households with elders as heads of households (see Fig. 5) travelled 26 per cent of the nine month period and households headed by young families travelled 56 per cent of the period (see Table 2). Of all the travelling which was done by the *kumpania* as a whole, households composed of younger families did 73 per cent of the total travelling. Old people often claim they do not like the rigours of being on the road all the time, and usually they are quite ill and in need of medical care. Many families settle into a *kumpania* when their patriarch or matriarch becomes old and infirm, but when he or she dies they will travel for at least several months, often up to a year because the place of death is *prikaza* (bad luck). In Barvale there were two exceptions to the general decline in amount of travelling by old people. Households 12 and 13 (Fig. 5) are composed of young families who care alternatively for a very elderly and senile old lady. Though they are constantly complaining that they cannot travel because of her, they spent 50 per cent of their time travelling.

TABLE 2   Amount of travel according to age of head of household

	Households	Months of travel	Average amount of time travelling %
Households with elderly person or couple at head:	15	35	26
Households with young couple at head:	18	91	56

The head of household 15 is also the head of an entourage of households (16–19) and often this old lady, who is quite agile, is the very one who is anxious to be on the move. These families (15–19) travel as a large group and are extremely mobile. They were absent 60 per cent of the nine month period.

Family groups (*familia*) varied according to the percentage of time which they spent travelling. Certain family groups were much more mobile than others. Table 3 gives a breakdown of the family groups according to the amount of time spent travelling.

There is no typical *familia* in terms of travelling. Some, such as the Machwaya were fairly settled, travelling about one-third of the time. The four *familiyi* who travelled the least, are all small single household *familiyi* headed by an old person or couple. At the top of the scale, *familiyi* 12, 13 and 5 travelled extensively and these *familiyi* were not stable members of the *kumpania* but were generally on the move from

TABLE 3   Percentage of travelling time by families

Familia (on Table 1)	Households (Fig. 5)	Time travelling %
12, 13	31–32	66
5	15–19	60
2	7–11	55
8	33	55
3	12–13	50
9	28	44
1	1–6	37
7	24–26	33
6	20–23	31
4	14	22
14	27	11
10	29	11
11	30	6

one *kumpania* to another. *Familia 2* on the other hand, is more permanently settled in the *kumpania*, and the old couple who head this large
familia (household 7) do not travel extensively anymore, though their
children (households 8–11) travelled to and from Barvale during the
whole nine months (Fig. 5). In general, it can be said that *familiyi*
2, 8, and 3 travel considerably, but they do have Barvale as their base
and eventually come back to it whereas *familiyi* 12, 13, and 5, which I
shall call travelling family groups, have no definite base and travel from
kumpania to *kumpania*.

Travelling family groups who have not chosen one *kumpania* as their
base generally have two patterns of travel. They may travel within a
certain area such as the West Coast, or the southern states of America,
or they may set up a winter–summer circuit between two places or
areas. Though I could not calculate what proportion of American Rom
are travelling family groups and what proportion live more or less in
one *kumpania*, I suspect that a majority of families are associated with a
kumpania.

Travelling family groups may be composed of one extended family
and may be very small, or they may be very large and composed of
several extended families led by the elderly parents. However, no
matter how large they become they should not be confused with a
European *kumpania*, as described by Yoors, for they are merely a large
group of closely related families on the move whereas a *kumpania*
refers to a group of several *familiyi*, not necessarily related, occupying
a certain territory.

Travelling family groups have several schemes for making a living,
but the one they used most often in Barvale is what the welfare department calls the "pending transfer system". They establish a residence for
a few weeks, receive their first cheque, and then transfer to a new place
before a social worker can visit them. It take two months to transfer
their case, and meanwhile they can receive their cheques for these
months. Before the two months are up, they transfer to another place.
One social worker told me she had several cases in which a year passed
before the family was visited by a social worker the few times necessary
to write up a social study. In this way, they not only avoided the questions and interference of a social worker, but they were able to keep
their income from welfare cheques while working on the move. Alternatively, they may come to town, hide their cars and/or trailers, stay
with friends or relatives in order to have an address long enough to get
their first cheque, and then move on to the next place. For large families
this can be a profitable and quick way to get money.

Other travelling family groups adopt a slightly different pattern of travel. These families establish a regular circuit, usually spending the winter in one area, involved in a certain occupation, and the summer in another place doing something else. By combining two occupations and two areas they are able to make a better income. In Barvale many families were on welfare the year round but spent several months in the summer, camping in fields and picking crops along with other migrant labourers for extra income. One group of Kuneshti families set up a circuit between San Francisco and Hawaii. They spent the summer in San Francisco where they established residence and received welfare cheques supplemented by occasional trips to engage in farm labour. In the autumn they would fly to Hawaii where they were able to make a good living at fortune-telling. The occasional *bujo** helped them to get their tickets back to the mainland. In one lean year they did not earn enough in the fields to get to Hawaii and were forced to spend the winter in San Francisco.

Reasons for Travelling

Travelling family groups must have a source of income which they can rely upon while on the road. There are many schemes which they have developed to cope with this problem such as the "pending transfer scheme" and a summer–winter work circuit. The amount a particular market has been tapped in one area is a factor in travelling. For example, families who travel around picking up auto-body work, tarring roofs and driveways, fortune-telling or selling plastic flowers may find an area overworked by other families, and this will make them move on to new areas. In almost any area, they may supplement their income with a welfare grant.

Families who choose one *kumpania* as their base of operations, travel for short periods to pick up extra income. They may take off several months in the summer to work in the summer harvest or to pick up body and fender work. In Barvale, for example, they have so over-worked the auto body repair market that young men will travel fifty to a hundred miles per day seeking jobs in nearby towns. These trips are limited in duration because after a certain absence they will be likely to have their welfare cheques discontinued: therefore, they tend to return at regular intervals.

Families in the Barvale *kumpania* travel for a variety of reasons besides economic ones. Travelling is socially imperative and is incorporated into the whole structure of law, social control, morality and religious beliefs. Specifically, an illness or a death requires the presence

* A *bujo*, translated as "switch the bag", is a swindle involving a large amount of money from a gullible fortune-telling customer.

of close relatives. Families will travel thousands of miles to New York, Mexico or Alaska to be near a sick relative. If death occurs they will stay for the three-day and nine-day *pomana* (death feast). Later they may take another trip to attend the six-week *pomana*, usually in a different area, to allow friends and relatives there to attend. One family, for example, was in Hawaii when the father of the family died. The whole family (fourteen persons) returned to San Francisco with the body by air since it was more expensive for all the relatives to fly to Hawaii, and after the nine-day *pomana* they went to Texas for the six-week *pomana*, accompanied by several relatives from Barvale. Relatives of the deceased will travel long distances at great cost to attend a *pomana*, out of respect for the *mulo* (spirit of the dead). They may also flee the *mulo* if they feel they are being plagued by him, and they believe they can "outrun" a *mulo* by keeping on the move constantly.

Though families will travel for economic or religious reasons, travelling is also a social occasion. Some families travel to visit relatives, to contract a marriage for a son, to attend a wedding, a baptism (obligatory for the godparents of course), a *slava* (a Saint's day feast) or *pakiv* (party in honour of a visitor). At times several of these social events may be combined in one trip, or a family may visit several *kumpaniyi* on a trip. Women often visit their parents when they are about to give birth and return to their husband's family with the new baby after confinement.

Travelling also may have political implications. When there is a *kris romani* (trial), families who are closely involved will travel far to attend. They will also attend a *kris* nearby even if only peripherally involved. Many conflicts, of course, do not necessarily result in a *kris*, but relatives will go to each other's aid in difficult times. If a conflict develops in a *kumpania* over leadership or a new leader emerges, families will leave and join another *kumpania* according to their standing in the new situation, and new families may take their place.

In general, the most accepted and common way to solve any problem arising between two families is for the families to leave the *kumpania* until they can come back in peace. Travel is a major method of social control and is a time-honoured solution to pressures from both the outside and inside. Demands from school authorities that parents send their children to school, demands from vocational authorities that young men take a job or attend vocational training, harassment from the police, or any pressures from the welfare department, government authorities, neighbours, or irate landlords, usually are solved by an exodus of the family for as long as necessary.

It is surprising how well this technique works. A diligent truant officer has no authority or concern for a family once they have left town, and when they return he will generally have to begin all over again applying pressure to the family before threatening prosecution. Once the threat is made, the family takes off again. Of course, a person who is wanted for welfare fraud or a crime, whether innocent or guilty, is unlikely to return to the same place, at least not under the same name.

Any scandal which arises in the *kumpania* requires that the offender (and sometimes the offended as well) leave town. An illegitimate pregnancy, a wife who leaves her husband, a case of adultery or any such breach of morality will result in a re-sorting of the families in the *kumpania*. A person who becomes *marime* (rejected) will almost certainly leave town until his case is sorted out or his sentence completed.

Travel is a very effective way of problem-solving for the individual and a form of social control for the community. Any person who is a source of trouble, whether or not he is to blame, must leave town until the community decides to accept him again. In any fight between families, all parties disperse for a certain period of time and then return to town, usually with a compromise solution to the situation. For example, at the Easter *slava* a fight broke out among several young men over shared payments for a body and fender job. The fight soon involved two large *familiyi* of the same *vitsa* (descendants of half-brothers) numbering five to six nuclear families on each side. When it was finally stopped by the police, the nuclear families immediately involved left town for several weeks until their fathers (the half-brothers) could work out a solution. The problem of the money was finally settled, and a broken car window was paid for by collections from both *familiyi*. The charges made by the police were dropped and in a few weeks the fight was forgotten.

Finally, a word on the symbolism of travelling. Travelling for the Rom is associated with health and good luck, whereas settling down is associated with sickness and bad luck. Old ladies who feel ill will take a trip "to recover" against their *gajo* doctor's advice. One young mother remarked: "I am tired and run down. I want to get away, have a rest, travel." She took off with her seven children and came back looking rested. One old lady took a trip whenever she got depressed or felt sick, and another who was too ill to travel, would just go and sit in her car for hours with the door open when she became low or depressed. Another young girl remarked that the Rom used not to fight when they were travelling but now that they have settled in cities, they fight constantly. All Rom agreed that when they were travelling all the time they were healthy and never needed doctors, but now that they live in houses they are subjected to many *gaje* diseases.[15]

We have seen that a *kumpania* is a territory where various families live together primarily for economic reasons. But families in a *kumpania* reside there only in the sense that it is their base from which they travel for a variety of reasons. Some closely related extended families, which I have called travelling family groups, travel so much that it is difficult to say whether they "live" in a *kumpania*. The Rom usually adopt one of three patterns of travel. They may choose a *kumpania* to live in and travel only occasionally when necessary for social reasons. They may adopt two *kumpaniyi*, making their living in one in the summer and in the other in the winter. Finally, they may travel in large family groups continually between various *kumpaniyi* where they have relatives and will be allowed to settle for short periods of time.

I have mentioned briefly some of the ways in which travelling family groups and winter–summer circuit families are able to make a living. I should now like to examine more closely the economic activities of those families who choose to adopt more or less one *kumpania* as their base of operations. To do this I must begin with the rules governing their economic relations with one another in the *kumpania* and the rules governing their economic relations with the *gaje*. Finally I shall describe how these rules are carried out in practice.

ECONOMIC RELATIONS

With few exceptions, the Rom establish relations with *gaje* only because of some economic or political motive. The *gaje* are the source of all livelihood plus a certain amount of political power. The Rom have developed one set of rules for behaviour in obtaining economic or political gain from the *gaje* and another set of rules for the same behaviour with their own people. The *gaje*—the policemen, social workers, politicians, newspaper reporters, landlords, shopkeepers, doctors, teachers, neighbours and social anthropologists—on the other hand, each have their own motives and self-interests in their contacts with the Rom (for example, getting their children to school, getting their votes, making them comply with garbage regulations, preventing them from stealing, finding out how they live). The Rom understand these motives and, rather than ignore them, play an active role in controlling and manipulating these necessary *gaje* contacts in such a way as to diminish the threat of control from them. For example, harassed police com-

---

15. This is not borne out by medical records in Barvale which show an improvement in health due to regular medical care.

munity relations officers, despised by most minority groups, feel flattered to be invited to a Gypsy *slava*. Imagine his pride at being able to say to his fellow police officers that through his friendship and understanding the Gypsies are practically free of crime.[16]

These relations with *gaje* are of an opposite nature to their economic relations with each other. Economic relations between Rom are based on co-operation and mutual aid, and it is generally considered immoral to earn money from other Rom. The *gaje* are the only legitimate source of income and skill in extracting money from them is highly valued in Rom society.

There has been much written on "Gypsy occupations" and the problems that arise in trying to list Gypsy occupations illustrate the pitfalls of approaching Rom society from the outside. Rena Cotten[17] has made a four-page list of Gypsy occupations without beginning to exhaust them all. Clébert[18] is typical of attempts to give some order to Gypsy economics. In his chapter on occupations he generalizes:

> With a few variations, the Gypsies are first and foremost smiths and workers in metals, musicians and mountebanks, horse-copers and dealers, exhibitors of animals and fortune-tellers.

He explains that all these occupations were condemned by the Laws of Manu (*Manava Dharma Sastra*) in India, and that the "Gypsies have followed precisely those occupations that were cursed by Manu" (p. 129). This explanation of traditional occupations, which Clébert links with the suggestion by Mircea Eliade[19] that there is close bond between the art of the smith, the occult sciences and the arts of song, dance and poetry, is interesting for an historical perspective. However, it does not explain the many changes in occupations which have occurred among all Gypsies, and it leaves out many recent skills and schemes (peg-makers, basket weavers, travelling movie showmen, farm labour and welfare). Also, it does not provide an understanding of what all these occupations have in common.

To analyse "Gypsy occupations" merely by listing the numerous occupations and dividing them into categories such as "musician" or "workers in metals" is not only inadequate, it is misleading. To understand Gypsy occupations, or better, Gypsy economics, it is necessary to

16. Recently in Oakland a Black leader suggested that it would improve the situation of the Blacks if each person would invite a policeman to dinner. He was hooted off the rostrum.

17. Cotten Gropper, Rena M. (1954). "An Anthropologist Looks at Gypsiology", *J.G.L.S.* Vol. XXXIII, pp. 113–116.

18. Clébert, Jean-Paul (1963). *The Gypsies*, p. 129 (Trans. Charles Duff) Penguin Books, Harmondsworth.

19. Eliade, Mircea (1956). *Forgerons et Alchemistes*, Flannarion (*Collecion Homo Sapiens*), Paris.

outline the jural rules for economic relations. The first and most basic rule is that the code of economic relations among Rom must be viewed in opposition to the code of economic relations with *gaje*. The opposition is simply that between co-operation Rom to Rom and exploitation Rom to *gaje*. Within the limits set out by this code, there are a large number of ways to make a living available to the Rom in America, and new sources of income are always being sought within these limits. The first step is to understand the nature of economic relations between Rom.

Economic Relations Between Rom

In the *kumpania* men and women co-operate with each other in exploiting the economic resources of their area. Any job, scheme or source of income may be exploited individually, but the Rom prefer to work in groups rather than on their own. These groups are called *wortacha*, or partners, and are always formed between members of the same sex. Men work in teams of men, and women work in teams of women though women often take along children of either sex. *Wortacha* also include young unmarried males (or females) who learn the skills of the adults.

Adult partners work as equals and divide the expenses and the profits from a job equally; however, an older person may be given a small amount extra as a token of respect for his age, and unmarried trainees do not get a full share but receive what the others will give them. The Rom do not work under the employment of another Rom for a wage, even if one person has located and organized a job. If a man wishes to "hire" someone to parts of a job he has no skill for or does not wish to do (for example, a "dirty" job), he hires a non-gypsy labourer (Lee).[20] This distinction is crucial, for a man may be honoured to join a group of men as a partner, but he would lose his self-respect if he were being employed as a labourer for them.

All the men in Barvale worked with partners most of the time although occasionally a man went out alone. Some men worked with adult sons, but often partners were cousins of the same age. For example:

(a) Nicky usually did body and fender repair jobs with his second cousin Billy and his first cousin Jimmy. All three men are just under twenty years of age and are recently married.

(b) Harry and Tom are brothers with large families and usually work as partners with Toma, a cousin of similar age. On one job they each got $50.

20. See footnote 2, op. cit., p. 1.

Women also worked in groups when telling fortunes around town or dealing with the social worker for welfare in the home. Women in the same household generally team up and do not work with women of other households unless they are close relatives. The most usual team is headed by an elderly woman and includes her adult daughters and daughters-in-law. Katharine, for example, always works in collaboration with her daughter Mary and daughter-in-law Rachael. Her social worker described the team thus:

> Rachael, Mary and Katharine are a formidable trio and they usually travel together. They are all experts at wheedling and begging. Sometimes they will work in relays, and at other times they employ siege tactics, that is, they all talk at once and it is very difficult to separate their needs from their desires.

The *wortacha* in each *kumpania* (and partners are usually formed with members of the same *kumpania*) have the right to exploit the territory that their *kumpania* covers. Rom from another *kumpania* are not allowed to move into their area without prior permission, and they do not go to the territory of another *kumpania* unless it has been approved there. Rom who do infringe this rule will be severely criticized by the local *kumpania*, and if they ignore this criticism they may find that they have been turned in to the local police for fixing fenders or for fortune-telling without a licence. Informing to the local *gaje* authorities on a person who infringes on the economic resources of a *kumpania* is generally considered acceptable; however, the objective is only to harass the person and not to get him arrested. Only just enough information is given to the authorities to arouse their suspicions, but not enough to warrant a conviction. Welfare is included in the resources of a *kumpania* and in Barvale a stranger coming to town has to get approval from some prominent and respectable *phuro* (elder) and the *rom baro* to get on welfare.

The Rom in a *kumpania* not only work together, but they co-operate economically in several other ways. Though ideally all Rom should help each other, in practice, apart from relatives, it is the Rom of the same *kumpania* who come to each other's aid. This is accomplished by means of collections (*kidemos*) among the *kumpania* members and the idea is to pool enough money for the needy without any single family being too debilitated by the expense. (See also Lee, 1967, p. 44.) Collections are a kind of insurance scheme because a Rom who gives freely in collections can expect to get help himself at some time in his life. Those who are mean with their contributions lose respect in the community.

Collections are made at every *pomana* to help the family of the deceased to pay the expenses and at weddings to help the new couple start their own life. A *slava* may be presented in a *kumpania* with the help of a collection though more often it is several relatives who join together to give a *slava* rather than the *kumpania* as a whole. At the Easter *slava*, everyone in the kumpania gave his own *slava*, and each family visited the *slava* of the other families. Collections taken up in Barvale over a period of three to four months included:

1. *Pomana*
   (a) A collection was taken to send Stevan and Yana to the *pomana* of his nephew in Oregon because they did not have the money to get there.
   (b) At the *pomana* in Oregon three collections were made to pay for the food and expenses. The first brought in $2,600, the second $1,500 and the third (from people arriving later) about $2,000. Each adult gave about $5.
   (c) When Marco died, his body and his wife, mother, children and daughters-in-law and their children were flown from Hawaii to San Francisco, paid for by a collection taken among relatives in the Bay area and the *kumpania* in Hawaii.

2. *Wedding*
   (a) When Sandra and Steve married, there was a collection at the wedding table. Each man gave $10 to $20 and about $600 was collected.
   (b) At a wedding in Fort Worth $225 was collected for the bride and groom and at a wedding in Oklahoma, $1,350 was collected.

3. *Slava*
   At the 28th August *slava* to St. Anne, four families pooled funds to give the *slava*.

The *kumpania* will also make collections on non-ritual occasions. If someone needs a private doctor's care or hospitalization, and the immediate family cannot afford to pay for it, the *kumpania* will take up a collection to help. The person's relatives in another *kumpania* will also send money. If someone in the *kumpania* is arrested and needs money for bail or must pay a fine, again a collection will be made. If there is a fight or disagreement in the *kumpania* and property is damaged, the *kumpania* will make a collection to pay for the damage and settle the fight. Finally, if a genuinely destitute family arrives, the *kumpania* will help them out not only by sharing a home with them but with a collection to get them started again. Spiro once said that any Rom who comes to Barvale and is desperate can expect help and that he personally knew of four or five collections being made on such occasions. It is the leader of a *kumpania* who handles the collection. In Barvale, both Big Mick and Stevan have been responsible for the collections. Examples of these collections include:

1. The Rom will often prefer to pay for private medical care with a collection rather than be cared for by a welfare doctor if they feel this care may be better. (Tompkins, 1965b: p. 8). In 1966, Marcia needed an operation for mastoids. A collection of $50 was made as a deposit on her operation; the balance ($400) was never paid.
2. Fines and traffic tickets are paid promptly in Barvale by the Rom. Stevan personally takes up a collection and pays the fines (usually for breaking garbage regulations) about once a month. (Tompkins, 1967: p. 11).
3. At the Easter *slava* fight, Spiro's car was smashed and no one would claim responsibility for it. Stevan, to end the argument, took $10 from each person involved in the fight to pay for the damages to the car and everyone was satisfied with this solution.
4. When a couple and their four children arrived in Barvale, expecting their fifth child and completely out of cash, they were taken by Stevan to get their first welfare cheque and were given the rent and a house full of furniture through donations from relatives and friends.
5. When Dorothy decided to leave her husband, his relatives demanded $150 for her return to compensate for the loss of their *bori*; her relatives in Barvale and New York made a collection to pay for her ransom.

In summary, the men and women of a *kumpania* co-operate economically in several ways in order to ensure a living. They not only share economic resources, homes, and income, but through this system of sharing, they avoid extreme want and the necessity to abandon their way of life and take employment from the *gaje*.

Although men and women work in separate unisexual groups as partners and although men generally take up certain occupations and women others, basically men and women use the same techniques to make a living. They rely on their wits and a forceful personality to make the *gaje* give them money. This requires considerable skills which must be learned from elders over a long period of time. The techniques used [21] are based on close observation and knowledge of the income,

---

21. There is no word in *Romanes* that I know of to describe this technique. In English the best word is "to hustle". Hustling is a time-honoured technique and even the earliest accounts of Gypsies describe the same methods of making a living.

status and aspirations of a given *gajo* combined with behaviour from the Rom which is most likely to break down the non-gypsy's resistance to the pressure put on him by the Rom. This behaviour includes creating a loud commotion to embarrass the non-gypsy, switching from flattery to hostility to confuse him or begging and pleading to invoke sympathy. To earn money with one's wits is highly valued and admired while to be a slow-witted or shy person is considered extremely bad luck.

The Kalderash in Barvale maintain that women are primarily responsible for supporting their husbands and family. This does not mean that men do not work, only that the primary moral responsibility to provide for the family falls on the women of the household. The ability to make money is still a major criterion in choosing a daughter-in-law for one's son and a major obligation of a wife. On the whole, this ideal corresponds with practice. Women still provide the largest amount of income in Barvale though men may earn most of the money when the family is travelling. Even on summer work in the fields, women generally work the hardest (Tompkins),[22] and in welfare, with few exceptions, the woman handles everything. In case after case in welfare records, the wife has also provided the major support of the family before welfare, whether by telling fortunes, working in the fields, selling flowers or begging. A woman who fails to provide for her family is in a sense a failure as a woman, wife and mother. A family which rises economically generally invests in the woman's occupation rather than the man's, even if their wealth was originally acquired through his efforts. Men do not value their occupations over the woman's but consider it more as a temporary measure in bad times. Except in the few cases where a man takes a pride in some skill such as coppersmithing, it is felt that a rich man would be foolish to work.

It is difficult to divide occupations strictly into male and female work. Basically, the women are fortune-tellers and handle welfare negotiations. In some cases, the man always dealt with the social worker. In these cases, the wife generally was considered a "bad" wife, that is, shy and unable to hustle for more money from the social worker, but the man was not condemned for taking over this role, only pitied for having a bad wife. Occasionally, men will tell fortunes as well, though they do not set up an *ofisa* (fortune-telling premises) or make a regular practice of this. They do participate in their wife's business by building the booth in a carnival or setting up the *ofisa*. Both men and women also engage in farm labour though again some men will leave this mostly to their wife and children. Male occupations are more exclusive and

22. Tompkins, Janet (1965a). *Gypsies in Barvale*. Report to the Welfare Department, Barvale, California. Part I, p. 3.

most male occupations are never done by women. Coppersmith work, tarring roofs and driveways, body and fender car repairs, trading cars and trailers, are all men's jobs.

Economic Relations with gaje

We have seen that the Rom co-operate with each other in a number of ways, including extracting money from the *gaje*. Both men and women use similar techniques to achieve this aim, techniques that require the ability to convince a non-gypsy to part with his money. This technique might be called "hustling". Whatever the method used to achieve this aim, it is always one which does not require the Rom to undertake employment from a non-gypsy and which allows him freedom to travel. The preferred arrangement is to charge a fee for a service (such as fortune-telling) or to obtain a contract from a non-gypsy for a specific piece of work (such as fixing a fender).

In times of extreme want, it is not always possible to avoid employment, but in this case it is taken for a few days to get enough cash to reach a relative who can help the needy family. Some men will take short-term jobs with construction companies or do gardening work. Some women have taken piece-work in a factory, but only when they can work in groups together and are physically removed from non-gypsy women. In general, any employment which requires close contact with non-gypsies or puts a person under the direction and authority of a non-gypsy is avoided. This kind of employment is considered *marime* because it requires some kind of commitment to American society and contradicts important values of Rom society. For example, most regular employment would interfere with the mobility required of any Rom. A Rom who does take employment is considered "Americanised", and his behaviour is taken to mean that he "rejects" Rom society and therefore is *marime*. One girl who took a position with the Job Corps (a programme for training young people) was treated as if she had committed a breach of the sexual code, and she and her family became *marime*.

Though money must be earned from *gaje*, but not by employment, it is immoral to earn a living from another Rom. There are certain times when money exchanged between Rom is considered legitimate and is not viewed as money earned. The brideprice should not be considered a method of financial gain (when this does happen it is highly unethical) but is an exchange between two families. The extra amount given to an elder *wortacha* in the *lovoro* (division of the take) is not viewed as money earned but as a sign of respect for his age and experience. When a leader gets a certain cut from new Rom coming into a *kumpania* to use the economic resources of that area, whether for welfare or fortune-telling, this also is considered a token of respect to the *kumpania* for the use of its resources; however, here the line between respect and earning money becomes very fine.

The legality of a scheme or occupation is not an important consideration for the Rom except when this is an inconvenience to them or when they are likely to be arrested. Avoiding arrest is extremely important; jail means being denied social contact with one's own people and being forced to live among the *gaje* (which is *marime*). Stealing from other Rom is wrong, but it is not necessarily wrong when it is from the *gaje*; although one should not be too greedy. "The story of God" is a myth which provides an explanation and justification for stealing for the Rom and there is no man, woman or child who does not know it.

> Jesus was going to be crucified and a Gypsy blacksmith, who was a slave, was ordered by the Roman soliders to make four nails, three to go into his hands and feet and one through his heart. The Gypsy stalled and stalled but the soldier whipped him so he made the four nails. He asked God to help him and to help the Gypsies. God cried and the Gypsy cried. When he was to deliver the nails he swallowed one and told the soldiers he had lost it. When God saw that he had swallowed the nail for Jesus' heart, he said "Gypsy you are free to go and travel anywhere and you can steal your food and take what you need to live." And that is why Gypsies travel and why they steal.

Actually the Rom in Barvale are relatively crime-free compared with the rest of the city. They are not involved in felonies, armed robbery, rape or murder, and their most serious offences have been traffic tickets, garbage violations and stealing from shops. An old crone once said to me: "Gypsies never kill someone. It is the worst crime. The next worst crime is betraying one of your own people." Although they are mostly involved in questions of fraud, in three years the welfare department found only ten instances of welfare fraud, nine of which involved unreported late model cars (Tompkins, 1967, op. cit., p. 11).

Murder is so serious a crime that there is no specific punishment against it since no Rom will admit that it can happen. However, there is no doubt that the person who committed such a crime would be a total outcast (*marime*) though this would hardly be effective since if he were socialized properly enough to fear *marime*, he would never have committed the crime in the first place.

Extortion, blackmail or coercion of other Rom, are strongly prohibited but not unheard of. When they occur, it is always a method, though considered an immoral one, of getting or keeping power among

Rom. The late Tinya Le Stevanosko used these techniques to relieve the powerful Machwaya of some of their wealth for his poorer relatives and increase his own power. The Machwaya themselves may not be entirely ignorant of these tricks as a recent newspaper article indicates:

CRIME FIGHTERS OR EXTORTIONISTS? The National Gypsy Crime Investigators' Inc. claims the first; other Gypsies claim the second.

Boto Adams claims his organisation is dedicated to "clearing the names of the Gypsies" and to exposing certain con-artists who are "extortionists in the guise of fortune-tellers." But the Corporation's dedication to the routing of the "renegades" has placed its own actions in the spotlight of illegality. Since its founding in February, 118 extortion charges have been filed against the group.

Some observers have voiced the opinion that the NGCI Corporation is just a way in which Boto and Mike Adams can better their (power) position in the Gypsy nation. But the two Adams deny this accusation. "We're out to prove to the courts", Boto Adams said, "that the self-appointed (Gypsy) kings, or rulers, are in the confidence game." (Jones)[23]

Within the general principles of economic co-operation between Rom and economic exploitation of *gaje*, the number of schemes for making money and the number of occupations is very large and very flexible. In Barvale, the most important source of income is welfare. The rest of this article concerns the methods of eliciting welfare.

Welfare

It is the obligation of the woman to get welfare and to protect her husband from any interference from the Welfare Department in his life or activities. She must use her skills as a "hustler" and her knowledge about welfare policy acquired by word of mouth from other Rom to be effective in her job. The women have many techniques for keeping the men out of welfare negotiations and for convincing the social worker to deal only with her. She may claim her husband is deaf, mentally retarded, senile or physically disabled, or she may simply take over all negotiations while he stays in the background. A few examples of intake interviews from welfare records in 1965–1966 show the effectiveness of this policy by the attitude and conclusions of the social workers.

1. The ———— are a Gypsy family and take full advantage of the fact in trying to avoid questions put to them. They have supported themselves largely as fruit pickers but in the seasons, Mr. ———— does body work and Mrs. ———— a little sewing.

23. Jones, Greg (1970). "Crime Fighters or Extortionists?" *The Houston Post*, September 24, 1970, p. 1/sw.

Mr. ———— allowed his wife to dominate the interview and at times she said he could not hear, but it seemed more his custom of allowing her to be the spokesman for the family than his failing to understand what I was saying. If anyone is hard of hearing, it would seem that Mrs. ———— was the one because every question I asked her had to be repeated. I felt this was in order to give herself time to think of an answer rather than because she did not understand the question.

2. Mrs. ———— is truly the leader of this family. She is a rather aggressive 25 year old woman. She makes capital of the fact that she is a Gypsy and that Gypsies have a much more difficult time in life than other people. She seemed extremely protective of her husband and evidently has accepted her family pattern that the woman, not the man, is the breadwinner and the agency representative for the family. Mr. ———— appeared to know nothing or to be unwilling to say anything. He conversed with his wife several times in a language which I think is Romanian. As far as the family was admitting he has never worked one day in his life for any organised employer. Mrs. ———— kept saying that Mr. ———— was extremely nervous and that he couldn't work because he had bad nerves.

3. Mrs. ———— has a very cloying wheedling personality and it is difficult to interview her. She is very grim and serious when she is performing; has no sense of humour unlike most of the other Gypsy women I have had dealings with lately. Mr. ———— has a pleasant, undemanding personality, but he gives free rein to his wife and he usually sits in the car while she takes one of the children to bombard an agency with pleas and threats. He has, I believe, always lived with his mother and it sounded like she supported him more than he supported her.

4. Mrs. ———— is the most powerful procurer. When she wishes to perform, the others stand back with awe and admiration. She never gives up. If three blankets are approved, she wants four. Mrs. ———— has been successful earning money in Hawaii as a fortune-teller. Mr. ———— seems ineffectual and simple-minded in contrast to the women. He is usually not around during contact with the social service and will not show up at all unless you specifically insist. According to his own statement he has never worked more than two or three days for any employer. It does not appear he would be capable of earning the thousands it has taken to transport his family so many times to Hawaii.

As an occupation for the women, welfare requires the same skills as fortune-telling: she must convince the *gaje* to give her money. Although the Rom are informed of their legal right to welfare by their social workers and have an amazing knowledge of the very complicated bureaucratic procedures involved, most Rom do not believe that simple legal entitlement to welfare is the only condition necessary for them to get their "little cheque". Of course this is perfectly true since welfare procedure is so complicated and changes so frequently that often the social workers themselves are not sure of the legal conditions.

To the Rom, personal contact and influence with the social worker is the most important condition for getting welfare. They believe that the way the social worker feels about them and the amount of pressure or flattery they give to her will affect the expediency and availability of their cheque. Some believe that she can cut them off any time she desires, and they often recommend that she do this to punish someone who has breached their moral code. Consequently, they are cautious never to offend her. If someone does offend her, the others hasten to apologize for him adding that he was *dilo* (crazy). Many newcomers to Barvale believe that they will not be able to get a cheque without Stevan's influence since it is well-known that he and the social workers are on friendly terms.

For example, one family came in with Stevan and applied for welfare. When the worker got their case from another county she found great discrepancy in the birth dates and called them up to question these. The man immediately said, "you mean Stevan doesn't want us to get welfare." The worker explained this had nothing to do with it, and she was sure they could straighten things out. He replied, "I thought Stevan had it fixed". He must have concluded Stevan was against him because he left town without ever getting his cheque. In one intake interview, a woman who was nine months pregnant offered to get down on her knees if the social worker would issue her a cheque that day.

All of these beliefs have a certain basis in fact. Many social workers are strict about establishing eligibility and can delay or deny welfare because forms are not filled out properly or information is not given correctly. Since most Rom cannot read or write (and certainly cannot read the forms given to them) they often give very contradictory and incomplete, sometimes false, information to the Welfare Department, and an unsympathetic social worker can deny them assistance. Generally, they also lack many of the documents required by a bureaucracy such as birth certificates, driver's licences, credit cards and draft cards. This means that residence requirements must be gleaned from pawn tickets, traffic tickets and landlord's or shopkeeper's statements. In Barvale the social worker is very sympathetic to them, and as she has years of experience in sorting out their confusing statements, she speeds up their applications by filling out the forms for them.

In counties where "special needs" such as bedding, furniture, refrigerators and washing machines are issued, the sympathy of the social worker is essential for obtaining these items. Some families get more special needs than others, and the ability of the women to hustle the social worker can make an important difference. In Barvale, "special needs" are only issued to the old people (which all the Rom accept as fair) because it created such competition in hustling the social worker. However, this is only the policy of an individual social worker and has little to do with legal entitlement.

Acquiring welfare, therefore, entails the same kinds of skills that other occupations require, that is, the ability to understand, convince, flatter, cajole, pressure and manipulate the social worker. Welfare is not considered a hand-out; it is money which they convince the *gaje* to give them. The legality or illegality of their position in welfare is contradictory and arbitrary to them, but as in other occupations, they learn to avoid arrest.[24] They do not consider themselves a depressed minority having to beg for charity from the middle class majority. On the contrary, welfare is to them an incredible stroke of luck, yet further proof of the gullibility of the *gaje*. Of course, there are problems connected with it. The *gaje* want them to send their children to school, the young men to vocational training, and the *gaje* in general want a lot of information which the Rom do not wish to divulge. However, as long as these pressures can be delayed or avoided, welfare is a reasonably good occupation for the Rom.

Perhaps the best illustration of their attitude towards welfare is the English names which they use for social workers (who in *Romanes* are simply *gaje*). Since they cannot read, the Rom rely on the spoken words in English, and this, plus perhaps a good sense of humour is possibly the reason for the homonyms which they have substituted. Most Rom in Barvale refer to "welfare" as the "world's fair" and hence a welfare worker becomes the "world's fair worker". Sometimes they may use the expression "the wealthy worker" and some skip the difficult pronunciation (for a *Romanes* speaker, "w" is very difficult to say) and call the social worker simply "the money lady". Whether these substitutions are conscious or unconscious, they concisely express the general attitude of the Rom towards welfare. Once, when I asked a young girl of eighteen what she wanted to do with her life, she replied, "go on welfare". She could not see why she should take up any other occupation and risk failure when there was a perfectly secure and reasonable one at hand.

24. For example, they are allowed to have as much wealth in jewellery as they like, but they are not allowed to have new cars. The Rom, who put their savings in gold and cars, consider this absurd, but accept the practical consequences of being seen with a new car.

Income is generally very difficult to determine since most Rom will not discuss what they earn; but, income from welfare is available from welfare records. Welfare cheques depend on what category of aid the recipient is eligible for and, if a family receives 'Aid to Families with Dependent Children' (AFDC), how many children they have. Welfare rules fit amazingly well with Rom family patterns. When a family receives AFDC a child will be cut off welfare at age 16 if he or she is not in school and at any age if married. The Rom will not send their children to school but prefer to marry them at a young age; therefore a young boy or girl can marry at 16 (since they would be cut off anyway), and once the wife becomes pregnant she can begin getting her own cheque. The Rom also have large families and of course this gives them a larger cheque. They share houses and meals, and therefore they are able to make their money go further. They pay very low rent, and are not interested in acquiring the usual material possessions an American family is accustomed to, although they do have other big expenses such as *pomana* and *slava* feasts, gold, new cars and travel expenses. They also know how to find jewellery bargains and stretch their money further by buying food and supplies at wholesale prices.

On AFDC the average Rom family of seven children and two parents received $373 per month. This figure seems small, but it is deceptive because most households do not contain so few persons. An older man or woman in the house may be eligible for Old Age Security (OAS), Aid to the Totally Dependent (ATD) if he is physically disabled (as most old people are), or the Blind Aid programme if he can convince a doctor that he cannot read an eye chart. Consequently households which pool their funds can manage fairly well. The income from welfare by household (see top of page 34), gives a more accurate picture of the financial situation.

These figures do not include income from able-bodied adult men in the household. Welfare policy requires that an able-bodied man must at least be seeking employment. Only three Rom in Barvale are considered employable by the Welfare Office. The rest have been able to claim some kind of exemption, either a physical disability or the physical disability of a wife or parent, for whom they are caring. Most men are quite ill and can get a legitimate doctor's exemption. Those who cannot often prefer to "desert" their wives (i.e., keep away from the social worker), not to avoid work which they are doing anyway, but to avoid the kinds of employment which the employment office might force them to take and sometimes to avoid reporting their own income. It is also quite common for a married son living with his parents not to be

1.		$114	ATD to head of household for obesity
		80	AFDC for her two minor daughters
		148	AFDC for her adult daughter and child
		148	AFDC for an adult daughter-in-law and child
		114	ATD for an adult son with cerebral palsy
	TOTAL:	$604	per month.
2.		$142	ATD to head of household for obesity, diabetes and heart trouble.
		172	AFDC to wife and two children
		221	AFDC to a daughter-in-law with three children
	TOTAL:	$535	per month.
3.		$180	to wife for Blind Aid
		221	AFDC for her husband and three children (one an adopted granddaughter)
	TOTAL:	$401	per month.
4.		$173	ATD and OAS for head of household
		172	AFDC for her two dependent children
		221	AFDC for her son and three dependent children
	TOTAL:	$566	per month.

claimed at all, and his wife (usually claimed by his parents as an unmarried or divorced daughter with children) therefore has all the contact with the Welfare Department, while the man is free to come and go as he pleases. If the man cannot claim any physical disability and it is already known that his wife is not a sister, he can arrange intelligence and psychological tests to "prove" he is of moronic intelligence and not capable of taking a job anyway. An example of such a test is the following:

Description and Behaviour

Mr. ———— was a short, slight, pallid, aged looking man, with pockmarked skin and a weak voice. He arrived clutching his chest and looking as though he was about to expire. Asked about retraining he shrugged with helpless resignation and said farm work was "all I've done all my life". Co-operation with testing was good and scores appear valid.

Test Findings

An IQ score of 64 was obtained. This is in the retarded range (69 and below), ranks in the lower 1 per cent of the general population and represents a mental age of about ten years. Thinking was markedly concrete with the lowest scores in phases of testing requiring abstract thinking. Visual motor performance was also poor. These results raise the question of organicity. Other phases of testing such as vocabulary, general information, long and short term memory, judgement, etc., were consistently in the retarded range.

Personality tests do not reflect severe pathology such as psychosis. Responses suggest a semi-plastic childlike view of the world, lack of maturity and a moderate ego weakness. Diagnostic impression is inadequate personality and possible non-psychotic organic brain damage in a retarded person. Retraining does not seem feasible. Instruction of the subject and his wife in birth control methods is strongly recommended. This man has nine children.

This kind of report is typical of test results on Rom. They always appear extremely co-operative with the tests and always are declared mentally retarded with a "childlike" personality or a "passive-dependent" personality. It is fairly obvious that the Rom, who are generally extremely intelligent, extroverted and aggressive, are simply acting in a manner which is the opposite of their usual behaviour. I am always amazed at the consistency of the results, and although I could see what kind of act this particular man was exhibiting in the interview, I asked him how he was able to manage such advantageous test results. He told me proudly:

> The trick is never to protest anything but act like you are doing everything right and are, you know, simple-minded and good-hearted about it. Anything she asks me I just give some wrong answer. For instance there was a picture of this doll, and I was supposed to connect the arms and legs. Well I put the legs in the armholes and the arms below. She kept trying to help me but I stuck with that like I was sure it must be right.

Of course, the fact that he could not read or write was also an advantage since this immediately classed him in a sub-normal intelligence group. One crafty lady went to Sacramento for a few months where she convinced her social worker that she was a retarded Cherokee Indian and obtained this pyschological evaluation:

> ... her manner was childlike, "mental age of about eight years". Personality tests "suggest a simple, childlike, not very competent person who is anxious and self-preoccupied. Diagnostic impression is passive dependent personality and probably organic brain syndrome in a retarded person.

The fact that this result is so similar to the other (the two people are not consanguineally related) suggests some kind of similar technique on how to manage the tests. This "Cherokee Indian" was able to get such sympathy from her social worker and keep her so occupied in providing special needs (which require a large number of forms and estimates) that she was unable to get any information on the family or observe them long enough to find out their true financial situation. When the social worker began to see the light, the family left Sacramento and returned to Barvale.

If, however, all other methods fail and a man is unable to have himself or his wife declared physically or mentally disabled, then he can try passive resistance. Stevan's son-in-law, is one of the three "able-bodied men" in Barvale, who have to either be looking for a job or training themselves so that they are employable. (Illiteracy counts as a social disability, but the person must go to night school.) He first said he had back trouble, but the doctor found him perfectly fit. Then he had to go to night school, but he missed most of the classes and only went just enough to keep them from dropping him. Then the employment officer said they must find him a job. He always missed the first appointment with them and then went to the second. Finally when they were ready to discontinue his cheques he moved away, but he stayed less than two months so his case was not transferred, and when he came back the pressures on him to get a job had to begin all over again.

Most of the families were on Aid to Families with Dependent Children (AFDC), but all the old people not yet sixty-five and therefore ineligible for a pension (OAS), generally had obesity related illnesses and could get disability aid (ATD). Physically fit elders always had at least one adopted grandchild and therefore were eligible for AFDC. One lady who had no adopted grandchild (which is quite rare) immediately had one flown out from New York City so that she could have a means of support. One woman was able to prove that she was blind because she "could not read the eye chart" and was eligible for the Blind Aid programme. Several were able to get ATD simply for obesity which they considered a wonderful joke since to them obesity indicates health and prosperity; thin people are thin because they cannot afford a good meal or else are extremely ill. In most cases obesity, heart trouble and diabetes went hand in hand, and the disability was genuine.

1. Tom and his wife came to Barvale with their son Johnny who they claimed was 15 (he is probably about 18). They produced a midwife's certificate from Tom's sister who said he was "born in 1954 or 1955 but I know he is 15." This gave them a year of AFDC until they could get through an application for ATD. At 16 Johnny would be discontinued because he was not in school.

2. Ruby, Tom's eldest sister, was on AFDC for her grandchildren until the last one became 16. Then she brought in an affidavit from Lalie, the only person old enough who could have delivered

her, stating that she was midwife at Ruby's birth and giving her age as 65. Consequently, Ruby qualified for OAS and her cheque went from $138 to $173.

Young people who have just married and therefore are discontinued from their parents' cheque and have no way to get a cheque of their own, are eligible for General Assistance (GA) ($30 per month) until they conceive their first child, usually within the first year of marriage. Even this short interlude between being on one's parents' AFDC cheque and getting one's own can be avoided by keeping the marriage a secret or calling it a betrothal until the girl has conceived.

We can see that practically all Rom can claim some aid from the Welfare Department. Besides the normal support programmes, AFDC, ATD, OAS and GA, there are also special funds and programmes in the Welfare Department which the Rom make full use of. These special funds are more difficult to get, require special application by the social worker and special approval in Sacramento. Of all the people in Barvale on welfare (and a large number of non-gypsies are on welfare in Barvale) the Rom are by far the most effective at acquiring these special funds. One large factor in their favour is their social worker who is very helpful and always informs them of funds which are available. The way in which the Rom make use of these funds is unique, however, and even their social worker can never predict what scheme they will come up with when they get the information. Every law has a loophole and the Rom seem particularly good at ferreting out these loopholes.

1. *Urban Renewal* When the urban renewal programme began, a fund was established to aid families being forcibly moved from their homes to a new area. Each family was given $500 for the expenses and psychological disturbance of moving. The Rom, who preferred the condemned housing in the centre of town, would move into one of these houses, which, of course, had very low rent and which they could alter to fit their needs, knocking out all the inside walls. Approximately six families received their $500 compensation.

2. *Special Housing Needs Fund* This is a fund established to help welfare recipients to buy their own house if they have problems in getting a house to rent (usually because of racial discrimination). The Welfare Department provides a certain portion of the downpayment if the recipient can get a loan. Staley put in a claim on this fund on the basis that he was constantly being evicted for "garbage problems" and "noise" and that he was being discriminated against because of his cultural pattern of life. He has now bought two houses with this fund,

negotiating a personal loan from the owner of the house. Since he is the only Rom in Barvale who owns property, his prestige has been considerably enhanced and his leadership reinforced.

3. *Travel Money* A welfare recipient who finds himself stranded away from his "state" and applies for welfare in another state can usually convince the Welfare Department there to send him back "home" because it is cheaper for them than supporting this person for a long time. The Rom, who travel constantly, often use this system when they are low on funds and want to return to the *kumpania*.

(a) Anna attended Big George Adam's funeral in Los Angeles in 1964 and had to leave Los Angeles when the Welfare Department threatened to take away her children because of "neglect". She arrived in Barvale and went to the welfare office with the story that she and her husband were driving along the highway and he unhitched their trailer and left her pregnant with seven children. She wanted the Welfare Department in Barvale to return her to New York (where she would join her husband presumably). They decided it was cheaper to send her back, even though she had to fly because a doctor declared she had a stillbirth in her womb.
They bought shoes and clothes for the children (who could not fly in "rags"), took them to the airport, bought their tickets and sent them on their way.

(b) One family claimed to the Cleveland Welfare Department that they were from Barvale although the Barvale Welfare Department did not know them. The Cleveland Department was so anxious to get rid of them that they bought all six people bus tickets and gave them $50 in cash to send them to Barvale.

(c) Another woman went to Chicago twice to visit relatives. Each time, when her money ran out she went to the Chicago Welfare Department and created such a scene they sent her back. The second time "stretched" welfare policy considerably.

CONCLUSIONS

The purpose of this essay is to describe as accurately as possible the economic organization of a group of Rom in America, but since I have emphasized throughout that the Rom are making a successful adaptation of their own economic norms and practices to the technologically complex economic situation in America it is not inappropriate to end with a few words on the future relationship between the Rom and welfare departments.

I do not wish to give the impression that in Barvale the Rom are receiving welfare benefits illegally or that they are "hustling" the welfare department there better than anywhere else. The contrary seems to be the case. In Barvale where the caseload is still concentrated under one social worker, fraud is at a minimum because of the personal attention and general knowledge of Gypsy society of the resident social worker.

In other counties on the West Coast, fraudulent practices increase when impersonal bureaucratic methods of handling welfare cases are employed. Recent welfare legislation in California, for example, has split welfare caseloads among several eligibility workers, who deal only with the financial transactions, and the social worker, who has contact with families only in crisis situations. The result of this split for the Rom, as for any nomadic group, has been a recent surge of fraud, primarily in the form of collecting cheques in several counties. One investigation in Los Angeles discovered forty Rom families collecting cheques from two counties simultaneously, and one woman was collecting aid from four offices within L.A. country for a total of $14,000 in fraudulent payments (Tompkins, J., personal communication). It has become obvious that loopholes in welfare law can only be corrected by a policy which encourages consistent personal contact between the welfare department and Rom clients.

CHAPTER TWO

American Rom
and the Ideology of Defilement

Carol Miller

According to Mary Douglas,[1] rituals of purity and impurity create order and unity in experience; they are the means by which symbolic patterns are worked out and publicly displayed. "Ideas about separating, purifying, demarcating and punishing transgressions have as their main function to impose system on inherently untidy experience, exaggerating difference between within and without, above and below, male and female, etc."

The ideology of defilement, or *marime* as defilement is called in Romanes, is pervasive to Rom categories of belief and thought, and extends to all areas of Rom life in some way, underwriting a hygienic attitude towards the world, themselves, and others. Pollution ideas work on the life of Rom society, especially in the sense of symbolizing certain dangers and expressing a general view of the social order. Lines are drawn between the Gypsy and the non-Gypsy, the clean and the unclean, health and disease, the good and the bad which are made obvious and visible through the offices of ritual avoidance.

The map upon which these lines are portrayed is the human body itself, certain areas of which are designated as sanctified and pure, notably the head and mouth and, in somewhat lesser degree, the entire

---

1. Douglas, Mary (1966). *Purity and Danger*, Routledge and Kegan Paul, London.

upper body region. Rites of purification and separation protect the auspicious power associated with the upper region and, the Roma believe, the health and well being of the person performing them. Items that come into contact with these areas are separately maintained, washed in running water or special basins and stored apart from ordinary items; items like soaps, towels, razors and combs,[2] clothes, pillows, furniture like the backs of chairs, the tops of tables, tablecloths, aprons, sinks, food utensils and, of course, food itself, which is prepared, served, and eaten with the greatest consideration for ritual quality. Body orifices that give access to the inner body are defensively guarded, some from further pollution and some from any pollution at all. Because the process of ingestion breaches the margins of the inviolate body area, eating is a delicate and closely regulated matter.

Numerous rituals of avoidance dramatize the different character and what the Rom understand to be the naturally disparate and opposing functions of the two body areas. Any contact between the lower half of the body, particularly the genitals, which are conceptually the ultimate source of *marime*, and the upper body is forbidden. The inward character of the genitals, especially the female genitalia which is associated with the mysteries of blood and birth, makes them consummately impure.[3] Items and surfaces that have contact with this area are carefully segregated because they contain a dangerous potential to the status of pure items and surfaces. The most dreadful contact, of course, would be between the genitals and the oral cavity.[4] Every

2. The following conveys something of the feeling state associated with *marime* rituals of separation:

> The one thing I always do . . . I'm strict . . . is to wash my face and take care of my razor right. If there isn't a face towel, I use my children's T shirt. Sometimes when the soap falls out on the floor and I don't have any more, I look at it and it's hard (to refrain from picking the soap up), but like the razor falling on the floor or being used for something else (than intended ritual use), I can always tell if it's *marime*. I break out in a rash. From *Machwaya Gypsy Marime*, Miller, C. A., unpublished M.A. Thesis, Univ. of Washington 1968.

3. Any reference, by word or by gesture, to the genitals, to defecation, or sexual intercourse is a shame, particularly in cross-sex situations or between Roma in different age categories. Taboos extend to such matters as yawning or looking sleepy at the table, because "it means you're thinking about going to bed". Beds and bathrooms are impolite topics of conversation, as are childbearing and babies. Daughters are not likely to mention pregnancy to their mothers, largely because of the relation of pregnancy to intercourse. When the baby is born, it is better for someone of the same age and sex to report the news, rather than either the girl or her husband. "Where were you found?" is preferred to the question "Where were you born?" according to Jan Thompson, a social worker with many years contact with Gypsy clients in both business and social situations.

4. The fellatio cunnilingus contact. Needless to say, the article is dealing with a discussion of Rom cognitive structures, beliefs and rituals. It may well be that in private life these taboos simply increase the titillation of such contact.

precaution is taken to increase spatial and temporal distance between each of these.

Under normal circumstances, the status of the adult body areas are conceptualized as relatively permanent and stable. Ritual separation is assumed to maintain the purity of one, by containing the impurity of the other. The transitional status of the hands, whose qualities can be improved by rinsing under running water and washing with "face" soaps and towels, permits the hands the necessary task of ministering to both body regions. In order to bring the hands into consonance with the goodness of the upper body, and to avoid injury to this goodness, washing ritual is performed with regularity after contaminating contact with the lower body [5] and before preparing food or handling the religious icons.

During certain progressive periods of the life cycle, the ratio of purity/impurity is automatically altered. At birth, the infant is regarded as entirely *marime* upon the entire body surface owing to the polluting nature of the site of recent origin. The mother, owing to her intensive contact with the infant, is also thought to be dangerously impure. Both are isolated for a period of time that varies from the three days of post-partum hospitalization to several weeks if the family has other female members to assume the household duties of washing and cooking. Subsequent to this period, the infant, and later the child, is not *marime* at all [6] although, as much of the child's contact is with the floor and other polluting surfaces, the Rom recognize the logical inconsistency of this singular condition by admitting that "he should be". Children are believed to be blameless to sin, including defilement, because they are new and innocent, and not yet fully aware of the consequences of their deeds. Their purity tends to ameliorate defiling contacts; they are usually forgiven if they come to the table without washing, and are permitted many freedoms of speech and movement that the adults of the family are denied. [7]

Innocence ends with marriage which properly activates the full capacity for pollution. At the same time, these powers are contained by the complementary structure of marital roles and responsibilities.

---

5. For some examples, washing the hands is recommended after touching the belt, putting on shoes /or making a bed. See Thompson's article (1922) for an appreciation of more elaborated rituals of separation among the English Gypsies.

6. Some few families still use separate tubs for adults and children to protect the children's purity from contamination and separate portable toilets for the same reason.

7. Other people's children are criticized in private for their bad manners, dirty appearance and foul language, however. Similar mistakes by their own children are likely to be tolerated. The Rom are generally very indulgent with their children. They try to please them and give them everything they want because love is largely expressed through being "unable to refuse anything". There is little teaching or disciplining by verbal direction. Children are expected to learn indirectly and by mimicry.

Marriage is the *rite de passage* to adulthood. A girl becomes a Romni with marriage, a woman and a wife; a boy becomes a Rom, a man and husband.[8] An important aspect of their adult responsibilities involves segregating the two sexes, as well as the two body areas. The etiquette of respect avoidance restrains and minimizes cross-sex contact between Roma of adult status, and gives additional opportunity for expression of belief in the superior qualities of Rom ritual purity by "putting a face on things". Even the married couple are respectful and decorous in approaching one another; they are not allowed to touch or display affection overtly, either in public or at home in front of their children. Among the many proscriptions upon association, they are prevented from eating together; to remark the difference in purity, privilege, and authority, men eat first and are served by their wives.[9]

Innocence is gradually regained, in some measure, with old age, a stage in the life cycle considered as spiritually elevated. The *phurotem*, the elders, are close to the gods and the ancestors, a condition of great gravity and potential danger to the living. Avoidance is publicly augmented in order to show the *phurotem* a respect consistent with their advancing years. As the powers of purity increase, the powers of impurity would seem to be in decline. Because they do not bear children or menstruate, old women no longer have the power to *marime* by "tossing the skirt" (see p. 51). The *phurotem* themselves are not criticized for slighting avoidance. Old men, for example, can flirt with young women with impunity.

Under normal circumstances adult men and women, as well as children and *phurotem* are assumed to be reasonably clean, the latter because of their innocence and presumed lack of interest in heterosexual contact,[10] the former because they are careful to confine their contact to the appropriate connubial time and place. The burden of avoidance obligation rests with adult Rom, who are at the most dangerous and most endangered stage of life. It is apparent from the changing intensities of power and danger at various stages, infant, child, adult,

8. The transition may be dramatic for the boy that marries young. One 14 year old husband, small for his age, dresses in a suit, tie, and hat, and drives a late model Cadillac to conduct business transactions with the *gaje* used-car dealers. The older Rom are careful to treat him as an equal, and he is given a man's respect by adult Rom women.

9. Eugene Hammel has kindly pointed out that the tradition for modesty of demeanour toward the opposite sex, particularly the modesty of women, is pervasive to areas around the Mediterranean, the Middle East and most marked in the formal avoidance characteristic of upper caste Hindus. Linguistic evidence suggests that the Rom are of Indian origin and their history of cultural contact has been largely in the areas mentioned.

10. The Rom like to believe that their elders have no interest in sexual relationships. The marriage of widowers over 40 years old, or couples with grandchildren, is explained charitably as "They just need a little company because they get lonesome now that the children are big."

and elder, that the ritual separation of the body areas, upper from lower, inner from outer, and male from female has a primary function to the control of sexual behaviour, and that sexual desires are conceptualized as potentially threatening. Improper sexual contacts spread shame and defilement throughout the kin group. They are frequently contacts that Roma regard as bordering upon the incestuous because they involve couples whose status is inappropriate to sexual contact, e.g., a Rom and his daughter-in-law (see p. 54, Case 5) or a couple related in *shevrimos*, cogod-parenthood, a sacred relationship that is protective to the health and wellbeing of the godchild. Relationships between a Rom or Romni and a non-Gypsy also join what should not be joined and offend Rom ideas regarding appropriate sexual union (see p. 54, Cases 2 and 3). Sanction is applied discriminately to males and females. Upon occasion a Rom marries a non-Gypsy woman, has children and, over a period of years, is permitted to return to public life and public favour as a married man. (His wife may even be treated with toleration.) The Romni is not allowed this privilege. A Romni has the burden of responsibility for the purity of the race, and is vulnerable to irreparable damage by contact of such kind. Parents are said to forget the name of daughters that marry non-Gypsies; runaway daughters lose their families, their rights as Rom citizens, and theoretically are ruined "forever". Parents are normally too soft hearted to conform to the letter of the law, however, and daughters are gradually reinstated after they have left their non-Gyspy husbands, presented medical evidence clearing them of any trace of venereal infection, and demonstrated remorse.[11] Punishment is likely to encourage their remorse. The girl is often married off at a low price to the first family that asks for her, a family that may be poor and lower-class.

The *gaje*, as the Rom call non-Gypsies, are conceived as a different race and kind of being whose main value is economic, and whose *raison d'etre* is to trouble the Rom. The major offence of the *gaje*, the one offence that the Rom can never forgive, is their propensity to defilement. *Gaje* confuse the critical distinction between the pure and the impure. They are observed in various situations which the Rom regard as compromising; forgetting to wash in public bathrooms: eating with the fork that they rescued from the floor of the restaurant: washing face towels and tablecloths with underwear at the local self service laundry: relaxing with their feet resting upon the top surface of the table. Because they do not protect the upper half, the head and mouth, from damage, the *gaje* are construed as *marime* all over, head

11. The family of the runaway girl is automatically isolated from public commensal association when she returns (see p. 54).

to foot. This condition, according to Rom belief, invites and spreads contagious disease. Rom tend to think of all illness and physical disability as communicable and treat them accordingly. The classic disease that the *gaje* convey is venereal disease. This is not limited to sexual contact. The Rom that eats with *gaje* or works for them is usually libelled as *marime* by some segment of the Rom community. Theories of disease dictate a caste-like separation of the two kinds of people, Gypsy and *gaje*, along a spectrum of opposition that is analogous to the distinction that is made between upper and lower. In either case, the danger of one, must be contained to protect the power of the other. Consequently, with the exception of the most expedient and profane of circumstances, making money or by reason of economic neccessity, the *gaje* are forbidden to Rom contact and association.[12]

Categories of thought that rank the *gaje* as inferior to the Rom in the many attributes associated with purity and health have an obvious significance to pride and self-respect. During the period of written history, beginning with the fifteenth century, the relationship between the Rom and their hosts has been one of persecution, enslavement, and a variety of abuses which have their culmination in the Nazi pogroms against Gypsies.[13] In most European countries, they are traditionally a low status group. By believing in the protection of a power that is equivalent, or greater, the Rom make symbolic defence against the inroads of the larger and politically more powerful society. The smaller is permitted to nourish confidence in their own systems of belief and values by avoiding challenge. The result is that despite demeaning life circumstances, which include frequent and irritating inequities, morale is maintained at a favourable level. When a Romni is arrested for telling fortunes, or a family is forced to move because the landlord has discovered that ten children, instead of the two or three expected, are living in one house, the aggravation can be lessened by a counter offensive of verbal abuse in Romanes concerning the appearance of the skin, the odour, moral character, and personal habits of the *gaje*.

For a variety of reasons, business and social, the majority of Rom prefer to live in the context of the city or in towns that approximate

12. An outspoken Rom describes the *gaje* as follows:

You know what we think of Americans? We think they're stupid, crazy, ignorant, filthy, and no good. Why? Because Americans always have syphilis and clap. They go down on each other. We throw the glass they drink out of away. They're filthy. It's not the same as clean and dirty. It's a lot worse. Americans wash their face with the same towel they wash feet with. Ugh! The old folks didn't have anything to do with *gaje*, but now we have to work with them in the car business.

13. Clébert, Jean-Paul (1963). *The Gypsies* (translated, Charles Duff), Penguin Books, Harmondsworth.

to large urban centres.[14] The urban world is perceived as pervasively *marime*, filled with items and surfaces that are subject to use and reuse by careless *gaje*, polluted, diseased, and therefore dangerous. In making their way through this unfavourable environment, they are forced by their circumstances to rely much upon the appearance of surfaces in gauging their merit. Rom prefer to shop in stores, rent houses, and travel in cars that "look clean", because, hopefully, they are. Ritual precaution and proscriptions serve as perpetual reminder to the rules of dissociation, however. A working Rom washes his face and hands whenever he feels his luck leaving him during the day; he washes again upon returning from his work. His children are normally not allowed to play with *gaje* children; they are even less likely to be allowed to bring a *gaje* child into their home. Animal, vegetable or mineral, whatever crosses the doorstep is carefully scrutinized. Only articles that are newly manufactured or freshly grown are considered entirely safe. Even so, those things that can be washed are subject to thorough cleansing; food, including meat, is most notable in this regard.

The home is the final bastion of defence against defilement, and the only place that the Rom feel altogether at ease. For the religious holidays that relate to the slava feast of southeastern Europe, a section of the house is transformed into a church. The Saints, who are "up", are supplicated for the good health and well being, *Sastimos* and good luck, *Baxt*, that forms the simple central theme of ritual and doctrine. On these occasions the appropriate condition of the house, the inhabitants, and the table, is as close to an immaculate condition as is attainable by the measures that the Rom know, namely, washing and scrubbing, as well as airing, disinfecting, painting walls and ceiling surfaces, sewing new covers for furniture and beds, replacing draperies, rugs, and dishes. In a degree depending upon the family's social standing or social aspirations, ordinary daily household maintenance will also require similar improvement efforts. Purchase and replacement is laborious and costly if the family is particularly mobile; only the wealthy are able to move often and present an estimable household appearance; usually the wealthy, for some of these same reasons, fall high on the scale of purity and respect.[15] The moral worth of the Romni is sup-

14. Cotten's ethnography of the Bigby family describes the transition and adjustment to an urban and semi-nomadic lifestyle. Cotten, R. (1968). "Urban Nomads—Gypsies of N.Y. City" *Transactions of N.Y. Academy of Science* II No. 29.

15. Nothing succeeds like success in the eyes of the Rom, and a healthy, wealthy and "lucky" appearance is considered as visible confirmation of merit. Nowhere is this more tangibly apparent than at the larger public events that attract hundreds of Roma, the men in expensive, well tailored suits and diamond rings, the women wearing voluminous dresses of sparkling fabrics and dazzling jewels. (For reasons relating to defilement custom, the

posedly incremented in proportion to her efforts to fight dirt and decay, and she makes a good public impression if she appears continually engaged in these sanitary activities. She makes an even better impression if she can sit and talk with guests while food and beverage are served, and the house is impeccably maintained by a bevy of unobtrusive and obedient daughters-in-law.

The Rom household is open to hospitality visits from other Rom; at any time of the day or night neighbours or travellers may drop in and, in this sense, the home and its occupants are always on display. A place that looks new and fresh is associated with people who look healthy and good. These are ranked as more prestigious on the scale of purity and social value than people and houses that appear neglected or disordered. For reasons of contagion, the latter are avoided by upper-class Rom who express their distaste by complaining of feeling unlucky, upset or nauseous after visiting them. Complaints of this kind are also frequent when Rom eat with *gaje* in restaurants.

Wherever food is served, at home or in public, the delicacy of feelings towards the process of ingestion is indicated by ease of insult. It is important to the Rom that commensal conditions be favourable. Food in *gaje* restaurants will go untouched or be thrown away if the atmosphere is strange, the room is crowded, or the food is suspect. Well lighted restaurants where the food preparation can be easily observed are preferred. Coffee is somewhat of a fetish; if the cup and saucer, the taste, the cream, etc., are inadequate in any way, the Rom refuse to drink it. These same beliefs and feelings are closely associated with customs of hospitality. With fellow Rom, the eating situation is *ideally* relaxed and unstrained because the kitchen is presumably maintained according to standards for purity and the company is ritually correct.

In addition to hospitality events, the Rom come together in a common and spiritual purpose upon socio-ceremonial occasions which involve feasting and special foods. The *pomana* makes feast for the dead and invites them to eat in heaven, even as the company assembled eats at the table. The *slava* feast is preceded by coffee and prayer; a candle coaxes the saint in the direction of the commensal table. The *slava* foods include the auspicious foods, *sarmaa* (cabbage rolls), *gushvada* (cheese strudel), and a ritually sacrificed animal, most often a lamb. At ceremonial events, the eating is less important than an ample presentation for all attending to see. A stingy feast is expected to please no one, including the supernatural guests.

---

dresses cover the legs but bare the bosom.) The ability of the Macvaia to display to better advantage than any other group is likely connected to their superior status in terms of ritual purity.

Good food in generous amounts has congruency to good health. Until recently, when a number of the larger Rom died from heart attacks in their prime, the size of a man was a measure of his strength, power and wealth. The word for "big man", or *baro*, suggests corporeal size, as well as political importance. Nurturance and affection is expressed through gifts of food, just as they are in many societies, but with particular emphasis by the Rom. When greeting an intimate, the most popular inquiry is to ask whether or not he ate that day, and what. The expression has a practical basis. Middle-aged and older, Rom have memories of many days when food was unobtainable. They report that nothing is harder for parents to endure than the sound of children crying from hunger. Lack of food is associated with bad living, bad luck, poverty and disease; if a person loses weight, even if the weight loss is reasonable from the standpoint of western medical norms, the presumption is that they have been sick. It is entirely appropriate at such times for the public to express concern about what is considered an inadvertent lack of appetite, or a shortage of food, either of which may portend failing health. Food is recognized as the most basic human need. Hunger is feared and ungratified appetite is dangerous. Supernatural sanctions are associated to these concerns. People that don't get what they want to eat become *postarniko*, obsessed by their need to taste a particular food that they have recently seen and have in their mind. *Postarniko* people can get sick, die, and become the ghosts that will haunt the living. The dream of a dead relative asking for food is especially fearful and requires appeasement with food offerings and fasting.

Commensality makes an important statement concerning altruistic attitudes towards other Rom, as well as the purity and equivalent respect of those that eat together. These are linked to the good health and vitality of the community-at-large as is particularly apparent upon socio-ceremonial occasions. Rituals of commensality work upon the body politic through the symbolic medium of the physical body. The act of eating together conjoins communion with the Rom public, with generations that are gone and generations yet unborn. The Rom present are reminded of their common destiny and their obligation to guard the strength, unity and goodness of the corporate unit from damage. The ritual of commensality is primarily the business of male Rom. Men represent their families at all public affairs, are responsible for their families' protection, as well as answerable to the public for their offences. The men meet at the table as equals in respect and privilege, none with more power than the other except by reason of the increased spirituality associated with age. As has been indicated, food is a primary medium of *marime* and disease. It is consumed with equanimity in the company of responsible and congenial Roma. Eating together denotes trust. The presence of one disgraced or sickly Rom in the commensal company is believed to be polluting to the rest. Each Rom has the same potential for damage to the others in these regards. On the other hand, the proper sensibility for custom is demonstrated by always accepting food that is offered by a Rom in good repute.[16]

In addition, commensality makes important statements about the distinction between the Rom and the *gaje*, the inner and the outer group, by emphasizing commensal separation. The minority standing and vulnerability of the smaller society in the context of the larger, the need for protection and for unity, is reflected in exaggerated concern with the exits and entrances of the human body. Proscriptions on contact provide focus to fears of political absorption; behaviours most apt to betrayal—eating and making love with the *gaje*—are subject to penalty by law. To remark the difference, Rom do not eat in *gaje* homes; they offer *gaje* hospitality in their own homes by service from china and eating utensils that are specially washed and segregated from other household items.

As is typical with many small scale societies, gossip and scandal are a main source of social control and public opinion is continually engaged in sifting reputations through the exacting sieve of Rom norms and values. A Rom, fallen into disrepute for any reason, is liable to commensal isolation. He may learn of his disgraced condition when his hostess presents him cold coffee in a cracked cup, or fails to serve him when everyone else is served. Worse, he may suspect that he has been drinking coffee from the cup reserved for *gaje*. Treatment like the *gaje* indicates that the Rom is graded low on the scale of purity and respect, that he is dirty, disreputable, diseased, in fact *marime*.[17]

The crimes of *marime* are moral crimes, or "shames". These damage the cherished image of the body politic, even as they threaten the carefully enlisted powers of Sastimos. According to Rom belief, the attributes of a good life, health, wealth, and happiness, are locked into a clean and moral family life.[18] Shames join what should not be joined

16. To refuse to eat with another Rom imputes not only his ritual habits, but his character as well. "Everyone always tries to take a little food anyway. If you turn somebody down altogether, it's not a good idea . . . makes you feel like you think their food is *marime*." Conversely, to be asked to leave a Rom house implies rejection for reprehensible reasons.
17. The Rom also say "reject", "blackball", or "he's out".
18. Health is often a good indicator of the condition of household affairs. If her husband, son, or daughter ignores her admonitions and is disobedient to moral precepts, the Romni is apt to experience health affliction. She is well within the limits of her role to cry hysterically for days, behave erratically, lose interest in making money or paying bills, forget to eat, lose weight and become sickly. If the problem continues for any period of time, the entire

and upset the recognized order of things and events, so that calamity visits the family in a form of Sastimos reversed, illness, loss of money, bad luck, unhappiness, insanity, even death. The most vulnerable to these supernatural sanctions are the children of the *familia*, the extended family. For these reasons, whenever shames of any size become public knowledge, in order to protect the *familia* and to stay the tide of unpropitious events, the agent of the shame is libelled as *marime*, dangerous to himself and others.

In this context, the stigma of *marime* is understood by the Rom as an official state of social disgrace. The stigma serves social ends as a kind of impersonal punishment for wrongdoing. Because they have a public status that women lack and because of their superior ritual purity, *marime* sanction applies primarily to men. The Rom *marime* is outcasted from social and political affairs. To remove the stigma and restore his respect, the Rom is compelled to face his accusers, and make public denial or public redress. In cases of *marime*, pollution taboos buttress and supplement a serious shortage of punitive sanctions. The court, that otherwise would be limited to an advisory and counselling capacity, is provided the means for redress of moral crimes through the offices of ritual avoidance.[19]

Beliefs about purity/defilement are associated with standards of morality/immorality, but not in a one-to-one relationship. Moral situations are not always easy to define; pullution rules are unequivocal. An interesting example of how these can work together to social purpose when ordinary means have failed is the sanction of skirt-tossing, a power for penalty by pollution afforded to women. Skirt-tossing creates a scandal that focuses public gossip upon disputes and inequities. The method is simple. Anything having contact with the lower female body, traditionally the underskirt, is deliberately juxtaposed upon the upper and saintly extremity of the Rom.[20] When news of the event reaches

---

family may suffer a general decline in health and living conditions. As one elderly Romni explains, "That's their belief. If you live in the home right, all go together. If (the husband or son) chase women, spend money, family get sick, lose business and happiness. All go together. That's the way it happens".

19. Brown mentions a Rom who is eventually punished by *marime* accusation after committing a number of crimes against fellow Gypsies. He writes that "it is not always easy to convict and punish such crimes by *Romani kris*: but to pronounce the parties marime is simple and effective" (165).

20. Skirt tossing pollution was probably more effective before the days of sanitary pads. Shoe tossing seems equally common these days, and the exposure of the female genitalia, although less lethal is also popular. A pubic hair, applied to the face of a Rom, is also a very strong sanction at present, and indicates "real hate". Yoors, Jan [(1967). *The Gypsies*, Allen and Unwin, London.] who spent the large part of his youth with the Lowara Roma of Europe, is of the opinion that their uncleanliness "assured Gypsy women an absolute sense both of privacy and of protection among their own kind anywhere at large" (p. 150). He

the community, the Rom is ostracized. It is traditionally his responsibility to call the court together that will help him clear his name. If the Rom is found guilty, the court recommends public apology, the payment of a fine, or a period of isolation. If the Rom complies with the court's decision, the Romni forgives him by admitting that the skirt-tossing story was fictional. This admission is essential to the peaceful settlement of the case. The Rom do not know any purifying ritual that will cleanse a man's head, the nexus of respect and honour, of such impurity. In fact, skirt-toss *marime* "never happens . . . it's a lie (because) if she really did it, he's out . . . no one could eat with that family forever . . . generations".

In keeping with Rom ideology, social isolation is expressed, in large part, by commensal isolation. *Marime* status extends to the household and, if the Rom is suspected of having eaten with them, the *familia*. Even distant relatives become somewhat apprehensive about commensal refusal and hesitate to visit other households. Until the slander is forgotten or publicly forgiven, any uncertainty about the legitimacy of respect status in the community is apt to result, according to the relationship with the Rom *marime*, in a variable degree of withdrawal from public life. Because kinsmen are affected, they will encourage the Rom to a quick settlement of the case.

Processes of ingestion have been described as portraying political incorporation. The ritual of reinstatement is, appropriately, the ritual of commensality. The decision of the court is expressed in a similar manner; those voting for the defendant will drink coffee with him: those voting against will not. The subsequent gossip that circulates the community regarding who is guilty and why; the extent of guilt and the manner of settlement is tailored, and retailored, to agree with various viewpoints about the proceedings and the temper of personal relationships with the defendant. The important piece of information, for those not participant to the trial, is whether or not the Rom ate or drank with the defendant before they left the courtroom.

According to the best reports available, the sanction of *marime* has been applied locally in the following situations and with the following

---

describes an incident involving a young man whose brutal beating is ended abruptly when the young man's wife began flailing the attackers with her skirt. Similar incidents are reported in the States. One young girl stopped a fight by disrobing and yelling for the combatants' attention. The men, she said, ran in all directions. The woman's power to reject is complementary to her husband's susceptibility to rejection. Rom will take his wife along when he visits stranger Rom, not only to make the proper public impression, but also to be assured that in the event of hostilities, he is armed and can retaliate in kind.

kinds of results during the past eight years (see Appendix, p. 54). The relevant population of approximately 1,000, encompasses four of the major cities in the northwestern United States. In four of the cases mentioned (2, 3, 5, 6), the court of elders was involved in the decision making process, either as a proper *kris romani*, with the members of several families represented, or as a smaller, more informal grouping classed as *deswato* or *diwano*, according to Kalderash or Machvaia dialects. In only one instance did the court agree upon a finite period of isolation (6). Two of the defendants have chosen to live elsewhere (1, 5). Half of the cases involved *gaje*, or problems with outsiders; the other half related to internal affairs exclusively. Of the former, cases involving outsiders, isolation continued in two until the defendants desired reinstatement and made conciliatory overtures to the public (2, 3).[21]

The cases studied are few, (only six), and not remarkable from the criminal cases and conflicts that might be found in any American lower or working-class community. The record clearly indicates that the inflexibility of pollution beliefs is easily adapted to a variable punishment that fits court and community decisions regarding the nature of the crime and possibilities for settlement and reconciliation. The sanction's clear intention in the context of "keeping Gyspies good to other Gypsies" is to modify behaviour, not to outcast indefinitely.

The formality of isolation is of course, only a small part of the penalty. Most humiliating is that lower status Rom and despised enemies gain ascendancy over the *marime* family and that the extended family is subject to contemptuous treatment by other Rom. Further, the period of isolation that the court specifies only begins the penalty. The shame lasts as long as the memories of the living, to follow the family wherever they travel. Even unsubstantiated rumours, if they become popular and are repeated often, can have a sinister effect upon a family's reputation.

The standards for propriety are high, and the reputation of the family is, in large part, the history of their scandals. But families are also ranked along parameters of more immediate kind—the clean appearance of the household, the skill with which hospitality ritual is performed, food generosity, the rectitude of women, their gifts for making money

---

21. Cotten (1950:164) found court verdicts involving *marime* of two types: a finite period of isolation, and permanent excommunication which required another trial to remand the verdict. She had the impression that verdicts were becoming less severe with the breakdown of some of the traditional lines of authority. This impression generally agrees with the experiences of my informants; only the eldest could remember a permanent *marime*. They also noted that court action on brideprice payment or brideprice return, which used to be the most frequent type of case involving skirt-tossing, had declined, and suggested that problems of such kind were being settled out of court.

telling fortunes, the family's appearance and decorum at public events. Gossip keeps the Rom under constant scrutiny. Any changes in appearance and deportment are evaluated according to ideas about the pure and good. Much stress is placed upon the ability to command respect by conveying a positive impression of health and prosperity. Efforts of such kind are part of a larger system of congruent beliefs and actions, and are instrumental to ordering, framing, and focusing experience to agree with ideas about the superior purity and superior morals of Rom.

APPENDIX

Marime Cases, 1965–1973

Case 1
Offence: Rape of the *gaje* wife of a Rom.
Result: No official court because defendant left the area to live elsewhere.

Case 2
Offence: Married a *gaje* and lived with her part of the time, returning to his wife upon occasion.
Result: Court threatened *marime* unless the Rom left his *gaje* wife. When he failed to comply, the community began the process of commensal isolation. During his five years of isolation, his brothers received him in private. Marriage to another Romni began reinstatement process.

Case 3
Offence: Married a *gaji*, but stayed with his Romni wife most of the time.
Result: Court decision split because defendant denied *gaje* relationship and Romni backed him up. Three years of isolation from the segment of the community that refused clearance followed. Household involved.

Case 4
Offence: Cursed a Romni during an argument; Romni said that she defiled him.
Result: No court. Public refused to acknowledge *marime*, largely because the offence was insufficient to justify isolation.

Case 5
Offence: Stole son's young Romni bride after the wedding.
Result: When couple found, girl's family reclaimed her without returning brideprice ($5,000). The defendant's household subsequently moved to another area.

Case 6
Offence: Beat up the wife of another Rom; Romni said she defiled her attacker.
Result: Court decision for isolation of one month which included the four households of the defendant's brothers.

Author's note: Although Roma of Machwaya affiliation were the major source of information regarding belief and ritual, the preceding cases of *marime* sanction include both Machwaya and Kalderasha.

CHAPTER THREE

Gypsies Travelling in Southern England[1]

Judith Okely

INTRODUCTION

All the travelling Gypsies I encountered during my fieldwork in South East England, frequented a wider area than one county. They cannot be labelled "local" Gypsies. So although this is a study of Gypsies or Travellers in a specific area, there may be aspects which are common to some Gypsies elsewhere in England.

The area lies near Greater London and is traversed by major routes to other parts of the country. It is a thoroughfare and convenient base for Gypsies, as well as commuter housedwellers. Formerly it had a mainly agricultural economy, with large country estates, isolated villages and a scatter of market towns. Industrial development was significant only towards the south west.

Between the wars came the first of several new industrial and residential complexes. Then after the Second World War, the area experienced the major effects of a government policy to redistribute employment and people outside London. New towns were established. Industrial expansion in the south west of the area also proceeded at a

1. All references to place-names in the area have been deliberately omitted in order to protect the anonymity of the Travellers. All names of persons and identifiable details have been changed. This essay is based on field work from 1970–1972. I am indebted to the Travellers for their hospitality; to the Centre for Environmental Studies, and the Rowntrees Trust, with whose project I was involved. I should also like to thank James Hopkins for comments on the early draft.

pace. This massive development brought dramatic changes for the Gypsies resorting to the area.

The new residential and industrial zones attracted skilled and highly paid workers, who, with the increasing number of middle class commuters, made a comparatively wealthy population from which the Gypsies could find profitable ways of earning a living. But while expansion brought economic opportunities, it reduced the availability of land for inconspicuous and casual encampments. Vast tracts of land, some of which had been occupied and occasionally owned by Gypsies were bought and developed. New roads carved up old haunts. With this development came tighter planning controls in the remaining rural areas.

As there are rural hamlets a few miles from large towns so there are contrasting groups of Gypsies in the area. Within an hour's drive from the heart of the metropolis, in the neglected woods and hills, there are a few Gypsy families whose habitat in all seasons is a "bender tent" of curved wooden rods overlaid with tarpaulin, shaped like an igloo. There may be rabbits or birds in cages and a dog, usually a mongrel. Inside may be a groundsheet and mattress, typically with neatly folded linen and blankets. (One old man managed with only straw for his bedding.) Cooking is done on an open fire, the black pot and kettle dangling from an iron rod. There are strict standards of cleanliness, particularly in connection with eating: food and drink are taken from shiny, unchipped china. At times a younger family may acquire an old van or pick-up with perhaps a trailer caravan. Others have no motorized transport and travel miles on foot with their possessions in an old pram or knife-grinding machine.

While this tiny minority of tented and non-motorized families are found in the rural pockets, the majority of families cluster near the urban centres. The vicinity of heavy industry and the major by-passes have attracted families who rely largely on scrap metal dealing. They have patched-up lorries and old but weather-proof trailer caravans. Pieces of scrap iron and overturned cars lie on the work space around their home. Large churns for storing water are near at hand. A horse used for pulling a trolley may be tethered nearby, and one or two dogs. These may be a variety of uncertain breeds; small lap dogs as opposed to guard dogs are allowed inside. The interiors of the trailers are neat and homely; bedding, clothing and other possessions are stored in wooden cupboards, and on the open shelves are family photos and china plates. There are calor gas cookers, and coal stoves.

Often in encampments off the roadside, there are other families with new lorries or Range Rovers and opulant trailer caravans worth between £2,000 and £6,000. These are laced with chrome and some have cut-glass windows. Inside are mirrored cupboards, glistening formica walls, satin covers, new carpets, cut-glass vases and Crown Derby China. Their dogs are pedigree and include Yorkshire terriers, lurchers and whippets for hunting and alsatians for guarding the property.

GORGIO–GYPSY RELATIONS

For the sedentary society, the Gypsies' nomadism has been a major source of conflict. As nomads, the Gypsies require to use land differently and the authorities in the sedentary society have found them elusive. Their way of life has seemed a mystery and an affront to the laws and values of settled housedwellers. In 1622 we find the Bishop of Lincoln writing to the Earl of Salisbury and other local J.P.'s in the area studied, urging them to put into effect the laws for "punishing, imploying, chasetising and rooting out" the Gypsies, or Aegiptians, as they were then called.

> His Majestie is justly offended at you, who . . . do suffer your countrey to swarme with whole troupes of rogues, beggars, Aegip-tians and idle persons . . . symptoms of Popery and blind superstition.[2]

In the sessions Rolls for the locality there are examples of Gypsies being "well whipped", dispatched to other counties or imprisoned in the local gaol. Nevertheless, it has often been claimed in the area studied, as elsewhere that Gypsies were tolerated in the past, particularly when they were "out of the way" in a rural setting. There were certainly examples of Gypsies having good relations with housedwellers, some of whom were prosecuted for "entertaining and harbouring" Gypsies. But there was also intolerance and conflict between the nomads and the sedentary population. William Ellis a local farmer in the eighteenth century, alleged that[3]

> These Miscreants and their loose women . . . travel in Terrorem to the country people. . . . A hard case indeed that the country should thus suffer by a parcel of Rogues and their Trollops who live like drones, on the labour of others without paying any Rent or Taxes.

His complaints are similar to those found in readers' letters to the local newspapers today.

---

2. The quotation by the Bishop of Lincoln is taken from a local County Records Sessions Rolls (1581–1698).
3. Ellis, W. "The nuisance and prejudice of the Gypsy vagrant to the farmer". Quoted *In* Bell, V. (1956). *To Meet Mr. Ellis*, Faber and Faber, London.

In 1816 John Hoyland[4] recorded the problems as described by a lawyer acquainted with Gypsies in the area;

> The situation of this people daily became increasingly deplorable in consequence of the establishment of associations for the prosecution of felons; and that the fear of apprehension as vagrants and the progressive inclosures near towns and villages had a tendency to drive them to a greater distance from the habitations of men.

A situation of conflict between Gypsies and gorgios in the area is therefore not new. Hoyland observed:

> It is worse than useless and unavailing to harass them from place to place when no retreat or shelter is provided.

His comments are echoed in the 1962 Ministry Circular.[5]

Policies of dispersal or elimination have proved unenforceable, so compromise and negotiation have been necessary. Officials and local citizens have tolerated Gypsies in certain places, if only for a while. Today the conflict occurs in a new setting. Official policy now includes accommodation in the literal sense. An attempt is being made to "settle" the Gypsies on council sites. The first of these in the area was opened in 1964, and by 1973 one local authority was managing six, accommodating a total of 83 families. Provision was preceded and accompanied by the large scale closure of alternative encampments regularly used by the Gypsies, so that the total number of camping pitches legal or illegal, now available is likely to have decreased in the last decade. The local authorities were sometimes directly or indirectly a party to this process of closure, using official site provision as their justification. One Gypsy put it:

> We had a grand time till this talk of sites. Now we can't go anywhere.
> They've closed our old stopping places.

With the effective closure of common, private and council owned land, the Gypsies tended to congregate on the grass verges of major highways where prosecution proved less efficient. Their immediate visibility and their use of the surrounding land for scrap work was provocative to passing motorists and local residents, so the authorities became increasingly impatient to acquire "control powers"[6] after making provision for 120 families. The police would then be able to take even more effective action against the remaining Gypsies not on sites.

---

4. Hoyland, J. (1816). *An Historical Survey of the Customs, Habits and Present State of the Gypsies*. London.
5. Ministry of Housing and Local Government Circular 6/62.
6. 1968 Caravan Sites Act.

The new emphasis on welfare and site provision can only be expected to mitigate conflict between the Gypsies and the sedentary society if the provision is consistent with the Gypsies' basic commitment to travel and independent work. However the sites are organised more in accordance with the requirements of housedwellers rather than those of nomads. The accommodation with bathrooms, kitchens and electricity are costly duplicates of portable facilities which the Gypsies must have in all circumstances if travelling. The Travellers themselves recognize the unsatisfactory compromise. One said

> Living in one of those huts . . . you might as well be in a house. You'd
> be better off in a house. But I'd rather travel.

Moreover, Travellers are allowed neither space nor permission for major scrap work, which consequently must be done elsewhere, usually the roadside verges, thus creating the kind of problems sites were meant to avoid. In many cases the Travellers or Gypsies I encountered, saw official sites as part of a pattern of increasing constraint and control. "When's the next reservation opening?" one remarked ironically to another.

ETHNIC IDENTITY

Outsider's View

It has been alleged that the majority of people on the road calling themselves Travellers are not "real Gypsies", not "real Romanies", but half breed "Didikois" or "inadequates" dropped out of housedwelling society; or foreign invaders, namely Irish Tinkers—none of whom are considered to have a distinct ethnic identity.

These assertions are not justified. Hoyland[7] listed the most common names of the Gypsy families who frequented the area at the beginning of the nineteenth century. The majority of these names were found among the families I encountered in field work.

Another critique is based on a pseudo-scientific theory of race which equates *social* groups of Gypsies with distinct *genetic* groups. The "real" Romanies are said to be those with no gorgio blood in their ancestry. Yet even the genealogies of celebrated Romany families collected by Gypsiologists in the past, have nearly all shown a scattering of non-Gypsy or gorgio ancestors. That the Gypsies in the area show a similar mixture is not new. Gypsies wishing to assert their identity emphasize

7. See Hoyland, footnote 4, p. 58.

their Gypsy ancestry and "forget" the gorgios. Both they and outside observers use blood and so-called "genetic inheritance" more as metaphors for their own social categories. Those used by outsiders can be understood in terms of the various problems which they pose to a sedentary and different society. The "real" Gypsy is identified by selective cultural traits which appear most exotic or picturesque; for example, a painted wagon or rustic setting, or paradoxically by the extent to which he conforms most to the norms and values of a sedentary, rather than to a nomadic society; for example, respect for private land. The "full blooded" Romanies are metaphorically the least troublesome group since they are imagined not to recruit members from the host society. They remain reassuringly separate and exotic, but subservient to the larger society.

By contrast, the fictional didikois, renegades or ex-housedwellers from abroad, alleged to be radically or ethnically closer to the sedentary society without apparently any redeeming exoticism, are alleged to have the most "anti-social" behaviour. The didikois, the so-called "half castes," are a disturbing mixture of "us" and "them," a reminder that Gypsies can cross racial and hence social, boundaries. The alleged drop-outs are denigrated because they have abandoned and rejected sedentary society of their own free will. The "foreigners"—also alleged to be drop-outs, usually from Ireland—are potentially the most nomadic, and are considered to have the least rights in the locality. These stereotypes have also been exploited by individual Gypsies in specific circumstances, to reassure officials that they themselves are not to blame, but some "other" groups.

Insider's View

Self ascription rather than "objective" traits is the most satisfactory means of identifying the group and its individual members.[8] Despite the temporary collaboration with outsiders, the Gypsies, or Travellers, have their own criteria as to who is a real member of the travelling society. The idea of a "full-blooded" Gypsy was not taken too literally. When a Gypsy used such a phrase he was not necessarily making a statement about the person's exact genetic inheritance but rather about his commitment to a Gypsy identity, or his relationship to the speaker. However, blood and heritage do have a role. A necessary condition for a person claiming to be a Gypsy or Traveller, and to be recognized

8. Barth, F. (1970). *Ethnic Groups and Boundaries*, see particularly Introduction, George Allen and Unwin, London.

by a Gypsy group of at least several families, was that he or she had to have one, and preferably two Gypsy parents.[9] The term "Traveller" carried the same ethnic requirements; it was often preferred, since it was free of the stigma attached by outsiders to the word Gypsy. A person with two gorgio parents cannot claim the right to be called either a Traveller or a Gypsy. Full membership can never be attained, despite marriage with a Gypsy, although he or she might participate more or less fully in the travelling society. The birth right of a person with one gorgio and one Gypsy parent was acknowledged, although he or she was sometimes called "half-and-half" or "Heinz 57 . . . She's all the varieties". If this person married someone claiming Gypsy parentage, preferably on both sides, the offspring would have the right to full membership, provided that they were brought up in the Gypsy way of life.

The principle of descent, which gives a right to membership by a biased selection of ancestors, should be distinguished from that of racial purity. Every group of Gypsies whom I encountered had a few gorgio ancestors mixed in. Of the 73 families with whom I had close contact, four were acknowledged as gorgio couples. They were temporarily or permanently attached to the Gypsies but they were never fully accepted, and they made no pretence of being Gypsy. Only four of the 73 families were originally from Ireland and four others originated from Yugoslavia one generation back. They appeared to have the same criteria. Of the 69 remaining families, most of whom contained a husband and wife, there were 15 Gypsy-gorgio couples: 11 where the wife was gorgio and the husband with Gypsy parentage, and four where the husband was gorgio and the wife with Gypsy parentage. Thus the majority of families whom I encountered living as Gypsies, fulfilled their own necessary condition for membership, despite the claim by many outsiders that the majority were pseudo-Gypsies.

Descent is a necessary but not sufficient condition. A Gypsy's identity is confirmed by socialization and a continuing commitment to the life style and those values and cultural traits deemed significant to the group. These traits may change over time. Among all the groups encountered, the following were considered important additional characteristics: an ideology of travelling; self employment; adherence to specific rituals of cleanliness and some knowledge of one or more of the Gypsy "languages", for example Anglo-Romany or Shelta.

9. Rehfisch, F. (1958). *The Tinkers of Perthshire and Aberdeenshire* (unpublished); see also Chapter 11 in this volume. For a fuller analysis, see Okely (1972). "Gypsy Identity" *In* Research Project of The Centre for Environmental Studies. (To be published by Heinemann as, *Gypsies and Government Policy in England.*)

Sometimes travelling was emphasized along with descent as a right to membership.

> A Gypsy isn't a Gypsy if he doesn't travel, that's why I had to pull off the site for a few weeks.
>
> I'm a real Gypsy, I was born in a wagon on the side of the road.

The Gypsies had distinct rituals of cleanliness in a system of beliefs which cannot be dealt with in this essay.[10] One aspect is that separate bowls had to be used for washing-up, personal washing and laundry. Ideas of cleanliness were focused especially on food and eating. Chipped crockery was jettisoned. The washing-up bowl was ritually clean and if used for another purpose was considered contaminated, i.e., *mockadi*. Dogs and cats were capable of contaminating utensils by contact, while horses were not. A Gypsy was expected to uphold these rules:

> He's a proper Gypsy. You wouldn't find him washing his hands in the same bowl as he washes his cup.

The personal washing and laundry bowls were not given the same kind of attention and were usually placed outside the trailer.

> Polly explained that previously both her washing up and washing bowls were stainless steel. Although she never confused them, she sensed that others accused her of doing so. She therefore threw away the expensive personal washing bowl and replaced it with an old plastic bucket.

Gorgios were considered ritually unclean because they did not make the same distinctions. Hand soap near a kitchen sink was an indication that the receptacle was used for personal washing and washing up. Fearing such an accusation among themselves, the Gypsies boarded up their caravan sinks and used several bowls. Wealthy Gypsies commissioned special trailers without sinks. "If you look at a Gypsy's trailer, you won't find a sink, that's what gorgio's use." Other cultural traits or values varied according to the group and their political rivals. A Gypsy who had very few possessions and could only make ends meet, drove me back to my camp in a car with no windscreen. He glanced at the flashy trailers and Range-Rovers belonging to the members of my camp at the time. "Those people aren't real Gypsies. Their trailers are

10. In accord with the Editor's suggestion, and in response to the questions most commonly posed by outsiders, I have confined myself largely to an ethnographic account for the general reader. For a theoretical analysis of, for instance, Gypsy–gorgio and male–female pollution, and the symbolism of the inner and outer body, see J. M. Okely: "Gypsy Women: Models in Conflict" *In Perceiving Women*, Ed. Ardener, S. and other forthcoming publications.

TABLE 1   Housing experience

	Women	Men
Main upbringing in a house	2	8
Some experience of housing	12	6
Never lived in a house	40	46
TOTAL	54	60

Thus only 14 out of 54 women and 14 out of 60 men had ever experienced housedwelling life.

too smart. Too much money. They've just come out of houses. Now take me, I'm a proper Gypsy. I was born in a tent."

Despite the emphasis on travelling as an ideology, upbringing or experience of living in a house did not annull a person's right to membership. Children born of Gypsies who had moved into houses could reactivate their membership in the travelling society by taking to the roads later. However it was difficult for them if they had lost contacts among travelling Gypsies. Also they were likely to be teased for their literacy, mode of speaking, dress and behaviour. Those wishing to be accepted had to change their ways. "John used to be more gorgio. But he's improved a lot since he's married Mary". In fact the majority of Gypsies I encountered had their main upbringing in the travelling community on the road. Information was available on the housing experience of 54 Gypsy wives and 60 Gypsy husbands. Fifteen gorgio women and eight gorgio men, all brought up in houses, were excluded from the figures. (See Table 1.)

Limited information seems to suggest that permanent sedentarization occurs mainly at the lowest and the highest economic level: the destitute take up welfare or council housing and wage labour employment or social security, while some extremely wealthy families invest in land, a house and a fixed business such as a scrap yard. This theory of sedentarization has been suggested already by Barth in a study of pastoral nomads.[11]

GYPSY–GORGIO RELATIONS

A fundamental expression of Gypsy identity was the ideological contrast which they made between themselves and the gorgio. This was reinforced by pollution beliefs. The Gypsy child soon learnt the words "Gypsy", "Traveller" and "gorgio". A two year old boy was asked proudly by his Mother "who are you?" His reply, as she anticipated, was "I'm a Gypsy". In general the gorgio was viewed with

11. Barth, F. (1964). *Nomads of South East Persia*, George Allen and Unwin, London.

suspicion and some contempt; Gypsies were hesitant to use the word in polite exchange with an outsider because of it's perjorative overtone. The term "housedweller" or the ironic "husseydweller" was preferred. After an acquaintance of several weeks, I was sitting talking with two women. One of them used the word "husseydweller", then she turned to me: "Let's not beat about, we call all your lot gorgios".

The rigid and over simple distinction between Gypsy and gorgio is maintained as a matter of ideology, despite cultural similarities between the groups and the lack of homogeneity in the housedwelling society. It is also reinforced by real institutional differences springing particularly from the Gypsies' nomadism and also maintained by their special economic niche in the larger society.

The contemptuous stereotype of the gorgio is functional and also maintained by the absence of relationships with gorgios based on equality or intimacy. The majority of gorgios calling on encampments were there in a hostile or interfering capacity: police officers, health inspectors, education officers and officials with powers to take the children into care. The few gorgios married to Gypsies were treated as anomalous members of the community, although their situation was improved if they demonstrated abilities in the Gypsies' terms. In addition there were gorgio "dossers"; vagrants or individuals on the run who were exploited as cheap labour. They were given shelter in the lorry cab at night, food and "a packet of fags" for a day's work. Gorgio women who drifted into the society without the formal status of a wife were sometimes exploited for casual sex. There were also a few gorgio married couples, some with children who had dropped out of house-dwelling society, usually after legal and financial problems. They were equally incapable of success within the nomadic society, partly because they had not been trained from early childhood in the necessary skills, and because they were linked to the society by neither descent nor marriage.

> A gorgio girl had been brought up in an orphanage. Paul, her husband, also a gorgio, spent much of his early life in care. They left their council flat after rent arrears. A Gypsy sold Paul a dilapidated trailer and they parked on the local by-pass. After being fined as Gypsies, they moved to a field. Eventually they were given a place on an official Gypsy site. But after a few months the Gypsy tenants, re-senting their presence, complained to the warden who ignored them. When the couple were out, the Gypsies towed their trailer off the site.

Few outsiders inspired respect for their gorgio qualities. Those who sought acceptance among the Gypsies could only do so via marriage and self conscious "Gypsification".

The other major point of contact with gorgios was in the work situation away from the encampment and on gorgio homeground. The Gypsies had to take this daily initiative to meet outsiders in a peaceable if not friendly manner and were prepared for hostility.

> You meet some real pigs sometimes. When we went out with my brothers we'd be driving down to the farm and they'd be standing there waving their arms saying "go back" before we'd even got there. Once when this happened, my brother drove right up to this man; "Are you the farmer?" The man said no. But you could see it was by his clothes. My brother said "Is he in?" The man said no. My brother said, "Oh, a pity, I've come to pay a bill". The man changed his tune: "I am the farmer really". My brother: "I can't pay you the bill". We drove off and the farmer stood there scratching his head.

The relationship was basically commercial and, while in most cases the Gypsies provided a genuine service, they were out to get what they could in cash or goods. The ability to get the better of outsiders was admired. "Trickster" stories were much embellished. It was also permissible to mislead fellow Gypsies, but sometimes within the context of certain rules; for example those associated with a deal which was completed by the two Gypsies "chopping" or clasping hands. There were few if any rules in an exchange with a gorgio.

Within the limits of their commercial relationships, the Gypsies gained considerable familiarity with aspects of gorgio society. The status, needs and personality of individual customers had to be closely assessed and turned to their advantage. Different roles were played to suit the circumstances, with the Gypsy acting inferior, if necessary. Sometimes the gorgio stereotype of the Gypsy was played up, other times concealed. Gypsies who tarmaced people's driveways were careful to put on smart and prosperous looking clothes.

> When we goes tarmacing we don't say we're Gypsies. We say we're from a private company. We offer to do it . . . then go away, telling them we'll come back with an estimate. We might get someone who can read and write to make out the bill.

A Gypsy woman, with whom I worked collecting scrap, told me about fortune telling:

> You have to put on a scarf, show off your gold jewellery, and say "Cross my palm with silver". Some of 'em says "Cross my palm with paper money now!"

In fortune telling the Gypsies were presented with gorgios' secrets and anxieties but the Gypsy remained aloof and manipulative. The gorgio had no comparable opportunities to observe Gypsy society, and the

individuals he met were likely to have adopted deliberately misleading
roles for the occasion.

Different from the "one-timer" on the doorstep, there were other
work relationships more obviously based on reciprocity and mutual
respect, that is where a gorgio and Gypsy came to a standing arrangement. These covered a wide range; a publican who offered his phone
number for tarmac advertisements; a breakdown service man who kept
his write-offs for one Gypsy; a garage-hand who sold, to select individuals cheap spare parts under the counter; a factory foreman who would
tell a Gypsy of a clearance job and a builder who sub-contracted small
tarmac jobs always to the same Gypsy who in turn did faultless work;
"It wouldn't pay me to do it badly". These contacts were to the economic advantage of both persons, but sometimes a closeness developed
which, for the Gypsy, was comparable only to that with near kin.

> Andy bought old cars, and those with potential he sold to a house-
> dweller to fix up. Andy looked out for buyers and would get a per-
> centage. He was given free run of the man's work yard and made
> welcome by the family in their home. Andy described the relationship:
> "I know him as well as my own brother."

In other situations, as when "weighing in" at the scrap yard, the Gypsy
was in an inferior position to the gorgio dictating the price. Generally
in work the pejorative view of the gorgio remained intact and was
hardly undermined by the few relationships offering equality and trust.

LIVELIHOOD[12]

Exploiting their mobility and resorting to a multiplicity of occupations,
Gypsies found and filled occasional gaps in the host economy's system of
supply and demand. All "Gypsy occupations", both past and present, can
be categorized in this way. Their work involves regular appraisal of
the local context and ready adaptation, whether the economy be
mainly agricultural or industrial. The Gypsies remained outside the
host economy as self employed individuals, free of the gorgio system
of wage labour which offered no scope for the initiatives and skills on
which they prided themselves, the fixed times and regulated conditions
were thought to be degrading, and invariably require an end to travelling. Wage labour is resorted to only as a temporary expedient or when
sedentarized.

12. For an analysis of the Gypsy's structural economic position in the larger society see,
Okely, J. M. (1971). "Work and Travel" *In* Research Project of the Centre for Environmental Studies.

The area studied was well placed for all kinds of work and probably more so than in the past. The highways led quickly to the industrial and residential estates of the locality and Greater London. The Gypsies exploited different stages of the motor and building industries. The growth in car production had brought a rapid turnover for second hand car dealing and scrap metal salvage. Increasing car ownership also stimulated the demand for tarmac driveways. Massive re-development in building brought lucrative pickings from demolition as well as sub-contracting for paving and hard surfacing. There were also openings in slating, decorating, fencing and landscape gardening.

The residential areas provided customers for hawked wares, hand-made or manufactured. Despite the claims that there was no longer a place for hawking, I found that female members of nearly every family earned money in this way. Flowers made from split wood or paper dipped in wax proved especially popular at Christmas. The door to door selling of lace and small factory made goods, like key-rings and combs, provided an entrée for fortune-telling which was still a lucrative occupation. The wealthier families with sufficient cash for bulk purchase hawked linen, blankets and carpets. Blanket selling was less likely to be connected with fortune telling. One woman said, "You've got to dress real smart, not look Gypsified." She described her work:

> We used to sell blankets and sheets and carpets. We'd find a village hall and go to the caretaker . . . hire the hall. We'd have cards printed advertising a sale and we'd stamp them with the place and a date. All sorts of people would come.

In private homes an abundance of consumer goods with built-in obsolescence provided an assortment of throw-outs: old clothing, televisions, carpets, bicycles, boilers, cookers and washing machines. Some of these items were useful for scrap metal, others for rag salvage or re-sale.

> When I went out "calling" with Aunt Jill we were asking at houses for "any old scrap". At one village we were given an old carpet and a heap of old clothing and rags. A few hours later in another village, Aunt Jill got talking with a housewife. The housewife had no scrap but Aunt Jill reassessed the situation and we were transformed into travelling salesmen. She sold the woman the carpet and several items of clothing from the rag bag.

The second hand market had in some cases drawn Travellers into the antique business. All these occupations whether scrap, tarmacing, hawking or re-sale utilized the Gypsies' mobility and required a minimum of equipment and capital. The only major investment was a reliable vehicle, already indispensable for transporting the family and towing the home.

The area was also strategically situated for casual agricultural work in surrounding counties and East Anglia. There were still opportunities in fruit-picking, beet-hoeing and potato picking, but the demand was declining owing to mechanization. This the farmer could exploit.

> In 1971 a local farmer encouraged all comers to pick his relatively small crop of potatoes. The rate, which was reduced 20 per cent from the previous year. On the first morning I arrived with a group in a dust storm of vans, pickups and lorrries. "There's loads of Travellers! That's no good. Why did 'e tell us all to come along? There won't be enough work for all of us." After a couple of days the members of my gang walked off the fields, one woman shouting "I'm not coming no more. It was never like this on the Fens. I'm a Fens picker." By the end of the week six of the 12 families had left and the remainder were obliged to accept the low payment.

The decline in demand for agricultural work has been incorrectly interpreted as a decline in demand for Gypsies' special skills. But agricultural skills among Gypsies of the past have been exaggerated. Their abilities never matched those of the sedentary work force.[13] The Gypsies' strength is their ability to apply themselves to a variety of jobs without specialization.

DISTRIBUTION AND NUMBERS

The Gypsies' dependence on a "host" economy and their ready adaptation to it, are illustrated in their general distribution. The figures obtained in the national census of Gypsies in England and Wales in 1965[14] indicated a concentration of 43 per cent in the more prosperous and densely populated South East, which included the area studied. It is likely that the Gypsies have slowly migrated with the host population.

The number of families at any given time in each county has been a matter of dispute, partly because the counting of a nomadic people is problematic, and also because it has been in the interests of the authorities to disperse and undercount those for whom they might have to make provision. For example, the 1965 census in one county recorded 98 families, fewer than those found in unofficial counts made even in the early 60's. Already at the beginning of the nineteenth century,

---

13. Vesey-Fitzgerald, B. (1973). *Gypsies of Britain*, David and Charles, Newton Abbot. See pages 191–192 for discussion on the limitation of Gypsy basket making as a craft.
14. Ministry of Housing and Local Government (1967). *Gypsies and Other Travellers*, H.M.S.O., London.

Hoyland recorded 60 families[15] in the same locality before the increase and migration of the host population to the South East, which the Gypsies are likely to have imitated. The authors of the National Census recognise that the number was an underestimate. The more realistic figure of 218 was obtained in a 1973 local survey carried out with the help of the Gypsy support groups, who were more likely to know the Gypsies' whereabouts.

Faced with this new figure, and with the more conspicuous encampments on highways, the authorities protested that site provision had attracted a mass "invasion" of "foreign" Gypsies and Tinkers who had never previously entered the County. But it would have been communicated among Gypsies that provision was for a minority and vacancies were immediately filled. I encountered no Gypsies who had risked an unknown region for the official sites. The likely shift towards the South East has probably been gradual and intergenerational. For instance, a few of the older Gypsies had conspicuous Northern accents and admitted that formerly they used to travel more in the North.

There may also have been a gradual migration from Inner London to the perimeter and beyond. Hoyland recorded how one third of the Gypsies in his nineteenth century survey moved to London in the winter where they took lodgings.[16] Post war development has made camping and makeshift lodgings more difficult.

When driving through the East End of London a Traveller was continually pointing out places once frequented:

My father was well known round here. There used to be rows of cottages all round here. Lovely for calling. There's still some. But there's a lot of flats now. There were a lot of Gypsies round here.

Then there were the M . . . s. They used to do horse dealing and run booths before the war. Then they took to the roads (outside London). The P . . . s always stopped near here. Look there's still one place on the corner." (He pointed to a trailer behind a fence, towered over by high buildings.)

The M . . . s chose the locality studied as a new base. Other groups have also said, "We're Londoners really, that's where our family came from." The movement from Inner London may be speeded up when "control powers" are awarded to each borough, after provision for only 15 families.

Meanwhile in the short run, the numbers in the county may have increased for a quite different reason; some families, especially those

15. See Hoyland, op. cit.
16. See Hoyland, op. cit.

taking up Social Welfare benefits, were encouraged to settle on sites and were less likely to travel great distances. Thus the number of families in the locality at any given time may have been inflated without the addition of newcomers.

TRAVELLING

The Gypsies' means of livelihood both utilized and required geographical and occupational mobility. Although the Gypsy family often had travelled only in order to find work, travelling obviously has further significance, some of which is noted below. The Gypsies work and travelling life had no simple ends-means relation; both were part of a pattern in which each exerted influence on the other in a number of ways.

Travelling Ideology

It is no coincidence that Gypsies often preferred to be called Travellers, especially among outsiders. Travelling marks them off most dramatically from housedwellers. In discussing the possibility of a house, one Traveller replied: "I wouldn't mind a house as long as it had wheels on it." Site provision posed new questions because of the idea of permanence attached to them and the awareness of pressures to "settle".

> Jack who, with his wife and two children had stayed on a site for several months was talking with some other Gypsies. He pointed to the tyres of his lorry: "My tyres ain't worn. You know why? Cos I ain't been travelling. . . . I gotta." He looked at the wheels of his trailer: "I've got 50,000 miles left in this trailer. You know what those wheels are for? To keep turning."

It is repeatedly asserted by Travellers in conversation with outsiders:

> They'll never stop us travelling. There'll always be Travellers on the road, that's for sure, no matter how many sites they build.

The desire to travel was considered to be an inherited quality:

> We have to travel. It's in our blood. . . . Children of Gypsies who've lived in houses all their lives take to the roads. It's in them to travel, maybe way back.

Travelling in itself was considered good and healthy, and in the case of certain illnesses the best way to effect a cure was to leave the encampment and keep moving. In contrast to travelling, living on an official site or in a house might bring illness or even death.

There's several Travellers who've died since these sites were opened. Something's wrong.

Travelling was also a means of avoiding the spirits of the dead. After a death and funeral immediate departure from the encampment was necessary, since it was believed the dead person would return to the scene. (Ideas on death and disease are part of a complex system of beliefs not covered in this essay.)

Travelling was considered a rational response to most situations of conflict, whether it occurred between kin, camp neighbours, feuding groups or with gorgio authorities. The majority of Gypsies on the roadside or on sites, even after a stay of several months, were able to pick up their belongings and leave within an hour if necessary. In the Gypsies' situation, versatility and flexibility were requisite qualities, whereas long term planning would often be irrational and sometimes was positively condemned.

Bill, a young married man, was complaining that the temporary site was soon to be closed.

"I'll be back here at Christmas, you see, even tho' it's going to be closed." John, an older and respected man, replied "You're here today and gone tomorrow." (This was not a criticism.)

His wife Laura said:

"Bill, don't cross your bridges . . . Wait till it comes . . . I never plan . . . You know Anne and Willie, well Anne's uncle had ordered a new trailer. He kept ringing up asking when it was ready. They said he'd get it in a week. The man came down to tell him the trailer was ready, but he met the wife—now a widow. Her husband had died, so she said "You can count me out . . ." *You must never plan, you don't know what'll happen.*"

The moral of this tale is applicable to many aspects of the Gypsies' life.

Travelling Patterns

The Gypsies' movements were not as clearly regulated, as for instance, those of pastoral nomads, who must to some extent follow the climatic and seasonal variations in pasture for their cattle. On the other hand, the Gypsies did not travel about aimlessly without any recognizable patterns. The majority travelled within a region consisting of several counties. Summer sorties were made out of the region; some only to neighbouring counties, others countrywide.

Within this main region they would be familiar, usually from childhood, with routes, stopping places and local context. Some would have established special work contacts. Specific routes within the region were often a matter of trial and error, governed by a variety of factors like proximity to a current job, harassment by police or other authorities, camp neighbours, the condition of the camping ground and a desire for change. The length of time spent in each place varied for the same reasons. Overnight stops usually occurred only in the case of harassment or in the course of a long journey. The general aim was to stay a few weeks in one place. In movements beyond the region there were seasonal regularities; families tended to cluster in areas near large towns in winter and to scatter over a wider area in summer, some families seeking work on farms. The warmer months were preferred for the exploration of new areas:

> They say when the grass is green and the birds are singing, that's the time to be going.

Proximity to known urban areas offered greater security in the face of harsh winter conditions. One local authority in the area studied had rough records of the monthly distribution of Gypsies in the County between 1970 and 1972. These revealed an influx in the winter months and a partial exodus in the summer, particularly June and July.

The area travelled by the majority of Gypsies I encountered between 1970 and 1972 may not have dramatically altered over the past 150 years, if Hoyland's information for the early nineteenth century is correct.[17] Hoyland also suggested that families tended to cluster in cities and towns for "winter quarters".

Motorization reduced the time taken for journeys and may also have reduced travelling within a region, since a greater distance could be covered in a day's work from the home camp. But it made travel beyond the region easier for the wealthier Gypsies.

Travel and Livelihood

Families were classified by travelling and work patterns interlinked with degree of wealth (see also Introduction).

Type A: The poorer and tented families, either not, or only intermittently, motorized. These were found mainly in rural localities near villages amd small towns. They were able to penetrate wooded and hilly areas not accessible to vehicles and there was little competition for their camping grounds from other Travellers. They managed to frequent several counties. Some travelled on foot or were given lifts by relatives; others made occasional use of run-down vans or pick-ups. (Some had

17. Hoyland, op. cit.

TABLE 2 Occupations, travel and economic status

Occupations	Husbands			Wives		
	Type A	Type B	Type C	Type A	Type B	Type C
Knife grinding	X					
Agricultural work	X	X		X	X	X
Minor scrap dealing	X			X		
Occasional wage-labour	X			X		
Hawking home-made goods				X	X	X
Hawking manufactured goods					X	X
Rag collecting		X		X	X	
Fortune telling				X	X	X
Major scrap dealing		X	X		X	
Second-hand goods		X	X		X	
Hawking blankets and linen			X			X
Car dealing		X	X			
Occasional tarmac		X				
Regular tarmac			X			
Occasional roofing			X			
Paving, small wall building			X			
Occasional painting			X			
Major dealing in horses			X			
Tree Lopping			X			
Total number of occupations in each type	4	6	10	6	7	5

once had horses and waggons, and the older men had not learnt to drive.) Their choice and number of occupations was severely limited by their lack of mobility, and so their poverty was perpetuated. (See Table 2.) The few Travellers in "regular" gorgio employment, for example, council gardener, grave digger, farmhand, labourer or domestic cleaner were more likely to be found in this group. It is possible that poor families in the past also resorted to tents in place of horse-drawn waggons.

Type B: These were motorized, although their lorries were frequently in need of repair. Some also had horses and trolleys for "calling". An important part of their livelihood was major scrap work. They congregated near industrial localities often on the verges of main highways. Individual members travelled considerable distances in a day's work.

The families also travelled relatively long distances in summer, mainly in pursuit of agricultural work. Since this had diminished, they were away from urban bases for shorter periods than previously. Lacking large reserves and good vehicles, few ventured far out of the region into unknown territory unless in a crisis, for example a dispute or to escape a serious prosecution.

Type C: These were fully motorized, often with new vehicles. They had the greatest variety of occupations, some of the newest as well as the most lucrative. They concentrated on tarmac, and also did scrap work, but only with the more expensive metals like copper and aluminium, which required less labour input than the cast iron and light iron worked on by Type B. Consequently, while they devoted less time in a week than Type B to scrap, they were able to earn relatively large amounts in specific jobs. Their economic superiority was perpetuated by interconnecting factors. Expensive and reliable vehicles gave greater mobility and access to a wider network of job contacts. A cash outlay was available, for example for tarmac or hawking blankets. Opportunity and flexibility in occupation in turn increased wealth. As with Types A and B, the wives played an important economic role, in addition to commitments to domestic work and child care. Although the males of Type C never bothered with casual agricultural work, they expected their wives to earn money that way. The wives in Type C were able to take advantage of their families' mobility for hawking and fortune telling and had cash for bulk purchase.

Type C were able to travel the farthest and to risk new regions most easily. Some of the places frequented included Hampshire in the South, Devon to the South West, the Midlands, Wales, Yorkshire and Lancashire, and as far North as Appleby for the Fair. Many tended to congregate near Greater London during the winter months. They selected and monopolized convenient plots of land near the major routes and were therefore less conspicuous than those forced on to roadside verges.

Table 2 indicates in generalized form the number and type of occupation likely to be found among husbands and wives of all three groups during the course of a year.[18] Husbands from Type C had over twice the number of occupations undertaken by Type A and also more than Type B. Moreover Type C had the more lucrative occupations. The wives in all three groups made a steady contribution.

18. This gives a more complex assessment of the Gypsies' work patterns than in the Government Report: *Gypsies and Other Travellers* (1967), H.M.S.O., London. Gypsies were asked to reveal only their "main occupation" at the time of the Census. The question presupposed the kind of qualitative and temporal specialization found in the larger society.

Most of the Gypsies I encountered fell roughly into these three categories; the majority in Type B, a minority in Type C and an even smaller number in Type A. In addition to these main types, there were other families who could not be so easily classified; for example, a family with showground connections who had travelled through England, Scotland and Wales doing a great variety of work, sometimes aided by their literacy. They were not as wealthy as Type C and were not associated with an active kin group. The Irish Travellers, nearly all of whom had travelled country wide, some poor, some wealthy, could not be classified in the same way. Without a long term familiarity with a specific region, they were geared to more frequent risk taking in all occupations.

THE FAMILY

Within the context of kinship, the domestic unit, usually the nuclear family, was relatively independent. (This has been misunderstood by observers who have confused the role of kinship as an organizational principle in Gypsy society with the structure of the domestic unit or family.) The domestic unit was taken to be those with shared cooking facilities. The majority of domestic units among Gypsies in the area were of a two-generational family i.e., husband and wife with children, some already adults. Table 3 gives the composition of 73 domestic units. Some consisted of nuclear families with additional members from a fragmented family, others consisted of fragmented families.[19] These tended to imitate the ideal model with a male and female adult, e.g., a widow with an adult son. The one domestic unit containing two married couples; an extended family in the strict sense, was gorgio.

Upon marriage, a young couple would immediately establish an independent unit, sometimes living in a van but usually with a trailer and vehicle. Cooking, budgeting and work arrangements were done separately. Thus the domestic unit was also the basic unit of production and consumption. Individual members of the family, especially adult sons, often earned and retained their own money and owned individual property.

Usually each domestic unit or family, earned a living independently of others. No family or individual Gypsy was found to have worked for another in the relation of boss and labourer. Where required, gorgio "down-and-outs" or "dossers" were used for cheap labour. In certain

---

19. A fragmented family consisted of an incomplete nuclear family which did not contain both a husband and wife. For a similar use of this term see: Arlo Nimmo, A. H., *The Sea People of Sulu*, Intertext Books, London.

TABLE 3   Composition of domestic units (total 73)

NUCLEAR FAMILY	
Husband and wife, plus children own or adopted and unmarried offspring	52
Husband and wife, offspring now left	3
Husband and wife, no children	4
Sub total	59
NUCLEAR FAMILY PLUS ADDITIONAL FRAGMENTED FAMILY	
Husband, wife, children; plus unmarried daughter and her child	1
Husband, wife, plus divorced daughter and her daughter	1
Husband, wife, child, plus wife's father	1
Husband, wife, child, plus husband's male cousin	1
Wife (husband imprisoned), son; plus married daughter, her husband and their children (all gorgio. Temporary arrangement in crisis)	1
Sub total	5
FRAGMENTED FAMILY	
Widow plus adult unmarried son	1
Widow plus adult unmarried son and daughter	1
Divorcé plus unmarried adult son and nephew	1
Units containing only one adult	
Divorcé	1
Widower plus children	1
Wife (husband imprisoned); plus children	2
Widow plus grandchild and young nephew	1
Widow	1
Sub total	9

circumstances work partnerships were formed. It was often convenient for a tarmacer to work with another man, dividing the labour and splitting costs and profit, but the partners never formed a joint domestic budgeting unit. Often partnerships were of short duration; the work situation changed, one of the families wanted to travel to another place, and joint decision-making proved difficult, since the individuals were taught and accustomed to make independent decisions. Work contacts could be a source of rivalry and suspicion instead of co-operation, even between close kin. Families would exaggerate the extent of their earnings and mislead others:

> I told her we'd sold our flowers at 15 pence a piece. Then she'd think we'd done well. But if she asked the same price for hers she wouldn't sell any.

Work contacts, new jobs and special arrangements with patrons or clients were protected when possible.

Each domestic unit also retained some independence as a travelling unit. It was rare for two or more families to travel permanently together. Each family was flexible in its choice of travelling companions, and for parts of the year might travel alone, joining up with others, usually kin, at specific encampments. In some exceptional cases a family took the responsibility of towing an additional trailer belonging to a widowed parent or sibling. Usually such a dependent relative would alternate among families.

Socialization and Education

The nuclear family has a crucial role in the socialization of the young and has many functions which, for non-Gypsy and housedwelling families, are fulfilled by organisations external to the family, namely the school, college and place of work. Only a minority of Gypsy adults encountered had ever attended school. An even smaller number were literate.

Gypsy education and training were different both in form and content from that of the larger society. The Gypsy child learnt by direct participation. There was no situation comparable to that of the classroom where 20 or 30 children are separated in one age group with one adult. Most Gypsy children spent the major part of the day with a parent or substitute parent, and at times were in the charge of older siblings. The skills required for earning a living were learnt when "calling" at houses or factories with parents or relatives, from the age of a toddler. Often the father took the boy and the mother the girl, but the sexual division of labour was not rigid. For example: a young mother would make her eight year old son sit next to her while she told fortunes: "I take him everywhere with me, so he learns what to say."

Children were encouraged to handle and earn money from an early age. They often had their own possessions such as poultry or ponies which only they had the right to "chop" (exchange) or sell. They bargained and "chopped" between themselves and with adults. The children made creative use in play of any available objects, rather than tailor-made toys and had a variety of inventive games often connected with travelling and reflecting the preoccupations of their society.

In education, one Gypsy made a distinction between "the gorgio craft" acquired in school and the "Travellers craft" acquired via the family. The first involves specialized training within a system dominated by the division of labour. The second is unspecialized. Some of the

Gypsies' skills or cunning have already been illustrated, especially the
need to have a variety of occupations. Also to be included are bargaining
skills, a disciplined memory as an alternative to literacy and mechanical
ingenuity; a bricoleur's ability to make do with minimum tools and
machinery.

Children were also socialized into Gypsy life and values by long
hours of observing and listening to adults' conversations and exchanges.
Inside the trailer they were expected to sit quietly, giving priority to
the adults (although outside, among themselves, they might indulge in
boisterous play). Very few subjects or situations were concealed from
the young. Parental quarrels, neighbours' disputes and scandals,
financial hardship, arrests, death and violence were freely discussed or
enacted before them. Greater reservation was displayed on the subject
of sex and reproduction.

The children were generally treated as "little adults", being entrusted
with secrets and given early responsibilities. Used as messengers
between families they reported back on private discussions and learnt
also to give partial information both to gorgios and rival families. Both
girls and boys were encouraged to develop abilities in physical combat;
to bear pain and hardship with stoicism; and to keep a cool head in the
face of hostility.

KIN GROUP CO-OPERATION AND COMPETITION

At this stage of research only tentative observations can be made about
the Gypsies' social organization. They face a number of problems such
as the allocation and exploitation of opportunities for work and encampment, the provision of welfare and mutual assistance and the settlement of disputes, all of which require for their solution the co-operation
of groups of families. The mechanisms of co-operation found in the host
society are largely unavailable and unsuitable.

The Kin Group

Although the Gypsies demonstrated solidarity in a confrontation with
gorgios and indicated a degree of national identity at the large fairs
such as Barnet, Epsom and Appleby, this did not amount to any effective
organization, and indeed fairs were often the occasion for a confrontation between groups. More significant was the type of organization
found in a loosely formed kin group using the cognatic principle for
recruitment. A number of families claiming descent from a common
ancestor would regularly associate with each other. Membership in
such a group could be traced through either or both the maternal and

paternal line. Families might choose to ally with either the wife's or the husband's kin.

As was fitting to their economic and travelling patterns, membership was highly flexible and had to be confirmed by active participation. Long term absence from the region suspended membership and could be revived on return. Locality was important, but did not always entail participation. Even close kin might be estranged from the group for a number of reasons: difference in wealth; conflicting loyalties to the spouse's kin, or personal incompatibilities, all of which might result in a major dispute. An estranged individual and family would seek, where possible, other alliances, for example with alternative kin groups of the spouse.

These kin groups would band together to reserve encampments if space was at a premium, ward off others and offer mutual aid of all kinds. Each found ways of resolving internal disputes and might defend its members in a dispute with others of another group. A kin group did not own property in common. The degree of independence of each family as a domestic, work and travelling unit should be seen in the context of this co-operation among kin, and the competition with other kin groups. When a family chose travelling companions or camp neighbours they were more often from kin, either on the wife's or husband's side. The regularity in such choices was one practical affirmation of a kin group.

The wife was not usually incorporated into her husband's family upon marriage, and often retained her names for her own and her children's use.

> Barbie, a married woman usually used her mother's father's name to refer to herself. She and her husband formed a kin group with her mother's brothers who had the greatest prestige and reputation for fighting in the area.

The wife's continued identification with members of her own kin reflects the way in which the individual family's choice of allies is left open for strategic purposes. The best situation was obtained when both spouses had many siblings offering a multiplicity of close kin as potential allies. These would inevitably be scattered over a wide area.[20]

Active localized kin groups varied in composition: a complete or partial set of married siblings; parents and some or all their married offspring, or siblings with cousins, uncles and aunts. The number of families also varied considerably.

There was no rigid system of leadership within the group, except

---

20. See Chapter 12 in this volume.

perhaps the "Elders" whose specific powers were hard to ascertain. Certainly deference was given to age and experience but senility eliminated authority. Some elderly women were credited with supernatural powers, but this might induce or coincide with their isolation from the group. Specific individuals enjoyed a degree of charismatic authority inspired by exceptional abilities, as in bargaining, conning or in physical combat. But if an individual attempted to dominate kin outside his domestic unit, he risked their departure to another locality and other allies.

These kin groups consisted broadly of families of the same economic level, usually within one of the three types A, B and C, classified earlier. There were several distinct kin groups in the area within the middle economic type B, a small number in type A and type C, both members occasionally overlapping into type B. There were no examples of a kin group consisting both of members from the poorest (A) and the wealthiest (C) families. Where there were kinship links between Gypsies in types A, and C, these were not sufficient for membership within the same active kin group. Because of the extreme contrasting wealth and associated differences, these connections were only publicly acknowledged on occasions such as funerals.

Localized kin groups played a major role in mutual assistance; in addition a family might call upon all the members of its wider kindred at times; and also non-related neighbours on a particular encampment would help each other in small ways. Nearly always some reciprocity was expected, in the long run. Care and assistance were offered in the following ways: If one spouse was ill or imprisoned, kin would camp alongside the family offering domestic and financial help. Children were temporarily fostered or permanently adopted, ideally by kin. (A popular criticism of gorgios was that they abandoned their children to official homes; "but we look after our own kind".) Financial gifts or loans were made more often between members of a kin group. Kin would peddle influence with site wardens to obtain tenancies for relatives. They would also take the main responsibility for sheltering those on the run from either Gypsies or gorgio authorities. To ensure proper care for a widowed parent, the youngest offspring might delay or forgo marriage. Otherwise the aged and less mobile were encouraged to settle on sites or in houses. Offspring and other kin negotiated places for them and then made regular visits. The kin group, joined by members of an individual's wider kindred had special duties upon the death of a member; at the deathbed, wake and funeral. Other Gypsies showed solidarity by attending the wake and joining the funeral procession, but they were expected to give priority to the kin group and kindred at all stages in the ceremonies. The main contribution towards the funeral expenses and gravestone came from the kin who also had regularly to visit the grave.

The Gypsies on the road made little use of the Welfare State. A rare few were registered with doctors. Hospitals were used for childbirth, otherwise only in real emergencies. Social Security was avoided. New council sites, however attracted the aged, the sick, and members of fragmented families, who found it easier to take up welfare benefits. In addition, families normally self sufficient, often from type B, were encouraged to accept Social Security and official unemployment pay, mainly because scrap breaking was banned on sites and the new expenses upset their budgeting habits. The wealthier families, of type C, with neither rent nor employment problems maintained their independence.

Inter-Group Conflict and Compromise

Links of consanguinity or marriage were useful for negotiating between competing kin groups. It seemed that kin of the same economic level in the locality were more likely to be members of the same kin group. So when there were no consanguinal links between different groups of the same economic level, alternative links had to be created by inter-marriage. A popular form of marriage was where two or even three brothers from one group married two or three sisters from another, or alternatively where a brother and sister married a sister and brother. Generally marriages between close kin; for example first cousins, and within a kin group were discouraged, while kin group exogamy was favoured. (Gypsy endogamy was maintained—marriage with gorgios was neither favoured nor frequent.) Marriages took place more often between groups of a similar economic level and where further consoli-dation of existing marital alliances between the two groups continued to be beneficial. The Gypsies were explicit that a marriage had important implications beyond the union of two individuals—"The K...s used to marry the M...s now they seem to be marrying the L...s".

Sometimes marriages occurred between two kin groups in a state of feud. Direct conflict was softened, although the feud may not have been resolved. In other cases where there were several affinal links, two kin groups might fulfil jointly some of the functions of a single kin group; for example, in choice of travelling companions and occasional work partners, and in the temporary reservation and defence of an encamp-ment.

There were some exceptional cases of first cousin marriages, but even the groups involved, expressed disapproval. Instances were found more frequently among groups in the poorer, type A. They had fewer potential partners to choose from, and fewer kin groups to negotiate with, since they travelled over a smaller area. First cousin marriages occurred least among the wealthier, wider travelling groups of type C who encountered a greater selection of Travellers and needed to make contact with more groups. Nevertheless they were more likely to choose partners from groups who regularly frequented the same region, rather than groups only briefly encountered. The occasional encounters between kin groups from distant regions were marked by caution if not tension; both marriages and direct confrontations, such as fights between them were avoided. (The resolution of disputes, both within and between kin groups in the area, cannot be fully analyzed in this short essay.)

Frequently vulnerable to some prosecution arising from their travelling and work patterns, the Travellers did not regard the institutions of gorgio law as a source of protection and they rarely resorted to it in disputes. Territorial claims had to be made by surreptitious and independent means. In such competition for land, the interests of different kin groups in the same locality were directly opposed.

Tacit agreements seemed to exist between some: the poorer, less mobile groups of Type A stayed in territory for which there was least demand, while the wealthier kin groups of Type C with a superior reputation for physical combat were able to select the most desirable territory. Thus any group facing contact with another of superior fighting reputation adopted a policy of avoidance. Between groups of equal force, direct confrontation and threats, if not acts of force, were more likely to occur. Alternatively, a representative (often a woman), from each group might meet for negotiations. Even on official sites, methods independent of the authorities were used to further group interests or resolve disputes.

Contrary to the fears which Gypsies seem to have aroused in outsiders, in a conflict with officials or other gorgios, Gypsies rarely resorted to any form of violence. Faced with the superior force of gorgio law and state institutions, including the threat of arrest and imprisonment, all groups of Travellers found their most satisfactory tactics to be avoidance, evasion, and dispersal.

CONCLUSION

The Gypsies or Travellers in Southern England have adapted, on their terms, to the demands of an industrial economy. They are the descendants of the now romanticized Gypsies or Romanies who, for a brief period in their history, travelled in horse-drawn caravans (previously they travelled with tents and pack-horses). Contemporary Gypsies have become motorized, continue to travel, and have found new, lucrative ways of earning a living. Despite the continuing economic exchange between the Travellers and the larger society, relations continue to cause friction. With increasing planning controls, bureaucratization and urban development, the Gypsies face greater difficulties in camping legally, even on land which they themselves have purchased, or where the owner consents to their presence. They are also victim to discriminatory prosecution on the highway.[21] (Not defined in law as an ethnic group, they cannot seek protection under the Race Relations Act.)

Costly official sites with elaborate equipment, suited more to the needs of potential housedwellers, and which require excessive supervision and controls by outside officials, should not be considered a workable policy for all Travellers. It cannot be assumed that the vast majority of those travelling will opt for permanent settlement in houses, or on sites which do not allow for travelling. Flexibility in movement is often necessary for the Gypsies' livelihood, as this essay has demonstrated.

One solution might be to give Gypsies, whose preferred life-style is caravan dwelling, special priority in planning applications for camping on land which they have either rented or purchased. This they can equip with minimum or more elaborate facilities, according to their needs, and in consultation with the authorities. There are often parcels of land in or near urban areas, considered unsuitable for building, or temporarily vacant, which could be made officially available to Travellers, until needed for other purposes. Alternative camping land might then be found.

For centuries, policies based on the dispersal of Gypsies to other localities have proved ineffective. Alternative policies of enforced settlement will either fail or bring demoralization, and high costs in welfare support. It is likely that many Gypsies will wish to continue travelling, and to retain their ethnic identity. If given legal access to suitable land for living and working, the opportunity for self determination and co-operation, the Gypsies might come to be tolerated by gorgios on a more realistic basis, not only as objects of fantasy.

21. The Highways Act 1959.

CHAPTER FOUR

Some Notes on Gypsies in North Britain

Anonymous

The Gypsy population of the region studied, is as typical of the national Gypsy population as any other regional group, in terms of the basic cultural characteristics of Gypsydom. Most ethnological details of the local group to be described would approximate to the general characteristics of Gypsies elsewhere in England and Wales. However, there are some minor differences that will at some stage need qualification.

This essay confines itself to a detailed description and analysis of the "Gypsy situation" in the geographical area of Hometown and the region surrounding it. The area itself has some ecological implications as far as migrations go, but more will be said of this at a later stage. Suffice it to say here, that it is a relatively isolated area bounded on the west and south sides by the sea and a large river estuary respectively.[1]

It has been said of Hometown that nobody goes there unless they have lost their way. The town itself is geographically isolated in being some forty-five miles from the nearest large town. Hometown is surrounded by a wide belt of agricultural territory which extends eastwards to industrial towns of the west, and northwards to an industrial conurbation. For this reason the region is fairly insular but at the same time demonstrates a clear division between town and country in that urban development is mainly restricted to the Hometown area. Because of

1. The geographical descriptions and place names have been changed to avoid the particular group of Gypsies being identified.

Hometown's vast rural hinterland and the fact that the whole area is relatively underdeveloped, it has not, as a region, suffered the same degree of post-war urban redevelopment as have other parts of the country.

This situation which is in many respects atypical of the national post-war scene, has allowed the indigenous Gypsy population to maintain a more traditional way of life. This relative lack of urban development has meant that many of the Gypsies' traditional camping sites and occupational opportunities have been kept open. Besides their traditional camping sites and occupations, there are three other factors which demonstrate their traditionalism and which tend, in some respects, to make them atypical of the national Gypsy population. The first is their living accommodation. Twenty per cent of them still live in "Bow-topped" canvas wagons which are horse-drawn.[2] This is certainly an atypical characteristic. Secondly, their general level of affluence appears to be comparatively low. This seems to be an indirect result of their continued dependence on a more traditional ecology. Many of the families have no motor vehicle whatsoever. Casual agricultural work and door-to-door hawking are probably not as profitable as the other occupational adaptations that other Gypsy groups have made since the end of the War, such as scrap-dealing and tarmacing. Motorized transportation is necessary for these latter occupations. This apparently slow adaptation to more lucrative occupational modes may, in some cases, be owing to the lack of economic pressure to change from traditional ways.

The last factor which renders these ethnological details atypical of the national picture is that of the size and density of the Gypsy population. Owing to the region's relative geographic isolation, the number of Gypsies who are part of extra-regional migrations are few. The majority of Gypsies are indigenous to the region. The density of the Gypsy population is comparatively lower than in other areas.[3]

ENVIRONMENT AND ECOLOGY

The general geographical details of the area have already been outlined, but there are a number of additional points that it might be useful to mention. The first is related to the agriculture of the region. The

2. For a full description of Gypsy wagons see *The English Gypsy Caravan* by Ward-Jackson, C. H. and Harvey, D. E. (1972), David and Charles, Newton Abbot.

N.B. The number of families living in wagons seems to diminish each year in favour of motor drawn "trailers".

3. See Ministry of Housing and Local Government. *Gypsies and other Travellers*, H.M.S.O. (1967), Map 1, p. 6. "Distribution of Gypsies and other Travellers", for variation in density patterns.

nature of the agriculture carried on in the large belt that surrounds Hometown is, of course, a major factor in determining the occupational activities of the Gypsies and thus some discussion of this is not only of general interest but also highly relevant. Traditionally, the area has had horticultural/agricultural practices that have been labour intensive with large numbers of acres devoted to fruit and vegetable husbandry. At the same time, therefore, while being labour intensive, the labour demands have also been seasonal. This has provided a set of circumstances conducive to a mobile work force which has been available at short notice. The Gypsies' migration and earning patterns have, indeed, been closely allied to the various regional locations demanding such seasonal labour.[4] It might be added, however, that the Gypsies' involvement in agricultural work is a relatively recent phenomenon following the shortage of labour experienced in rural districts as a result of rural depopulation during the nineteenth century.[5]

In recent years, the great advances in agricultural and horticultural technology have produced machinery capable of doing many of the tasks that once needed a large number of hands. The trend to mechanization has not been as marked in this particular region as in many others, for example, the South East. But there are still many farms and small-holdings which have either not yet become highly mechanized or still grow crops for which there is as yet no machinery for the harvesting. The one apparent variation in this general pattern is that climatic factors affect the feasibility of machine usage. The main example of this situation occurs in the potato harvest period (approximately the three autumn months starting in September); if there has been too much rain and the land has become very heavy, then the new automatic potato-lifting equipment cannot be used, and the traditional labour force is once again required to perform the back-breaking tasks.

The non-Gypsy population of this agricultural hinterland is mainly associated with rural occupations, although nearer to Hometown there is a greater incidence of rural-dwelling city commuters. At a national level, residential development on the outskirts of towns has been one of the main factors contributing to the post-war plight of the Gypsy population with regard to camping sites.[6] The same development has occurred in villages which have found themselves within striking distance of towns via the motor car and which, as a result, have

---

4. The radius of the general migration pattern has a maximum distance of approximately sixty miles, but, of course, a few families travel farther afield.
5. See Saville, John (1957). *Rural Depopulation in England and Wales*, Routledge, London.
6. *Gypsies and other Travellers*, op. cit., pp. 17–24.

eventually become engulfed by such development. This trend has been at a slower pace than in other parts of the country, but nonetheless it has had an impact on the local Gypsies. In what was once country areas adjacent to Hometown, there is now considerable suburban development. This has put a premium on land and many of the Gypsies' traditional, unofficial camping locations have been eaten away by house-building and road construction.

With a sparse agricultural population in the rural areas, and thus with less of a premium on every scrap of land, the Gypsies have been able to remain an acceptable part of the traditional rural scene. Their migration patterns, which have been established over many decades, have been continuously facilitated by their locally acknowledged traditional camping places. In the main, these camping places have not become victims to development in the post-war years. Villages and other small urban settlements have, at least up until very recent times, accepted the seasonal arrival of the Gypsies. This may well be owing to the fact that their economic role and its function to the rural community was obvious to all concerned. The decreasing demand for their labour in the rural areas has apparently corresponded with the declining willingness to accept them in a community when now only a minority of that community may have any employment for them. If the number of farmers who still want and can use this form of labour is very small, then it does mean that the Gypsies will, in the course of their migrations, have to camp in areas where their utility to that particular community has long since passed. In these situations it seems to be the case that the Gypsies are becoming less socially acceptable.[7]

Some reference has already been made to the Gypsies' occupational activities when they are in the rural areas. But a more comprehensive account is now required in terms of their ecology. The section which follows later on the Gypsies' migration patterns will give reference to their particular agricultural work, but besides this activity, in which most members of the family take part, there are other occupations carried on while the Gypsies are residing or travelling in the rural locations. The women go hawking and some of the men may, when agricultural work is slack, do scrap-metal work. This is only carried on by those Gypsies who have motorized trucks. They visit farms and villages in search of scrap metal which will then be taken to the unofficial camping site and sorted and broken up as necessary. With a "saleable" load, a journey will be made to the nearest outlet for such commodities —usually Hometown. Besides this type of scrap work there is another

7. This may also be a consequence of fewer "safe" camping locations being available and thus the Gypsies tend to stay in areas longer than the occupational needs demand.

which consists of scavenging on local authority rubbish tips. This is often carried out by the younger members of the community and salvaged material is carried home on prams and bicycles. This occupation is often carried out to the great annoyance of local authorities responsible for the tip.[8]

Their rural ecology, therefore, involves the children in a number of ways. Firstly, in the scavenging activities on the rubbish tips, and secondly, as assistant labour to the adults in the work of "scrapping". This is usually reserved for the older children from about eleven years upwards. During the strawberry and potato harvests, however, even younger members of the family participate. With a limited period in which to pick, combined with a wish to maximize family income during the period, it is important that all the family as far as is possible should help "pull". Lastly, the children may be taken on hawking expeditions and used in the capacity of soliciting sympathy from the people called upon. In the knowledge that society is usually concerned about the welfare of children, irrespective of other considerations, it is not surprising that presenting a picture of a "destitute" mother with a babe-in-arms and perhaps another six or seven-year-old by her side, they are awarded greater hospitality than if appearing as single trades-people with apparently no obvious symbols of a domestic background. The amount of hawking done by adult women whilst in the country districts is limited, as it is probably the case that the income from agricultural work, when assessed in terms of collective family earnings, is relatively large. In view of the fact that the family may also be in receipt of social security, for example, family allowances, the necessity or incentive to go hawking may not be great. The main disadvantages with hawking when in the country is that it involves a great deal of walking and/or expensive bus fares which in contrast with the high density of population to be found in the towns, makes the activity less practical and profitable.

The occupational pattern in the urban and suburban setting is more varied. In fact, each family has its own occupational range and the factors affecting this will include family structure and material possessions; for example, whether the family has a lorry or a "dray".[9] The families that are motorized are generally active in the field of scrap metal. This is dealt with in the same way in the rural and urban settings, but the type and quantity of scrap is different. There is more chance of the valuable metals like copper and aluminium being obtained in the town and, of course, there is usually a greater quantity of such scrap available. It

8. In some cases it is this activity which local councils use as the sole excuse for "moving the Gypsies on".

9. A four-wheeled tradesman's cart called a "dray", "trolley" or "lurry".

should be added, however, that in the city there is more competition for valuable scrap.[10]

The motorized families will, when the opportunity arises, travel from the suburban camping sites to do casual agricultural work if they hear of a farmer or market-gardener who wants a small job done—for example, singling sugar beet. Very few families carry on the occupation of tarmacing. Of the families who live in horse-drawn wagons, some have additional vehicles which are often drays. These are used for "tatting" or "calling" around the streets in the city and suburban areas. All manner of materials are collected—scrap metal, antiques, rags and resaleable "junk" of one description or another. These cargoes, once collected by the men, often assisted by adolescent boys, are brought home to be broken up and sorted. The resaleable goods and commodities are transported to the appropriate market place, usually a scrap-metal depot or a rag factory. The residue may contain articles that can be utilized by the Gypsies themselves, but the rest, which is small in quantity, is usually left discarded on or near to the unofficial camping site.

Those who do not possess drays earn a large part of their income during urban stays, by their womenfolk hawking. Nearly all Gypsy women go hawking but the regularity of the latter group is greater than many of those whose menfolk are making additional earnings in ways already described. The hawked materials usually comprise pegs, lace, charms and trinkets and home-made flowers which are manufactured by the women (the pegs, although more often made by the men, can be made by both using a simple division of labour). The hawking, or as it is referred to by the Gypsies, "calling", is conducted methodically. The women usually go in groups of twos and threes and will travel by bus between 9.00 a.m. and 10.00 a.m. to a specifically selected residential area. The wares are carried in large wicker baskets and covered with a sheet or cloth. When calling at the doors, threats, curses and "bad" language are often used if the residents refuse to buy; begging may also be practised, especially if the resident buys something and thus may be indicating a degree of sympathy. At the end of the day, the women will use some of the takings to buy provisions at supermarkets before returning to the camp, which may be as late as 4.30 p.m. to 5.00 p.m. There is, thus, a degree of sex segregation in the social organization of "production" and earnings.

In many ways, with obvious and notable exceptions, the Gypsies' ecology bears many resemblances to a hunting-gathering technology.

10. Hometown has a number of non-Gypsy scrap/rag/bone collectors.

This basic technology, however, has, through the centuries, been overlaid by systems of barter and money economics, but the essentials are still to be seen as there is the qualification of nomadism and a limited inventory of tools. In the economic aspect of their ecology, they are subject to a fairly vigorous environmental determinism: this is usual with a simple technology. It has already been stated that the distribution of suitable economic opportunity within the area has a direct influence on the migration patterns of the Gypsies, and indeed, the same factors play a not inconsiderable role in shaping kinship relations and also the spatial relationships of social units.[11]

Additional income is generated within Gypsy families by application to the Department of Health and Social Security for benefits of one kind or another. "Family Allowance" is drawn by all families. It is the impression that during the periods of agricultural work, a substantial increase in family income is achieved and this provides a capital sum which is used to create or replenish savings. It is also at this time of year that many families indulge in purchasing domestic durables like television sets and record players. Motor vehicles are often purchased at the same time, when there are sufficient funds for the necessary tax and insurance charges.

Migrations

The Gypsies' migration patterns present a highly fragmented and complicated picture about which generalizations are difficult to make. This is mainly because each nuclear family, which is usually the basic economic unit, will have its own pattern of migration. Despite this, some general comments on the Gypsy migrations in the region are possible because, irrespective of family composition, the general pattern of migration is the result really of wider ecological determinants. A distinction is perhaps usefully made between the migrations of the Gypsies who are actually based in Hometown and those who mainly live either in the suburban areas or the country districts of the region.

Firstly, Hometown's Gypsies have been resident in caravans (or houses at different times) in the town for many decades. Some of the Gypsies who still live in the area were born within the town boundaries; many of their traditional camping places and permanent dwellings have been slowly eaten away by modern redevelopment schemes. Some of these Gypsy families now live in the country districts all the time. But the rest still live in the town on a number of unofficial sites. Some of these families may, at certain times of the year, venture further afield, especially during the spring and summer months.

11. "Social units" refers for the purposes of these notes to groups of caravans and wagons.

The country-based Gypsies have a somewhat different pattern. Some families' pattern of migration is east/west, moving from the Hometown suburban area in the spring and making their way fifty miles to the east where they will stay until the strawberry season.[12] For this short season, they may go just across the border where most of the strawberry fields are. After the strawberries, they return mid-way into the region to wait for the autumn potato and sprout harvests. This is only one migration pattern, but there are also other smaller groups with different movements. One group will stay in the Hometown area all the year round with perhaps a week's visit to another small town to see relatives. Another group will stay in Hometown all the winter from late November to August, when they will then go out into the region for the potato and sprout harvests. In November, all these groups, with one or two exceptions, will migrate to the Hometown area for the winter period. The groups of Gypsy families who have trailer caravans and are motorized, are obviously more mobile than the families solely utilizing horse-power. The only difference in their migrations will be that the former tend to move around the region from one camp site to another, at more infrequent intervals and seemingly at random.[13]

One or two families also seem to migrate independently of the general migrant routes already described. They will winter outside the region and come to Hometown during the early spring.[14] They may, after a few weeks, move northwards out of the region. Another family will spend the winter months on an official but temporary caravan site at a town some sixty miles from Hometown and in the spring return to spend a few weeks before going further north. Towards the middle of the summer, they may return to the area and wait for the potato harvest when they will join some related groups in the country district. The last group of Gypsies are a separate branch of the same regional group, but who have their own particular migration pattern. They travel throughout the year by themselves within the region, but have little if any contact with other groups.[15] Apart from all the groups mentioned above, there are a number of Gypsies who are related to the Hometown ones and who come into the region just for the summer period. They join the indigenous Gypsies at a particular village but leave towards the end of the summer season. It is worth remembering that the Gypsies

12. Such migrations usually start in the spring—April or May, but there is no collective movement at one fixed time. A large number of factors will be influential in relation to each family.

13. Random migrations could be caused by feuding; death; illness; getting wagon wheels repaired etc.

14. These families have kinship ties outside the region but come to Hometown during the summer for the fruit picking season.

15. This very traditional group have all horse-drawn wagons and no motor vehicles.

are culturally a nomadic people and, although it is ironic, it is true to say that their mobility brings them the economic and social security that others seek in the permanent character of their own solid immobile homes. It should also be remembered that the migration pattern established by one family, or small social group, during the course of a year may not be identical each year. Indeed, during the period of fieldwork, there was no identical recurrence in any particular family migration. Although in retrospect it is possible to state various similar aspects of the migrations such as geographic locations and routes, it is not possible to say with any certainty that the same families will be involved next year or that there will not be variation in the dates of departure. Changing migration patterns should not be thought of as significant aberrations from tradition, but only part of a continuing process of adaptation to the wider changes that have been endemic to the Gypsies' environment over the centuries.

The timing of migrations are of some relevance to their understanding, and while in many cases this will be related to seasonal change, there are other factors which precipitate migrations, and which now require identification and illustration. There are undoubtedly a large number of reasons why Gypsies travel at any particular time or to any particular place. It may also be the case that many of the direct or subsidiary reasons for migrations will remain unknown to students of Gypsydom. It is possible, however, to try and explain some of the reasons as they manifested themselves during the period of fieldwork. Of prime importance in the rationale for migrations is the economic motive. This has been briefly documented above, but must not be seen in isolation to other social, cultural and political factors. It is the intricate and complicated interplay between all these factors which will, in the end, produce a decision to "move on". Apart from the economic factors which have already been considered, there are a number of social factors which have appeared to be significant at certain times in causing or contributing to family migrations. Interpersonal and inter-group conflict, with the resulting necessity to create distance between the conflicting parties are most certainly factors which may cause movement. Belligerence can be a powerful factor in creating change in all social groups and its potential is ever-present when the traditional environment changes to produce new and adverse conditions for the social groups that live within its influence. As kinship conflict can cause migration, so equally can kinship ties and affiliations. Both the above factors will, it is worth noting, further influence the participants in choosing a particular migration. Unilateral causation, apart from death and sickness, is unlikely since, in the case of migrations caused by conflict, the willingness to move and the eventual destination will be determined by other factors. For example, migrations are more likely to result from conflict if there are other economic opportunities offered by potential new camping sites. If not, then the movement might only be in the nature of a hundred yards or more down the road.

Another social cause of migration may be one which seems to the observer at first consideration, no more than capricious behaviour, but which, on closer investigation, is related to the state of the immediate environment. This may be too polluted with rubbish; rats may be attacking the pigeons; it may be too muddy and dirty; or there may not be enough good grazing for the horses. On the other hand, however, Gypsies may move just for the simple reason that they "feel like a change". Often a relevant reason for migration is that the Gypsies may desire to take advantage of certain social and educational provisions which may or may not be facilitated by a particular move. Two other factors which may be responsible for migration are horse fairs and the transfer of siblings. At various times in the year, children will go to stay with different sections of a family group. Kin relations in which this individual movement takes place, will be with relatives such as grand-parents, aunts, and sisters.[16]

The "external" forces affecting migration patterns may now be enumerated.[17] These comprise mainly the police, council officials and local residents. Residents may consider the proximity of Gypsies to be offensive, and may refuse to give them water and threaten to complain to the police if they do not move on. The camping families may also meet with physical violence from residents, who have been known to throw bricks at the windows of the caravans and wagons. Farmers, who traditionally have utilized their labour may find their service no longer needed and so ask them to "move on". Council officials, usually from the Clerks' or Public Health Departments, visit their encampments and inform them that they have to move. No reasons or Court Orders are given, but if resentful questioning follows, the Gypsies are told that they only have their job to do and that the "orders" come from above. Despite the questionable legality of these practices, the Gypsies comprehend the officials as being the front-line men of the vast and united body of officialdom and law and order which, in the end, is not to be tempted or seriously questioned.[18]

16. In one example, a child from a nuclear family of seven was left some fifty miles away with a housedwelling grand-parent (see p. 106).

17. "External" refers to the migrations of the Gypsies enforced by the Gaujos: i.e., non-Gypsies.

18. The degree of departmentalization within Gaujo society is a factor the Gypsies find difficult at times to comprehend. To the Gypsies one official is the same as the next.

The police are responsible for the larger number of family movements. Their actions are usually precipitated by complaints from the various departments of the local authority, or from nearby residents who complain over factual or imaginary incidents.[19] It is the impression that the police usually act on complaints from the local authorities but balance the complaints by individual residents with the total number of complaints, and the length of the Gypsies' stay in any one particular camping place. If there are a growing number of complaints and the Gypsies' immediate environment looks to the police to have deteriorated, then they usually ask them to "move on".[20] Summonses for offences against the Highways Acts are seldom issued. Another reason motivating the police to ask Gypsies to move on is that they may consider the Gypsies' groupings are too large or that a particular caravan may pose a traffic hazard.

Relationships between the Gypsies and the police are usually cordial and even friendly. Certain officers have been responsible for dealing with them over the years and have come to know many of the Gypsies by their first names. The police will come along and say, "Come on Freedom—it's time you were moving on—go by Sunday". In most cases this seemingly friendly advice is passively accepted and by the Sunday the Gypsies have quietly moved away. The excuses for objecting to being moved on are many, and although they may rarely prove to be substantive, will often include such factors as sickness; having a baby; "full employment"; poor water supply or poor grazing at alternative locations, and interrupted school attendance.

Each family or small kin group's change in migration timing and direction may be a combination of factors, some trivial, others crucial to their survival. Job opportunities are, of course, very important in precipitating movement. In the last year of observation, a combination of factors resulted in quite significant changes in one particular pattern of migration. One September, the writer expected, in the experience of the previous two years, for most families to move to the potato and sprout fields within a radius of 50 miles from Hometown and return in mid-November. This did not happen for three reasons. Firstly, some friends of the Gypsies had persuaded the local police to suspend the practice of moving the Travellers on. Secondly, nearly all the families had acquired motor vehicles of one type or another. In the case of the

19. Local residents are often very vocal to young and enthusiastic press reporters about the alleged assaults made on them or their children by the Gypsies or their dogs. From the writer's experience, such allegations are unlikely to have little foundation in reality.

20. The state of "deterioration" may be assessed by the amount of scrap and other waste material, or by the local Public Health Inspectorate informing the police that the area has become fouled and thus a public health hazard.

horse-drawn wagon families, the sons had bought cars or vans.[21] Finally, added to these two developments was the fact that the children had been kept interested in education during August by some teachers visiting their site. This was followed in September by the starting of a special class set up for the children by the local education authority.

These three factors were responsible for breaking a relatively well-established migration pattern. Most of the families "stayed put" as they wanted to camp on the site for the rest of the winter, and the police had told them that they would not ask them to move on. The labour force for potato and sprout picking could be taken to the farms each day using their own transport. Finally, the parents were anxious and pleased for their children to attend school.

The factors outlined above relating to migration patterns, by no means pretends to form an exclusive list. The distinction has been drawn between the self-determined migrations and the external social/political causes. External causes of migrations have a significant effect on the lives of the Gypsies in several ways. They affect the access and utilization of social and educational services. They may exacerbate already difficult living conditions, but more importantly, enforced migrations create social friction between the Gypsy and the non-Gypsy communities. This area of interaction between the two communities influences the attitudes and perspectives of each to the other and thereby the nature of relationships and behavioural responses which they make towards each other.

External factors requiring the Gypsies to move, have more often than not an adverse effect on the lives of the Gypsies. They may complicate illness, and in any case, will cause strains and tensions in individuals and within families. They may be forced to move to a dangerous new camping site such as the verge of a major road and this, inevitably, poses many problems for the care of children and livestock. New camping sites may offer poor grazing and thus precipitate further migrations. Each migration necessitates the packing and unpacking of their possessions. Although nomads are used to this, it is not readily accepted or desirable if it is forced upon them with too great a frequency from outside forces beyond their control, and often for reasons they do not understand. On one occasion, a Gypsy family which had two broody hens nesting in the long grass by the caravan near to the verge, were moved on by the police—unrestrained petitioning on their behalf had no influence—they had to move, which resulted in the eggs becoming addled. These moves may deprive the Gypsies of more substantial

21. Many of the senior male members of such families were too old to learn to drive and thus, until their sons reached a "suitable" age, the family was dependent upon horse-power.

economic opportunites; not only by jobs being lost, but also because "a move" may involve one or two days' income being lost. The new camping position to which they move may be more distant from shops, bus routes and water supply, and so for that period of stay, domestic and economic operations are made that much more difficult.

Compulsory migrations, however, do not have a totally negative effect. Sometimes the police will move the Gypsies when local residents' complaints begin to mount and, also, in the light of subjective observations (by the police and local residents) that the immediate environment has become too spoiled and requires cleaning up. It is only when the Gypsies have moved that the local council are called in to clear the so-called "rubbish and filth" which has been left. The justification for moving them on in these situations is usually on public health grounds. Again, the enforced "moving on" may tend to ease community relations and thus benefit the Gypsies; certain residential areas are often prepared to accept the Gypsies for a while, but after a period feel that it is time another area should have their share of the "burden" of "Gypsy occupation". The implied tolerance of this community relationship may be attributable to the fact that the Gypsies have long traditions of "belonging" to the area and so gain a higher degree of acceptance than perhaps others do in different parts of the country.[22]

LIVING CONDITIONS

Major differences in the living conditions of the Gypsies are primarily influenced by whether they live in a canvas wagon or a trailer caravan. Apart from this basic difference, their immediate environments are alike. But their existing unofficial sites merit some comment and description. They are usually either by the side of small roads, large grassy lay-bys, or common land, Council lands, or in small lanes or "drifts". Dykes, hedgerows or small copses are usually present and facilitate toiletry. As the Gypsies live in the open most of the time, apart from bad weather, and as their homes are relatively small, many of their possessions are placed out in the open and around the respective caravans. Visible evidence of their economic activities is seen in the form of piles of "junk and scrap" awaiting sorting and which may also include larger scrap such as parts of broken cars. Waste from domestic and occupational activities, such as the manufacture of pegs, is deposited on

22. This tolerance of the Gypsies in one area, at least for a while, may well be related to (a) many of the residents had lived in the area for long periods and thus stories of Gypsies present in the area have been passed down from generation to generation, and (b) the fact that many of them still live in the "real Romany wagons" and thus are "true Romanies".

fires that burn continually by day near most caravans. Livestock is usually kept outside and includes horses (which are tethered at spacious intervals along the verges), dogs, chickens, pigeons and sometimes cats. The exception to this is caged birds which are very popular and are usually kept inside the caravans. Protective "house dogs" are always tied up, but the chickens do run free and, in a strange way, all keep to their own caravans and also seem to have a road-sense! Without official waste disposal facilities and with no apparent concern for orthodox means of disposal of what Gaujos would call "rubbish", it is not surprising that their immediate environment often tends to appear chaotic and hazardous.

The living conditions inside the caravans vary according to whether the living accommodation is afforded by a modern trailer or a traditional wagon. The trailer is, of course, larger than the wagon. The former may allow some compartmentalisation with the use of built-in screens and curtains, while the canvas-covered wagon can only be used as one living area. This means that at night or in bad weather, all the inhabitants share the same, small living area. Cooking facilities are present in both types of accommodation; in the wagons, they consist of small solid-fuel stoves with side ovens, and in the trailers they are usually calor gas cookers, although the former is sometimes used for cooking. Space heating is provided by solid-fuel stoves in both types of living quarters. Electric power is provided by car batteries and in a few cases, little generators driven with petrol engines are used. This source of power is used to work night lights, television sets, and some non-transistorised record players. There is no running water and supplies are brought in by the children who go and beg for it from nearby households and wheel supplies home in milk churns on old pram chassis or small hand carts.

The interiors of their homes are kept clean and tidy in terms of their own standards and there is often great pride taken in the setting out of pillows, bedding, china and other ornaments. Tremendous pride is also taken by a few in the exterior condition and attractiveness of their wagons. One Gypsy man with a canvas covered wagon spends considerable sums of money on the purchase of gold-leaf which he will use in the designs and motifs which decorate the wooden parts of the exterior.[23]

As well as the different types of accommodation the Gypsies' material possessions are also limited by their nomadism and by the possibilities of transportation. If they have trailers they have motor vehicles of one type or another. More often than not these will be Ford Transit

---

23. See *The English Gypsy Caravan*, op. cit., especially illustrations.

trucks, but the range of vehicles among the Gypsies as a whole will include cars, vans, pick-ups, trucks and lorries. Cars and vans are more usually owned by those with canvas wagons. Vehicles are always parked alongside the owners' living accommodation.

The familiar domestic commodities such as cooking utensils are commonly used but some families seem to be short of crockery. Cutlery is limited in quantity and use. The more interesting feature of their possessional range is the number of domestic durable goods. These feature as an important part of their lives and include transistors, record players, televisions, records, tape-recorders, car radios, car accessories, artificial Christmas trees and decorations, watches and clocks and bicycles (which are used a great deal as a means of transportation). The range of these types of goods in conditional first and foremost by whether they can be moved easily, and secondly, by whether they can function without mains electricity supply. Very few of the goods are purchased new, but are mainly bought secondhand. With their need to be mobile at fairly short notice, their material culture will be limited by what they can take with them. With the advent of adaption to lorries, trucks and trailer caravans, it is now the case that more can be carried than traditionally when the sole means of transportation was the canvas wagon.

SOCIAL STRUCTURE

The social unit within one caravan tends to be for the most part the nuclear family. There are, of course, many variations to this basic structure and it is worth noting a few of them. Despite the paradox, the exceptions to the norm are common and, although in some families they will be only of a temporary character, in others a different structure may amount to a permanent arrangement. In some cases the extended family is too large for one wagon and, in these circumstances, two wagons are usually owned and utilized for sleeping and for the storage and transportation of goods. Another two-wagon situation may arise with a four-generation family structure. Another exception to the basic rule of a nuclear family per caravan is where old parents are cared for, or children are looked after by the grandparents or other relatives. A nuclear family may take into care the children of a deceased brother or sister. The size of these family units will vary greatly and it is unwise to generalize. There is, for example, the case of a childless couple who have taken the responsibility for an orphaned niece. There is also a nuclear family of nine who live in one canvas wagon. Nuclear occupation tends to be more common, if anything, among newly established couples who have one or two children.

It is difficult to make any hard and fast rules regarding patterns of marital residence, but the more common one may be described as bilocal residence.[24] First : this form of marital living pattern is compatible with migrations and the possible need to travel at different times to different places and in different groups. Thus, social groupings prior to migrations may be different from the groupings that eventually form at new camping locations.[25] Second : it allows for an ease of mobility which is necessary for facilitating exploitation of economic opportunities when discovered. Third : the possibility of both patrilocal and matrilocal residence is compatible with the processes of conflict resolution.[26] In some examples of bilocal marital residence where the mother/daughter bond is strong, it is clear that in a number of cases the girls stay with, or near to, their family of orientation. If the latter case applies, then the young couple are more likely to have their own caravan and travel round with her immediate kin rather than his kin if their migrations differ. In some cases, where the girl has a baby but is not married, and has not decided to pair-off with the biological father, he may be incorporated within the girl's family and live in the same accommodation as part of the family, but not necessarily as sexual partners.[27]

No marriage occurred during the period of fieldwork; one young man was to be married to a Gypsy girl at a local registry office, but called it off at the last minute. According to one informant, the marriage was called off because the young couple would have had no separate living accommodation and neither kin group wanted the young couple to join them. It is the writer's impression this may well have been a valid reason militating against the marriage as both families were very large and had limited accommodation, i.e., one trailer with ten occupants and two wagons with thirteen occupants respectively. In relation to the above case, it is interesting to note that Farnham Rehfisch, in his work on Scottish Tinkers, reported that he knew of no cases where marriage was postponed because of shortage of material resource, such as accommodation.[28] The writer was shown many family documents but, at the time of writing, had not been shown any marriage certificate.

---

24. Bilocal residence is favoured by groups with migrating habits, but some may argue that the Gypsies have no particular type of marital residence. Although there seems to be no rigidly adhered to practice, there are examples of neological residence. The pattern, no doubt, will be influenced by the physical environment and its camping possibilities.

25. The type of vehicle may determine the distances travelled.

26. See later section on the resolution of conflict.

27. "Not married" in this particular context refers to no explicit statements or ceremonies on the part of the couple or their kin.

28. Rehfisch, F. (1961). *Marriage and the Elementary Family among Scottish Tinkers*, School of Scottish Studies, Vol. 2.

It seems that the majority have just paired off and bought a caravan and thereafterwards been considered as married by the community. It has been explained by informants that many couples are not "properly married". These statements have often been mentioned in the course of discussions relating to social security claims. It is felt that the Gypsies believe the romantic myth about "marriage" within the settled society: that they always get married in church and stay with each other for life. This is the sort of impression they would be eager to give a Gaujo about Gypsy marriage. The impression is that the Gypsies who marry Gaujos are more likely to be legally married, while only two cases of legal marriage were known between Gypsies. It is the impression, therefore, that common law marriage predominates, as the majority of them do not seem to be legally married. In many cases the creation of married partners comes about after a child has been born.

Marriages within extended family groups are not uncommon. The rules of exogamy within the Gypsy community suggest that relationships of a procreative character are accepted if they are outside the family of orientation. First and second cousin marriages are common and the findings regarding marriage patterns in the region studied, seem to fit in with the other national research findings. "There is considerable marriage between and within extended families. . . ."[29] Marriage, whether legal or unofficial, is monogamous, but conjugal breakdown does occur.

Although there were no obvious cases of marital breakdown during the period of fieldwork, there were family histories that implied separation and realignment of partners. There were quite often discussions reporting or alleging cases of past or present adultery. Information in this area is, however, very difficult to obtain and appeared generally unreliable.

When the Gypsies refer to their surnames, there is a tendency for the children to take the mother's name if the parents are not legally married. This is, of course, only noticeable in the families where the parental surnames differ. This happens when a Gypsy marries a Gaujo or when a different Gypsy name is involved. The implications of matrilineal tendencies may not be totally attributable to the absence of legal marriage, but may also be related to the Gypsies tendering the most Gaujo sounding name when in communication with the settled society. It thus may be used to disguise the fact that they are Gypsy or to deceive true identification when being questioned by agents of "officialdom". Within their own community, the Gypsies do not use

29. *Gypsies and Other Travellers*, op. cit., p. 28.

their surnames, but refer to each other by their Christian names, or, more commonly, by nick-names. Nick-names are awarded to people for many differing reasons. It may be on account of one's dress or for one's idiosyncratic mannerisms. If further clarification is required in reference to another Gypsy whose nick-name has not brought immediate recognition, then kinship ties will be mentioned as additional clues. This always ends the mystery of identification. To strangers, however, the Gypsies' names assume a common character and in such instances of questions by the alien, an anonymous curtain is drawn so as to render individual identification virtually impossible. If asked their names by strangers they will say "Smith" or "Jones" with such singleness of mind and so emphatically that one is reluctant to even consider the slim possibility that they could have another name. If further questioned however, they will avoid giving an answer or will say "just Smith". This use of a common pseudonym is possible with a common community surname which is used to avoid individual identification. Their surname is also used at other times when it is needed for official requirements such as for answering questions in connection with claims for family allowance and social security, birth certificates, and pedlars' licences etc.

The dangers of generalization are never so present than when the discussion focuses on the nature of conjugal roles and relationships. Some mention has already been made regarding the division of labour within the family. Women's roles clearly have a dual function: economic and domestic. Their economic roles have been considered, and it was observed that they are a highly functional part of the family economic support system. Some economic activities are shared with the menfolk, potato-picking for example, but whether or not specific activities are shared, the family's economic viability undeniably depends on close co-operation between men and women. In the domestic sphere too, there does not seem to be any clear-cut line between the duties of men and women, except that in most cases the women are responsible for the purchase and preparation of food and drink. The care of children can be performed by parents, siblings or other kin, and when the mother is out all day hawking, her husband may be left at home to make pegs, to look after the children, and other domestic tasks. In many cases the children will almost exclusively be brought up by the grandparents. In some families the women and children will go with the menfolk hunting for scrap; the older children helping by "calling" with mother, or by looking after the younger children in the cab of the truck. Although housework, or rather caravan or wagon-work, will usually be carried out by the women, there seems no rigid practice as in one case the father of six was left at home in the mornings and one of his duties was to tidy up the wagon and all the bedding etc. The bedding in almost all wagons is meticulously folded and arranged as in the style of an army "bed-box" on the bunk at the rear of the wagon. At the times of migrations, the man will be concerned with the moving of the caravan; either preparing the horse and fixing the harness or latching the trailer to the truck. The women are responsible for loading the goods into the wagon, including the children and livestock.

Conjugal roles do not, for the most part, comply with any rigid segregated form, apart from some of the general patterns outlined above. Sex segregation, however, does take place during leisure periods. Fireside gatherings and other entertainments do seem to divide social groups on sex lines, with, for example, a group of men round one fire and all the womenfolk gathered around another. This is not a hard and fast rule but the writer has witnessed it on many occasions, especially Sunday afternoons.

Information on sexual behaviour is very difficult to gather and thus limited in these pages. It is the impression that the most common form of birth control practised is abstinence. It may be that the younger members of the community practise other, more modern methods of birth control, but there is only limited evidence to support this supposition. The fact remains, however, that there are now more channels of communication and information available to the community on this subject. Records, television, social and romantic contacts with Gaujo boys and girls, and contacts with official agencies such as doctors and hospitals, all have an influence in this direction. Despite this, Gypsy families are large and the number of young girls who become pregnant are too many to provide any real or plausible evidence to suggest that up-to-date methods of birth control are used. One day, a young Gaujo couple called to see the Gypsies. They all knew one another well and there was a high degree of trust in the relationships. A Gypsy father of six asked the couple why they were not having a family, he went on: "Why? Are you not lying together?" This comment is the only real clue to birth control practices that the writer came across during the period of fieldwork. But it does indicate that physical separation and abstinence are the order of the day in some families. It would, however, be dangerous to generalize from rather limited data on this particular matter.[30]

Decision making within the family is again a topic about which information is difficult to gather, especially if the observer is not

30. Some mothers of large families are reputed to have been offered sterilization operations when in hospital having their latest addition to their family.

actually involved in the domestic structure of a family. The information obtained, however, seemed to suggest that there is again no hard and fast rule. Both parents will chastise the children; both will make decisions regarding their activities, such as whether they will be allowed to go to school or on a school trip. It is the impression that decision making in the economic spheres may well be on a unilateral basis—the women deciding when and where to go hawking and the men deciding independently when and where to look for scrap. Unless a family is widowed, it appears general that the man will make the decisions regarding migrations, the routes and locations to be taken etc. Other major decisions regarding sales or purchases of caravans or trucks are also ultimately taken by the male head of the family. In widowed families, however, although there may be an adolescent son, the mother will make the above decisions for her family. Ultimate authority within the family certainly appears to be awarded to the father as senior male member of the social unit.

Families tend to live from day to day and there is little detailed, long-term planning with regard to such factors as family size, acquisitions, or migrations. This diurnal character of their existence is, however, contradicted in a number of instances. First: there is the capital surplus that is generated during the fruit and vegetable picking seasons; thus, there is a degree of economic "storage" to guard against seasonal shortage or unexpected emergency. Money may also be saved with the idea of buying an expensive item like a new truck, and in this sense economic planning is in evidence. Again, a family head may take a decision early in the year to make a different migration from the previous year. The more general picture, however, is one in which planning and deferred gratification is relatively limited and usually specific.[31]

When talking about Gypsy social structure, it is important to consider the kinship obligations that are implied by the structure and which, at the same time, help to explain it. But unfortunately, the nature of the fieldwork was such that the writer was only able to gather limited information on this subject. Thus, it is difficult to be very precise or definite, but some details were gathered.

Except in special circumstances of serious illness requiring hospitalization, older Gypsy members of the community who are either widowed or too old to carry on the central role duties of a nuclear structure are always looked after by their own family. It may be a son or a daughter, but it is not necessarily the eldest or youngest. Often there may be

---

31. Savings only being made with a specific future purchase in mind, e.g., a grave stone, new caravan or television set etc. The gratification of such purchases, however, tend to have to be a short term, i.e., a few months.

sharing of the responsibility so that the old couple or surviving spouse will spend so long with the family of one of their children and then spend the rest of the year with another married child and his or her family. There is no practice of shifting the responsibility away from the immediate kin to either distantly related kin or to outside agencies such as old people's homes. Although a case was not recorded, it is expected that if an old member of the community has no brothers or sisters alive or any children of his own, he or she would be cared for by their deceased siblings' children. The obligation to care for the old is certain, but exactly whose obligation it is, is not culturally specified. In deciding which of his children an old Gypsy person will live with in old age, a wide range of factors will, no doubt, be considered. Such factors may include: degree of mobility; living accommodation; family size; relationship with child and his or her spouse; personal choice; economic standing of family; where he can be of most use; and where their spouse is buried if widowed. Any one of the factors included on this rather limited and arbitrary list, may be significant in determining whose obligation it is to care for aged parents or other old members of the community, but the choice of the old person, himself, seems to have considerable influence on the outcome. The study records no instance of where an old person was put in an old people's home. This would not only be contrary to traditional kinship obligations, but it would also be a most difficult course of action to take. Not only would the Gypsies have little knowledge about these institutions and how to gain admission, but also the old Gypsy is much more likely to be the "traditional" Gypsy in terms of dress, behaviour and attitudes. It is exceedingly unlikely, therefore, that they would be accepted or even happy in such homes.[32]

In one case of widowhood, where there were two children and three grandchildren still at home, there seemed to be no economic support from kin outside this depleted family. The widow had to make ends meet by making her own pegs and flowers and hawking them. In this particular case, income was supplemented by social security benefits and the income generated by the older children in her care. When they were told to "move on" by the police one day, the eldest married son came with his van from another camping site to take many of the goods that would not fit into the wagon, and helped out generally in other ways. It is thought that, despite this apparent independent family responsibility, in times of gross need, other kin will help out and assist less able family units.

32. Hospitals are disliked generally—attended only when seriously ill and seeking discharge as soon as possible.

Kinship obligations are also observable in cases of orphaned or fatherless children. In these cases the obligation seems to be on the aunts and uncles to share the burden and so it may well be that an orphaned family will be split up. Once placed with the particular fostering family unit, there is a tendency for them to stay with them although the children do visit each other for short holidays. If grandparents are not too old then it is very common for such children to be cared for by these senior members of the families. With regard to orphaned children, therefore, there seems no set pattern of care except that the children are cared for by one or more closely-related kin, and are never taken into care by a local authority children's department. This is certainly the last thing they would do with the children of the deceased or deserted kin. Even very difficult children with physical or mental abnormality, are cared for by somebody. It is worth noting that one child, from a viable nuclear family, was sent to stay with grandparents because the child had been in full-time attendance at a local school near to where the grandparents lived. As she had made such impressive educational headway, she had been singled out from the rest of the large family as worthy of special treatment. Grandparents are always seriously concerned about the welfare and care of grandchildren.

Kinship obligations also define themselves when unmarried daughters become pregnant. In all the cases that materialized during the field work period, if the girls did not want to leave the family of orientation to set up home with the biological father, or if the father had disappeared as a result of a migration, then the girls were accepted and cared for by their family of orientation. There seemed to be no stigma attached to this occurrence, but in one instance it was explained to the writer that "She has been a naughty girl". It is thought, however, that this was an excuse manufactured to meet the Gypsies' expectation that the writer would be morally shocked by this apparent behavioural indiscretion, but that in their own community the occurrence was not treated with great moral indignation or embarrassment, but accepted as a normal part of social life.

Death is, of course, also an occurrence demanding kinship obligations. All kin and friends are expected to pay their respects to the dead person and are further expected to bring flowers and attend the funeral. One exception to this seems to be if there is a section of the community which "keeps themselves to themselves" and are geographically distant at the time of death. Another exception will be if there is a current feud raging, in which case the kin of the dead person may object to the presence of the feuding person or group. As only one death and funeral was witnessed, it is difficult to be more definite about generally expected behaviour in these situations.

At a more general level, when the community as a whole or one of its members is in conflict with the settled community, there is a discernible fusion of ranks and the obligation to protect the community is universal. This obligation even transcends internal conflict and feuding, and is irrespective of closeness in kin relations which is so significant in other social obligations. Two examples illustrate this. The first is when the local Criminal Investigation Department made a so-called "friendly" call on the Gypsies and then after some small talk, asked where D was. All knew which D they were enquiring after, and all knew where he was, but to the police the response was simple and clever. "D . . .? No we don't know a D—not our little D? Ha, go and fetch little D." Whereupon a small boy of six was produced. The police were intuitive enough to realize that they had drawn a blank. The second example is perhaps more interesting, in that it demonstrates that the mechanism of fusion in response to threats to the community works on occasion to include non-Gypsy friends who are considered to be part of their community. The writer was, for a period, driving the children to their school in a hired bus and it was the custom to stop at the village shop to allow them to spend their money on sweets etc. The shopkeeper, intrigued by seeing these Gypsy children regularly all together in a bus with a driver who did not, on most occasions, look like a typical Gypsy, happened to ask one of the older girls who had gone into the shop, "Who was that chap and what was he called?" Her prompt reply was: "I don't know". This protection against individuals being identified is part of the social obligation to protect kin and associated members of the community in an environment where there is a clear and distinctive dichotomy between "them" and "us"—"Gaujo" and "Gypsy".

There are other instances where it is possible to witness family and group co-operation and solidarity in the face of unfriendly external influences and threats. When families have been asked to "move on" there has often been inter-family co-operation in packing and carting. It is not unusual to see two or three families help another pack up and catch all the livestock; or for a man to help a widow harness the horse for her wagon. Social behaviour in hunting and gathering economies are strongly conditioned by factors of environment and it appears that the Gypsies' ecology affects the nature and degree of social co-operation between family groupings. The Gypsies' economic unit usually being the nuclear family often means that in an environment where there is a scarcity of economic opportunities, there will be competition between families. When normal economic conditions prevail, nuclear families do compete with each other and individual fathers are expected to go out and find the sources of scrap, and agricultural work for themselves. It is the impression that this competition between families gives way to co-operation and egalitarianism (as is common in hunting and gathering economies) when sections of the community find themselves physically threatened by acute social and economic need or when certain job opportunities are plentiful. The diurnal and thus vulnerable nature of each family's economic support system and that of the community as a whole, demands on occasions, egalitarian distribution and co-operation. This also militates against the formation of exclusive groups and helps to establish reciprocal rights and obligations to be called upon in times of need. With the ever present potential enemy of the Gaujo society, this need for potential social unity is never more necessary than with the Gypsies. The basic insecurity of life itself and the inevitability of old age are ever present reminders of the dependence of one human being upon another.

It is perhaps valuable to postulate further reasons for their social cohesion. It is certain that a small community in almost perpetual conflict and competition with a larger, more powerful society, must have satisfactory methods of resolving conflict and maintaining a sense of community that will allow for the economic, domestic and social functions to be carried on without serious or prolonged interruptions. It is possible that their sense of community comes firstly from the clear characteristics of their environment. The social and political opposition and economic competition with the settled society, often couched in behaviour demonstrating obvious hostility and prejudice, helps to create a feeling of comradeship, group identity and unity. There is the economic environment which is often far from benevolent, and has inevitably a day-to-day insecurity. It has already been mentioned how these factors foster co-operation and how this can parry some of the harshest effects of the environment.

Gypsy attitudes towards their treatment by the settled society manifest a strong sense of injustice and, central to their idea of this injustice is the fact that many of their menfolk fought in the two World Wars and are now treated with derision, social exclusion, distrust and hostility. In repayment for their contribution to "their country", no tangible reward has been received. Another cause of resentment and feeling of unjust treatment is that the children are "not allowed to go to school".[33] Similarly, they feel they alone get blamed for many of

33. Some gypsy children are often refused admission to local schools either because of catchment areas, prejudice or the school being "full", etc.

the wrongs which, in reality, are committed by the sedentary community, such as petty crime and the indiscriminate dumping of waste materials, often near to their own encampments. This sense of unjust persecution adds to the feeling of belonging to a minority which they feel is despised by the Gaujo, and which must be considerable in creating a sense of collective identity and unity within the Gypsy community.

Another factor which should not be underestimated in explaining the persistence of social cohesion in the Gypsy community, is the fact that kinship ties exist throughout, and beyond the regional area. Although there is a feeling of belonging to a geographically fragmented community, at the same time it is considered to be a very real community. Thus, kinship ties play no small part in creating unity within the region. This is not to say, however, that they do not recognize kinship links with other Gypsies outside the area. In fact their inter-regional links are extensive and of some considerable importance.

The kinship links with groups in other regions provide lines of communication that are functional in many ways. They facilitate an extension of kinship ties and affiliations; they provide information about economic opportunities outside the region (which may be exploited by the more mobile families); they are channels for communicating news about kin, births, deaths and marriages etc. Such news is transferred surprisingly rapidly throughout a community which is after all geographically fragmented.

Communications are not always carried out by the actual physical movement of individuals or families. There are a limited number of cases in which letters are written, usually to be collected at post offices, but this form of communication is used more by the settled society for the purpose of making official contacts with the Gypsies for such things as the issuing of social security, Giro cheques, etc. The Gypsies will, on occasions, use the public telephone to ring a hospital to enquire about sick relatives or to ask a blacksmith if a wagon wheel has been repaired etc. But the most common means of communication is by travelling in person.

The Gypsies' communication network is, in fact, an important factor which fosters their strong sense of community. The network is continually functioning despite its fragmented character and is, of course, only changed in structure by further migrations. To elucidate this statement; if, at any one time, the migration pattern results in the Gypsies in the regional area being divided and grouped in a number of different locations, there will be almost constant physical communication between the different camping locations. The means of communication will usually be by motor vehicles or, in some cases, bicycles. The frequency with which these "inter-camp" movements take place will vary, but it is observed that most will take place at weekends and especially on Sundays.

It is suggested that these inter-camp movements are highly functional in relation to social cohesion. As in the case of extra-regional movements, they facilitate an extension of kinship ties; they may strengthen existing relationships, and allow for the temporary suspension of feuds. They provide opportunities for news and gossip about other groups and members of the community; they give information and advice about various economic opportunities (such as when soft fruit is ready for picking); they provide the separate camps with social stimulation; and they facilitate the exchange and sale of goods. The children, who will go in large numbers in the back of the vans, enjoy the excitement and play with their friends. Such constant links of communication help to keep all members of the groups informed as to where everybody else is. This in itself emphasises and strengthens the bonds of their community.

The temporary change of environment and excitement that inter-camp movements must provide, may, to some extent, help to resolve the day-to-day frictions that are present in any small closely-related social group. The fragmentation of the community into different groups situated at different locations is, to an extent, conditioned by economic factors, but also by kinship ties and affiliations which obviously influences the composition of the different groups. The perpetual contacts between the different groups creates a "web" type structure which is always changing in design as the groups keep migrating, but these constant lines of communication, with their multiplicity of functions, are of prime importance in creating a sense of community identity, social vitality and a dynamic kinship structure.

It is, perhaps, interesting to ask at this juncture how the community is able to reduce and contain internal conflict.[34] Brief mention has already been made on this topic, but a further analysis is now useful. For a society to have unity and solidarity, it has to be able to resolve conflict in a way that does not threaten the long-term cohesiveness and persistence of that community. Some factors of social control have already been outlined above, and they included the need for friendly and co-operative relations in the face of the ever present hostile Gaujo society; the need to co-operate at certain times in economic activities; and the need for communications and co-operation at other social events such as funerals and forced migrations.

Despite the forces of social control, however, it is inevitable that

34. Conflict within their own ranks as opposed to conflict with the non-Gypsy world.

conflict will break out in any community. A number of examples follow
to illustrate some points of conflict which often arise. The Department
of Health and Social Security, on one occasion, stopped payment to one
client because they found out they were making payments on false
information provided by the client. The disappointed client then
proceeded to tell the Department of other clients within the Gypsy
community who had been doing the same thing, "and why should they
still be getting their money?" This resulted in further investigations of
other claimants and consequently, other payments being stopped.
Conflict back at the camp soon emerged. Another example is when one
family's child is hit by another parent, and if relations are already tense,
this may precipitate group conflict and ill feeling. Yet another example
is when one small group are camping quietly, unharassed by the police
and then more caravans or wagons arrive, thus increasing the numbers
sufficiently to encourage the police to move them all on. This again can
cause much ill feeling. Conflict is created also by their own status distinctions based upon cleanliness. Sometimes when the Gypsies are
"moved on", the members of the group who have spoiled the immediate
environment with the remains of scrap-metal breaking, are blamed by
others in the group for being untidy and thus causing their enforced
movement.

Whatever the exact cause of conflict, it certainly seems as if the
quarrel is made explicit to all present within the camp. The gravity of
the quarrel will influence how many Gypsies hear about it at other
camping locations. There seems to be a number of different methods
for resolving conflict which are related to the seriousness, or degree,
of the ill-feeling. Ridicule and ostracism are possible "punishments"
within the immediate camp. Minor conflicts are resolved by the individuals making the issue public and positioning themselves at a distance
from each other and then conducting the arguments by shouting across
to each other, often using strong language. The parties may be sitting
by two different fires or just standing at a distance. Observers do not
seem to be excluded from the controversies, but in the cases witnessed, it
was mainly conducted by the individuals who started it. This shouting
match may be continued for some minutes. If this does not result in
each side feeling avenged or in one side withdrawing in submission,
then physical conflict may be threatened or even embarked upon, but
this was rarely witnessed. If the conflict is not resolved to the satisfaction of the parties concerned, it may then progress to a further stage in
that one of the parties with family and sometimes other kin, will move
their caravan to a new position. This may be only two hundred yards
down the road, but it appears to be efficacious in reducing or suspending

the conflict. The distance to which one of the parties may move might well depend upon the need for them to be in that particular area: job opportunities, police activity, and alternative camp sites, will be factors taken into consideration. It may also be that if the conflict offends or influences the immediate kin of either side of the "warring parties", the resulting social divisions will have greater significance, as it may provide the basis of a feud. The numerical involvement, the intensity and occurrence of feuding appears to be closely related to the serious- ness of the cause, and they may last for very long periods of time. The existence of feuds may help to explain some of the social and geographical groupings and migrations within the region. Thus, if conflict cannot be contained within particular groups, there is always the possibility that the groups will divide and move away from each other. This has the functional advantages of reducing, or at least suspending, feuding tendencies. At the same time, seen in the context of the amoeboid character of the existing communication network, this helps to maintain the essential unity of the total community.

There is a difference between the serious conflict and ill-feeling which has been talked of above, and the sometimes violent discussions that will take place around a camp fire. This level of argument appears socially harmless in terms of relationships and may revolve around any issue under the sun. Usually, however, it is over a trifling point of detail. For example, there may emerge a discussion about the makes and value of the watches that are being worn by those present. The heat of the argument will go steadily upwards involving claim and counter- claim of value and number of jewels etc. To settle the argument an independent arbitrator will be called to the fire (perhaps someone who can read) and the dispute will usually be settled when the words on the watches have actually been read aloud. Such "gospel" words are accepted without further question.

It is suggested, therefore, that the seeming fluidity of the social structure afforded by the possibility of easy migration is an essential factor which has enabled the Gypsies to resolve and contain conflict. The mobility that is precipitated by conflict is not therefore evidence of permanent or irrevocable social dislocation, but is more a constant adaption of social groupings which enables the maintenance of kinship ties and an overall sense of a "stable" community.

Because of the public nature of social conflict, social groupings are determined in a manner that is compatible with the overall successful functioning of the social and economic structure. The factors of distance and time, militate against an uncontained and destructive escalation of conflict. What at first sight may look like social disruption is, in fact, a highly functional feature of the social system. If it were not so, then unresolved conflict would eventually lead to increasing restrictions on possible migrations and social groupings. For the sake of a viable social structure and economic survival, such restrictions must, somehow, be avoided. With very few social contacts with the settled population, the Gypsies' social structure has had to function to give a real sense of internal cohesion and lineal persistence.

The question of social cohesion and the resolution of conflict has been consciously laboured owing to its importance as a factor in the Gypsy's culture. It plays a significant part in their relations with the settled society and also in the nature of their responses to social and educational provision that is made available for them by the settled population from time to time.

There appears to be no formal or institutionalized legal system among the Gypsies, any more than there is any recognizable, representative or direct government. As the nuclear family is the effective economic unit, leadership tends to be based upon it, and in most cases this will fall to the senior man (or in the case of a widowed family unit, the mother). There is no discernible wider group leadership except that in some social situations involving dialogue with members of the settled society, such as the police, some charismatic Gypsy personalities will emerge and appear to be vocal on behalf of the group. There is really no wider recognized representation apart from the spokesman for individual families. The family will call on any member to speak or take a leading role depending often on who is available and what the situation dictates. Where special skills are required, for example reading or writing, then a member of the group who can render such services will be called upon. There is only one man in the area to whom the Gypsies award any degree of authority. He is middle-aged, intelligent, and economically successful. On some occasions, such as evictions, he will be the only one to act as spokeman. There is no election to such a position and it is the impression that it is merely that he is their best spokesman in such a situation. In a different context, however, this passively-awarded representational authority vanishes. For example, when he was asked if the group as a whole would like the local authority to organise schooling for the children, he said he could not speak for other families, but that each individual family would have to be asked.

An important part of the Gypsies' social structure which should not be underestimated in helping to explain its form, is the subject of its own social distinctions and status positions. Although research material is thin with respect to this area of investigation, it is possible to make one or two general comments. There are two predominant criteria for

determining social distinctions; cleanliness and affluence. Each family
or small social group will make distinctions between themselves and
other families and groups in terms of these factors. It is difficult
however, to discern any set pattern of application of these criteria.
There is no uniform standard either of wealth or cleanliness which is
universally accepted by the Gypsy community. All assessments therefore
are purely subjective and peculiar to each family or grouping. Thus,
each family or small social grouping will "look down" on other families
by awarding themselves a higher status distinction using the criteria of
wealth and cleanliness in whichever way it is seen necessary to establish
such distinctions. For them to be able to do this, it requires an individual
manipulation of the meaning of wealth and cleanliness. Thus for example,
the poorest family, in pure economic terms, with the most traditional
living accommodation in the form of a horse-drawn wagon and with
lowest standards in home and personal hygiene, will look down on the
cleaner and more economically affluent groups who have progressed to
living in a trailer caravan. This distinction is based on the grounds that
because of the nature of the affluent families' work (scrap dealing) they
have fouled their immediate environment and, because of their dirty
habits, have brought social condemnation on all the Gypsy community
from the settled population. The wagon-dwelling families derive their
status from their self-identified sense of tidy habits, and their imaginary
tidy and clean immediate environment. It is alleged that the dirty
behaviour of the scrap dealers is the root cause of forced migrations by
the police and council officials. On the other hand, the economically
more affluent groups of scrap dealers see the distinction in a different
light, and derive their status by making sharp distinctions between
them and the poor, traditional families. This is on the basis of the
wealth and cleanliness as clearly demonstrated by their modern living
accommodation in trailer caravans with their "smart" motor vehicles.
They feel that the Gypsies who still hang on to the "poor" way of life
and still live in the old wagons with horses, let the Gypsies down in the
face of Gaujo society.[35]

Between the Gypsies who live in trailer caravans, the same sort of
distinctions operate, in that the families with the more expensive
trailers will see themselves as superior to the ones with cheaper trailers,
and thus the latter are supposedly more dirty. The traditional family
groups who still travel and live in the canvas wagons have, similarly,
felt distinctions between them. Mention has been made of their con-

35. One "affluent" "clean" Gypsy man with a good trailer caravan complained bitterly
when a television crew were only interested in the traditional wagons. He said, "It let us
sort of people down so much."

demnation of the Gypsies in trailers, but between themselves there are distinctions made again on the basis of cleanliness. Irrespective of the state of their wagons, immediate environment and personal hygiene, some feel themselves to be superior to the other families, and at times call each other dirty and filthy. Unwashed children or the lack of elaborate paintwork on the wagons are the focal points for these criticisms regarding cleanliness.

These status distinctions in many cases also help to explain the social and spatial divisions which exist among the Gypsies, but it would be unwise to suggest that these factors alone are responsible for such social divisions, for in many cases, as aforesaid, kinship ties and the climate of relationships play an important role in the geographical creation of social group structures. This is demonstrated by the fact that a family who are relatively clean and with a trailer caravan, will closely associate and camp with their kin who may still live in a canvas wagon.

Religious beliefs among the Gypsies are common and there are many visual and explicit religious symbols, such as crucifixes above the bed, pictures and simple pictorial story books about Jesus. In one wagon in which a bunk bed was shared by an old couple who slept at either end, two crucifixes were lodged in the roof rafters above their heads. Great delight and pride was taken in telling why the two crosses were so placed. In other wagons and caravans there may also be small roughly-framed pictures of Christ. These will not take pre-eminence in display, but will be put with other family photographs or prints of horses etc. One family had a picture story book of Jesus which was kept with other papers as part of the permanent archives of the family.

Belief in the supernatural and in the Christian tradition, was verbally witnessed by many families. The incidents in their lives that defied natural explanation were accounted for in terms of supernatural actions. Predestination was not an uncommon belief and in response to the unreasonably many tragedies that seem to impinge upon their lives, they would attempt to interpret them totally in the actions of the Lord who is awarded the wisdom to know what is best. Such phrases as "'im up there, 'e knows best''; "The Good Lord 'as decided'', were often heard. It is not suggested that they attempt to transfer blame from themselves or others on to the better judgements of a supernatural being, for it was very clear that worldly events which could be explained in terms of human fallibility and misdemeanours were directly apportioned to the alleged guilty party. For example, the "mismanagement" of their immediate environment by ill-advised disposal of dangerous waste, like broken glass bottles, inevitably resulted in serious injuries. One small boy needed medical treatment which included twelve stitches on the sole of his foot. In this case, they blamed the boy for being careless. Again, by way of example, one night a car driven by an unknown Gaujo smashed into one of the wagons parked at the side of the road. This not only startled all the occupants who were asleep, but it also nearly turned it over and damaged much of the undercarriage. In this instance there was no reference to supernatural ordinance, but blame was put on the unknown offender. It is mainly in death or serious illness that "supernatural" actions are given expression and credence.

Church attendance is not regular, and indeed there was no evidence of it at all apart from ceremonial events such as christenings and funerals. In being shown many of the family documents (including all papers; old newspaper cuttings, pedlars' licences, old accounts for funerals, photographs, etc.) which are usually stored under the bedding or in some small corner of the wagon and wrapped in two or three pieces of cloth to keep them clean, certificates of christenings have been found, but they usually refer to older children and it is the impression that children are, nowadays, no longer christened. It may well be that because of the seeming lack of legalized or church weddings, there is an understandable lack of interest, and even reluctance, to have children christened.

Church funerals are the common practice for their departed loved ones, and indeed, death, more than anything, demonstrates the expression of their religious beliefs and the strength of their kinship structure. After the deceased has been laid out, the coffin is returned from the funeral directors to the Gypsy encampment and placed in the wagon or trailer of the deceased. The lid is removed and the walls of the wagon are lined with white sheets. All the community will, and are expected to "pay their respects" to the deceased by going to look in the coffin. The news of the death will rapidly be transferred to all sections of the community. Thus, visits by members of the community to the bereaved encampment to pay their respects will follow almost immediately. The wake will last all night and many of the visitors will stay the whole night through by a big fire. This practice is known as "sitting up". Children, young people and adults will stay up and all sit around the fire, but in the one case witnessed, by the early hours of the morning, most of the other families, apart from the immediate kin, will go to their own wagons or trailers for a few hours' sleep. It seems as if a mark of respect is paid to the close kin of the deceased if visitors and fellow campers at least stay by the fire for some time and look in the coffin to pay their respects. The immediate family seem, for their part, to be expected to stay up all night by the fire which is constantly made up by the young men present. As night approaches, two white candles are placed in candlesticks and lit. These are placed at each end of the coffin together with a plate of salt. It is stated that the reason for this practice is that these symbols represent sorrow, and it was a custom which was always complied with. When the writer was being shown the coffin by the step-daughter-in-law of the deceased, the sadness of the situation was explained and concluded in the following manner, "Well, 'e 'as gone to a much better place". While the writer was paying his respects to the deceased, some children were eager to enter the wagon to see things for themselves, but this move was resisted by the older lady. The resistance proved negative and the step-grand-daughter and step-great-grand-daughter surreptitiously slipped their way into the wagon which by now seemed crowded. They looked with unstartled interest into the coffin. Their ages were thirteen and five respectively.

The social atmosphere around the fire was free and easy. Most of the discussion was of a trivial character, but it was friendly and there was surprisingly much fooling about and joking. Weeping was not observed until the following day when all the visitors reappeared some hours prior to the funeral. Only then did the immediate kin show visible signs of personal grief. About one hundred and fifty people attended the funeral and the cortege was watched with interest by many Gaujo people outside the church. The service was short and simple, but the singing of two hymns was poor. One informant said that they always had a funeral service in church and that it mattered a lot to them. The informant further commented upon the poor singing, saying that it was because most could not read the hymns and this was a pity. "Especially on occasions like this. This is why we want the kids to go to school."

All the individual families within the community brought flowers to the funeral and there were some very expensive-looking sprays, the most elaborate of all being called the "Gates of Heaven". This is a wreath of white flowers in the shape of an archway about a foot high and at right angles to a base of more flowers. There was a small cross on the top of the archway. It is placed on top of the coffin and afterwards placed at the head of the grave. This wreath was a point of interest in conversation and is usually provided by the next of kin or other immediate relatives. The cost of this is in the region of £4 to £5 and this again is a fact that is brought up in conversation. It is certain that the relatively high cost of the "Gates of Heaven" and other flowers bear witness to the respect that they have for the deceased. In the months, and even years, following the funeral, there are very regular visits made to the grave (which, in some cases, can be a family grave). Fresh flowers are always placed on the grave on the occasions of these visits.

RECREATION

The Gypsies recreational activities are extensive in character, and in many cases are similar to those of the settled population. In many of the activities there is observable sex segregation and age setting, but it appears that neither of these are a result of any rigid compliance to traditional custom. Age and sex difference in interests and participation seem more to be related to individual preferences. Gypsies practice a large number of games and sports which include "Cowboys and Indians," snowballs, curling and homing pigeons. These games are usually played by children and adolescents. Once a game of "horse-shoes" was played in a field by a group of the adult male members of the community. It is not known whether there was any gambling in connection with this game. It is the impression that they do engage in cock-fighting with their highly-prized "gaming-birds". One indication that this particular sport is a part of their leisure-time activity was witnessed on one Sunday afternoon. The writer made a visit to one of their encampments which was located out in the country. On arrival he asked for one of the senior men who had expressed a wish to see him. There seemed to be no menfolk present at the time, but the women gave hesitant directions as to where to find the person. They said that he was fishing over near some old railway lines. The writer made a long trek across the fields in the direction advised. The whole area was searched in the hope of finding the Gypsy man quietly fishing in one of the flooded gravel pits. The search proved unsuccessful and so he returned to the area of the caravans. Nearing this latter location, a large group of adult Gypsy men were seen approaching from the opposite direction. Their number included the person sought, and it was fairly obvious that neither he nor the others had been fishing. No discussion followed as to where or what they had been doing and why the writer had so obviously been misdirected. On another occasion, some of the Gypsy children showed their teacher how cock-fighting was done, by holding two cocks face to face and then letting them go. On this occasion, a mother came out of a caravan and shouted at the children to stop it. It was also interesting that sometimes the children in their school situation asked the teachers to draw pictures of fighting cocks. It may well be, therefore, that in the quiet of the countryside in summer, perhaps on a Sunday afternoon, the men will have an enjoyable but clandestine and illegal sporting session.

Despite the possible inaccuracy of the story given to the researcher on the particular occasion, many of the Gypsies reported that they went fishing, but it seems not to be a common practice. Bathing and swimming, especially by the young men and boys, is very popular on hot summer days. They will bathe in small rivers and use their trousers and pants as costumes—few of them can actually swim. Another sport that is also popular with the men and boys is that of hare-coursing. The hunted creatures are not always hares, but may include game birds or rabbits. When the Gypsies are encamped in country districts, they will sometimes engage in poaching activities. Dogs are mostly used and especially whippets and lurchers as they do not bark and will take non-verbal instructions from their handlers. It is difficult to say whether these activities are carried out for the sake of economic necessity or merely for sport. When there are public events such as meetings for hare-coursing, some of the Gypsies will enter the competitions. They will train the dogs with an electrically-operated rabbit skin. Long distances may be travelled to attend these meetings. Similar distances may be covered in order to go to horse fairs, county shows and race meetings. Regular attendance at horse fairs is a strong and traditional part of their culture, but these days the families who attend have trailer caravans and motor trucks, and it is often the case that they will only stay for one or two days. In some cases the men may go alone on a day trip. The families in wagons tend not to go; the reason given being that it is too far to travel on the increasingly dangerous roads; it takes too long to get there and costs too much to feed the horses. It may be true also that some poorer families are reluctant to suffer the possible loss of earnings. Spending a leisurely three or four weeks on the road, and being able to find plenty of camping places en route, with possibilities for odd jobs on the way, is no longer such a practical possibility. Each autumn, a large fun-fair comes to Hometown and the Gypsies eagerly await this event. It is interesting to note that they seem to have some social contact with the fair people but make no attempt to exploit any economic opportunities offered. They enjoy going for the excitement and entertainment.

Public houses known to be friendly are frequently attended, but drinking is sometimes done at home. Apart from "pubs" the Gypsies will often attend "clubs" of various kinds. One club at Hometown is very popular during the period of the potato harvest when, on a Saturday evening, large groups of young people will go and drink, sing, dance and take a delight in the cabaret show. Dancing is a popular activity especially among the teenage girls. Some Sunday afternoons they will get a record-player outdoors and dance, "jive" and "rock" to very loud pop music. Onlookers are invited to join in and much delight and laughter was had on one occasion when the writer was thus persuaded. Another club of a different type is also very popular—this is a working men's club which they often patronize. The Gypsies have a great interest and liking for Country and Western music and this particular club specialises in this type of music and entertainment on Tuesday nights. In fact, some of the Gypsies joined with the club's Gaujo members for a trip to another town one night in the winter. The trip included a meal and a concert at a similar club where a famous Country and Western star was performing. The inclusive charge for the trip per person was £1·25. A pastime that is popular among the young is going to the cinema. Strong attractions are films starring Elvis Presley, but war, horror and cowboy films also command great interest.

The major part of their leisure time is taken up by sitting round the camp fire. The open fire by the side of the wagon or trailer is a very important part of the Gypsies' life. It is the focal point around which most of their everyday experiences are centered. Almost all social intercourse and domestic tasks are carried out within its warmth and light. At most times in the day, and especially in the evening, Gypsies will be seen sitting around the fires. They will talk, tell stories, have arguments, nurse babies, love and chastise children. In the spring, summer and autumn they very much enjoy sitting by the fire and watching the battery-worked portable television sets which many of them own. Often whole families will sit and enjoy an evening's viewing. The commercial stations are watched more than the BBC. In fact, television is watched a great deal and it is not uncommon to see teen-agers watching a film in the middle of the afternoon. At night time, the sets will be kept on until very late. Of course, some programmes are more popular than others, for example, "Family at War" and "The Virginian", were highly rated; the general pattern of viewing is action films and money-quiz programmes—the more serious programmes, like discussions, being turned "over". They do, however, watch the News programmes. Commercial advertisements are watched with great interest and amusement. It is interesting to note that a number of children are given names of famous entertainment personalities, the most common being Alan Ladd, Kay Starr, Elvis Presley, and Jason King. The full name is given to the child and the star's surname becomes the child's middle Christian name. From some of the famous namesakes used, it is clear that this practice is well-established. Traditional Gypsy names, for example, Liberty, Wisdom, Sophia, Abraham, Lisa, appear to have given way to more contemporary names and particularly the names of popular entertainers as above.

Other activities include listening to records, mainly Country and Western, outside in the open. More organized activities have been witnessed such as playing cards and dominoes. Whether much money is involved is difficult to say, but the impression is that, apart from pennies and ten-penny pieces, there is no heavy gambling. This rather limited list of the Gypsies' recreational activities is, of course, not exclusive, but it does help to give some indication that from the point of view of leisure, their culture bears a remarkable degree of vitality and a healthy diversity. It is clear that the traditional leisure-time pursuits of Gypsy folklore are not greatly in evidence, such as the traditional stereotypes of story-telling, violin-playing and dancing. No evidence was gained to suggest that they had ever engaged in these activities, but it is also worth noting that even if they had, and are thus now less traditional, this would be little different to the changing patterns of leisure-time activities of the settled population. The latter group demonstrates a remarkable susceptibility to rapidly changing fashions in entertainment, so much so, that relatively few today play the piano or other musical instruments—most have record-players, radios and television sets.

CHAPTER FIVE

Boyash Gypsies: Shantytown Ethnicity

William Kornblum

The ability to get along well with people whose cultures and values are quite different from one's own is a highly prized talent in modern society. Among diplomats, anthropologists, and international salesmen, for example, it is either developed into a practised art, or it is codified in elaborate protocols. At the other extreme of society, in the marginal and often violent world of the urban migrant, existence among strangers may be the key to a group's survival in a new social environment. At the grey edge of the commercial metropolis and in the factory zones of industrial centres, the need to understand the ways of foreigners assumes a desperate and yet mundane urgency. Perhaps for no other group is this observation more appropriate than for the Gypsy tribes which inhabit the fringes of great Western cities. More than any other diaspora people, the Gypsies have remained in the slum world of the urban migrant, and their cultures have become remarkably adapted to the delicate negotiations among strangers which so often settle the fate of urban migrant groups.[1]

Gypsy groups in the major cities of Europe and America have tended to remain in immigrant neighbourhoods over many generations, long after other newcomers have either disappeared culturally into the larger

---

1. For further comparative analysis of the relationships between Gypsy cultures and structural dimensions of Western society, see William Kornblum, "Urban Gypsies and the Culture of Poverty", *Urban Life and Culture*, spring 1972.

society, or have at least relocated their communities in somewhat more "respectable" quarters of the city. Undoubtedly this aspect of Gypsy life is due in large measure to the history of discrimination and racism which have made the Gypsies a pariah group *par excellence*.[2] It is also true, however, that the Gypsy cultures are based on the corporate family economy, tribal endogamy, and a fatalistic rejection of the values of non-Gypsy society. These characteristics of Gypsy culture have survived over centuries of nomadism through the peasant agricultural lands of Asia, Europe, and North Africa. Theirs is a culture most adapted to an environment of peasants and small shopkeepers. Thus Gypsies in the city thrive best among new urban migrants, people whom they understand and who have need of the Gypsy's particular style of folk urbanity. The seeming paradox here is that on the one hand the Gypsies generally avoid prolonged attachments with *gadje*, non-Gypsies of all description. On the other hand, the Gypsy's daily existence depends on their intimate understanding of non-Gypsy society, or at least that stratum of it which they frequent. Especially in the cities, the Gypsies must live among strangers, under the most crowded and competitive urban conditions, while they attempt to maintain their own distinct culture.

During the late spring and summer of 1968 I lived with a large family of Boyash Gypsies on the industrial outskirts of Paris.[3] The family inhabited a Parisian shantytown (*bidonville*) at La Courneuve, a camp which they shared with a number of other immigrant groups, as well as with various types of Parisian *demi-monde*. While recognizing that there may be quite wide divergence in the manner in which various Gypsy groups manage their relations with outsiders, study of the relations between Boyash Gypsies and other cultural groups at the camp in La Courneuve does offer insight into a number of dimensions of Gypsy–gadje ethnic relations. Among the most important of these is the relationship between Gypsy dealings with other groups and the maintenance of the nomadic features of Gypsy culture, including the Gypsy's ability to maintain family solidarity in the face of conflict, and their skill at the use of symbolic cultural displays. These aspects of Boyash culture are particularly important in allowing the Gypsies to thrive in what for other groups is a hostile human environment.

2. The best scholarly treatment of racism as it has affected Gypsy cultures is Kenrick, D. and Puxton, G. (1972). *The Destiny of European Gypsies*, Basic Books, London.

3. This research was conducted in connection with a Documentary film project which I undertook with my film-making partner, Yehuda Yaniv. Our expenses were paid by the Walden Film Co., which unfortunately dissolved before the entire series of planned films were completed, an unfortunate hazard of anthropological cinema. Two short documentaries on the Ivanovich family were completed and are available from the author or at the office of the *Bulletin Des Etudes Gitanes* in Paris.

THE IVANOVICH FAMILY:
BOYASH GYPSIES OF THE PARISIAN REGION

Boyash Gypsies speak a dialectic version of Romanian, and they have traditionally worked as animal trainers and circus performers. Although they are famous as bear tamers throughout the Balkans, there are only two Boyash families in the region of Paris. The Ivanovich family with whom I lived make their home in the working class regions of St. Denis and La Courneuve. During 1968 there were 51 family members living in the shantytown at La Courneuve. Organized into seven nuclear family units all were to varying degrees subject to the authority of Alexandre Ivanovich, the elderly family patriarch, and his wife Marie. In addition to the parental respect they could command from their children, the couple was by far the most skilled at animal handling and could offer necessary guidance and advice to other members of the family whenever problems in husbandry arose. Together the family cared for a large assortment of performing animals, including a bear, two llamas, a pony, five monkeys, and assorted goats and dogs.

The care and training of animals still occupies a central place in the European Boyash culture and is the mainstay of their family economy. Whenever money is needed, small groups of Ivanovich men and boys stage animal shows in the working class market areas of Paris. In addition to these itinerant shows, the family members also engage in other economic activities, including some trade in gold, auto parts, and used wagons. The Boyash women typically remain in the camp and do not go out to tell fortunes as do the women of the Kalderash and other Rom groups. Instead, the Boyash women normally care for the camp and attend to the details of obtaining food for the family's livestock. On occasion they do accompany the men and boys to different Parisian neighbourhoods where they perform. Normally the women remain in the camp and thus may become quite deeply embroiled in the politics of life in the migrant camps, as will become evident presently.

In contrast to the more settled life of the Montreuil Kalderash, the Boyash remain nomads. Even though the Ivanovich family has lived almost continuously in Paris since the Second World War, they inhabit the highly transient world of the Parisian *bidonvilles*, they send nuclear family units out of the city on periodic tours of the countryside, and to the best of their ability they remain ready to move on short notice. Their homes are the traditional roulottes, or converted buses which they group around two or three common courtyards, an ecological strategy which also clearly marks off their domain within the migrant camp.

Finally, many of the families continue to cook their meals over open fires within their yards.

Although they often become involved in a wide variety of petty business transactions with other immigrant groups in the camp, the Ivanovich family economy still depends quite heavily on the entertainment which they bring to the inhabitants of market neighbourhoods in the working class Portes de Cligancourt, d'Aubervilliers, Clichy, and other similar areas.

The entertainment which the Boyash men and boys provide is far from elaborate and suffices only to provide some momentary diversion for the crowds which jam the open air stalls of the market streets. As a teenage boy taps a snare drum roll, an adult man guides a trained goat up a ladder to a high pedestal, all the while maintaining a steady patter of jokes and exhortations to the crowd. This goat act is generally followed with a few tricks by a trained monkey, as the young boys circulate through the crowd with tambourines to collect coins from the audience. The show terminated, the band moves two or three blocks into the street and begins the routine anew. On special occasions, such as the annual Communist Party fair at La Courneuve, or other gatherings which attract large groups of working class people and immigrants, the family may present a more elaborate performance. Here the elder Ivanovich couple themselves will present their performing bear for the finale, an act which is generally too strenuous for the normal sunny day outings into the Parisian neighbourhoods.

Adult members of the family recognize full well that the entertainment they provide, and the more general conditions of their existence depend on their intimate knowledge of working class French, West Indian, Algerian, and other groups which frequent the congested areas of the city. For example, on one warm summer day during my sojourn with the family, we set up the props and animals on a busy thoroughfare in the neighbourhood of La Motte Piquet, in the shadow of the Eiffel Tower. Here crowds of good humoured pedestrians of every ethnic background stopped to watch old Cortez, the oldest Ivanovich son-in-law, as he coaxed his little goat up the ladder to her pedestal. Generally the shoppers gave rather generously to Babosh and Nené, the young boys whose job it was to pass the hat.

During a break from this routine, as we stopped for a glass of wine in a café where Cortez knew the owner, I asked the older man why he didn't wander over to the tower itself where there would no doubt be crowds of well-heeled tourists. "We don't go near the tourists," he explained, "because there the cops will chase us away, and besides the tourists think they do us a favour when they throw a penny. In this neighbourhood the people appreciate what we do and they don't sit on their pocket books like the tourists."

Boyash relations with non-Gypsies in the streets of Paris tend to be confined to fleeting relations with old acquaintances, and bantering with inhabitants of the various neighbourhoods. Back at the camp in La Courneuve, however, relations with gadje may take on a much more serious tenor. Although all the camp's inhabitants share the general conditions of lumpenproletarian life, each group also attempts to maintain its own distinct culture and social organization. Success in this regard is reflected in the physical division of the camp into more or less segregated ethnic territories. In general, in this social environment where they are a distinct minority among minorities, the Gypsy family nevertheless manages to have its own way on most issues which it deems important. Thus, for example, the family occupies proportionally much greater space than other groups, and within that space it also houses its rather impressive menagerie. Of course Gypsy success at survival in the migrant camp is only partially based on their experience and skill at the migratory life. It is also based in some measure on the specific problems which confront the other groups with whom the Gypsies must co-exist.

OTHER IMMIGRANT GROUPS: PROBLEMS OF STATUS AND COHESION

Despite their relatively greater numbers when compared to the Gypsy family, each of the other immigrant groups, Serbians, Algerians, Spanish, and French is confronted by serious problems of inexperience, foreignness, or status deprivation. These problems differ in degree for each of the groups, but, in comparison with the Gypsies, each group is confronted with difficulty in communicating with other groups in the camp, difficulty in establishing the solidarity of their populations, and a deprivation of honour in the outside society which often leads to extremes of self-hatred and instability. Of course all the groups which compose the camp's population share the need to find food, shelter, and safety in a difficult environment. *Bidonville* La Courneuve is small and homey in comparison with the much larger squatter settlement in St. Denis, but like its larger neighbour the camp offers no electricity, no running water, and no formal organization of authority or responsibility. Water is available at one common faucet, a row of pit toilets serves the entire camp.

Whatever common morality and trust emerges among the camp's inhabitants is almost entirely a matter of their own negotiations. In consequence, if any of the various groups are to attain a decent level

of living even by the lowest standards, some mutual aid and co-operation is necessary. The first line of mutual aid develops around common
ethnicity or national heritage. The camp is roughly divided into dis-
crete quarters according to the ethnicity of the residents as Algerians,
Serbians, Spaniards and Gypsies, each attempts to locate their temporary shelters within the areas "reserved" for their members. This
style of "neighbourhood formation" is the primary basis of social order
in the camp. Each group comes to defend a specific section of the terrain
within which their members feel a sense of relative security and ease
of communication. On the other hand, the general security of the camp's
inhabitants also depends on the overall moral order of the shantytown,
an order which develops out of the negotiations among the various
groups. These negotiations, in turn, are necessarily based on the particular problems which confront each of the various immigrant groups.

Serbian immigrants, who have come North in search of better occupational opportunities, inhabit the central alleys of the camp. Generally
these migrants from the industrial centres of Bosnia and Southern
Serbia hold menial jobs in Parisian metal shops or fabrication plants.
Since the work is highly susceptible to market fluctuations, the group
is highly transient. Despite this transiency, the Serbian immigrants
attempt to recreate a squatter ecology within their section of the camp
which corresponds to their ideas of respectability. Crowded into
dilapidated buses and vans, the Yugoslavs nevertheless go to great
lengths to attach wooden entrances and porches to their sagging quarters. Further simulating the private dwellings to which they aspire,
the Serbians plant little flower gardens along the steps leading up to
their converted vans and truck-body bedrooms.

This group of Serbian immigrants, numbering approximately 800
residents, accounts for the largest single ethnic group within the camp
although it is only slightly larger than the North African population.
In comparison with the single Boyash Gypsy family, the Serbians and
North Africans are numerically the dominant groups. On the other hand,
the Serbians in particular are plagued with difficulties in establishing the
solidarity of their population, a problem which is seriously aggravated
by a shortage of available Yugoslav women.

In comparison with the Boyash Gypsies and their well organized
extended family, the Serbians are typical of the immigrant group whose
members seek better economic opportunities and have little intention
to remain in the host country. For this reason most of the Serbian
immigrants are men, many of whom are married and have left their
families behind with the intention of returning to their homes. Often,
therefore, a group of men will live with one woman. This creates

domestic situations which often lead to severe jealousies, conflict, and a sense of shame. Deprived of both the satisfactions and the responsibilities of marital and parental status, the Serbian men suffer from depression and ennui. Their leisure time, made meaningless in a culture they do not share or understand, is often occupied by stories of home, heavy drinking, and arguments over relations with each other. It is not surprising, therefore, that in their dealings with more organized groups in the camp, particularly the Gypsies, the Serbian migrants often find themselves in highly dependent positions, a situation which they often come to resent.

In contrast to the highly transient Serbian migrants, the Algerian and other North African immigrants who inhabit one corner of the camp are more permanent residents of France. Often they are people who have migrated to Paris from other French towns and whose search for jobs and housing is frustrated. Others are families whose members have had troubles of one kind or another and are unable to marshal the resources necessary to leave the camp. Like the Serbians, the North Africans are somewhat plagued with the problem of lack of women and the attending difficulties of establishing the solidarity of their numbers. But this is not nearly as severe a problem for them as it is for the Serbians. The greatest difficulty the North Africans face in the camp stems from the manner in which the ecology of their settlement reinforces the other residents' stereotypes of the North Africans as dangerous and untrustworthy.

In their corner of the sprawling *bidonville* the Arabic speaking residents have constructed a packing crate and canvas facsimile of the North African casbah. Families from specific North African cities group their members around common courtyards where the rooms are constructed of crating wood and an occasional truck body. These individual clusters of dwellings are connected by a tortuous system of covered passageways and blind alleys. This recreates an urban environment which is quite familiar to the North Africans but entirely strange for the other residents of the camp. The Yugoslav immigrants, the Gypsies, and other groups in the camp do not like to enter the North African quarter. They complain they often become lost there, or they do not feel they have any control over whom they will meet once inside the narrow alleys and crowded courtyards. As a result, the North Africans are rarely hosts to others in the camp. They are much more likely to visit others on neutral ground or to be guests in other camp neighbourhoods. Thus while the North Africans generally manage to maintain the order and security of their own quarter, they rarely play prominent roles in the larger camp society.

In addition to the Gypsies, the Yugoslavs, and the North Africans, who because of the numbers or their influence are the most important groups in the camp, there are also smaller ethnic groups which attempt to claim a portion of the common terrain. At the outer most fringe of the camp is a highly mobile group of Spanish and Portuguese immigrants, for the most part composed of small family units. These are perhaps the most unfortunate of the immigrants because they are generally illegal aliens, and cannot obtain the all-important working cards which would permit them to pursue legitimate occupations. Lacking even this meagre prop against poverty, the Spanish and Portuguese immigrants tend to drift from one bidonville to another. More than the other groups represented in the camp they tend to become involved in petty crimes, particularly traffic in stolen merchandise. In this respect the Southerners have some affinity with the least reputable and most disorganized group in the camp, the superannuated prostitutes, the alcoholics, and the petty criminals.

This latter group of underworld characters is also distinguished from most of the other migrants by nationality and culture. For all the personal troubles and misfortunes their individual biographies reveal, they are nevertheless citizens of France. Their citizenship guarantees them the common rights of all Frenchmen, including access to social assistance agencies. Ironically, their citizenship also deprives the French underworld inhabitants of a social psychological defence which often makes life bearable for immigrants. The foreign groups who inhabit the camp may rationalize the grim conditions of their present lives with favourable comparisons to their past lives in other places. As immigrants they may attribute their troubles to their displacement and their persistent problems in mastering the subtleties of a new culture. Above all there is always the hope that conditions will improve with time.

None of these defences against the harshness of present reality exist for the broken French men and women of the camp. While the aged *putain* or Parisian *clochard* may mock the broken French of the immigrants, their citizenship alone provides little ground for solidarity among them. They are down and out in a milieu which for respectable Frenchmen represents *la lie du peuple*, the dregs of society. An indication of their demoralization is the fact that the French citizens do not command a specific territory within the camp and generally depend on the aid of other more organized groups for their security. Thus the Boyash "employ" three or four such individuals as servants. They do much of the most onerous labour for the Gypsy family in return for the barest necessities of food, lodging, and a sense of belonging in human society.

In summary, the Algerians, the Serbians, the Portuguese, and

Spaniards, and the disorganized representatives of the Parisian under-world, constitute the immediate social environment of the Boyash Gypsies in this Parisian shantytown. While some representatives of the dominant society, particularly welfare workers, police officials, and shopkeepers also have some contact with the Gypsies, the immigrants are their neighbours in the camp, the people with whom they live their daily lives. Bidonvilles such as this one at La Courneuve are isolated immigrant enclaves. Their impoverished, makeshift dwellings, and their reputation as dangerous places tend to discourage both the casual visitor and the inquiring functionary. Therefore, to a greater degree than is true in most urban slum areas, the inhabitants of the shantytowns must create and maintain their own very parochial moral standards and their own pragmatic notions of interpersonal trust. In these matters the Gypsies excel. Unlike the other groups who are plagued with problems of organization, or who attempt to adapt their former cultures in an unhospitable environment, the seemingly Hobbesian world of the shantytown has become the Gypsies' permanent habitat. As one might expect, therefore, the Gypsies almost invariably take on roles as central figures on issues of morality. Their transactions and negotiations with representatives of the other groups are central to the emergence of a moral order in the camp, even if that order is based on arrangements which would not be considered respectable against the standards of public morality in the larger society.

GYPSY NOMADS AND PEASANT MIGRANTS

Much of the influence of Gypsy groups in migrant camps derives from the organization of their nomadic cultures. Although the Ivanovich family members are not nomads in the classical Gypsy manner, they maintain a nomadic style of existence. Their family economy and their relations with other groups in the camp are very much grounded in the rootlessness and disruption of the other immigrants' lives. The other groups in the camp are not "at home" in the migrant camp as are the Gypsies. In consequence they often have need of advice and material support which the Gypsies are in a position to provide.

On a typical morning, beginning around 11 a.m., after the social and physical soreness of the morning has somewhat dissipated, Alexandre Ivanovich holds court around the fireplace in his family's main court-yard. A group of Serbian men, newcomers to the camp, arrive to ask his advice on the purchase of an old truck which they will make their home. The conversation is held in Serbo-Croatian and adheres to the pro-prieties of Balkan custom. The Serbian men have brought a bottle of

Slivovitz and the men carefully introduce themselves. They recount the story of their recent travels, detail their present life situations, and offer toasts to their host and his family before beginning serious discussion of business. After the men discuss their choice of vehicles, most of which they have located outside the camp, Alexandre offers the thought that he might have an old trailer of the desired dimensions which he could possibly rent to the men. After all, he reasons, they may not be in the camp very long if they find good jobs and can afford, after a few months, to move in with some of their countrymen in one of the nearby housing projects. On the other hand, if they cannot find good jobs they may wish to move on to another city, in which case ownership of a trailer or bus would be an encumbrance. This argument convinces the men and a deal is struck.

By this time it is already lunch hour and the women are admonishing Jean, a Parisian *clochard* who is one of the family's servants, for not having bought an adequate supply of firewood. Grumbling that he is always the scapegoat, Jean nevertheless prepares to push the heavy hand cart along the muddy road which leads to the vacant military land to the rear of the camp. Shortly thereafter, Tony, one of Alexandre's literate grandchildren arrives with the newspaper and is asked to read the gold quotations on the financial page. Marie Ivanovich, her ancient face furrowed beyond her fifty-seven years, explains to me that the family generally converts its assets into gold, usually in the form of rings, bracelets, watches, and even nuggets. "We don't trust this French paper," she explains, "even if we are citizens of France. In the hard times gold is the only thing that counts. If we travel to Romania soon, or to the Voivodina where my family is, they will not take this paper, but gold is always of value."

References to the family's travels, or to the uncertainty of life in gadje society reinforce the family's nomadic culture. Adult members of the family always think of themselves as on the verge of a voyage even if they have not moved from the camp for four or five years. The imminence of displacement, in turn, is further justification for their reluctance to commit themselves to the institutions of gadje society. For example, Richard, one of the literate Ivanovich grandchildren explains:

> I finished the Brevet (primary diploma) and I've been to technical schools to learn auto mechanics. I could work in any garage around here but what's the point? I can fix cars right here in the camp. I work on my own time and make money when I need it. The family needs me here and this is my life. What would happen when we move. I wouldn't be happy staying behind while the family goes elsewhere.

Sure we get disgusted with this life sometimes. I'm ashamed to bring girls here, to show them that my bedroom is this rotten *mil kilo* (van). But I'm not happy away from here for very long. It's the same with most of us. Look at Tony (his older brother). He married a French girl, left the family, and got a job *chez* Renault. In six months he was back here with the wife and baby. He was going crazy in the little apartment, nothing to do but work and watch television. He was afraid that the family would move and leave him in Paris staring at the four walls.

By remaining in the camp where their services as itinerant auto mechanics are in constant demand, the younger generation boys and men contribute a great deal to the status of the family in the *bidonville* society. People throughout the various settlements owe them favours, and they are in a position to cultivate the friendship of young men from the other groups who might otherwise threaten the family's safety. Surprisingly, these friendships do not heighten the conflict between the young Gypsies and their parents, as is evident in the comments offered by Lou Lou, a Gypsy boy from another family who lives with the Ivanovich family:

When you first started taping the old man and the others we felt terrible. That's why none of us younger guys came around the fire for quite a while. We were so ashamed. We would walk around on the other side of the wagons and pull our hair. The old people are not singers or musicians. Their old songs and jokes must be like nothing to someone from America where you have all the stars of rock and roll.

Then, when you began coming to spend time with us, the young, it was fine. When we sang and told stories together we saw that you understand these things and that you were not scornful of the old people.

The shame these young Gypsy men felt is hardly akin to that of adolescents from immigrant families who in Western cultures tend to reject the "old world ways" of their parents. Gypsy adolescents generally express a great deal of pride in the solidarity of their families and they identify their futures quite closely with that of the entire family. Thus the young men and boys could accompany their elders and their animals into the streets of Paris without feeling shame. Like their parents they believed their performance was appreciated among the immigrant and working class people for whom they performed. "When we first began to show the animals," Lou Lou explained, "we felt some shame, but it passes quickly. After all we have been doing this since we were young boys. We are used to the crowds and we enjoy being out in the street. We like to watch the people watching us. When the day is over we feel proud to return to the camp with stories of the day's adventures for the old people."

As these comments and examples suggest, the Boyash Gypsies' nomadic culture is sustained even though the family has long ago ceased to circulate widely through the agricultural lands of Southern and Central Europe. The family nevertheless continues to believe in its nomadism and even if the family itself does not voyage regularly, the others who inhabit the migrant camp are continually transient. Indeed, the Ivanovich family economy is rather dependent on the transiency of the other groups in camp. Also, as long as family members believe that they will be displaced in the near future, their relations with out-siders will remain tentative and instrumental. Finally, and perhaps above all, the family's success in this social environment depends upon the maintenance of generally high levels of inter-generational solidarity, no small accomplishment in this age of adolescent rebellion. These specific features of Boyash society, all of which are closely tied to the cultural adaptations of a nomadic culture, assume particular importance at times of stress or conflict when the security of the family is threatened.

DEALING WITH CONFLICT

Bidonvilles such as the camp at La Courneuve have the reputation as dangerous places where the inhabitants live outside the norms of re-spectable society. In fact shantytowns such as this one are no more dangerous than the average urban neighbourhood; there is a readily identifiable social order in the camp which is based upon informal institutions and norms which govern the interactions among the various groups. During the time I lived with the Ivanovich family there was only one serious fight in the camp, and even that incident of conflict was more a symbolic display of the readiness to use force. When it was resolved, the conflict served more to reinforce the basis of trust between the groups than it disrupted the safety of the camp.

Despite these qualifications, there is no escaping the fact that the overall safety of the camp depends upon the ability of various groups to resort to the use of force. The safety of particular individuals and families rests on their access to larger organized groups who can, as a last resort, call upon the strength of their numbers. In this respect, group solidarity and the skilful use of timing and illusion are also essen-tial in instances when a group is forced to fight for what it considers its rights or its honour. This last point is extremely important for the Gypsies because although they lack the numbers of other migrant groups, their family solidarity compensates for this deficiency. This should become evident in a narrative taken from the author's field notes:

Shortly after ten o'clock this evening, as we were sitting around the main camp fire trading stories with the elder Ivanovich couple, Lou Lou was struck in the arm by a rock thrown into the camp from somewhere outside our circle. Even as the family members jumped to their feet two or three more stones landed near our fire. In what seemed like a matter of seconds, all the Ivanovich men were gathered in the courtyard.

Amid much shouting and speculation about where the stones were coming from, everyone ran to the main road which runs through the camp. They expected to find an opposing group mobilized for combat outside their section of the camp. Instead they found only two or three Serbian men who were on their way home from work. The men claimed no knowledge of the incident.

Back at our camp fire again, the remainder of the evening was spent in angry speculation about who could have thrown the stones. The general consensus was that the stones had come from the direction of the Serbian settlement. Alexandre proclaimed loudly that the honour of his family had been damaged. He blamed the Serbians and promised to see to it that they punished the guilty party in their midst.

The next morning a small delegation of Serbians, men whose long standing relations with the Gypsies made them familiar figures, arrived before the senior Ivanovich quarters. While protesting their innocence and that of their group in general, the Serbians attempted to assuage the Gypsies' feelings. They promised to co-operate with the Boyash family in locating the guilty party. Thus for the remainder of the day Alexandre Ivanovich proudly proclaimed the matter settled and the honour of his family repaired by the Serbian "apology".

As we sat around the fire that evening we heard a sudden loud commotion from the Serbian section of the camp. Three of the Yugoslav men came running down the main road shouting obscenities at the Gypsies. With his sons surrounding him, the elder Ivanovich confronted these men and listened to them accuse his family of having thrown stones into their neighbourhood.

Although he was not certain of his family's innocence, Alexandre protested the accusation fiercely, and the two groups parted on less than friendly terms. For the remainder of the evening the Boyash adults questioned the younger family members until they were satisfied that none of them were guilty. Alexandre explained to me that if they had found any of their children guilty they would punish them and then apologize to the Serbians. "We are not savages", he explained, "We know how to settle these matters like men."

The following day was spent in an atmosphere of restless tension.

When night fell the family gathered around the camp fire and when the early part of the evening passed without incident, the young adults drifted beyond the limits of the fire. The older Boyash continued to trade stories over the remaining wine and coffee. Then, just as they were dispersing a small hail of stones landed around the main courtyard of the camp.

Within seconds the family was readying itself for bloody battle. Most of those who had lingered around the fire were women and, incensed at the resumption of hostilities, they ran from wagon to wagon summoning the men and gathering all available weapons. I had retired to my roulotte and was about to undress for bed when Persa, the eldest Ivanovich daughter burst into the wagon. She shouted that the Serbians were throwing stones again; we were going out to stop them. I would have hesitated, flattered that the family felt so comfortable with me that they would ask me to fight on their behalf. I was also worried about getting hurt. But Persa had no sympathy for the distinction between participant and observer. She thrust a heavy stick in my hand and shoved me toward the door.

As I found my way to the main road through the camp my worst fears were confirmed. It seemed there would be a pitched battle, for the Boyash men and women were grouped about fifty yards away from a much larger group of Serbian men. Both groups were heavily armed. I saw Cortez flick open his switch blade. Tony was holding a shotgun. The Boyash women kept up a steady barrage of violent oaths and insults. As we slowly advanced toward the Serbians I attempted to find a place in the second ranks, but Persa was there again to shove me to the front. Tony, whose infant daughter was sleeping in his wagon, looked at me with a grim smile and a shrug which told me he had as little heart for the combat as I did.

Our band of Gypsy warriors advanced steadily as I prayed for some miraculous truce. Persa was walking next to me holding a heavy club as were the other women. Now the Serbian group was more visible. I could see that many of them had no intention to fight for they were clad in pyjamas. Others in the front ranks seemed ready for the battle but many of the stragglers were dropping away from the group. Now it was clear that despite their numbers we would win. Too many of the Serbians did not wish to fight.

As we stood facing each other a quiet came over the Boyash and the elder Ivanovich addressed the Serbians. "We have not wished to have this fight," he began, "But you can see that we are ready to die to save the honour of our family which you have dirtied with your cowardly stone throwing."

After some shuffling and discussion among their group, a Serbian man finally shouted back, "We are as innocent of this as you are and we also do not want to fight over something we have no knowledge of. Let us return to our beds and discuss this in the morning." There was some grumbling and more sighs of relief when we turned from

the Serbians and walked back to our fire. As we walked Persa thanked
me for coming out with them. She explained that since I was taller
than any of the Gypsy or Serbian men it had been necessary for her
to push me to the front in order to intimidate the Serbians. We
reached the camp fire in a festive mood and celebrated our "victory"
long into the night.

For the Ivanovich family the important aspect of the conflict was that
they had demonstrated their solidarity and their readiness to defend
their status in the camp society. While the question of who was throwing the stones lingered, Alexandre claimed to have some idea of what
was happening and promised to resolve the matter shortly. After a day
spent consulting with friends and debtors throughout the camp,
Alexandre that evening announced he had solved the mystery. A
Serbian woman who had been spending much time with the Ivanovich
family had spurned the attention of an Algerian man of doubtful mental
stability. This man felt wronged by the Serbians and by the Gypsies,
since the woman he loved preferred to spend her time with them rather
than with the Algerians. For this reason he had attempted to create a
dispute between the Gypsies and the Serbians.

Having found the guilty party, another day of negotiations among
representatives of the Gypsies, the Serbians, and the North Africans
was necessary to decide what to do about the Algerian man. These
discussions were held mainly around the Ivanovich main courtyard, with
the aged Alexandre acting as mediator, aggrieved, and judge. All sides
in the case were heard at great length. The Gypsy woman wanted the
man and the woman banished from the camp for having disrupted the
smooth course of relationships among the groups. The Serbians,
anxious not to lose one of the few women of their group, defended her
innocence and asked that the Algerians themselves punish the guilty
man. The Algerians claimed no responsibility for his actions since he
had a history of irrational acts and had not been behaving as a representative of their section of the camp. When Alexandre heard this last
position it was clear to him what the compromise should be. The man
should be banished from the camp and the woman should be required to
remain among her own people, the Serbians, where she would no longer
arouse the jealousy of non-Serbians. This solution was accepted by
the spokesmen around the fire, but privately Alexandre confided to me
that the North Africans should not have abandoned one of their own so
easily. This was further proof for him that the North Africans had little
solidarity and could not be trusted to ensure the safety of even their own
area of the camp. In this way, after a round of negotiations among the
three major groups in the camp, a potentially dangerous pattern of

conflict was avoided, and each of the groups reaffirmed the need to reach understandings which would preserve the safety of the camp without having to make appeals outside their own society.

GYPSY SOCIETY AND SHANTYTOWN MORALITY

The refusal of Gypsy groups such as the Ivanovich family to enter into the "mainstream" of Western societies is too easily romanticized into a modern version of *la vie a la boheme*. After all, members of the family themselves are quick to point out the limitations of their life style. "You see the mud on my legs?" states a young woman of the family who is concerned about her chances of finding a suitable husband, "We can wash ourselves all day long but what good does it do with the way things are in this camp." On the other hand, the alternatives open to her are quite limited. Unskilled and generally illiterate, she and her Gypsy sisters can barely hope to find work which is more favourable than what the family can offer within its own economy. Worse yet, the young Gypsy adults face not only the prospect of a menial job, but the possibility of estrangement from the family, a situation most find extremely difficult to even contemplate. Thus most of the family members accept their lot with a Brechtian sense of resignation and fatality rather than any romantic ideals of primitive rebellion. In one sense this is a necessary feature of their culture, for it makes them masters at finding pragmatic solutions to everyday troubles and avoids unnecessary idealistic anguish.

Were it not for the Gypsies' somewhat cynical skill at the politics of bluff and illusion, and their willingness to negotiate pragmatic arrangements among the various immigrant groups of the camp, incidents such as occurred between their family and the Serbians would more often end in violence. Camps such as the one at La Courneuve would more likely merit their poor reputation were it not for the folk "professionalism" with which the Gypsies approach their dealings with their gadje neighbours. Now that free access to the peasant villages of rural Europe is a thing of the past, the Boyash Gypsies have learned to make the best of a less desirable environment in order to continue the only life style they have ever known and could ever seriously contemplate. A direct consequence of this adaptation, is that the Gypsies play prominent roles in establishing the basis of trust in the everyday life of the migrant camp.

CHAPTER SIX

Some Mānuš Conceptions and Attitudes

Aparna Rao

In his article, *Principaux Groupes Tsiganes*, Matéo Maximoff,[1] the well known Romani writer, attempts a classification of Gypsies. Throughout this article, I shall use the word "Gypsy" as a general term to cover all persons claiming to be "Rom", irrespective of their cultural, linguistic[2] or religious differences, and whatever the degree of their nomadism or sedentarization. For convenience I have adopted Maximoff's classification as regards the group of persons sometimes called "the Alsatian Gypsies" and who would, thus, be the "Gāygikānes Mānuš". The members of this community, who refer to themselves as either the Mānuš, or the Sinté, can be distinguished from other Gypsies and form a distinct social group. This group is largely endogamous. In cases of exogamy, such alliances take place with the Gādjé (non-Gypsies; in this case either Alsatians or other local people), or alternatively with the Yénisches", who form a marginal population of unknown ethnic origin, and many of whom are found in the Alsatian regions. Mānuš society is composed on the one hand, of nomads, whose area of travel is rather ill-defined, but whose base is nevertheless situated in and around Alsace and the Rhenisch regions of Germany and Switzerland; and, on the other hand, of sedentarized and semi-sedentarized families who reside in Alsace. All the patronyms

---

1. *In Etudes Tsiganes*, No. 1, 1956.
2. For further reading on this subject, see Luc de Heusch (1965). *A la Découverte Des Tsiganes*, p. 17, University of Brussels.

to be found in this group, are germanic in consonance and for most of
the older members of the community, German, or one of the Germanic
dialects is the second language, the first, of course, being Mānuš.
Without going into details about the Mānuš language, I would like to
mention that a very large proportion of its vocabulary is of directly
Germanic origin. The other major linguistic influences are those of
classical Sanskrit and classical Greek.

THE HISTORICAL BACKGROUND

Although results of research done in the fields of language and philology
point to the certitude of a common Indian origin for all the Gypsy
groups, no one knows exactly when, how or why, the Gypsies did
leave the Indian sub-continent to come further and further west, to
ultimately create temporary or semi-permanent settlements across the
entire globe. In certain Gypsy communities, myths are current about
their "country of origin", or their "first king", and so on; but in
actual fact, the early history of the Gypsy people remains totally
shrouded in mystery. The first written records mentioning groups of
persons whom we can now identify as Gypsies, date from the fourteenth
and fifteenth centuries. In these records, the names of the different subgroups are, I believe, never mentioned; hence we can not be sure
whether the first group of Gypsies who came to the Alsace region,
for example, were Mānuš or Kālderāš, etc.

All we do know is that Gypsies made their first appearance in the
Rhineland region between 1414 and 1418: "En cette année arri-
vèrent à Strasbourg et dans tout le pays les premiers Tsiganes. Ils
étaient environ 14,000 et dispersés ça et là. . . . Les Tsiganes sont,
donc, apparus dans les pays rhénans entre 1414 et 1418, première incur-
sion suivie d'une seconde en 1422, d'une troisième en 1428 et d'une
quatrième en 1433."[3] Around the same time, we have the following
reference: "Anno Domini, 1418, gentes plebe sive nobilis . . . terram
nostram applicant."[4]

THE SITUATION TODAY

I had my first contact with the Mānuš some three years ago. They were
in all about three hundred persons living either in caravans or in little
houses in an area called the Polygone. This is a district of Strasbourg
which was planned and built by Bismarck in 1871–1872 for his soldiers.

3. See H. Dubled (1961). *Etudes Tsiganes*, Nos. 3/4.
4. Ibid.

In addition to the barracks, there was also a large field used for military exercises. In 1945, the army gave a part of this field to the City of Strasbourg, which built a number of temporary houses to shelter people whose houses had been destroyed during the Second World War. Gradually, with the reconstruction of the town and the rebuilding of houses, these people left the Polygone and the shelters fell vacant. But they did not stay so for long. By 1950, the majority of the original occupants had been replaced by immigrant workers, mainly from North Africa and Portugal, as well as by families of Yénisches. During the next five years, many sedentarized Mānuš families had also moved into the empty houses and by 1960, a large part of the empty space opposite the houses was being used by nomadic and semi-sedentary Mānuš to park their caravans and reside.

Although the occupants of all the houses have always paid rent and electricity rates, the City of Strasbourg has all along tried to evict them. There are two reasons for this. The first of these is that the new occupants pay the same amount of rent as the original occupants, although the actual value of the houses has certainly increased enormously during this period. The second reason is that the authorities have received complaints from inhabitants of nearby districts, who did not want these minority groups as neighbours. Unable to legally evict the occupants, but reluctant to provide them with alternative accommodation, the City authorities decided to try and "persuade" the new occupants—more especially, the Mānuš and the Yénisches—to leave. This policy of "persuasion" consisted primarily of neglecting minimum civic maintenance of the area. However, these tactics failed to persuade the inhabitants to leave. All that did happen was that the Polygone became one of the most dirty, underprivileged and marginal districts of Strasbourg. This, in turn, helped enforce the image of the Mānuš, the Yénisches and the others as dirty, diseased, dangerous and generally "undesirable" members of society.

As I have mentioned earlier, among the Mānuš we find nomads, sedentarized and semi-sedentarized families. The nomads live in caravans all the year round. The semi-sedentary families spend winter in Strasbourg (from November till about May), either in houses or in caravans, and in summer they travel around and live in their caravans. The sedentary people, of course, live in houses all year round. These categories, however, are not strictly divided or mutually exclusive, in the sense, that a family which has been nomad, may become semi-sedentary, either temporarily, or semi-permanently, and vice-versa. Generally the transition from a nomadic way of life to a totally sedentarized one is gradual and may take more than one generation. The transition from the nomadic to the semi-sedentary way of life is usually more rapid and also more easily reversible.

Apart from the travel-aspect, is there a romano way of life? Rather, is Mānuš society just a sub-product of the Alsatian social pattern, or has it an identity and a structure of its own, no doubt influenced by, and, to some extent, adapted to the surrounding Alsatian environment? In this essay, I shall try and show that in spite of the numerous social, economic and political pressures they have endured, the Mānuš have succeeded in conserving their distinct identity as a socio-cultural group. This I shall do by referring to my personal experience, observations and friendship with some Mānuš families in Alsace. It is obvious that the scope of this essay does not allow for a thorough analysis of all or even several aspects of Mānuš life and society. I have therefore chosen a few important themes and tried to discuss them at some length.

SOME SYMBOLIC SYSTEMS

The majority of the Alsatian Mānuš are baptized as Catholics. A large number among these prepare for and take Communion. Almost none have a church wedding; but all demand, and receive, a church funeral. Thus, they are supposed to be Roman Catholics; moreover, they claim to be so. It is a notorious fact that Gypsy groups have freely adopted the religions of the people among whom they found themselves; some accounts even go as far as to say that, as they crossed borders, the same families changed their faith. It is thus obvious that any deep study of Mānuš religiosity would necessarily have to take into account the diverse religious influences and the varying degrees of syncretism that their basic religious and spiritual notions underwent as they travelled further and further away from their "native" lands. We know next to nothing about their original religious attitudes and beliefs; we do, however, have some ideas of the different religious and cultural influences they must have met in the course of their travels from Asia to western Europe.

Present day Mānuš spiritual notions are the result of this extreme syncretism between their original beliefs and practices, Islam, Judeo-Christian conceptions and local pagan customs and beliefs which they encountered among the sedentary populations with whom they came into contact. My discussions with several of the Mānuš have convinced me that by far the majority among them have only a very vague notion of Christian theology or even of basic Christian doctrine. What, in fact, does the Christian religion represent for them? In other words, what do they mean when they say that they are Catholics?

Being baptized brings the Mānuš child into the Catholic community. But what does the ceremony of baptism mean to them? We do know for certain what the fact of not being baptized implies in Mānuš society. It means that the child is exposed, more than all others to the malevolent intentions of various evil powers. Who or what are these powers? In order to answer this question, let us see what happens to the child who has the misfortune not to be baptized.

As soon as a child is born, he is in danger. Hostile powers surround him and try to trouble him in various ways. On his first night, evil powers—whose names I have not as yet been able to identify—attempt to steal him away from his mother. Either they take him away altogether or else they replace him by another child who resembles him but who, in reality, is a creation of these evil creatures. Alternatively they may take away his *dji* (heart, spirit) and leave his body intact. To prevent these powers from doing such harm, the child's mother must keep watch on him all night; if for some reason she cannot, another woman of the clan—preferably a *pūri dāi* (literally: old mother, term of respect for all old Mānuš ladies; also means grandmother)—must guard the baby. A child who has not been baptized is also likely to be very sick, and though indigenous pharmacopoeia and medical aid are sought to cure him, nothing will be able to save him unless he is baptized as well. The child who is baptized also has the great advantage of having Godparents, the *kirvo* and the *kirvi*. Godparents may be either Mānuš or Gādjé; most often, however, when there is a Gādjo Godfather or Godmother, there is, in addition a Mānuš also filling the same role. This could indicate that the role of the Gādjé Godparents is purely an economic one; on the other hand, the Mānuš Godparents do not in any case take the spiritual responsibility they are supposed to. They are however highly respected by their Godchildren and have considerable authority over them.

Even the baptized child is, however, not altogether out of danger; and this is where we see that Mānuš demonology runs parallel to their acceptance of certain Christian rites. Everything is of course done to prevent the Mānuš child from falling ill. When he is a small baby, his mother ties a little red thread round his wrist or his neck to keep away all illness. But, in spite of all the precautions that his family may take, he often does fall sick. Above all, say the Mānuš, little babies always have lung disease. Gādjé doctors never seem to know the cause of these illnesses, nor are they ever able to prescribe the remedy. Only certain *pūri dāi*, who are recognized by the community as healers, can find out the cause of the trouble. They alone know the cure. This they do in the following way: they cover the child's body with goose-oil, starting at the head and finishing at the toe. They do this three times, on three successive days. This massage is accompanied by certain incantations known and understood only by the *pūri dāi*. On the third day, after the last drops of oil have been put on, they wrap the baby up in some dirty garment, preferably a shirt already worn by the child's father. In a few hours time, the child suddenly shows signs of improvement, and after a few days he is completely cured. It appears that this practice was resorted to formerly, immediately after the umbilical cord had been cut, irrespective of the health of the new-born baby.

In fact till he or she reaches the age of puberty, a child is in perpetual danger from the evil powers. Thus, if a child ever happens to leave his toys and playthings outside after dusk, these are thrown away— preferably burnt by his mother next day. If he played with these again, he could very easily come to harm, as it is probable that the evil powers would have contaminated these toys in some way during their nocturnal wanderings. But the relationship which the child has *vis-à-vis* these supernatural beings is of a passive nature. His acts in no way attract or repel them, no ritual taboos govern his behaviour and none of his voluntary or involuntary acts can endanger (morally or physically) anyone else. He is only a target for the evil powers, and since he is largely incapable of protecting himself against them, others must protect him. As we shall soon see, this passive role changes totally as soon as the child reaches puberty, for then all his acts are governed by rigid categories of prohibitions and permissions.

Few, if any, Mānuš children receive formal religious instruction.[5] And yet, every child has a few spiritual notions which he has received by word of mouth and by observing customs practised and observed by the Mānuš society as a whole. Let us now examine what these basic notions consist of.

THE MĀNUŠ PANTHEON

The Mānuš are implicitly monotheist, believing in one God, who, in spite of at times appearing to be unjust and unkind, is ultimately kind, forgiving and protecting. He is called the "Bāro Devel", (the Great God) and linguistically the gender applied to him is masculine. He lives above the stars in an unknown abode, which, however, is supposed to be a *shukar ker* (beautiful house). Mānuš cosmogonic myths speak of

---

5. Although the Mānuš in Alsace have their own chaplains, none receive any religious instruction from them. The chaplain baptizes their children and officiates at funerals and generally helps them in other spiritual or social matters; but he does not, as a rule, intervene in their private lives or beliefs; nor do they hide from him some of their non-Christian customs.

this Bāro Devel and his unique relationship with the Sinté (the true Rom). In fact all Mānuš cosmogonic legends, in addition to being of interest to mythologists and anthropologists are also interesting for someone wanting to study how a minority ethnic group, much discriminated against, creates internal means to fight against external pressures, by persuading itself of its intrinsic ethnic superiority. One such myth known to all the Mānuš I met, tells of the creation of the world. In the beginning there was nothing but water, then God created sand. From this He fashioned the earth. On the earth He planted a tree and from this great tree He drew out all men and women, that is, all but the Sinté. Then, when He had made all this, God looked on His work and was pleased. Soon, He began to feel that something was missing. He thought about this for a while and then, suddenly one day, He realized what it was that was missing, for His great and beautiful work to be really complete and perfect. This was a true Rom and a true Romni. And so, He created a Sinto couple, more beautiful than all the other couples, and He created them, not like the others, but individually from His own hands. Now his work was perfect. Another story explains the brown skin of the Rom. When God decided to create human beings to live in the world, He took some heavenly clay, shaped it and decided to bake it. However, He took his handiwork out of the oven a bit too soon, the baking was underdone and the result was the white man. Then God tried again, hoping to get it right the second time. But this time, He left the clay in the oven for too long and the result was the black man. Finally, God decided to really try and get it the way He wanted men to be. He tried a last time, and lo and behold, He made it just right this third time, for there was the much-longed-for brown man: the Rom.[6]

This Bāro Devel, although in supreme control of the universe, appears, in practice at least, to have less direct effect on the world and its goings-on than would be expected. Nonetheless, in times of need and distress, the Mānuš prefer to appeal to, and invoke other powers, who thus appear to be the Bāro Devel's more accessible agents. These agents are above all great protectors from danger of various sorts. On the other hand, once faced with danger, direct communication is sought and battle or appeasement arranged with the sources of the danger concerned. At that stage, special protection is not sought either from the Bāro Devel or from any of his agents. Nor are these agents and the Bāro Devel ever invoked "needlessly", that is, unless some precise boon or favour is asked to be granted, either to the individual or to the group. Communication with transcendent forces in the form of

6. Father Barthélémy was told a similar legend by some Gypsy groups whom he met in Chile.

adoration, thanksgiving or purely spiritual contact is unknown in Mānuš religious life.

Principal among the Bāro Devel's sublime "agents" is the Virgin Mary. She is important, not as the mother of Christ, but in her own right. Linguistically, this does seem strange when we remember that the Mānuš word designating her as *Debleskri-Dai* (literally The Mother of God), but in actual practice, she is known as, and referred to by the Mānuš as, *I Hailigi* (The Holy One). Besides, we cannot be sure that "The Mother of God" is interpreted by the Mānuš as "The Mother Of Jesus", for Jesus Himself is called *O Devlesker Čāvo* (The Son Of God). In any case, Jesus has little, if any, importance in their cultic or religious life; and even those who give the matter any thought, seem to see his importance only in that he is the son of the Virgin. The majority of pilgrimages which the Mānuš organize or participate in are to the Virgin. Almost all have been to Lourdes and on several graves we can see plaques bearing inscriptions such as; *Bénie pour toi à la grotte de Lourdes*. On the contrary, crucifixes are never to be found in caravans or elsewhere; these are reserved for tombstones.[7] Confirming the extreme importance of the Virgin in Mānuš spiritual life is the fact that all caravans have as a part of their essential decor, a statue, however small and insignificant, of the Virgin.

There is nothing special about the external appearance of the Mānuš caravan. Inside, however, what does strike the observer, is a corner, generally above the T.V. set, which is reserved for divers objects, which may seem trivial at first sight, but which, in actual fact, play an important part in the emotional life of a Mānuš family. Photographs cut out from magazines of actors, actresses and pop-singers jostle with pictures of Saints and perhaps of some of the living members of the family. Amidst advertisements displaying women (Gādji) in more or less provocative clothing, a vase of artificial flowers, newspaper cuttings of some Mānuš musician, a few pheasant feathers and postcards sent from friends and relatives around the world, stands, invariably, a statue of the Virgin, sometimes accompanied by a card, a picture, or a little plaque from Lourdes, or by a pair of holy candles. As far as one can tell, neither these objects, nor the corner in which they stand, are subject to any specific consideration or ritual behaviour. That the statue of the Virgin is however, considered as being endowed with some special powers of protection and conservation, is amply borne out by the following incident. A Mānuš family was travelling in Central France. One day they met with an accident. The caravan was over-

7. See page 158.

turned and badly damaged, with three small children inside it. Nothing however happened to the children and to the wooden statue of the Virgin which is said to have stood still and unaffected in its corner. The father of the children imputed the safety of his family to the benign presence of the statue. Since then, this statue has been carried during processions at various pilgrimages organized by the Mānuš. Whereas few of the Mānuš know the story of the Bible, or for that matter, believe in almost any of the Christian doctrines, or identify with any of the Christian symbols, all of them fully believe in the miraculous powers of healing and protection of the *Hailigi*. Although the Alsatian Mānuš deny any allegiance to, or belief in Sainte Sara, diverse information and observations that I have gathered persuade me that the idea of an original Romano Mother-Goddess-cult are not altogether to be dismissed. Further research in the field will of course be needed to confirm or disprove such a possibility.

Another important member of the Mānuš cosmos is "O Beñg".

THE BEÑG

The etymological origin of this word is *bañka*, which in Sanskrit means crooked. This original adjectival root has developed two meanings in many of the modern Indian languages, *bāñkā* or *bañgo*, which means crooked, twisted and *bañg*, *beñg*, etc., which means frog. The Mānuš do not use this word to designate frogs. But I do not yet know to what extent they associate frogs with their word *Beñg*, for they translate *Beñg* as meaning the "Devil". I have not yet been able to ascertain whether or not they believe that the Devil is frog-shaped; he is however known to be crooked and twisted. But to what extent does this *Beñg* really correspond to the Devil as described in Judeo-Christian mythology? The *Beñg* is supposed to be the master of a place called *i Beñgeskeri-kisinā* (literally the kitchen of the *Beñg*) and identified with the conception of Hell. And yet, no one believes in the possibility of ever having to go to this "kitchen", for the Mānuš believe in the ultimate kindness and forgiveness of *O Bāro Devel*.

Certain mishaps and illnesses are however imputed to this *Beñg*. These are happenings which cannot, for some reason be fitted into the cause and effect chain, which governs so much of Mānuš life. These are not the result of the transgression or non-obedience of any stricture. These are uncontrollable occurrences, although this does not mean that their source is unknown.

The most important among these acts of the *Beñg*, inflicted on a very

large percentage of the Mānuš population are cases of what is supposed
to be a kind of madness, i.e., epilepsy.[8] Almost all families have at least
one or two children who are subject to epileptic fits of varying degrees.
In the Mānuš language, epilepsy is called *Beñgālimātā* (drunk with the
Beñg). Strangely enough, to cure a person of these fits, no charms or
spells are recited, the *Beñg* is not exorcised, and no indigenous phar-
macopeia applied. Instead, "charms", in the form of old, local (Alsatian
or German) Christian (although these, too have a heavy dose of pre-
Christian spirit left in them) prayers are worn as protection against
the evil influences of the *Beñg*.[9]

The *Beñg*, is in fact, primarily the agent of "madness". As he has
certain affinities with, or at least as he can be to some extent made to
correspond with, the notion of the Devil, he must be combated with
Christian "weapons" i.e., Christian prayers. On the other hand, other
evil powers unknown to the Gādjé, but well known to the Mānuš, must
be combated with old traditional remedies, with on occasion an additional remedy borrowed from the Gādjé.

The *Beñg* can also be voluntarily attracted by eating any "black
meat", i.e., the meat of a black hen, a black or dark-coloured fish, and
so on. In such cases, the colour black is obviously identified with the
Beñg and this could perhaps be an influence of the Devil-image. It is
believed that if one ate such "black meat" one's own body would turn
black or, alternatively, that one would contract some unidentified
disease. The *Beñg* would then enter into one's body and take possession
of it. This purely physical act would have a purely physical effect, that
of rendering the body "impure". This "impurity" would, in turn, be
manifested by the body turning black.

But what is this notion of "impurity"? This, and its complementary
notion of "purity" are, in fact, the most important conceptions in
Mānuš ethics and are of the utmost importance in everyday Mānuš life.
As in all archaic societies, there is no hiatus between the sacred and the
profane. The domains of the secular and the ritual are not separate.
Religious and spiritual beliefs are an integral part of everyday life.

No particular time is set apart for the observance of purely ritual or
cultic acts. As I have mentioned earlier, communication is established
with transcendental powers when the absolute need arises and thus,

8. A mad woman is called *beñgli*.
9. All Mānuš men, women and even little girls wear jewellery. The girls and women
wear earrings, bracelets, rings and necklaces. The men and pubertal boys wear rings. All
the jewellery is made of gold and often encrusted with precious or semi-precious stones,
especially jade. The extensive use of jade springs from the belief, common to many oriental
peoples, that this stone protects its wearer from epileptic fits. Incidentally, an ornament encrusted with jade has also become a symbol of prestige and even some authority in the group.

this communication also falls into a general pattern of life and is in no way separate from it, or in conflict with any part of it.

This kind of religiosity is at least partly due to the fact that, in spite of the Mānuš calling themselves Catholics, they have not basically been affected by the body of Catholic doctrinal thought. Their religious beliefs and spiritual needs govern not so much their abstract thoughts or inner feelings, but their physical acts and their immediate physical needs. Let us now try and analyse the obviously traditional aspects of this religiosity.

Purity and Impurity

Everything operates within Mānuš society on the division made between these two categories. Some acts are classed as pure and thus permissible; others are classed as impure and are thus not allowed. The distinction made between these two categories is an ancient one, no one knows by whom. The fact remains that they are scrupulously observed and even the young people do not question them. Such categories are obviously bound to be rather arbitrary. By what function are they determined? External powers, transcendental or otherwise, are never evoked to justify these categories. I do not think that the infringement of either of these categories is supposed to bring down the wrath of either the Bāro Devel, or the Virgin Mary, nor would it specially attract the various evil powers. In fact, from my personal observations and conversations with the Mānuš, it appears to me that these categories are closed and self-evolving. If anyone does something which is classed as impure, he becomes impure. In more practical terms, what does this imply? It means that he is considered a danger to the rest of the community, because in most cases at least, impurity is contagious through either direct or indirect contact with the impure person. Social sanctions are turned against the culprit. Formerly, such sanctions had a more judicial nature and the *Romano Kriss* could even condemn a person to death, in extreme cases. Nowadays the culprit is banished from his clan (this means in practice from the entire group), temporarily or in serious cases, permanently. The social danger is thus quite effectively eliminated. There does not appear to be any method of expiation of such infringements.

It would be extremely difficult to draw up a list of acts classed as impure. I shall, therefore confine myself to giving a few examples and trying to analyse them. No object is thought of as intrinsically impure, but some can become so, if used or acted upon in a certain way, or ways, by certain persons. On the other hand, some things such as fire are intrinsically pure and can never become impure. These can also be used for purifying purposes. Another important fact to note right away is that impurity can not be contracted through physical proximity with an impure person or object. Impurity can be contracted either by one's voluntary act or by oral, verbal, or vaginal contact with an impure person or object. Moreover, a person, or women in particular, can be overcome by impurity involuntarily, and through no fault of their own. This impurity is then only temporary, although strict measures must be taken so that she may not contaminate other members of the community. Finally, impurity is not a characteristic only of the living, for a dead person is in a constant and irrevocable state of impurity, at least in terms of those he leaves behind on earth.

Women, more than men, are liable to become impure. In fact, each pubertal woman is always in a latent state of impurity, i.e., till she reaches menopause. As we have already seen, in the case of children, these categories cannot be applied. These can be applied only after puberty, and in the case of a woman, till she reaches menopause. Before and after a person is individually pure. He or she can of course become impure by contact with impure persons or objects, as mentioned above, but is not capable of doing acts which would render themselves and others impure.

Let us first see why and how pubertal women can become impure and how they can contaminate others.[10] When a young girl has her first menstrual flow, her mother tells her that now she is grown up. No explanations are asked for or given. The entire subject is surrounded by taboos. Most important of all the girl knows that from now onwards she may not do a certain number of things which she could previously do with impunity. She also learns that if she does a certain number of things, not only will she be endangering herself, but she will be considered a menace by the whole society, and thus the society will try and eliminate her in some way. In all this there is no thought of punishment in after-life, nor even of punishment by the Bāro Devel, in this life. She and she alone will be responsible for her acts even though, in certain cases she may very well be able to hide the facts from the others, the fault would have been committed and this would suffice for some unknown punishment to be inflicted by unnamed powers not only on her, but on the entire community.

She must thus learn that she is impure and a threat to the life of the group, in the following circumstances: when she has her menstrual

10. The whole idea of contamination by genital and vaginal means is extremely interesting. Indeed, it expands at times even to influence certain preferential alliances within the kinship system. This would require a longer discussion than is possible here.

periods, after sexual intercourse, immediately after she has given birth
to a child until she has her menstrual period once again, etc., etc.
Apart from such special circumstances, a pubertal woman is in a constant state of impurity, or rather, her body is an eternal source of
possible impurity; this is particularly true of "the lower part" of her
body, as the Mānuš say. Thus, objects which may have come into contact with the lower part of a woman's body are impure and are regarded
as bearers of this contamination. By extension, objects which may have
come into contact with her skirts, or other garments draping the lower
part of her body, as well as all underwear, are considered impure.
Physical contact with such objects would not contaminate a pure person,
but oral or genital contact would. Hence, culinary objects must never
come into contact with a woman's lower garments. Thus, if one happens
to leave a pot, a plate, a cup, or other such items used for cooking in, or
eating out of, on the floor, or elsewhere where it may have come into
contact with a woman's skirt, this object must never again be used for
its original purpose. A second factor contributing to the contamination
of such an object would be that it would have been in direct contact with
the floor and the floor is regarded as dirty and impure, as distinct from
the earth which is considered sacred. Formerly, such objects were
immediately broken, or destroyed in some other fashion, lest they be
used by mistake. Nowadays, it is more common to use them for some
other purpose, where one can be sure that no contamination can take
place. Similarly, women's underwear may never be washed in the same
bowl as men's or those of pre-pubertal children. Although we have seen
that simple physical contact does not induce contamination, there are
certain agents which render even physical contact dangerous. This is
because, although pure themselves, they are highly liable to become
impure. Water is the most important of such agents. Thus physical
contact in water can lead to contamination.

WATER AND IMPURITY

We have already said that water, as opposed to fire can easily become
impure, thus one may never spit into water but one may spit into the
fire.[11] Water becomes impure when any impure person or object is
partially or wholly immersed in it. In this context it must not be

11. It must also not be forgotten that spit is identified in the Mānuš mind, as in many other
archaic minds, with semen. The following Mānuš phrase bears out this idea, "He is the spit
of his father". Would the ban on spitting into water result from the identification of the
latter with Heavenly semen, as among so many other archaic populations? Spitting into fire
could then mean ejecting semen into Mother Earth's bowels and a re-enactment of the primordial act.

forgotten that in the archaic mind, notions of cleanliness and ritual purity are closely bound up. Thus, an impure person or object is automatically dirty and vice-versa, a pure person or object is automatically clean.

All stagnant water is supposed to be impure. The Mānuš therefore always use running water to bathe themselves and for all general washing purposes. In fact, they think that the Gādjé are very dirty as they "try and wash themselves in their own filth", when they use bath-tubs, etc. The Mānuš obviously never use swimming pools either, for this would not only involve bathing in stagnant water, but the additional risk of being contaminated by the water in which women have swum.

This is also why water in which women's garments, and more especially underwear, have been washed is thoroughly contaminated and if men's clothes are washed in this water, either simultaneously or afterwards, they would invariably get contaminated. As a rule, therefore strict sexual segregation is enforced in laundering. On average, a Mānuš mother washes from twelve to twenty-five pounds of clothes every week and she does it all by hand. Usually, she does the washing twice a week. She divides it all into three lots: women's and pubertal girls' clothes and underwear; men's, boys' and non-pubertal girls' clothes and underwear; kitchen and table linen is also washed apart. Each lot is washed, rinsed and dried separately to avoid all danger of contamination. Most often the women's and girls' clothes are washed on a day when the men of the family are sure to be out at work. In any case, no man may see women's clothes or underwear, either wet or dry, when she is not wearing them. If he did, it would be a matter of *lādj*,* another complex notion of supreme importance in everyday Mānuš life.

All water which may have been used for washing, bathing or other similar purposes is highly impure. It therefore poses a certain threat to the entire community, and must be disposed of as soon and as efficiently as possible. When in caravans, the Mānuš throw this water as far as possible from the encampment; when in houses it is disposed into the toilet, and in no circumstance must it be thrown into the washbasin or sink, or on the ground near the house or caravan, for then its impurity could still affect the group in some way.

We have so far seen how water, which is essentially pure, can be contaminated. Let us now see how an impure person or object can be purified or at least be rendered less impure by the use of water. A Mānuš woman who has her menstrual periods, or again, a woman who has just given birth to a child, being considered to be in the state of impurity, *par excellence*, must take all possible precautions not to con-

* See page 154.

taminate other members of the community. One of these precuations is washing as often as possible. I have already mentioned that contamination is caused by oral contact as well as by genital means. Hence, such a woman must not cook food for uncontaminated people around her, nor is she allowed to use the same cooking pots and pans as the others. When a married woman is in a similar state of impurity, she is, in fact, replaced in all her household chores by another pubertal girl or woman. The impure woman then either eats elsewhere, or she cooks herself a meal and when she has finished, she washes her pots and pans. These objects are reserved for this purpose. Often on such days mothers suddenly absent themselves, and the elder daughters, or on rare occasions, the husbands, do the cooking and washing.

Another example of the purifying powers of water may be observed in the daily Mānuš rite of the morning-toilet. Although the length of the present essay does not permit any elaboration on this subject, I might mention here that the Mānuš believe that when a person is asleep, he has direct communication with various spirits and other supernatural beings. Dreams too have an extreme importance, and great credit is given to the dreams of elderly women in particular. One should never ask a Mānuš whether or not he has spent a good night, for this would be a covert reference to the activities the spirits may have carried out within him while he was asleep. In fact, a Mānuš never speaks to anyone in the morning before he has washed his mouth. The mouth, being the seat of both Spit and Word (two fertility symbols of prime importance, in nearly all archaic societies), occupies a very special place as an intermediary between Life and Death, between the natural and the super natural. During the night, the Mānuš is in contact with spirits, many of them probably evil and he remains under their influence until he liberates himself from their hold. If he speaks while still under their influence, it would amount to their, and not his speaking, and this would be harmful for all. Hence, he must liberate himself from their influence before he utters his first word. To do this, he must undergo an act of purification, and this he does by thoroughly rinsing his mouth as soon as he gets out of bed. He never uses a washbasin or a sink, for this purpose. He takes running, or fresh water from a pail, and pours this over his face and rinses his mouth with it. The used water is collected in another receptacle reserved for this purpose and like all other water used for washing, this too is never thrown in to the sink or washbasin, but either outside far away from the encampment, or else, into the lavatory.

The eating of certain foodstuffs, especially certain meats, also causes impurity, and any offenders to these bans are said to be very severely punished; by capital punishment in former times, and nowadays by heavy social sanctions. The most important of such bans is on horse-meat, a meat common enough in many parts of France and Switzerland. The greatest humiliation that anyone could inflict on a Mānuš, would be to force him to eat horse-flesh. What is the origin of this ban? The Mānuš give an economic reason. In former times the horse was the Gypsy's constant companion. To kill a horse, would mean to stop travelling. This ban unofficially imposed by "the ancestors", would now have taken on the form of a very formal interdiction. I do not know of any conclusive explanations for such a ban. However, it may perhaps be interesting to investigate the eventual connection between this ban (and the fear of impurity, resulting from the violation of this ban), and the superstition current in post-Vedic and some parts of contemporary India about horse-meat: a person who ate horse-meat would contract either leprosy, or would go mad. In the case of madness, it would be of interest to see whether this could be extended to cover the cases of epilepsy. This could then be of special interest in the context of Mānuš society, as I have already mentioned.

"LĀDJ" AND SEXUAL SEGREGATION

Another very vital notion in Mānuš society is that of *lādj*. Literally translated, this word means "shame", but its actual use in Mānuš language goes far beyond the scope of the English word. *Lādj* is used to cover acts, behaviour and sentiments ranging from dress-habits to relations between the generations and the sexes. In the present essay, I shall attempt to describe its application only in the domain of sexual segregation.

Until puberty boys and girls are brought up in exactly the same way. No formal discipline is meted out to them as the Mānuš themselves put it, "among us, a child is a king". This is true in as much as they are rarely if ever, scolded and absolutely free to do what they like. Strict discipline however starts as soon as a child reaches puberty. Even at this stage Mānuš education does not consist of teaching a child what to do and what not to do; he simply falls into a pattern of life, takes on new responsiblities expected and demanded of his age group, and obeys a certain number of interdictions applicable to all adults. A pubertal person, whatever his or her age, is considered to be an adult. As long as a girl is pre-pubertal she may wear what she likes. She is free to expose parts of her body which she would not be allowed to do were she pubertal; but above all she may wear the garments which are the exclusive dress of males, i.e., trousers. As soon as she reaches puberty however, she may no longer wear trousers, she must dress as only a woman may, i.e., in dresses and skirts. To do otherwise would be a matter of *lādj*, not only for her, but for her entire family.

There is also a very distinct sexual segregation and mutual avoidance in the use of the caravans and of the different parts of the house. The two rooms most used in the house are the living room and the kitchen. When both men and women are at home, the former becomes the exclusive domain of the men, and the latter of the women. The men sit and chat among themselves and eat in the living room, while the women stand in the kitchen and watch the men, without in any way participating in the conversation. A similar thing happens in the caravans; men and women never sit and talk or eat together. But there is one moment at which the caravan and the living room are turned into common meeting places for people of both sexes, when in the evenings or on Sunday afternoons, almost everyone watches T.V. It is as if the darkness in the room cancels out all differences between the sexes. No one talks, although, now and then, there are interjections of *"Bāro Devel!"* or exclamations of joy, admiration, fear or surprise. When the programme is over no one discusses what they have just seen, no one talks at all. Either the women go off leaving the men alone, or the men leave and the women stay among themselves. It is as if, with the sudden transition from darkness to light, we come back to the domain of sexual segregation. The roles of light and darkness as makers and breakers of temporal and place structure in Mānuš life are extremely interesting in the context of sexual behaviour and attitudes within the group. Any attempt to transgress one or more of these social codes, would be a cause of *lādj*, both for the individual and the group at large.

From these few examples we can see that any misdeed on the part of the individual is a threat to the entire community. The guilt of the individual becomes a collective one, unless appropriate steps are taken by the collectivity to protect itself. This it can do in two ways: by punishing the individual committing such a crime or, by preventing it from happening by forbidding it altogether. The former would serve two purposes, that of serving as an example to others, and symbolizing the expiation of the sins of the collectivity. The latter, apart from avoiding more unpleasant measures being taken, would enable the social authorities to determine and control all the activities of the group and thus act as the unique judicial, economic and religious power which all the members of the group would have to obey.

This social authority, which in time becomes tradition, governs all aspects of social life, including the kinship system. It governs a person's life from birth, and even conception, until his death. This is true of all archaic societies, and Mānuš society is no exception in this respect. Let us now briefly discuss some attitudes and behaviour towards death, in Mānuš society.

DEATH IN MĀNUŠ SOCIETY

Each society has its own ideas and explanations about death. The Mānuš too have a whole philosophy of death which is extremely complex and which would be impossible to describe, let alone analyse or explain, in a few paragraphs. I shall therefore briefly describe the external behaviour and some of the social attitudes and ceremonies manifested towards and related to death.

E. K. had been ailing for some time. Everyone knew that the end was near, but no one spoke of that. One day, her friends and family had to accept the fact that she had but a few more hours to live. She was taken out of her caravan and laid on piles of thick, soft mattresses inside a tent, especially bought for this event the day before. It was an expensive and large tent and all the grown-up sons and daughters of the ailing woman had contributed to buy it. She thus lay in the tent, with her feet and her face turned in the direction opposite to that of the door of the caravan owned by her and her husband; but she could not die in the caravan. Death is almost the embodiment of impurity and hence the place wherein a death actually takes place is forever soiled and may never again be used as a habitation. Moreover, the spirit of the dying person is not free to leave its body, if the latter is confined within four walls. Meanwhile all friends and relatives from far and near have been notified. They will all come to the funeral, wherever they may be, whatever they may be doing and however poor they may be.

The death took place at about 3 o'clock in the afternoon. At once ritual wailing began. These mourners were exclusively women and were led by the oldest surviving female member of the nuclear family. They moaned and wailed and tore their hair and rolled on the ground. The men on the other hand, including the deceased's husband, kept a strict silence and showed no outward sign of sorrow or emotion at all. Simultaneously all the windows and the door of the deceased's caravan were opened wide in order to let her spirit leave it completely.

The burial usually takes place three days after the death. And this is when the official period of mourning begins. This mourning period lasts for ninety-nine days if the deceased is a child, and one full year if an adult. Those who go into mourning are the members of the nuclear and extended families. But only the female members of the nuclear family wear the mourning black for the full mourning period. During the actual mourning period no member of the nuclear or extended family may play a musical instrument, sing or dance. As can easily be imagined, this causes a considerable economic loss to people whose means of livelihood depend upon music and entertainment and from this real sacrifice, their sincere attachment to the deceased can be gauged.

From the time of the death until the corpse is buried, preparations are made for the funeral. Much money is spent, and a three-day period begins which may be described as an intermediary period of mourning. During these three days and nights no one may eat or drink anything except water. One may not comb one's hair, change one's clothes, bathe or wash. This period and these observations seem to be a pre-Christian survival among the Mānuš. Once again we come up against the problem of impurity, for death has soiled the entire family and they will remain soiled till the burial. After all is over and the spirit of the deceased is sure to have really departed, purification will take place. In fact, these rites and beliefs may be compared fairly closely to certain Hindu mourning customs.

The body of the deceased is washed, irrespective of sex, by the older female members of the clan and it is then dressed in its best clothes. Among the Mānuš these clothes are not new ones bought specially for the occasion, but it appears that formerly this was the practice. No special colours appear to be prescribed for these clothes, although red is not allowed, as being the sign of joy. It is clear from this, that the deceased, and not only those she leaves behind, is supposed to be sad at the parting. The funeral has been arranged by the most important male members of the clan. Here again as in the case of the tent, the more expensive, the better. In fact several clans have family tombs which are built and maintained at considerable cost. The coffin is ordered and made either of oak or if the family is really poor, of pine wood. In former times, it appears that most families could not afford other than pine wood, hence even today pine trees and pine wood in general is associated with Death and shunned for every day use. Thus, for example, the Mānuš will never camp near a pine-wood forest.

The Funeral

At the cemetery, the *rāšāi** conducts the ceremony. The Mānuš men form themselves into an orchestra and play solemn music. This is the last time they will play for one whole year. As the coffin is lowered into the grave, the music stops. Handfuls of earth are thrown on to the coffin and with the first handful, friends and relatives throw in coins. These must

* Priest.

be either gold or silver and are intended for the use of the deceased on
his or her journey. The grave is then closed and the tombstone laid.
Masses of flowers, both fresh and artificial, are arranged and planted on
and all around it. Plaques from Lourdes, bearing various inscriptions
are often added. Sometimes, a few crucifixes are also arranged on it.
In this connection, it is interesting to note that for the Mānuš, a crucifix
is a symbol of death and not of resurrection (incidentally, as mentioned
earlier, few of the Mānuš know the Bible story). This object is never
to be found inside a caravan. Even on the graves, the crosses used are
mortuary ones. A little *bénithier* is also placed on the grave, containing
holy water and a few tufts of grass. No explanation was given to me for
this last detail, but I believe that for the Mānuš of old the proximity of
water and grass represented horses and thus, travel. This "offering"
could therefore have symbolized the journey of the deceased. Alternatively, grass here could symbolize food and secondly, the direction
to be taken by the deceased on his future travels. For even today,
grass is often enough an important component of the *patrin*, the signs
and symbols the Mānuš use on their journeys through the countryside.
The *patrin* are left on footpaths, at crossroads and elsewhere to indicate
to other members of a clan which direction to take if they want to catch
up with, or meet different relatives and friends.

With the lighting of twelve holy candles arranged around the grave,
the funeral ceremony is over, and the person is really dead. The official
mourning period can now begin. The first acts of purification are gone
through. Everyone washes, bathes and changes. The clothes worn at
the funeral and since the death took place are burnt and destroyed. A
final act of purification, which in modern terms may be judged as an act
of catharsis, takes place when a feast is prepared by the survivors of the
deceased. It is arranged by the nuclear family and is held in a café or
restaurant. Much eating and drinking then takes place and very few
people sleep that night. This also saves the nuclear family of the
deceased from having to sleep in the old caravan. For although the
actual death had not taken place in it, it is in some way affected by the
death. It is not, however, impure as it has not been contaminated by
death. The tent in which the death took place has been irrevocably
contaminated and is burnt immediately after the funeral. But no Mānuš
would ever again like to live in the deceased's caravan. This is due to the
various beliefs about the "Mulé", who may be compared to ghosts. We
shall soon see the extreme importance this "Mulo" occupies in Mānuš
life and thought. For semi-sedentary and sedentary Mānuš living in
houses, it is not possible to get rid of their dwellings or shift each time
that there is a death in the family. They therefore keep their houses, but

caravan dwellers dispose of their caravans as soon as possible, usually within the twenty-four hours immediately following the death. Along with the tent are burnt all personal effects of the deceased, such as clothes; jewellery personally owned and worn by her is sold to the Gādjé, and it has been reported that even bank-notes belonging to the deceased have been burnt.

If one visits the grave the morning after the funeral, one will invariably find there the following objects. (As yet, I have not been able to ascertain when they are placed there, nor by whom): Bottles of beer, presumably to quench the thirst of the deceased, baskets full of fresh hens' eggs and some slices of bread, presumably for the deceased to eat, and finally, two identical vases which have obviously been deliberately broken. But the broken bits are often enough put together again to make them look like intact vases. These vases were empty each time I saw them but were they full at the time at which they were broken? And if so, did they contain water? Similar customs are of course prevalent throughout the Islamic world and the passage of the Gypsies through countries of Islamic culture could be a clue to this custom.

Mānuš graves are always very well looked after, as friends and relatives go to the graveyards almost every day when they are in the area to tend them. Every anniversary of a death is invariably observed and there is a certain re-enactment of the original scene. Holy candles are lit on the grave, as well as at home. Members of the nuclear family abstain from eating meat or drinking alcohol; the nuclear and to some extent the extended family unites at the site of the tomb, which itself is thoroughly arranged and decorated. In most cases the nuclear family also requests the local Catholic priest to say a mass for the departed soul.

Incidentally a Catholic priest is also asked to bless the caravan which is bought to replace the one owned by the deceased. After he has done so, on the first night of its occupation, the head of the household proceeds to a ritual conjuration, in order to protect the caravan and its occupants from the "Mulé", i.e., from ghosts in general, and from the spirit of the defunct, in particular. While the conjuror goes around the caravan three times from left to right, sprinkling it with holy water, those inside the caravan make the sign of the cross.

From what we have said so far about death among the Mānuš, the following assumptions could be made. It seems that inside the body of every human being there is something which gets liberated at the time of physical death. Let us call this "something" the essence of the person, for the sake of convenience. On the other hand, at the moment of physical death, the person is not esteemed wholly "dead" because if he were, mourning would begin at once. We may thus assume that the

essence, once having left the body remains somewhere and retains a
certain amount of contact with the body. At the same time, although
liberated from the body, it does not travel far, or else it would already
need money at this stage, and this it does not. Secondly, it does not
seem wholly independent of the body, as far as nourishment is concerned.

The community, or at least the family of the deceased is in a state of
impurity. This comes to an end only with the burial. From the time of
physical death till the burial, the deceased either needs no external
nourishment, or else he too is supposed to be fasting like those he has
left behind.

As soon as the burial is over, the person is really esteemed dead. At
this moment, either the essence joins the body and both travel, or else
only one of the two travel. It is not yet clear to me where exactly their
travels lead them. In any case, at this stage, the deceased needs both
money and external means of sustenance.

Mānuš beliefs and customs about death are the result of an inter-
mingling of Christian and non-Christian beliefs, some of which may be
of Islamic or generally Semitic origin, and others of possibly pre-
Christian, Asiatic and European origin. An example of such an inter-
mingling would be the fact that the Mānuš place twelve burning
candles on the graves of their dead. The practice of putting a lighted
holy candle on the grave is a Christian one. Twelve is a mystic number
recognized universally, but for the Mānuš these twelve lighted candles
mean more still. They symbolize the twelve camp fires their ancestors
lit during the twelve months of the year.

Let us now try and briefly analyse the importance of fire in Mānuš
life, and especially the symbolism it calls up.

THE IMPORTANCE OF FIRE

Yāk is the word the Mānuš use for fire. This word is of direct Sanskrit
origin, from the word *agni*. All Indo-European scholars are aware of the
supreme importance of fire in the Aryan and more particularly, in the
Indo-Iranian civilizations. And, although in modern India the original
nature-worshipping cult of the Aryans has been replaced and synthe-
tized into other pre-existing religious forms and beliefs, Fire still
maintains a considerable amount of importance. Fire plays a predominant part in all religious ceremonies, ranging from the "rites de passage"
to marriage, and death.

In olden times, fire was of utmost practical importance in their
everyday life. It was their only source of light and heat and their only
means of cooking as well. Nowadays, at least for a large percentage who

live in caravans, fire is perhaps less indispensable. It is no longer a source of light, everyday cooking too is no longer done over the open fire, although all ceremonial cooking, on festive occasions is still done in the open over the flames. It is still, to some extent at least, a source of heat. But the real importance of fire for the present day Mānuš arises from its inherent symbolism which is part of the structure of Mānuš beliefs and practices.

This is why, the first act that a Mānuš accomplishes when he decides to camp somewhere for the night, is to light a fire irrespective of the time of year and the weather. This he does just in front of the door of the caravan. When several caravans are parked near each other the fire is lit in the middle, in such a way that the door of each caravan faces the fire. As evening progresses and if the weather is fairly warm, people gather round the camp fire to sit and chat. Long logs are usually found and arranged as seats. The men sit on one side of the fire and the women sit opposite. Once again, men and women may not sit next to each other. One notices however, that the people are never grouped round the fire in a circle. The seats of the men and of the women run parallel to each other and ample space is left at either end.

Another striking fact is, that as night approaches and deepens, instead of trying to increase the intensity of the fire, the Mānuš reduce it intentionally to a smouldering heap of logs. This is done irrespective of the outside temperature and weather. What is the reason for this? There are actually several reasons for this and they spring from the intensely ambivalent nature of Fire. On the one hand, Fire is a symbol of life, and thus of the Mānuš. The light and heat it gives protect the Mānuš from various natural and supernatural dangers. In this connection, it is interesting to note the expression the Mānuš use for "putting out the fire" *"mé marāwā o yāk"* (literally, I kill the fire), which implies a personification of Fire. On the other hand, Fire is also a symbol of death and thus of that strange creature known to the Mānuš as the "Mulo". The Mulo is supposed to be as much attracted by the Fire as the Mānuš himself. The Fire gives light and heat to the Mulo as much as it does to the Mānuš; besides, as we shall soon see, the Mulo always appears to be seeking the company of mortals. Whenever it spots a camp fire it knows that a Mānuš is somewhere nearby and it does its utmost to come and join in the company. And yet, the Mulo, being a supernatural being, is essentially a creature of darkness and cold. And so, although it is attracted by light and heat, its natural haunts are where cold and darkness reign. Therefore, if the Mānuš were to put out the fire completely, or not light it at all, he would be absolutely sure of encountering the Mulo in his own domain. It is

obvious from all this that the Mānuš find themselves in a dilemma
caused by the dual nature of fire. The solution lies in reducing the flames
to embers, and this is exactly what he does.

Fire is the supreme means of purification and thus it would seem
logical enough that no contagion could take place were persons of the
opposite sex to sit round it together, or even side by side. And yet this
is not done. Why not? This is because fire is also probably the very
personification of purity and hence sacred. It must thus be treated with
utmost respect and deference. To integrate the sexes in its presence
would amount to an act of profanation. Besides it would be impossible
to form a complete circle round the fire. First of all, the circle is by far
the most prominent of fertility symbols and a circle formed round a fire
would invariably represent the womb, i.e., the beginning of life, and
simultaneously and inevitably, therefore, it would also represent death.
Finally, it is believed that were the Mulo to come near the fire, he must
be allowed to pass by without directly encountering any of the Mānuš
on his path. Hence a free passage must be left for him at either end to
enter and leave. I have spoken of the Mulo earlier on in this article. Let
us now try and understand this complex notion.

THE NOTION OF THE MULO

Each and every adult Mānuš I know and even some of the children, has
seen, or in some way felt the presence of a Mulo at least once in his or
her life. What is a "Mulo"? This word could more or less be translated
by the English word ghost, but this translation would not I believe
completely convey the sense of the original word. Every Mulo has at
some time previously been a living creature, man, woman or child,
Mānuš or non-Mānuš. They also appear as men, women or children.
As far as I know they never appear in animal or bird forms, nor are they
mounted on any bird or animal. There is however a bird which is
closely associated with the Mulo and is called the *Muleskročirklo* (The
bird of the Mulo). This is the owl. It is hard to say why this bird
in particular is associated with the Mulo. I can only refer to the Alsatian
custom of nailing stuffed owls on the doors of stables, for it is believed
that this will protect the horses and keep away all evil spirits. On their
journeys through the Alsatian countryside, the Mānuš may have
frequently noticed these birds and thus associated them with Death,
and hence with the Mulo. The magpie, although not directly associated
with the Mulo, is also believed by the Mānuš to be dirty and a bearer
of sorrow and bad luck.

The Mulo live in mountains, woods, near rivers and old castles, and in numerous other places known only to themselves. When the Mānuš manage to find out about these dwellings, they avoid going near them. How does a Mulo make his presence felt? He has three means at his disposal. He can either appear before one or more persons in a human form and most often, I believe, in the form of the human being he once was; in this case he will be "seen" as a very vague and misty greyish form. Alternatively, he can choose to make himself heard and then one hears a strange sound like the howling of the wind. Apart from this, even when a Mulo decides to be seen, he is often enough preceded by a sudden storm (a classic procedure used by various supernatural or diabolic creatures even in non-Gypsy mythology). He may also be seen sometimes wading through a vast amount of water, proof, that in Mānuš cosmogony as well, a vast stretch of water separates this world from the world of the dead. A third way in which a Mulo may manifest his presence is by his breath or his touch. This would then be felt by a living human being as a sort of ticklish sensation or a little shiver. The Mulé can appear at any time of the day or night, but they appear mainly after dusk.

Mānuš oral literature in which the Mulo appears quite frequently is of two types. Some stories depict the Mulé as doing a kindly service for the Mānuš they meet, others show them as maleficent creatures. Although I would not, as yet, attempt to draw any final conclusion, I would like to point out that as far as I have been able to notice, the "good" Mulé are always women and the "bad" or "harmful" ones, always men. In any case, the Mulo (the word is almost always used in its masculine form, although the feminine does exist), is an object of real terror for all the Mānuš. He appears to be of special danger to young virgins, as he seems to be eternally in search of fulfilling his sexual urges at the expense of the virgins of the Mānuš community. He thus appears before these girls as an attractive young man and woos them. When he is quite sure that they will comply with all his wishes, he changes back into his real, horrible self. But it is of course too late and the girls cannot escape.

Mānuš society also makes use of the Mulo to explain, justify, and "rationalize" some of its own practices. For example, the plight of the barren woman. If a married woman has sexual intercourse with a Mulo she is invariably supposed to be pregnant. But the Mulo is, after all, not a living human being, thus although she conceives his child, it is that of a dead man, and cannot be born as a mortal to live among mortals. And she, having once come into direct sexual contact with Death, has become impure and will remain so forever. Thus, whatever she conceives will forever be dead, i.e., the child will die in the womb at the very moment of conception. Gādjo society would call such a woman barren, but the Mānuš know that she is simply a woman who has had sexual intercourse with a Mulo. What happens to such a woman? All I can give as an answer to this question, is that in the rare cases known to or heard of by me, a barren woman has always committed suicide. From the Mānuš point of view, such a woman is more than likely to give herself up completely to her Mulo lover one day or another. In this respect she is also considered to be mad. The Mulo therefore finally takes her away one day to live with him as a Muli. Such is the mythical explanation invented for a sociological phenomenon within the group in which a barren woman commits suicide under social pressures. Predictably, no such myths are known about relations between the Mānuš man and the Muli.

ATTITUDES TOWARDS THE MULO

It is now obvious that the Mānuš are afraid of the Mulo. When a group of people are afraid of something, be this a real and objective phenomenon, or an idea or notion created by themselves, and hence of subjective value, what do they do? Either, they try and suppress this object (and subject) of their fears, or they try not to think of it; alternatively, they try and placate it, so that it may do as little harm as possible. The Mānuš know that they cannot suppress the Mulo, for all human beings are Mulé-in-waiting. Nor on the other hand, do they stop thinking about it. In fact, the Mulo is an object of great interest; often enough when men or women sit around a table chatting and drinking, the favourite topics of conversation are sex and the Mulo. Conversation then takes on the form of stories told by each of the persons present. As the night grows deeper and the glasses fill up, the accounts of personal (or a relative's) adventures and experience with love and death grow wilder and wilder. When finally these little parties break up and the guests and friends are about to leave, the host goes out of the caravan with a jug of holy water, which he sprinkles all around the caravan to keep away the Mulé and the evil spirits. The guests, too, sprinkle themselves with this water before they leave, to protect themselves on their way home.

We have seen that as a group, the Mānuš are obliged to try and reduce the Mulo's harmful activities. How do they set about doing this? They have three methods. The first and most obvious is of course to try and avoid all contact with it, or at least try and keep this contact to a minimum. This the Mānuš do by not going to places which are known to be the haunts of these creatures. Another means of doing this is by not travelling at night. For at night the Mulo are most restless. It is then that they search for human company most of all. If they find a caravan on the road, unprotected by fire, they will certainly try and follow it. What then should the Mānuš do? The best thing is to try and find a camping place as soon as the sun starts to sink and light a fire as soon as possible after encampment.

A second attitude towards the Mulo is to actively try and keep it away from all Mānuš habitation and frequentation areas. For Mulé in general, conjuration with holy water, etc., is done. Alternatively, certain traditional (non-Christian) ceremonies are performed to "frighten off" these creatures, if they have already manifested their presence in some manner. Two such incidents have been narrated to me, although I myself, was not present on these occasions and would thus not be able to confirm or disprove their validity: one evening strange noises were heard near a house. Soon it was "confirmed" that a Mulo was prowling around the area. Some had seen it and others had heard it, even the dogs had seen it and were barking loudly, for they could smell it. The Mānuš decided to deal with the matter. The family who lived in the house, near which it had first been noticed, volunteered to get rid of the obnoxious creature. They owned a cock. The head of the house took this cock and held it over the window and cut its throat. A few seconds later all the strange sounds and smells and sights ceased. The Mulo had disappeared. The cock too, which had been left under the window, had gone by the next morning. Other similar incidents narrated to me mention the use of cloves of garlic and fresh eggs. Are these sacrifices made as offerings to placate the Mulo, or do they for some reason, frighten away the Mulo? To answer these questions, we would need to go much deeper into the analyses of Mānuš demonology.

So far we have seen how the Mānuš protect themselves against Mulé in general. Let us now see what they do to keep away the "family Mulé", i.e., the Mulé who were known, or unknown members of their own families. It is not very clear whether these old kinsmen are as harmful as strangers. It is however believed that dead men and women often try and visit their husbands and wives on earth. They even try to "take revenge", if these widows and widowers have since remarried. In any case, be they harmful or not, the presence of these kinsmen is not greatly appreciated. Thus everything must be done to see that they do not come in search of their families. Apart from their own natural tendency to visit kinsmen, certain acts on the part of these same kinsmen would invariably attract a Mulo. These acts are above all, pronouncing its name. Hence, once a person is dead, he is never again referred to by name, the name, in this case, being the epitomy of the Word and the essence of the Person. In fact, a person can change his name at each *rite de passage*. Almost no one acquires his or her final name till the age of puberty, i.e., adulthood. Also, before a child has been given a name, he possesses no identity and thus a child who dies before being named cannot become a Mulo. It is clear, that pronouncing the name of a dead person would amount to calling him. When obliged to refer to a dead relative the Mānuš always use the term of kinship and add a very deferential adjective to it. It is believed by some, that formerly, the graves of the Mānuš did not bear the names of the dead. This practice was recently attested as well in one Strasbourg cemetery. On the day following a burial, the warden of the cemetery found that the name on the Cross had been erased and only the dates of birth and of death remained to be seen. However, my visits to other Mānuš tombs in Strasbourg and elsewhere have not borne out this fact. Another immediate way of attracting a Mulo, is to display a photograph of him. The Mānuš thus destroy most photographs of their dead. If at all they keep any as souvenirs, they keep them hidden and never carry them around. As we have already seen, the Mānuš never keep any objects which belonged to their dead.

CONCLUSION

In these few paragraphs I have briefly tried to give an account of certain aspects of Mānuš life and thought, but, as the reader can well imagine, much remains to be said.[13] The complex kinship system, with the closely-knit and well structured clans and the vestiges of what may have been a matriarchal system would be worthy objects of deeper studies. As we have seen, Mānuš society has conserved many of its most traditional aspects. It remains an independent social, economic and ethnic entity. Throughout several centuries, the Mānuš have fought certain Gādjo values and this constant struggle has obviously had both positive and negative results. It has resulted in a certain economic backwardness of Mānuš society. At the same time, it has helped to forge their spirit of economic independence, for even today, a Mānuš man or woman will never work as a salaried employee of a Gādjo. Though living within a capitalist society, their economic life runs parallel to it and up till now, they have categorically refused to fall victims to the temptations of materialistic western society and its accompanying values. The traditional education which the average Mānuš child receives at home, is ample proof of this.

13. The present article is part of a larger study of the Mānuš carried out by the author and presented at the Univ. of Strasbourg, France.

But for how much longer will Mānuš society be able to safeguard its identity? Today, Mānuš society has reached an extremely interesting and crucial stage in its evolution. Today, more than ever before, Gādjo society with its own cultural and social values, is imposing itself on the Mānuš. Direct force may have become less frequent, but persecution, born of centuries of prejudice and the inherently ethno-centric attitudes of those in power, is no less than it was when Louis XIV issued his edicts against the Gypsies. In addition, the Mānuš are subjected to new methods of dangerously subtle persuasion, through the mass media and other channels diffusing and preaching Gādjo values. Social patterns within Mānuš groups are evolving more rapidly than ever before and we cannot rule out the possibility of adaptation and partial acceptance giving way, ultimately, to total assimilation with Gādjo values. This would not necessarily be a good thing, and is not, I believe, something to be hoped for.

What the Mānuš themselves, and all those who are interested in the matter should work towards and fight for is the creation of equal opportunities in all fields, and for the right to be treated as full citizens. Differences in social structure and cultural values should be fully accepted and respected, rather than become a means of exploiting them and converting them into objects of overt or covert racial and socio-economic discrimination.

CHAPTER SEVEN

Kinship, Marriage, Law and Leadership in Two Urban Gypsy Settlements in Spain

Teresa San Román

No intensive anthropological research has been done in Spain among the Gypsies (*gitanos*), nor has their history been written. They arrived in Spain about the beginning of the fifteenth century and, until 1499, they were welcomed and received many privileges as Christian pilgrims. From 1499 until 1783 there was increasing persecution and legislation against them; but from 1783 to the present day there has been a relaxation of restrictions. However, insofar as many of them have no settled mode of living, they have often been regarded as "a potential social danger". Since 1871, when a Civil Register or Census was established, all people have to be registered within fifteen days of birth, and later obtain a national identity card to be produced on demand and necessary for obtaining a passport, voting, holding political office and engaging in legal and business transactions. It is also necessary to have a civil record of marriage. Some Gypsies lack these documents, but a certificate of baptism by the Roman Catholic Church can often be used to establish legal status and obtain certain other documents. State welfare benefits are available for those in settled employment, i.e., those who have work contracts; but many Gypsies are irregularly employed or follow traditional occupations and for them there are only minor and temporary forms of assistance. However, many disabilities are suffered by them in respect of education, health and housing facilities. There is benevolent work done by the Roman Catholic Church in the parishes, and by religious orders and associations: one major institution is Caritas. The Pentecostal Church has some adherents among Gypsies, but lack of space precludes any discussion of its influence. Finally, a Church's Gypsy Secretariat was established in 1967 in Madrid, and later in other parts of Spain to deal with Gypsy affairs.

Most Gypsies are now permanently settled, but they visit relatives, attend weddings and funerals, and make pilgrimages to certain Spanish centres. They also participate in international pilgrimages to, for example, Banneux in Belgium and to Saintes Maries de la Mer in the Camargue in France; I was fortunate enough to attend these in 1969 and 1970.

The *gitanos* constitute the majority of Gypsies in Spain, as distinct from the so-called "Hungarian" group, and they are subdivided into Béticos, Catalans, Castillians, and Cafeletes, but differences among them are due largely to social class rather than to culture. Apart from nomadic Gypsies, few of them have a knowledge of Caló (the Romany language), and they resort to it mainly in the presence of *payos* (non-Gypsies) whom they may wish to mislead, and distinguish themselves from.

My main research from 1969 to 1970, and later from time to time as occasion permitted, was carried out in two Gypsy settlements, La Alegría in Madrid, and San Roque in Barcelona, but brief visits were made to Gypsies in Cordoba, Ecija, Seville and Granada.[1] La Alegría, with a population of about 500 Gypsies, was settled in 1964 by Gypsies from other parts of Madrid. In 1962 some *payos*, mainly university students, visited La Rivera which is near a rubbish dump in the southeast of Madrid. Appalled by conditions there, they constituted themselves as a Fraternity; funds were obtained from private, state and Church sources, and property was bought in the ward of Pozo del Tio Raimundo on which to build some small brick houses and huts and for which a nominal rent was paid to the Fraternity by the Gypsy occupants. This became the Gypsy community of La Alegría. The Fraternity is concerned to promote education and the economic development of the

1. This essay is based on material included in my thesis, "A Comparative study of Three Gypsy Urban Settlements in Spain", submitted for the degree of Master of Philosophy in the University of London in 1974. I am indebted to the Lake Barnett Folklore Research Fund for a grant towards field expenses. My thanks are also due to the late Professor Daryll Forde for his help and encouragement, and to Dr. Kaberry of the Department of Anthropology, University College, London, for assistance in preparing the essay. To those Gypsies who gave me their trust, friendship and co-operation, any expression of gratitude must seem inadequate, but I hope that this essay, and my thesis, will contribute something to an understanding of their values and way of life.

Gypsies; a school, nursery, training centre and social clubs have been set up. I acted as Adviser from 1971 to 1973.

San Roque is a ward in Barcelona where some 2,000 Gypsies live interspersed among *payos* and constituting a minority in the population. Most of the Gypsies formerly lived in Somorrostro in north-east Spain near the coast, until they were evacuated by the government in 1966. Most now live in flats but do not constitute a nucleated settlement, a grave disability in view of the Gypsy value attached to residence near members of the family and other kin. The necessity to pay rent, gas, electric and water bills has meant that many of them have had to seek some form of regular employment, but their standard of living is much lower than that of another Gypsy settlement in Barcelona, namely Hostafranchs, which has been in existence for about four generations.[2] Moreover, life in a city flat does not permit Gypsies to follow many of the traditional occupations which often involve owning a horse or a donkey and a cart for the collection of goods for resale, and a place where to select and prepare scrap metal for sale.

LINEAGE ORGANIZATION

Lineage organization is a most important aspect of Gypsy kinship, although in Hostafranchs it is of little significance these days. In San Roque and La Alegría, the term *raza* (race) means for the Gypsies a group of people who are descended from a common ancestor through male links. The name of the ancestor may be a surname, or, more frequently, a nickname, but Gypsies from a sense of insecurity often conceal lineage names from *payos*. Lineages are endogamous, and have a genealogical depth of from four to five generations, but it is almost impossible to calculate the average size of a lineage, members of which may be scattered throughout Spain. Gypsy estimates varied wildly, but the average size may range from 150 to 200 members. However, it is not uncommon to find a whole lineage in a certain area such as French-Spanish Catalonia, or like Madrid, Guadaljara and Toledo Provinces which border one another and are now part of the new Castille.

2. Hostafranchs is a ward in the south-west of Barcelona where about 400 Gypsies live who speak Catalan and having been living there for about four generations. All live in flats and, compared with Gypsies elsewhere, enjoy a higher standard of living. With a more regular income they are able to make use of government facilities and send their children to better schools than those in San Roque. Compared with San Roque and La Alegría, kin groups are smaller, but there is a tendency for sons to be living near their father and also near brothers. There is a strong sense of community among them though they lack the type of council found in La Alegría. In 1965, some of them took part in the activities of the Gypsy Secretariat in Barcelona, and later on in 1966 two representatives were elected to the Secretariat from each of the Gypsy settlements in Barcelona.

Because of the dispersal of Gypsies living in San Roque, I was unable
to identify more than eight lineages; members of these are to be found
also in other wards of Barcelona City and in Barcelona Province. In La
Alegría, where I was able to make a complete census, six lineages are
represented and members of these also live in other parts of Madrid and
elsewhere. I now give a list of lineages in San Roque and La Alegría,
placing in brackets other regions where they are represented.

San Roque Lineages:

Jacobo	(French-Spanish Catalonia, Andalusia).
Llamas	(Madrid, Spanish Catalonia and Andalusia).
Hormigas	(French-Spanish Catalonia).
Perez	(Spanish Catalonia).
Escopeteros	(French-Spanish Catalonia, the south of France from Catalonia to Marseilles).
Frutos	(Barcelona Province).
Tapias	(Spanish Catalonia)
Hilera	(French-Spanish Catalonia).

La Alegría Lineages:

Caballeros	(Madrid Province).
Comas	(Madrid and Guadaljara Provinces).
Barrenos	(Valencia, Madrid and Barcelona Provinces, Galicia).
Junquenos	(Madrid and Toledo Provinces).
Bobos	(Madrid and Logroño Provinces).
Flecos	(Madrid, Guadaljara and Toledo Provinces, Béziers in France).

This dispersal of lineages should be understood within the context of
Spanish movements of migration from such very poor regions as
Castille and Andalusia to, in the main, the two largest cities of Spain—
Barcelona in Catalonia and Madrid in Castille. These two cities have
received a very large number of immigrants in this century and particularly during the last thirty years. Among these there are many Gypsies,
many of whom are unskilled labourers and without permanent jobs.
However, in San Roque, for reasons I have mentioned, young Gypsies
are labourers working in permanent jobs, or working at a job for
part of the year and combining it with some traditional occupation.
On the other hand, in La Alegría, where rents are nominal and such
amenities as water supply and gas are absent, they follow the traditional
occupations for which they receive no regular payments; but, for this
very reason, there is a considerable incentive to take on seasonal employment at the time of the vintage in French Catalonia.[3] I shall discuss
this more fully later, but some San Roque Gypsies also go.

3. There is close contact between Spanish and French Catalonia which border one another
and extend north and south of the Eastern Pyrenees. The two Catalonias were a political

One reason then for lineage segmentation is the movement from one part of Spain to another in search of better living conditions. Whether connections are maintained is dependent in part on geographical distance and the length of time which has elapsed since separation. For example, the ancestors of Tapias lineage in San Roque used to live in Andalusia. One of them, now looked on as the ancestor of the lineage, left his brother and migrated to Murcia on the east Mediterranean coast. His descendants in their turn moved to Barcelona, but the present members of the lineage in San Roque do not know who the father and brothers of their ancestor were. One day a man, also called Tapias, arrived in San Roque from Andalusia and met a man belonging to the Tapias lineage there. After talking for awhile he said: "Then you must be a descendant of that brother who left Andalusia to go to Murcia in former times. I am a descendant of the brother who remained in Andalusia." The two men did not bother any more about their genealogical connection and did not fulfil the obligations carried out by lineage members for one another. Each considered that he belonged to a different lineage.

Another reason for lineage segmentation is for two brothers to adopt different attitudes in an important event in which they are expected to act together. For example, in San Roque a man from the Jacobo lineage did not attend his father's burial. Thenceforth his own brothers had nothing more to do with him and, with his sons, he lived apart from them. In La Alegría, a man of the Caballeros lineage had a fight with a member of another lineage who was a stranger in the ward. All the Caballeros brothers and their sons, except one brother and his sons, went to their brother's aid. This brother and his descendants are now called by another lineage name, and they do not co-operate any more with their erstwhile lineage fellows.

Lineages then have a depth of about four generations from the youngest member. At the fifth generation co-operation is likely to cease, although if a man's father is still alive he would assist him in aid given to lineage members more distantly related to him; when his father is dead he would probably cease to give help. However, if individuals in the fifth generation are related through marriage and *compadrazgo* (god parentage), co-operation is likely to be more enduring, but I am pretty sure it is for different reasons than that of agnatic relationship. The position is summed up succinctly by several

---

unit until the second half of the seventeenth century. The tradition of this unity is still maintained and is supported by community of language, Catalan, and many customs. Contact between the two has been intense for centuries and immigration has taken place in both directions.

Gypsies: "My father's father and his father's father were sons of two brothers, so we help one another."

It often happens that a genealogical relation has been discovered or is known between two individuals of different lineages. For example, a Flecos man in La Alegría was talking about another man from another ward in Madrid. He said, "He is not a relative of mine. Well, his father's father and my father's father were sons of two men who were children of two brothers. But he has nothing to do with me. He is *familia retirada* (i.e., a distant family relative)". The term *retirada* (distant) is not the word commonly used in Spain. Spanish people talk about *familia lejana*, which has a similar connotation. However, *retirada* implies "retired", which is not implied in the term *lejana* as used by Spaniards. *Familia retirada* is not only used for distant relatives of another lineage, it is used to mean any kinsman or kinswoman who is not considered *familia* (see below).

The Gypsies in San Roque and La Alegría are very much concerned with what they call "the strength of the *raza*". This strength is measured by the number of male members in a lineage; the children of a married couple belong to their father's lineage, even if husband and wife are separated, divorced or married for a second time. The fact that the children are living with their mother or father does not modify the rule. In La Alegría, Comas lineage with 87 men and 57 women is considered to be "strong"; and, indeed, few Comas people live outside La Alegría. Caballeros is also a very strong *raza* with 55 men and 40 women; unlike Comas, they have many relatives outside the ward. On the other hand, the Flecos have only 16 men and 10 women, but their lineage is said to be the largest in Castille; I know of about 80 Flecos living in other parts of Madrid and its environs, and about 30 more in Talavera in Toledo Province,[4] that is, a total all told of 136 and there are others unknown to me. In San Roque I know personally or by reference 126 Llamas people (65 men and 61 women); there are others outside San Roque and it is regarded as a "strong *raza*". Also in San Roque I know of 95 Jacobos, and others in other parts of Barcelona, as well as one in Figueras near the French border, and 4 near Perpignan in France. This is a total of about 145 Jacobos known to me, but there are many more in Catalonia and in Andalusia.

The 'strength' of a lineage supports the authority of the elders *vis-à-vis* other lineages, and the capacity of a lineage to defend itself against others. For example, a Tapias man explained to others that "strong" *razas* are very dangerous: "If you go to a market for business you must

---

4. Figures for the three other lineages are Barrenos: 10 men and 9 women; Junquenos: 17 men and 29 women; Bobos: 9 men and 10 women.

be very careful. It sometimes happens that a group of Gypsies is coming towards you with the elders and their men. They warn you that you are to give them a part of what you earn. If you answer that you do not want to give, they immediately ask which *raza* you belong to. If yours is a strong *raza*, then they apologise and they leave you alone. But if your *raza* is 'weak', then they will force you to pay them." Things like this also happen in La Alegría and among other Gypsies I met in Andalusia.

Members of a lineage have the obligation to defend one another when one of them is abused, insulted or beaten-up. Lineage kinsmen who are with him on the spot have to defend him against the other man and his relatives. The lineage members on both sides, who live in other settlements, are soon called in case a fight may take place. If the fight occurs and blood is shed, then the elders of both parties send telegrams to other lineage members who live in other villages or towns, inside or outside Spain, depending on the seriousness of the fight. If one man is killed, the lineage members who are present will go out and try to kill the murderer; if the murderer is not found they will kill a member of his lineage. When a fight is finished and if vengeance has not taken place, it is the duty of the father, brothers and sons of the dead man to avenge his death. This duty is not shared by other members of the lineage: that is, lineage members have the duty to defend each other, but afterwards the obligation of vengeance is shared only by the father, brothers and sons of the dead man.

However, when a man is wounded very badly by a member of another lineage, or when the man has been killed, the usual thing is for the elders of the two lineages to stop the vendetta. They call the elders of different lineages, who are not involved, to act as judges. The territory where blood is shed is divided into two parts: one lineage is given one part, and the other lineage the other. Members of one lineage are not entitled to pass through the territory given by the judges to the other lineage; the territory may be a section of a ward, a ward, or even a village. In this situation, one lineage is said to be *contrario* (opposed) to the other. All members of one lineage share the *contrarios* of their lineage. The relationship of *contrario* is inherited, as long as the genealogical links to the lineage men who had the fight are remembered. A woman is *contraria* to the *contrarios* of her own lineage; but, if she marries out of her lineage, then her sons are not *contrarios* to the *contrarios* of their mother's lineage. I shall discuss later, defence, vengeance and *contrarios*; here I wish to point out that these are situations which involve all lineage members.

There is another situation in which the lineage acts as a single unit. The worst insult which can be said to a Gypsy is, "I excrete on your dead". If a man of one lineage "names the dead" of a man of another lineage, any of the members of the lineage of the insulted man who know about it are obliged to kill the man who is known to have said the insult.

Another aspect of lineage rights and duties is the economic factor. Daily co-operation in work and everyday life does not take place at the lineage level, but at the level of the *familia* (family). Nevertheless, there are some situations in which lineage ties are claimed to demand some assistance.

Lineage members help each other in moments of economic difficulty. For example, in San Roque a man of the Jacobo lineage died who had a wife and nine children. The widow was helped in many ways, especially with money matters, by the lineage of her deceased husband. To help the widow of dead lineage members is proper behaviour. However, those who have not sufficient money to cover their own needs are not so required nor would a man living for example, in the south of France, unless he is asked because those living nearer the widow have not enough.

A wedding involves heavy expenditure; usually this is met by the groom's father. But if a man's father is dead and he himself cannot afford the money he would be helped by members of his lineage. Again, when a Gypsy is ill in hospital or is in prison, he expects to be visited by members of his lineage and they are expected to look after his wife and children. Similar action is taken to meet the cost of burial. A young Flecos boy in La Alegría died after a long illness. His father had no money left for the burial and was helped by lineage members in La Alegría, by a man living in another ward, and by another man living in a village in Toledo Province who gave about £70.

When a man makes a good business deal, he is expected to share it with members of the lineage who are with him at the moment; in some cases his own share may be less than that given to a relative. However, this is ideal behaviour and not followed in all cases. There are also other situations which involve relatives at the lineage level. Hospitality is very important and is specially symbolized by drinking coffee together. It is particularly manifested by lineage members when a man is away from his home. If a man needs to hide from the police or from other Gypsies, he may leave his town and go to live with some relatives.

The ceremonies of baptism, weddings and burials involve a gathering of lineage members. Baptism is usually attended by those members of the lineage who live in the settlement where the ceremony is held, and by those who live nearby. The same happens at a wedding, but I have been told that relatives of the groom and bride may come from distant places to attend the ceremony. The burial of a person is the most important ceremony which lineage relatives have to attend; not to do so may have serious consequences and those involved may be ostracised by the rest of their lineage. This is especially true when the dead is a *Tio*, meaning also a man of prestige or elder of a "strong *raza*"; relatives of his lineage attend his burial, travelling to his ward from distant places in Spain, and even outside Spain. I attended the burial of one elder who used to live in El Cajón ward in Madrid. Unfortunately his lineage, Cardos, is a very "weak" one. I went there with members of his mother's lineage, Flecos. There were about 70 Flecos present, more than any other relatives of the dead man who numbered about 40. In the case mentioned above of the Flecos boy who died, there were about 250 to 300 present, but these included in-laws and collaterals.

There are some other situations in which lineage members co-operate, as for example where many people are needed for labour. In this case, people are summoned irrespective of the distance which may separate them. One instance of this, a lucrative one, is employment in films as "extras". A number of westerns are filmed in Spain because of the suitability of the terrain and the lower costs of production. Many Gypsies are good jockeys and they enjoy a temporary job for which there is relatively good pay, a minimum of about £4.70 a day, and which permits them to bring in a number of their lineage fellows of both sexes and all ages.

Temporary migrations are also occasions when lineage members co-operate and three categories may be distinguished: first, many Gypsies go to the south of France during the harvest to do agricultural work; secondly, many people in La Alegría go to different villages in Castille towards the end of summer for the vintage; and, thirdly, those Gypsies in La Alegría who migrate to Central and South America for a period of time, usually from three months to two years.

In San Roque the movement of Gypsies to the south of France begins about the middle of May and ends during the first days of October. There are three main periods between these dates. From the middle of May up to the first days of June, some Gypsies work in the harvesting of beans, a rather poorly paid task and requiring few workers; from the middle of June to the middle of July in the collection of apricots and peaches; this entails a larger labour force and the remuneration is better. At the beginning of September they start the vintage which finishes in the first days of October. Those who go in the middle of June may return to San Roque when they have finished their work in the middle of July; but usually they wait for the vintage to arrive, about forty days later. During the interim most gather osier twigs to make baskets; the women sell them in the village or in nearby villages.

Gypsy workers in one particular village in the south of France are usually members of only one lineage. An elder goes in the spring to settle conditions with the owner or manager of the fields: wages, the size of the task force and accommodation. On his return the elder seeks out those in his lineage who may be interested in the employment, first among his nearest relatives and then more distant kin. If there is not sufficient work for the members of his own lineage, he will while in France have made arrangements with other employers. It is interesting to note that none of the Gypsies I met in France had temporary contracts, though these can be arranged through the Spanish Institute of Emigration in co-operation with French syndicates and which provide social security benefits while in France and the necessary money for the journey. But Gypsies prefer face-to-face agreements and the freedom to leave when they feel like it.

There are two kinds of labourers during the harvest: "cutters" who pick the apricots, peaches and beans, and cut the bunches of grapes; and the "carriers" who carry the produce to the lorry or cart. The latter have less work than the cutters since they have to wait while the cutters fill the lorry but they are higher paid. Women and children are the cutters; males, over the age of 15, the carriers. In 1971 for eight hours work, carriers received about 3,500 francs, and cutters about 3,000. Each elder gets the money for his wife, sons, daughters and unmarried children. In a family in which two men are carriers and three other members cutters, the earnings would be about £211 for 20 days. But they spend a lot of money while in France: they have to buy most of their food and, because of the desire to obtain prestige, they pretend to have no concern about money and will, for example, throw away the dirty dresses of a baby instead of washing them. However, the Gypsies of San Roque have a cycle of debts just as they have a cycle of earnings. When they return from the vintage, they pay arrears owing for rent, electricity, gas and water bills. They also repay debts to the ward food stores and to those persons from whom they usually buy things like pottery and cloth to sell. Gypsy occupations and jobs do not provide them with enough money to meet the expenses of rearing a large number of children, and those incurred for reasons of prestige and the fulfilment of kinship obligations. Thus they have to ask for credit and they pay bills and rent irregularly. About March one begins to hear comments about loans, credits and the lack of money which compel a temporary migration in the summer. With what they bring back from France they pay debts and use the rest to face the exigencies of the winter.

I shall now deal with the temporary migration of Gypsies of La

Alegría to Central and South America which they indiscriminately call "Piru" (Peru), especially to Peru itself, the Argentine, Venezuela and Mexico. Members of the Comas, Barrenos and Flecos lineages are primarily involved, and in each case two or three members may go to places where they have relatives, who can give hospitality and teach them how "selling" is carried out in the country. The period of residence in the Americas varies, usually from three months to two years. Their purpose is to earn money very quickly and to improve their standard of living in Spain. When they return they may buy a good flat or a small house, a car for business purposes, and especially an initial stock of cloth, iron, watches, etc: to sell in favourable markets in Spain. It is very rare for Gypsies to remain permanently in America.

There are three main differences between the temporary migration to French Catalonia and that to "Piru". As I have already pointed out, the temporary migration to France is part of the economic cycle of the year, but that to "Piru" is done to change the whole economic situation. Secondly, while the move to France is done by many lineage members together during the summer, that to America involves only a few lineage members who usually take the place of relatives who have returned from "Piru". Thirdly, the temporary move to France takes place on the basis of lineage organization and the pattern of dispersal. Thus lineage members who live in Spanish Catalonia join those living in villages in French Catalonia, while those going to "Piru" will not find a segment of their lineage living there. Finally, some of the Gypsies in San Roque have to migrate temporarily because the young Gypsy population are compelled to take on very poorly paid jobs in the factories surrounding San Roque. The only other occupation is trade from which the gains are small. As far as possible they rely on some work in France, which does not involve much improvement in their living conditions and is just the final part of the year's cycle.

Those in La Alegría who go to the vintage do so primarily to save and not to pay debts: those who temporarily migrate to America seek to change their standard of living when they return. La Alegría is more favourably placed than San Roque for eking out a livelihood. It is also surrounded by factories, is near markets, especially El Rastro (a market for antiques and second hand goods), and a dump from which things can be salvaged. All this, together with almost the absence of periodic payments, permit a man to be able to leave his family for a year (since they can support themselves), having saved enough to pay for the sea journey.

Authority increases in proportion to age; in everyday life, a man wields authority over his wife, sons and daughters, and his sons' wives

and children. But in those situations where lineage members act
together, the elders organize and give the orders to the younger
members. Lineage elders sometimes act as witnesses and enforcers of an
oath made by a member of their lineage. They also must be visited first
when a man from a different ward or town goes to see his kin, or on
business.

The prestige of an elder depends on certain personal qualities, but
his power mostly depends on the "strength" of his lineage, to which I
have already referred. Llamas and Jacobo lineages in San Roque, and
Flecos and Caballeros lineages in La Alegría, are the strongest in their
respective wards. The elders of these lineages may be called in by
lineages different from their own to act as judges in disputes. The
Gypsies, who do not follow their decision after asking them to arbitrate
in their concerns, will be attacked by members of the lineages of these
elders.

THE FAMILY AND MARRIAGE

The term *familia* (family) is used by Gypsies in different contexts: it
is used for the nuclear family, but it is especially the ego-centred group
constituted by a man's parents, grandparents, parents in-law, brothers,
sisters, brothers-in-law and sisters-in-law, children and their spouses,
and grand-children. It is also used to indicate the relationship among
members of the same lineage, and includes those in the mother's
lineage if this is different from that of the father.

The Gypsy *razas* are not necessarily exogamous: many marriages
take place inside the Jacobo, Llamas, Perez, Escopeteros and Frutos
lineages in San Roque, and inside the Caballeros and Flecos lineages in
La Alegría; it is highly probable that the same occurs in other lineages
in these communities. Gypsies say that they "belong to the father's
lineage first, and to the mother's lineage secondly." In fact, the father's
raza continues to exist through the generations, while the mother's *raza*
has significance only in a set of rights and obligations which an individual has during his lifetime; in some cases parents belong to the same
raza. Duties become apparent in situations of quarrelling and fighting:
a man supports his father's and his mother's lineages against others; if
a dispute occurs between the lineages of his father and his mother, he
must support that of his father.

As noted before, Gypsies are secretive about the names of their
lineages, but this is not so about their own surnames which are transmitted in the same way as among *payos*. The use of nicknames is very
common and two types are distinguished: *mote*, which describes the

characteristic of an individual, such as "the black one" or "artist"; and *apodo* which is transmitted through the lineage of the father or the mother. Thus the *apodo* is the *mote* of an ancestor. Gypsies say that there are certain rules of transmission, but in fact there are many exceptions. The first son inherits the name and nickname (if there is one) of his father's father; the second son inherits the name of his mother's father. But if the wife's father is dead, and the husband's father is alive, the first son is given his mother's father's name, and the second son his father's father's name. The same rule applies to women. When a couple think they are having their last child, they give it the father's or mother's name. Other children are called by the name of their godparents.

In addition to marriage within the lineage, intermarriage may be common between certain lineages: for example, in San Roque, Jacobo intermarry with Escopeteros, Llamas and Perez, and these three intermarry with one another. In La Alegría, Caballeros, Comas and Bobos intermarry, and Bobos also marry Flecos. It might be thought that this intermarriage is an alliance among the different lineages; but, in fact, I think this is primarily a matter of Gypsy preference for marrying close relatives. For example, it sometimes happens that a man marries his brother's wife's sister; and that the son's son of one of these couples marries the son's daughter of the other couple. I have also found cases of men married to their cross-cousins; and, less frequently, of marriage to a father's brother's son's daughter, father's brother's daughter's daughter, or to a father's brother's wife's sister's daughter. The Gypsies say they prefer their children to marry "known people", and needless to say many relatives fall within this category.

There is no bride wealth or dowry, and the relationship with the wife's lineage or the husband's lineage finishes as soon as the relationship between husband and wife comes to an end. But during their lifetime a man supports and defends his wife and also the member of her lineage, and she supports his lineage. A woman should not only take the side of her husband but do so even when close relatives are involved, however great the conflict of loyalties. However I give one case in which there was some difference of opinion. In San Roque, a woman had a violent argument with her husband and he "cursed the dead" of her lineage. This, as we have seen, is an act which must be avenged by those concerned. The woman called for her father and her brother, and they killed her husband and also the husband's father who came to assist his son. After some time, she defended herself, saying, "If there is a fight between a woman's brother and her husband, she has to think first of her brother. Blood ties are greater, and there is nothing like a brother.

You may change your husband, but your brother is always your brother." The men who were present opposed this strongly, and another woman said: "I never found myself in the situation of having to choose between my brother and my husband. But this happened to my mother, and I know that a woman must always be on her husband's side as long as he is her husband. And he is the only one who has the right to beat her, and the one who defends her first and foremost". Everybody agreed, and the other woman had to be quiet. A woman, when she marries, is said "to enter her husband's lineage". Nevertheless her ties with her own lineage do not disappear with marriage, and she will give help in cases of financial difficulty and other crises, and they assist her when her husband lacks the means. They will also defend her if he has beaten her without good reason, or if she is forced to seek sanctuary with them because of other forms of ill-treatment.

Gypsies marry young in comparison with the usual age for marriage in Spain: men from the age of 17 to 22, and women from the age of 15 to 17. There are few individuals who remain single, and I found only one case of a single woman in San Roque; she was about 45. For Gypsies, chastity is the most important virtue for a woman to have; and, if a woman is to marry with a wedding ceremony, she must be a virgin when she marries. It should be understood that the relationship between a young man and a young woman is very formal: young unmarried people of both sexes never go alone to the cinema or for a walk. They meet in the homes of their parents and relatives, but it is uncommon to find boys and girls chatting together in the street, let alone a bar. The girl who does such things will have a bad reputation in the community. There was a girl, 15 years old, in San Roque who had this reputation. She escaped from her home and went to Madrid where she had relatives. Her father said he wanted to know nothing about her anymore. After several days she returned, but she is now considered a bit of a *lumia* (Caló for prostitute) by the Gypsies, even though there is no direct evidence that she has ever had sexual intercourse. The formal relationship with unmarried girls is even so strict that no compliments, *piropo*, can be paid to them by members of the opposite sex, although this is common among *payos*. Finally, any kind of physical contact between a girl and a boy is forbidden. Dancing is not forbidden, but a distinction is made between "loose" dancing where the men and woman dance separately, and "engaged" or *payo* dancing where the couple dance in one another's arms. To dance "engaged" compromises both of them: "You only dance 'engaged' when you want to marry a girl. But if a girl agrees to dance in an 'engaged' manner, then she is considered a prostitute if marriage is not the purpose of her allowing a man to do so." The rules about dancing are beginning to be disregarded by some, but on the whole they are still observed.[5]

As I have pointed out previously, a Gypsy boy and girl should not marry without the consent of their parents; and marriages arranged by the parents are very common. When a boy and girl begin to "go out", i.e., walk together or chat, either their parents do not say anything about it or they forbid the relationship; but in the former case the fathers implicitly give their permission to the relationship. In any case parents must be told about their children "going out". As one Gypsy said to me: "A Gypsy cannot go with a girl without their parent's knowledge. That is something only *payos* do. The parents must choose whom they want them to marry." These ideas are also held by the young people even though these days they ask for more freedom of choice. In giving consent to a union, the parents not only take into account the character and reputation of the young man and woman but also that of their respective families.

There are several steps towards a marriage. First of all, either the boy's father or the girl's father send a common friend or a kinsman to the other. This intermediary is sent to find out if the marriage between the boy and girl is essentially approved by the other party's father. If it is approved, then both fathers meet. On both occasions the conversations usually take place in a bar. There the fathers fix a day for the formal "asking of the bride", but the actual "asking for the bride" generally takes place in the bride's house.

When both fathers are agreed on their children's marriage, the couple is said to be *apalabrada*. *Apalabrada* is a Spanish word, the participle of the verb *apalabrar* which means to make a verbal contract which will be carried out later on. I shall translate it as "engaged". When the couple are engaged they are allowed more freedom in their relationship: they may go to the cinema together, and may talk freely and alone; they cannot have sexual relations but some physical contact is permitted at this stage and is said to be "play", though it must not go so far as intercourse nor must it happen in the presence of the parents. If a girl's parents have reason to think that their daughter may have lost her virginity, the girl's mother "searches" her. On one occasion, a woman took her daughter to her room and "searched" her; the father, brothers and some other members of the family waited in the

---

5. Pitt-Rivers in his book, *The People of the Sierra* says that the people of Alcalá regarded the Gypsies as a race apart. They can be distinguished by their appearance, dress, gait and so on. A Gypsy who does "an honest job of work" is simply not behaving like a Gypsy! It is said they are shameless. However, their skill in dancing is admired and make them symbolical of gaiety (1954, pp. 186–187).

dining room. After a while, the mother came and said to them: "You can relax. She is alright."

As can be seen, a father is entitled to "deny" his daughter, i.e., he will not allow her to marry. But if he does this without any reason and several times to different men, he is looked down upon by other Gypsies and will be told: "Why don't you 'give' your daughter? Do you want her for yourself?" This would imply incest, and it would damage the honour and prestige of the man and his family. On the other hand, if a woman loses her virginity with a man, they have to marry; if he is married already, he would be killed.

There is not space here to describe the wedding ceremony, but in some cases it does not take place. In many instances there may be an elopement, *fuga*, and this may occur if the girl is not a virgin any more, though usually after the formal engagement; or if one or both parents are against the marriage. *La fuga* is traditional among Gypsies, but formerly when this happened there was no contact with the parents until a child had been born. Then the couple "returned to ask the pardon of the Gypsy woman", i.e., the girl's mother, and then the pardon of both families. Everybody looked on them then as husband and wife. Today only a few days may elapse before seeking pardon, the couple remaining in the interim at the home of the man's relative. Their children will be legitimate, but there are some consequences for the woman. For example, she must remain silent when a serious matter is being discussed in her husband's family; she cannot be the godmother of a bride or even be present in the most important part of the wedding ceremony.

Ideally, an individual should marry only once, but in fact it is permissible to marry more than once. When a young couple marry they are free to separate while they have no children, but if one individual abandons an old spouse, he or she is very much criticized and will be ostracised by the whole Gypsy community and more or less forced to leave the ward. The worst time for a couple to separate is when they have small children, though not much attention is paid if the children are more than fourteen years old. If a man leaves his wife and children, or if she still "wants" him, her father and brothers will look for her husband and bring him back. If he resists, the usual thing is for his in-laws to beat him up; however, Gypsy law entitles them to kill him if he leaves her when she has small children but I have no evidence of this. Similarly, if a woman leaves her husband and young children, he and his relatives look for her and bring her back if he "wants" her.

We can talk of divorce when the couple, their respective lineages and the public opinion in general, accept the separation. This does not happen immediately, but in all cases of which I have knowledge, the situation is eventually accepted. The children belong to their father's lineage, but, if he abandons them or does not show any concern about them, they live with their mother.

A widower may marry again after some years, but ideally a widow should not marry again: "She should remain with the memory of her husband". However some widows do marry again, but in this case, as for all second marriages, there is no wedding ceremony. They may be criticized at first but eventually they are referred to as being married.

It should be clear at this stage that authority rests essentially with the men. A woman is subordinated to her father and brothers in her family of orientation, and to her husband in her family of procreation. When she marries she becomes a member of her husband's lineage, though she still has rights and duties in her own lineage of which she will always be a member. It is only in the religious field that a woman seems to have more power than a man: her curse and her use of the "evil eye" is more feared than that of a man.

A man has the exclusive right to inflict physical punishment on his wife; a woman is considered "weak" and "inferior" to a man. As one Gypsy said to me: "As she is weak and subject to her husband, he is entitled to beat her, but he must always defend her". However, defence is less necessary now than in former times and seems rather incongruous in the case of some young Gypsy women. At the National Gypsy Conference of Spain held in Madrid in 1969, some young women said they did not agree with the way they were treated by men: they wanted more freedom in dress and in their association with boys, and the right to take the initiative since traditionally everything was planned by men.

A woman not only works in her house; very often she sells flowers in the streets, or sells plastic pots, stockings, china and garlic in the markets, streets, or from door to door. She generally has some freedom to use the money she earns: she contributes to household expenses, gives some pocket money to her children and fulfils kinship obligations, such as helping a relative in difficulty. The man who systematically lives on his wife's earnings is regarded as a bad husband by the community; but, if he is in jail, ill, or in circumstances which temporarily prevent him from working, she must earn sufficient to feed him and the children and even provide him with all the luxuries and comforts she can.

A Gypsy woman's standing in the community, then, depends on whether she has been married by the wedding ceremony, has married only once and remained with her husband, has not remarried when she has become a widow. When she has her first child, her marriage is consolidated; and, when she bears a son, her influence and prestige in

her husband's lineage and her own are increased. She must co-operate
with her husband to earn money when necessary; be obedient, and fulfil
obligations. These are accounted virtues in a woman; and although she
has no formal authority she may in fact, when she is older, have such
influence in her own lineage and in that of her husband and in his family.

RELATIONSHIPS WITHIN THE FAMILY

As we have already seen, the obligation of vengeance is shared by an
individual's father, brothers, and also by husband or wife. We have
already noted that segmentation of a lineage usually takes place through
the separation of brothers, either in residence far apart, or in differing
attitudes to a serious matter in which they are supposed to be at one.
Nobody is entitled to interfere in a discussion, quarrel or even fighting
between brothers. After the father, the eldest son has authority over his
brothers and sisters and usually acts as his father's executive in decisions
made by his father. An elder in San Roque was criticizing a man who
beat his children himself. He said: "A father must not beat his children
unless they have done something very bad. That is why the eldest son
is so important for a man. If a child is doing some bad, I shall threaten
him by saying that I shall tell his elder brother to beat him. It is my
elder son who educates them and beats them, and I tell him how to do it.
In this way a father reserves himself for more serious matters, while his
children learn to respect their elder brother." When the father dies, it
is the eldest son who takes decisions. He does so with his other brothers,
but he has the last word. His house is usually the place of meeting for
all his brothers, and the place other relatives visit when they go to the
ward.

A man's father-in-law does not have real authority over him though
he may influence him through advice. The relation between parents-in-
law and daughter-in-law is very different. The daughter-in-law is in a
subordinate position and must pay especial attention to her mother-in-
law. However, a man should respect his mother-in-law though he has
no duty to obey her or listen to her advice. On the other hand, there is
considerable freedom between brother-in-law and sister-in-law and it
can be regarded as a "joking relationship". A woman can refuse to do
something for her brother-in-law; she may change her clothes in his
presence; they kiss each other on the cheek when they meet; pay
compliments to one another and play jokes on one another. In general
it can be said that there is more freedom of action and expression in this
relationship than between husband and wife, and brother and sister.

Brothers-in-law must always defend each other when they are

together, but later on the obligation falls on lineage members, particularly father and brothers. The relationship between a man and his affines may be strengthened through *compadrazgo* (see below); a man's *compadre* is his son's godfather. Sometimes a man is not on good terms with his own lineage and family of orientation, and he may resort to *compadrazgos* to strengthen his relationships with his wife's family in which he will find help and co-operation. So when he has children he decides that his wife's brothers will be their godfathers.

As I have said before, economic co-operation in everyday life takes place among family relatives. It is common for two or more brothers and/or brothers-in-law to work together and this is especially found, in San Roque, among elders who deal in first and second-hand goods and sometimes act as intermediaries for other traders. In general these occupations call for a considerable amount of money to buy goods wholesale for resale. The situation is different for younger men who usually have jobs as manual workers, either temporarily or permanently. In this case they may help brothers or affines to find jobs in the same factory. In La Alegría, the situation is rather different. Only a few young men have jobs and that is in building. Many men are watch and cloth sellers; but nowadays ready made clothes are cheaper than buying the material, so dealers in cloth combine it with other occupations and go to small villages in Castille where there are no big stores. Some young men are learning new crafts, tapestry making and carpentry in the centre of Patronage of Worker's Promotion, organized by the Ministry of Labour. There is one other occupation which is highly valued among Gypsies: "to be an artist", that is to be a flamenco singer, a dancer or a guitarist. Artists usually continue living with their families or near them, and it is very common to find a singer whose guitarist and *palmeadores* (clappers) are family and lineage relatives. Spanish public opinion sympathizes with these artists and considers them to be different from and better than other Gypsies.[6]

Finally, something must be said about the institution of *compadrazgo*: it is a quasi-kinship relationship which is established through the rite of baptism between the parents of the child and the godparents of the child, who are usually a married couple. A Gypsy man, who is going to be a father, looks for his *compadre* among his kin and affines (especially brothers-in-law) and also among his friends. If the man chosen as a future *compadre* agrees, then both men "give their word to each other", i.e., they promise each other that the chosen man will baptize the child; baptism is not always a Roman Catholic rite. "The giving of the word"

---

6. See Pitt-Rivers (1954). *The People of the Sierra.*

may take place long before the child is expected and even before *compadres* are married: friendship, gratitude and complicity may all be reasons for this contract between two men. The baptism ceremony cannot take place until the two meet again after the birth of the child; when the people were more nomadic than now it might be months before it could be performed. *Compadre* is a term of address and reference for a man in a *compadrazgo* relationship. A man is godfather also to the child's mother. *Comadre* is the relation between the godchild's mother and the godmother; and the woman is also *comadre* to the child's father.

The *compadrazgo* relationship calls for the showing of mutual concern and respect. *Compadres* and *comadres* who are not members of the nuclear family use the forms of *usted* ("you") as soon as the baptism ceremony is performed. There is some flexibility in this, but I have often met two *compadres* who were father's brother's son to each other and who used *usted* to talk to each other. Sometimes this respectful treatment is only used when people whom the *compadre* does not know are present; in intimacy they may use *tu* (thou) in some cases. A person has to assist his *compadre* and *comadre* whenever they ask for help; they give hospitality to one another; when a *compadre* enters the house, the owner will attend to him before anybody else except elders of prestige. Another rule of etiquette between *compadres* is to ask permission to drink or eat. Thus before drinking it is traditional to say "with my *compadre's* permission", though this is less common nowadays. People linked by the *compadrazgo* relationship must never quarrel. Finally, in popular opinion, though no longer in canon law, it is considered among *payos* to create an incest taboo. Among Gypsies there is no incest taboo, but it would be rare to find such a marriage for it implies a considerable difference in age between groom and bride, and this is something which Gypsies do not like.

THE GYPSY CODE OF LAW AND MORALITY

In the section on lineage organization I have already discussed briefly offences, which are considered heinous by the Gypsies, and the responsibility of certain kin to exact vengeance. Here I shall deal with Gypsy attitudes to Spanish law and their own code of morality, before describing more fully leadership and methods of settling disputes.

The most frequent crimes committed against Spanish law are theft and fraud. For them, there is nothing wrong in taking fruits from the fields, hens or even a pig if this is to provide their children and themselves with food, as long as they do not hurt the person from whom they steal. They also steal metal scrap to sell, rods to make sticks, heath to make brooms, and material to make baskets without any notion of wrong doing. Swindling is more frequent, and is considered a means of earning a living; it proves to them the stupidity of the person swindled. These two offences are usually committed against *payo* people. Fortune-telling is, in most cases, a form of swindling and is done by women. It is contrary to Spanish law, but officials turn a blind eye to it. There are many forms of fraud and they frequently involve selling goods in short measure; Gypsy horse-dealers are notorious for their skill in hiding the defect of the animals they sell.

These activities of the Gypsies have two main implications. On the one hand, they increase the need of maintaining the *payos'* ignorance of their way of life and, in many cases, of the Gypsies' identities. On the other hand, there are instances in which some Gypsies denounce the behaviour of their fellow Gypsies to the *payos* to justify their own attitudes. For instance, a Gypsy in Madrid called Emilio had quarrelled with another Gypsy man. Emilio and his relatives expelled the other Gypsy and his extended family from their ward. The *payos* from the Gypsy Association of Madrid asked Emilio for an explanation of his behaviour. He said that the expelled Gypsy had stolen some scrap metal from some *payos*. In fact, for Gypsies there is nothing wrong in this kind of theft, and the real reasons for the expulsion were other than theft. But Emilio, like every Gypsy, knows that theft is prohibited by Spanish law, and he used *payo* law to justify his behaviour which was in fact based on Gypsy law.

There are many reasons for the Gypsies and *payo* authorities to come into conflict. One reason is that many Gypsy women sell goods without a document called a *patente de ventas*, which entitles a person to sell in certain places in the municipalities. The municipal governments of Madrid and Barcelona wish to reduce as much as possible selling in the streets and permits are extremely difficult to obtain. Offenders are punished by a fine. Again, Gypsies in La Alegría are permitted to light fires in their streets because these are almost isolated and surrounded by clear ground. But San Roque is an urban area which is surrounded by blocks of flats, and the police prosecute severely the lighting of fires in the streets.

We have already said that Gypsies often do not possess the documents which the Spanish state requires from all citizens, i.e., a National Identity Card and, in the case of men, also a Card of Military Service. The Gypsies are not always able to provide the data to obtain the identity card (Civil Register Certificate, place and date of birth, certificate of parents' marriage, etc.); at other times they are not interested in giving the personal data, as, for example, when they are being looked for by the police; on other occasions, they have all their personal documents but do not have jobs, or a permanent job or work contracts. This lack of documents, and the kind of offences committed against Spanish law, make it difficult for the Gypsies to have good relations with the Spanish authorities. The frequency of crimes is a reason for the Gypsies to be specially controlled by the Civil Guard and by the Municipal police. Moreover, in some cases police abuse their powers, and they sometimes have their informants who are Gypsies or, more often, *payos* who live in Gypsy settlements. Informers, *soplons*, are very much despised by the Gypsies but they are naturally feared. They do not get money from the police but they obtain privileges. Needless to say, Gypsies are very careful about what they say in front of an informer, but in some cases informers have been beaten up at night. To be an informer is one of the worst crimes that a Gypsy can commit against Gypsy law.

The existence of an institutionalized way of settling disputes among Gypsies, based on Gypsy law, prevents them from appealing to the police when crimes are committed against them, and secrecy about their own affairs is also another factor in this prevention. In most cases, *payo* authorities do not interfere at all in Gypsy judicial procedures and for the most part they are kept in ignorance of the facts. However, some serious matters, and very specifically murder, are generally known to the police and dealt with by the Spanish authorities. Nevertheless, the Gypsies act at the same time, and the consequence of applying *payo* law may not be in accordance with the consequence of applying Gypsy procedure. For example, a Gypsy killed another Gypsy and was sentenced to death; he subsequently died of poison contained in some food sent to him by other Gypsies while he was in prison. Again, the Gypsies are conscious of the power of the *payo* authorities and the difficulties they have to go through with Gypsy law when *payo* authorities interfere. Thus, there are cases in which a Gypsy elder commits a crime; the elders of the lineage may decide that, if the worst happens and the police discover the crime, one of the young members of the lineage, usually a son of the elder, will accuse himself and be accused by others of that crime. The elder is more important for the lineage than the young man is. The young man will be visited in prison and given anything that he wants; when he is released from prison he is treated with respect and gains much prestige. However it should be noted that Gypsies not only hide many things from *payos*, but they also hide many things from one another. It is not only that they do not trust Gypsies from other lineages and families; when a Gypsy is out of his ward he sometimes prefers not to know if the Gypsy he meets in a street is a member of a "strong *raza*" or is *a contrario*. I think that in general the need for secrecy is an element which has maintained their cohesion *vis-à-vis* the *payos*, and their marginal position with respect to the way of life of the Spanish people. Even their own language, Caló, is less a tool for communication than a tool to exclude *payos* from Gypsy affairs. Among themselves they speak Spanish.

The illegal activities of Gypsies in many cases, their rules of secrecy, together with the means used by the police and an occasional abuse of their power, become a vicious circle. Gypsies and *payo* authorities are not able to understand one another and they see one another through stereotypes which lead to inexact opinions and judgements in the majority of cases. This vicious circle is sometimes broken by what in Spanish is called *enchufe*. This word has two meanings: one is "to plug"; the other is "to exert influence". Thus in the second meaning an office obtained through nepotism is an *enchufe*.

The *payos* are often useful in acting as a liaison between the Gypsies and the Spanish authorities. Thus a Gypsy may ask a school teacher to speak for him to a National Health Officer. In this case the Gypsy only asks the *payo* because of his ability to communicate better than he can and his better knowledge of the bureaucratic machine. But, in fact, the school teacher also uses some aspects of his personality which are favourable to the Gypsy's cause: his higher class, status and more prestige. Bishops, priests and Church institutions have been the Gypsies' *enchufe* in relation to *payo* authorities. The state has given to the Church part of its responsibilities which the Church has tried to meet by charity institutions such as Caritas. Gypsy assistance and development have been one of these responsibilities, and the Church has, among other means, tried to solve it by the Gypsy Secretariat. Assistance also comes from people and institutions which are either directly or indirectly linked with the Church. In La Alegría, the Fraternity is neither dependent nor maintained economically by the Church: it is an association legally constituted as a Church institution for lay people. The Gypsy Association of Madrid is a civil institution, and is maintained financially by money from the state which is administered by Caritas. Gypsies very frequently resort to all these institutions as *enchufes*: thus to be a member of the Association is a guarantee for a Gypsy in relation to *payo* authorities. And the existence of some services in both wards has been mainly achieved by *payos* who work in these institutions.

As we have seen, the Gypsies' own code of law and morality is in large part circumscribed by relationships among Gypsies. Their law is in most cases based on a principle of objective guilt; the subject aspect of the intention of the person who commits the crime usually has little relevance. It is the wrong itself, independently of the intention to commit the act, that matters. For example, a man in San Roque was killed by accident, run over by a van. The dead man's mother said she would like to kill the driver with her own hands. Her other sons told her that the man was in jail and that was enough. She disagreed, for her son had died "killed by hand", i.e., by another man. In La Alegría, a very young boy was playing and throwing stones; one stone seriously injured the head of another Gypsy child. The father of the young boy, together with his wife and children, had to leave the ward and had to pay the hospital and other expenses. Even two years later, a close relative of the boy who had thrown the stone was forbidden to live in the ward by the father and father's brothers of the injured child. However, it should be noted that in minor offences other things are taken into consideration, such as the reputation of the guilty person, repetition of the offences and the circumstances in which the wrong was committed.

We can differentiate between two types of wrong in Gypsy law: first, those wrongs which have consequences for the culprit's lineage and the injured person's lineage; secondly, wrongs which have implications only for the culprit himself and the injured person's lineage. I shall deal first with the former category. As pointed out previously, murder, bloodshed, a serious beating up and "naming the dead" demand action taken by the lineage to avenge the wrong by killing the culprit or a member of his lineage. Murder and "naming the dead" have to be avenged. Bloodshed and a serious beating up may be avenged, but usually not. What happens is that lineage members of the two parties who are present fight and are quickly separated.

Secondly, there are wrongs which involve the culprit and the injured party and his own lineage; these offences are mainly sexual and are primarily the responsibility of the man because women are considered inferior and, to that extent, less responsible. Rape is the most serious offence that a Gypsy can commit; incest is also a man's responsibility although a woman may be strongly censured. In one case of incest between a man and his daughter, some Gypsies said: "poor girl, he is shameless. Of course, how could she expect her father to do something to her which is wrong?". In La Alegría, there were some cases of incest between a man and his mother-in-law. In one instance people said the woman was shameless, but it was the man's fault because he did not sleep with his wife for fear of having more children.

In adultery a woman has some responsibility and she may be severely punished. The Gypsies' idea of adultery is somewhat different from the Spanish one. The Gypsies prohibit sexual intercourse between a married Gypsy man and a married or unmarried Gypsy woman, and between any

Gypsy woman and any man other than her husband. The main difference between the Spanish concept of adultery and that of the Gypsy is that a Gypsy man, married or unmarried, may have intercourse with any *payo* woman, married or single, and his behaviour is not only accepted but encouraged: it shows the lack of morality of *payo* women, the lack of virility in *payo* men, and the superiority of Gypsies. Consistently with this, adultery committed by a Gypsy woman with a *payo* man is one of the worst crimes which she can commit. It should be noted that Gypsies do not attach much importance to the separation of a married couple (providing there are no young children) and second marriages; but adultery is severely sanctioned. What Gypsies do not accept is for an individual to be living with one person and, at the same time, making love to another. The crime of adultery involves the adulterer and the offended party and his or her lineage. When the woman is the adulteress, her husband with his brothers take action against the adulterers. When a man is the culprit, his wife's relatives, especially her father and brothers take action against him and his lover.

Finally, a man or a woman who abandons children when they are still small is considered a criminal. I think we can regard all these crimes (rape, incest, adultery and abandonment of one's family) as crimes against chastity. It is interesting to note the correspondence between rights or obligations acquired through marriage and wrongs against marriage. Thus marriage creates ties between an individual and his or her in-laws, but not between the two lineages of which the man and his wife are members. These wrongs are thought to be committed not only against the injured individual but also against his or her own family of orientation.

There are wrongs which involve only the individuals who take part in them and do not involve other relatives. Nevertheless, the offences committed by an individual may contribute to create a bad reputation for his or her family. Moreover, an individual dispute may develop into a wrong involving two groups, as when one individual later attacks the other; both lineages are then embroiled in the dispute because fighting has taken place.

Finally, it is clear that Gypsy law and morality and the sanctions applied to support their observance are less strict these days. There is much difference between what Gypsies say should be done and what really happens; even more, young Gypsies do not know clearly what should be done. This is true in both La Alegría and San Roque, but I think this situation is more marked among young Gypsies in San Roque. It is possible that *payo* influence is stronger there. Gypsies live dispersed throughout the ward and are in a minority. They live in blocks of flats and some dealings with their *payo* neighbours, although not desired, are inevitable. Similarly contact occurs in factories and in building jobs. In La Alegría, on the other hand, there are no *payos;* the huts and little houses promote constant contact, especially in the hot weather when people live more outside their homes than within them. Also, occupations of young people are carried on mostly among relatives.[7]

HONOUR AND PRESTIGE

The concept of honour and prestige are intimately related to what Gypsies call in their language, *lachi* or *lache*. It can be translated by "shame", and it means for the Gypsies a feeling of being in a position of humiliation and discredit, or a feeling of timidity. Thus the feeling of *lachi* has much to do with public opinion and in itself implies a proportion between the importance of the *lachi* and the publicity which causes the *lachi*. The difference between honour and prestige is expressed through the feeling of being offended (*offendido*), which defines better the situation of honour than the loss of prestige.

For a person to have prestige he must conform with the norms of behaviour and the fulfilment of his kinship obligations. He may have other things which help to achieve a prestigious position, such as money or "strength", but without this first condition he is not a man who has prestige. To do more than prescribed obligations require gives prestige. Another thing is to be clever in earning money and to be able to maintain one's family well. The man who avoids quarrelling has prestige because this is a generous attitude of benefit to the whole ward. Such a peace-maker may be called on to act as judge and go-between in the quarrels and fights of others.

Apart from generosity in fulfilling kinship obligations, wealth is very important for a person's prestige; this involves indifference in spending money, and in the making of gifts to relatives, *compadres* and sometimes to friends. They may prepare more food than is necessary every day because, as they say, "it would be a shame not to have food ready when a visitor arrives". Display is particularly important in feasts and cere-

---

7. A young Gypsy man from San Roque explained his confusion and that of others in this way: "My father's father was very different from my father, and I expect that my children will be different from me. Everything is changing and nobody is clear about what to do. If my father's father and my father would have told us how to do things, and both of them would have said the same thing, I would know what to do now. Each generation does things differently. Here we do not know what to do. This is the reason why it is very difficult to find a Gypsy, a real Gypsy anywhere." An exaggeration no doubt, but many of the young and indeed the old are perturbed by the changes taking place.

monies, especially during a wedding and in the burial of the dead. People vie with one another in the clothes they wear at a wedding, and men may tear new shirts to show they have more. But while rivalry is displayed among those invited to such an occasion, it is even more marked between lineages in the lengths they will go to provide very expensive gravestones decorated with angels, a cross and flowers, etc.

As I have said before, honour is deeply linked with the offence interpreted as an insult, and not necessarily as a crime. The wrong against a man's honour is an offence which is also extended to the members of his family who consider themselves also to be insulted. There are two types of situations in which Gypsies consider that their honour is damaged. First of all, there are those in which a woman is offended or commits certain offences which stain her family's honour. In general, they may be summarized as those which damage a woman's reputation for chastity. In San Roque a man was worried because his young daughter was not taking any care to protect her chastity. He commented that if she had sexual intercourse he would prefer to see her dead. "It would be too much for us all if she arrives home with a belly grown by an unknown man. What a shame for us!" This, I think, is the difference between honour and prestige. In matters of prestige, the shame is shared by all those who take part in the shameless activity; but this shame does not involve other family members, while, in matters of honour, it does. Thus, a person must not suggest to a girl, if she is already engaged, that certain boys would be good grooms for her. This implies that the person who makes the remark has doubts about the girl's behaviour in matters of chastity, and so it offends her and her family. In one case, a young man who was visiting friends in La Alegría commented: "I do not understand how *Tio* X is respected in this ward. His daughter is a shameless girl and he does not seem to do anything about it." When, on one occasion, the girl escaped from home, the elder who was her father said: "I do not want to know anything else about her. She is not my daughter any more." It seems that the only way of "cleaning" the elder's honour and that of the rest of the family was to reject the girl forever. Equally, adultery committed by a woman damages the honour of her husband, who is entitled to kill her lover to be able "to remain a man". The father and the brothers of the woman are not much involved in this situation of honour, because their responsibility for her chastity has ceased when they gave her to her husband.

Secondly, there are situations in which a man considers himself insulted by another man in such a way as to bring into question his virility. The reaction of the man whose honour has been impugned may be described in the phrase: "Do you think that you are more of a man

than I am?" As in the previous type of offences against honour, the
situation of insult is shared by members of the family, especially the
men. This kind of insult in which the virility of a man is doubted by
another man is called *faltar*; a *falton* is a man who has a reputation of
faltar. It implies a deliberately provocative type of person.

Up to this point the condition of honour among Gypsies is very
similar to that of the Spaniards. But there are special situations in which
Gypsies understand that their honour is injured. For example, to say to a
Gypsy that he is a *chivato* (informer) is an injury. In a way this offence
is similar to that of a man who has to compete with other Gypsy men: he
needs to resort to *payo* strength to compete with other Gypsies. The new
element here is the dichotomy between *payo* and Gypsy: the accusation
implies that the man is not only unable to compete as a man, but also as
a Gypsy.

"To have word" and "to fulfil one's word" means that a promise or a
contract is based exclusively on the man's responsibility; the "word" is
a guarantee because, if the man does not fulfil what he has contracted to
do, he loses his honour. Thus a man who "has word" is a man of
honour. For this reason, a man who has behaved in a way that shows
his honour not to be "cleared" and seems not to care about it is a man
"without a word".

Not to pay debts to Gypsies is considered a serious crime to them, and
also has implications for honour and prestige. Debts among Gypsies are
contracted with an implicit "word or honour", though it is sometimes
made explicit. He loses prestige also because his behaviour involves
lack of generosity, too much concern with accumulating money, or the
lack of it.

I think that for the Gypsies, honour is directly related to virility in its
two main forms: a man's capacity in relation to women, and his capacity
in relation to other men. Thus, the men are ultimately responsible for
the sexual behaviour of the women of the family; women, as we have
seen, are less responsible than men in sexual offences. So rape, adultery
and the provocation of another man have, for a man, something in
common. In my opinion, the offence against honour is, among Gypsies,
above all competence in the field of virility or man's exclusive capacity.
The offence is committed either against the woman (because the man is
responsible in any case) or against the man himself. In any case it
implies provocation and takes several forms, such as the capacity of the
father and brothers of the girl to control her chastity and to defend her
against other men, or the capacity of the woman's husband to satisfy her
in sexual relations and defend her against other men, or the capacity to
compete with other men of courage, or simply with other Gypsy men

and by Gypsy means. For Gypsy men honour is a ritual condition, insofar as it acts in part on a symbolic level: honour equals virility in its physical and social contexts. It can be "injured" by an insult or provocation; it can be "cleaned" by the reaction against the provocation in such a way that the offended man "remains over" the other man, that is, in showing an equal or more virile behaviour than the person who provoked him. Honour is a component of prestige, but a man may have honour without the other components of prestige such as wealth. But a man may have prestige by being "strong" and rich without being especially esteemed. A man who has honour is called by the Gypsies "a man of respect" and a "man of word"; a man with much prestige but without honour may be only a "strong man".

Both honour and prestige are means to achieve power and authority, but as already mentioned, leadership in the lineage will be dealt with only briefly here. A man has authority and is considered an elder when he is about forty years old, and is called *tio* by Gypsies younger than he, irrespective of whether or not he is their uncle. He will also have influence over younger men who do not belong to the same lineage. He has real power if he belongs to a "strong lineage". Sometimes such a lineage abuses its power to such an extent that a "weak" lineage prefers to leave the ward; this is particularly the case in a compact settlement like La Alegría where community life is more intense than in San Roque. An elder can lose his *tio* "title" and the main reasons are: alcoholism and drugs, stealing, swindling, non-payment of debts to other Gypsies, manipulation of other Gypsies to earn money, abandoning children when they are less than fourteen years old, insanity, provocation, and for a wife to have had several lovers. Some elders are called *tio* only when spoken to directly and are referred to by their names or nicknames. Some are so despised that they are not even called by their first names but are referred to as "the old one" or *fulano* (so-and-so).

Nowadays literacy is creating a new field for influence; the few literate Gypsies are able to perform services for illiterate Gypsies who thus become dependent on them. Moreover literacy and the ability to speak Spanish well (rare among Gypsies) are used as a means to create relations with *payos* who work in the Gypsies' development institutions. A literate Gypsy who knows a *payo* priest or social worker may act as a liaison between this person and other gypsies. This is a form of *enchufe*. A Gypsy from San Roque who is a member of the Secretariat of Barcelona and a Gypsy in La Alegría who is a member of the Association for Gypsy Development are able to manipulate their offices in two different ways: they are in a position to grant favours to other Gypsies such as gaining membership in the tapestry cooperative (after two years, nearly all members were relatives of one of the founders, who was vice-president of the Association); secondly, they may acquire privileges or favours from the *payo* authorities and act as guarantors for other Gypsies. Such men, "men who know", i.e. are literate, are not necessarily *tios* or "men of respect".

To conclude, I think that the authority exercised by some *tios* beyond the lineage level is the product of a new situation among Gypsies. The facts of living in permanent settlements and the actions of the *payos* to benefit their development are the two main reasons for the new fields of leadership. On the one hand, by living in permanent settlements members of different lineages are placed in relationships creating bonds of friendship, marriage, common interests, and the interest of all of them over ward matters (schools, problems of urbanization, etc.). On the other hand, the *payos* who work in Institutions dedicated to the welfare of the Gypsies, act in such a way that the plans are for *all* the Gypsies, not for certain lineages or for a certain area of the ward. Thus these *payos* have also contributed to Gypsies having common interests, and an image of themselves as being members of a single community in a way. In La Alegría, the results of these two factors are emphasized because there are only about 90 families, living in a compact settlement, and also because there is only one institution, the Fraternity, acting in the ward. The Association also acts but it is always through the personnel and with the approval of the Fraternity; i.e., the action is unified by a single institution. The Council of the ward and the existence of a common influence in the person of the "Lord Mayor" has, I think, clearly emerged in this new field of relationship among Gypsies.

In San Roque, dispersion, the life and work with *payos*, residence in blocks of flats in which a Gypsy family is sometimes alone among *payos*, and the fact of there being about 2,000 Gypsies make things different. Account must also be taken of the fact that the action of *payos*, who work for the development of the ward, has also been different. Caritas maintained in San Roque a social work service for the whole ward of *payos* and Gypsies, and the Secretariat has social work especially for Gypsies. Apart from this, the Catholic parish and several charity institutions acted in the ward (clubs for young people, charity activities etc.). Some political parties have also worked there. The different institutions and groups of *payos* did not always perform their activities among the same Gypsies; so there is a lack of unity in *payo* supra-organization, and of the activities, ideologies, etc., of the *payos* of the ward. This situation makes more difficult the establishment of extra-kinship ties among Gypsies, and it facilitates the interrelationship between *payos* and Gypsies living in the same ward or in the same employment. This is so, even if Gypsies, especially elders, avoid having much contact with their *payo* neighbours. And it also makes it difficult for the Gypsies there to have an image of themselves as a kind of community or unit. I think that is why there is no council of the Gypsies in the ward, nor a "Lord Mayor" of the Gypsies. There are only several *tios* who act at different levels of relations, but who do not have much cohesion among themselves nor a unique type of influence or authority over all the Gypsies in San Roque.

CHAPTER EIGHT

Ways of Looking at Roms[1]: The Case of Czechoslovakia

Willy Guy

THE IMPORTANCE OF AN HISTORICAL APPROACH

The Relevance of Historical Experience

Class happens when some men, as a result of common experiences (inherited or shared), feel and articulate the identity of their interests as between themselves, and as against other men whose interests are different from and usually opposed to theirs . . . Class-consciousness is the way in which these experiences are handled in cultural terms: embodied in traditions, value-systems, ideas, and institutional forms. (Thompson)[2]

What Thompson writes about class is equally relevant to minority communities if the positions of being a minority and also a dominated stratum or class coincide as they so often do. If anything, historical experience can often play an even more crucial role for such minorities in helping them understand their present situation.

The situation of Roms in what is now Czechoslovakia has long been that of a dominated minority. Being a Rom meant for many centuries seeing the world as hostile; as a place where gaining a livelihood was a precarious business, where you were always liable to be beaten up and

---

1. "Rom" is the name used by these people to refer to themselves. Names like the more familiar "Gypsy", etc. were coined by non-Roms.
2. Thompson, E. P. (1968). *The Making of The English Working Class*, Penguin, Harmondsworth.

driven away, where perhaps you and your family might even be drowned, hanged at the cross-roads or burned alive in your hut. It didn't happen all the time of course, but it had happened in the not too distant past and might happen again—perhaps quite soon—who could know?

Even in "good times", being a Rom meant seeing perhaps half of your children die young, of hunger and disease. To spare a weak child the prolonged agony of an inevitable death, nomadic Roms in Czechoslovakia used to plunge their new-born babies into icy water. If they could survive that, they had a chance on the road.

All this must have given these people a rather special way of looking at the world.

Nomadism and Persecution

When writing about Roms in general, two central problems always arise and are of course, linked—nomadism and persecution.

Despite presenting a wealth of comparative historical data, Jean-Paul Clébert is still able to write that "the Gypsy is primarily and above all else a nomad. His dispersion throughout the world is due less to historical or political necessities than to his own nature".[3]

Where settling has occurred, it is explained as being due to degeneration.

> The sedentary Gypsies are generally "excluded" people, groups or families or couples who have founded a family and who have been banned from the clans or made "marimé", that is, "unclean", because of serious violations of the Tradition.[4]

When you realize that the countries with the largest numbers of Roms are in Eastern Europe and that the majority there are "sedentary" and therefore that Clébert's "groups or families or couples" in fact number hundreds of thousands of people, you begin to feel a little uneasy with this explanation. Was it really like that? Who is excluding who? Perhaps Clébert is more a self-appointed custodian of the "authentic Gypsy culture", as he conceives of it, rather than a chronicler of choices actually made by Roms in concrete historical situations?

In his careful assessment of the problems facing Europe's Roms today, Gratton Puxon writes of anti-Rom prejudice as "a Europe-wide phenomenon which permeates all strata of society, regardless of political, ethical or religious systems".[5] As a way of stressing the extent and continuity of anti-Rom hostility this is excellent, but it also carries the

3. Clébert, J.-P. (1967). *The Gypsies*, p. 246, Penguin, London.
4. Ibid.
5. Puxon, G. (1973). *Rom: Europe's Gypsies*, Minority Rights Group, London.

suggestion that persecution of Roms is somehow undifferentiated and consequently inexplicable in historical terms. If no matter what the conditions, the situation, it was always there, how can you start trying to understand it? And what would be the point anyway, for perhaps it will always be there?

A more fruitful approach to both these problems would seem to be to probe rather the variety of Rom experience in specific historic situations rather than stressing its universal nature. For example: under what conditions did Roms settle? In what circumstances were Roms persecuted in certain ways?

General answers are difficult to provide but even particular answers are not easy to give, largely because of the way in which much previous data has been presented. Writers on history almost invariably, and understandably, ignore Roms. Writers on Roms frequently, and unforgivably, ignored history. They wrote myopically about these people almost as if the Roms were the sole arbiters of their fate whereas, as a small and vulnerable minority, it was far more likely that their history would be more a tale of what was done to them than of what they themselves had done. Even the tale of what was done to them must be seen in a broad context, for most authorities had far more pressing problems to deal with than complaints against a few Roms, so when they did act against the Roms perhaps they were playing a deeper game. The possibility is worth bearing in mind.

In an important sense the study of Roms is worthwhile not so much for its own sake but for what it reveals about the nature of the societies in which they lived and still live.

To take just one example, the Romantic stereotype of the Gypsy, as an exotic and noble primitive, wandering unconstrained as the mood takes him, tells us very little about the ways Roms managed to exist in England during the nineteenth century. Yet it comes as a shock to realize that this stereotype was cherished by members of a class which collectively owed its comfortable existence (including the leisure to fantasize about "Gypsy freedom") to the systematic imposition of long hours of daily, repetitive, soul-destroying factory labour on other human beings. This was not perceived as a contradiction.

Fanon (a black) commented aptly on a comparable romanticizing of blacks:

> To us, the man who adores the Negro is as "sick" as the man who abominates him . . . In the absolute, the black is no more to be loved than the Czech, and truly what is to be done is to set man free.[6]

6. Fanon, F. (1970). *Black Skin White Masks*, Paladin, London.

The Important Case of Czechoslovakia

The territory now known as Czechoslovakia should be significant for those interested in Rom history for at least four main reasons. Firstly it straddles the frontiers of what might be termed the "Western" and "Eastern" areas of Rom development in Europe.

In the Czech lands of Bohemia and Moravia, the development pattern is similar to those of Germany, France and England, where Roms were more usually seen as useless pests by the authorities, who ignored them or legislated savagely to expel them and deter new immigration. In these areas the Roms remained largely nomadic.

In Slovakia however, which until 1918 was part of the Hungarian lands, the pattern resembles those of the Danube lands and the Balkans, where Roms were often seen as useful and from their first appearance were permitted, encouraged and even forced to settle. They were also taxed by local authorities or the state. It is these countries that have the larger Rom populations.

It is not suggested of course that all Roms or all authorities always conformed to these patterns, but that as a model these rough generalizations prove helpful in understanding the varied trends of Rom history in Europe, including developments in particular countries since the Second World War. For this reason a fairly detailed account is given of Rom history in the Czech lands and especially Slovakia, the homeland of virtually all of contemporary Czechoslovakia's adult Roms.

Probably the general differences between "Western" and "Eastern" development are related to more fundamental modes of economic development (capitalist industrialization/feudal ruralism) and related methods of state formation (nation states/multi-national states) but this would need careful demonstration.

Secondly, on this territory were made probably two of the most widespread and systematic attempts to assimilate Roms—by the Habsburg monarchs Maria Theresa and Joseph II in the second half of the eighteenth century, and by the government of socialist Czechoslovakia from 1958 onwards.

Thirdly, we are fortunate in having fairly full documentation of both these attempts as well as having a number of general studies of Rom history in Czechoslovakia. At present the most outstanding work is Emilia Horváthová's excellent and painstaking *Cigáni na Slovensku*,[7] to which the following section is greatly indebted. However, a number

---

7. Horváthová, E., (1964). *Cigáni na Slovensku*, Vydavatel'stvo slovenskej akadémie vied, Bratislava.

of further studies are nearing completion, including one by the Rom historian, Bartolomej Daniel.

Finally, Roms are relatively well-integrated into Czechoslovak society, especially in comparison with the capitalist countries of Western Europe. For those interested in speculating on possible future developments of Rom communities, the situation in Czechoslovakia, where the majority of Roms participate in the labour market and where there is a small but growing Rom intelligentsia who still see themselves as Roms, should prove stimulating.

THE HISTORY OF ROMS ON CZECHOSLOVAK TERRITORY UNTIL 1945

Roms in the Czech lands before 1918

Shortly after the first undisputed reference to Roms in the Czech lands (1399), a large group arrived from the East in 1417 who were later to arouse the attention of Western Europe partly because of their numbers, novelty, and apparent nobility of their leaders, but also since they had been granted impressive letters of safe-conduct. After passing through Bohemia[8] they divided and various sub-groups travelled to North Germany, Bavaria, Rome, Paris and Barcelona. They were magicians, fortune-tellers, horse-dealers and apparently petty-thieves; occupations compatible with, or even requiring, nomadism.

Their obvious difference from Roms previously settled in Eastern Europe has usually prompted the explanation that they were simply a different tribe of Roms. Štampach, a noted Czech Gypsiologist, believed that they had not come from the Balkans but directly from Asia Minor with the Turks. However, a straightforward account of their appearance as the unplanned intrusion of a primitive nomadic tribe practicing their traditional occupations is inadequate, as Horváthová has convincingly argued, because the newcomers seem more, rather than less, sophisticated than most Roms in the Balkans at that time.

It almost appears as if they made a careful market survey before their arrival for they knew Western European languages and soon possessed accurate maps and almanacs indicating fairs (Clébert, op. cit., p. 68) and they included craftsmen who could make seals and write official letters. Even more remarkable was their initial success in obtaining powerful letters from such rulers as the Holy Roman Emperor

8. Hence the French term "bohémien" for Roms.

Sigismund[9] and Pope Martin V by means of an explanation of their origin and nomadism which was not only plausible but even meritorious in terms of current European values; they claimed to be religious penitants.

Poissonier even suggested that the apparent great difference in wealth between Rom leaders and followers was not so much a reflection of internal social divisions but a collective tactic to give these groups a better negotiating position. Although highly speculative this view is partially supported by the fact that in France at least Roms imitated aspects of the beggars' guilds which were in turn a parody of feudal society, having their own courts, kings, social divisions and systems of justice.

Whatever the origin of these Roms it is important to recognize that in any case contemporary conditions in Western Europe probably would not have permitted them to follow the pattern of Roms in Eastern Europe. In particular the more developed craft industries were better organized to resist penetration by intruders. Likewise prospects for settling would have been bleak during a period when hordes of beggars, discharged soldiers and pedlars often wandered the roads.[10]

Although legislation expelling Roms as alleged Turkish spies had been enacted at the end of the fifteenth century in neighbouring German lands, it was not until the mid-sixteenth century that similar measures were taken in the Czech lands, when Roms were accused of aiding the Turks by starting the fires which broke out in Prague in 1541. Official lethargy in implementing such laws is evident from their frequent renewal and despite a not unrealistic fear of hired incendiaries, it is probable that the legislation was intended largely as a sop to public fears, a convenient way of demonstrating that the authorities were taking some positive action against the growing Turkish threat. At times popular feeling must have been extreme, for in 1556 it was necessary to forbid the drowning of Rom women and children; yet during the same period there are records of alms and letters of commendation granted to Roms by town councils. Although some Roms were killed or driven out, others continued to travel the Czech lands supplying their usual services of horse-trading, fortune-telling and the like.

The late seventeenth and early eighteenth century is known as the "Age of Darkness" to the Czechs for the devastation of the Thirty Years War had left the country depopulated, plague-ridden, starving and continually troubled by serf uprisings and robber-bands recruited from discharged soldiers. Meanwhile the Turks (and French) mounted new and more menacing attacks. It was a terrible period for Roms.

9. At Spiš castle in Slovakia.
10. Clébert, op. cit., pp. 63, 134.

Once more the activities of foreign-paid incendiaries, including Roms, in Prague led to the expulsion of Roms, but this time accompanied by mass killings. Whole groups were hanged, shot or drowned and to discourage further immigration scores of Rom bodies hung from trees along frontier roads. Later signs were erected depicting gallows and bearing the inscription: "This is the penalty for Gypsies entering Bohemia"[11] (Šmerglová, pp. 50, 51)[12]. Youths and girls under eighteen were mutilated; in Bohemia the right ear was cut off, in Moravia and Silesia, the left.

This period of savage persecution came to an end some time after the accession of Maria Theresa to the Habsburg throne. Starting in 1761 she and her successor, Joseph II, made a systematic attempt to assimilate all Roms by settling them throughout the Habsburg lands and making serfs of them by prohibiting them from nomadism, horse-dealing, having their own leaders, and even from speaking their own language. Probably the most drastic measure was the forcible removal of children from their parents, fostering them with non-Roms to ensure a Christian upbringing.

Compared with what had gone before, these measures were enlightened, being based on the principle that integration would succeed only by settling, employing and educating the Roms or, as they were officially renamed, *Neubauern* (New farmers) or *Ujmagyar* (New Hungarians). In the Czech lands several colonies were founded to provide adequate accommodation, with apparently little enduring effect although one colony in South Moravia remained until the 1930's. But in any case the total number of Roms involved was relatively small; in Slovakia however the situation was quite different.

The nineteenth century, like the fifteenth, is remarkable for its lack of reports of Roms. Attempts to assimilate them lapsed with Joseph II's death in 1790 and they were left to wander around the rapidly industrializing Czech lands, apparently causing little more than occasional local aggravation.

> Gypsies often visited the villages, the men selling chains, axes and gimlets, the women telling the fortunes of senseless women from cards or palms and casting spells.[13]

In 1887 however, a "modern" policy of official registration and harassment was introduced. Similar measures were adopted by other Western European countries (e.g., Bavaria and France).

---

11. Similar treatment was sometimes given to vagrants. (Horváthová, op. cit., p. 57.)
12. Jamnická-Šmerglová, Z., (1955). *Dějiny našich cikánů*, Orbis, Prague.
13. Drobil, quoted in Horváthová, op. cit., p. 73.

Roms in Slovakia before 1918

Many early Rom immigrants to the Balkans (e.g., Serbia) managed to integrate themselves into the wider society, often forming their own quarters in towns and specializing in a limited number of occupations like other ethnic minorities. The commonest early settlement-pattern in fourteenth and fifteenth century Slovakia however was around feudal castles. There are frequent references to Roms as castle musicians and metal workers but an even more common occupation was that of soldier and Hungarian Kings commented favourably on Rom troops in 1476, 1487, 1492 and 1496.

Not all Roms settled for fifteenth century sources refer to nomadic bands who lived by fortune-telling, magical healing and theft. Social differentiation was therefore extreme among Roms from their first appearance in Slovakia for while some lived the precarious life of robbers in the woods, others sought service and protection with the ruling nobility and were fortunate that conditions permitted their skills to be utilized. However, the isolation of such newly-settled Roms from the Slovak and Hungarian peasantry made them vulnerable to manipulation by their protectors, a situation which feudal lords were not slow to exploit.

In 1514 a major Hungarian peasant uprising was crushed by the Palatine, Ján Zápolský. The peasant leader was gruesomely executed by being seated on a heated iron throne and having a red-hot iron crown placed on his head. These torture implements were forged by a group of Rom smiths.

Zápolský was later (1526) an unsuccessful contender for the throne of Hungary and to revenge himself on the Slovak towns which had supported his opponent, he used Roms to set fire (in 1534) to four important East Slovak towns. Some of the Rom incendiaries were caught and confessed that they had orders to burn a further nine Slovak towns.

Such manipulations of Roms in class struggles must have worsened relations with peasants and burghers, but evidently not to the extent of preventing further settlement during the sixteenth century. Roms were generally granted permission to settle beyond the outskirts of towns and villages, where they often made simple implements for local farmers, weapons for night watchmen etc. Larger scale and more profitable metal-working was monopolized by non-Rom craftsmen.

As in the Czech lands conditions rapidly deteriorated during the seventeenth and early eighteenth centuries as a consequence of the Thirty Years War. There was an influx of vagrants and nomadic Roms fleeing the savage measures of the Czech lands, which in turn provoked retaliatory legislation in Slovakia. Regional authorities passed numerous measures which although referring formally to all Roms, were usually only enforced against "foreign" nomadic groups. The difference between the Czech lands and Slovakia is well illustrated by the signs erected on the borders depicting the execution of Roms. In the Czech lands this fate awaited any Rom who entered the country, while in Slovakia the threat was to "all nomadic Gypsies who did not settle within three weeks of entering Slovakia" (Horváthová, op. cit., p. 113).

This differential treatment of Roms cannot be explained by greater devastation in the Czech lands, for Slovakia too was a battleground in the strange triangular struggle between Turks, Hungarians and Habsburgs, further complicated by peasant uprisings. However an economic explanation is strongly supported by contemporary documents showing the extensive taxation of Roms in the Hungarian lands. The slaughter or expulsion of Roms in Slovakia would have meant a loss of revenue; this deterrent did not apply in the Czech Lands.

The accession of Maria Theresa did not lead to any dramatic change in policy towards Roms in the Hungarian lands, but rather to an intensification of efforts to assimilate them by settling and employing them under an altered administrative structure. In 1758 the Imperial Council made local Diets of gentry responsible for Roms in their area, reserving a co-ordinating function for itself.

In spite of a wealth of statistics, it is difficult to assess the success of the policy for, as J. H. Schwicker demonstrated, Diets deliberately falsified their progress reports in the safe knowledge that the Imperial Council had no way of independently evaluating their work.[14]

In any case they enjoyed considerable autonomy for "Hungary, even in periods of absolutism, was administered by elected committees [Diets] of the country gentry, and these would never operate measures which ran against their privileges."[15]

There is good reason to suppose that the policy was not entirely welcome to the gentry, for although it might appear advantageous to landowners to gain new labour-power and feudal rent, this would only be the case if nomadic Roms could be successfully settled and put to work. The initial prohibitively high costs (new housing and training, as well as regular payments to foster parents of young Rom children) were to be met entirely by the landowner, while the first rewards went to the Imperial coffers in the form of tax. In view of these factors it is likely

14. Schwicker, J. H. (1883). *Die Zigeuner in Ungarn und Siebenburgen*, Vienna, quoted in Horváthová, op. cit.
15. Taylor, A. J. P. (1964). *The Hapsburg Monarchy*, Penguin, London.

that many gentry made a careful assessment of investment prospects before trying to settle groups of nomadic Roms; those who appeared a bad risk were simply moved on, despite Council instructions to admit them to serfs' villages.

Nor is it likely that many Roms were enthusiastic about the policy for while it is probable that some nomads would have welcomed the opportunity to settle (as they had previously), the harsh conditions, such as losing their children, would have been quite unacceptable. In fact Schwickert found statistical evidence of movement of Roms from regions where the policy was more vigorously enforced to those which were more lax. As well as the nomads, however, those Roms already settled opposed the policy since they probably saw any increase of their numbers in a particular place as a threat to their precarious social position and also to their livelihood through increased competition. They occasionally petitioned Diets to move bands of nomadic Roms from the district, usually with justifying accusations of theft.

The simplistic assessment that "Maria Theresa had very good feelings [but] . . . a complete lack of understanding in regard to Gypsies and their way of life"[16] fails to appreciate that many Roms were not at all opposed to settling *per se*, but more importantly overlooks the practical considerations behind the policy. Allowing Maria Theresa her "good feelings", her efforts must also be seen on a different level, as yet another move in the continuous struggle by the Habsburgs to extract money from their wayward Hungarian lands. As an important part of their jealously-guarded autonomy, the gentry paid no direct imperial taxes, although their serfs and the commoners did. To raise money from these lands therefore, Maria Theresa was forced to use a variety of indirect means, including the imposition of heavy taxes on imports to Hungary. To maximize these taxes Hungarian home industry was intentionally neglected.[17]

While the gentry was prepared to sacrifice the economic development of their country to maintain their own privileged position, they actively resisted more direct ways of raising imperial revenues and therefore any failure of the policy towards Roms were probably as much due to administrative sabotage by Diets as to resistance by nomadic Roms.

As in the industrializing Czech lands, the nineteenth century is remarkable for the lack of official attention paid to Roms in Slovakia. The country remained predominantly rural under the control of the gentry, but there was a little industrialization (mainly mining) in the east, although not enough to create much hope of a better life amongst

16. Clébert, op. cit., p. 102.
17. Taylor, op. cit., p. 19.

the Slovak peasantry. "Over half a million Slovaks, nearly one-fourth of the population, emigrated to the United States in the quarter-century preceding the First World War. Others streamed to Canada, South America and Russia".[18]

Meanwhile the numbers of Roms had greatly increased and an 1893 census revealed 36,000 Roms in Slovakia, of whom 2,000 were semi-nomadic and only 600 nomadic (less than 2 per cent). Even though a certain number of nomads must have escaped the census, it is clear that by this time the vast majority of Gypsies were already settled.

Roms in Czechoslovakia 1918–1945

Although Roms were recognized as a nationality in 1921, little was done to alleviate their poverty. This is hardly surprising since Slovakia and Ruthenia (now part of the U.S.S.R.), where most of them lived, were left undeveloped and in general "were regarded more or less like colonies"[19] during the First Czechoslovak Republic (1918–39).

In 1924 a Slovak local authority complained: "The penalty of imprisonment has no effect on them, because imprisonment only improves their living conditions. It often happens that a Gypsy without resources commits a crime only to escape the pangs of hunger."[20]

Yet the situation of many peasants was often little better, especially in Slovakia where some were forced to become itinerant pedlars and craftsmen, often working for food, not cash, and sometimes simply bartering fruit for grain. It was against such itinerants, as well as against nomadic Roms that the 1927 law controlling nomadism was directed. This was based on the old 1887 regulations and required all officially permitted nomads to be registered and carry a nomad's pass, which could be withdrawn at any time. Apparently 36,696 such passes were issued up to 1940[21] although a 1927 census of Roms in Slovakia had shown 60,315 to be settled and 1,877 nomadic.

Some newspapers justified the law as a new and humane approach, but a more reliable picture of the Roms' situation in these times of general unemployment and hunger is given by other contemporary events such as the 1928 Pobedim pogrom where, in reprisal for pilfering crops from the fields, Slovak villagers wounded eighteen and killed six Roms— including two young children. Commenting on this massacre, the

18. Straka, V. (1964). *Czechoslovakia Today*, p. 77, Artia, Prague.
19. Nováček, J. (1968). *Cikáni včera dnes a zítra*, Socialistická akademie, Prague.
20. Horváthová, op. cit., p. 155.
21. Šmerglová, op. cit., p. 65.

influential daily *Slovàk*, wrote "the Pobedim case can be characterised as a citizen's revolt against Gypsy life. In this there are the roots of democracy".

A year later a Rom robber band was accused of murder and cannibalism. The second charge was eventually dropped but not before the press had inflamed public opinion with sensational and inaccurate coverage reminiscent of its role at a 1782 trial where forty Roms were tortured and executed, being accused of identical crimes, before an investigation ordered by Joseph II discovered that all of the supposed victims were still alive.

While there is no evidence to suggest that the hostility against Roms was deliberately fomented by the government, nevertheless there appeared little official resistance to such developments and perhaps even some elements within the government welcomed them to divert some of the acute public bitterness over social and economic conditions. It is important to notice that since 1926 the dominant party in the bourgeois coalition had been the Agrarian Party which eventually took office in 1932. Since this party represented the interests of predominantly landowners and farmers, it was unlikely to have had much sympathy for Roms.

It is a commonplace to point to the manipulation of minorities as scapegoats in times of severe crisis. As might be expected therefore, pogroms against Roms were not limited to Czechoslovakia during this period but occurred also in Austria, France and Germany.[22]

Despite the generally bleak outlook it would be wrong to see the Roms' situation as entirely hopeless during this period for remarkable, if isolated, efforts were made to integrate Roms, especially in the field of education. After 1925 special schools for Roms were established in several towns in Ruthenia and East Slovakia and in 1929 a group of Slovak doctors founded what was later known as the "Society for the Study and Solutions of the Gypsy Problem." As well as concerning itself with health matters, the Society organized theatrical and musical performances by Roms in principal regional theatres in Slovakia and inspired the formation of a flourishing Rom football club which toured abroad.

The events of the Second World War are simple to relate, but less easy to forget for the Roms.

Soon after the start of the war, a register of Roms (1940) showed 60,000 in Slovakia, while only 6,500[23] (9.5 per cent) in the Czech

22. Nováček, op. cit., p. 87.
23. However, a 1939 police report estimates this figure at 13,000. (Kenrick and Puxon, 1972). *The Destiny of Europe's Gypsies*, Heinemann, London.

lands.[24] Although some Roms in the Czech lands managed to escape the register, these figures reflect the overwhelming pre-war concentration of Roms in Slovakia.

Of those 6,000 "Czech" Roms only a few hundred returned from the Nazi concentration camps to which they were sent, while under the puppet Slovak State Roms had been more fortunate. Some men had been sent to labour camps; there had been occasional pogroms, burning Roms alive in their huts and machine-gunning them as they burst out with their clothes aflame; fascist Slovak Hlinka Guards had delighted in beating them up—but there had been no mass extermination. The war had ended too soon for that.

ROM EQUALITY—BY ASSIMILATION OR INTEGRATION

The "Gypsy Problem" and the 1958 Assimilation Campaign

Immediately after the War, began what can only be described as a mass migration as thousands of Roms, often with their families, left their isolated settlements in rural Slovakia for the Czech lands. There they settled mainly in the industrial conurbations of North Moravia and North Bohemia, in the larger towns and in the border areas from which the former inhabitants, Sudeten Germans, had been expelled in 1946. For the first time Roms were participating in the general labour market on a mass scale, usually as unskilled factory or construction workers.

By 1947 of a total Rom population of 101,190, there were 16,752 in the Czech lands. They comprised over 16 per cent, already nearly double the pre-war proportion, although for an obvious reason they were virtually all migrants from Slovakia. It was noted that these new migrants were forming Rom concentrations, or even minor ghettos, in the Czech towns rather than dispersing amongst other non-Roms. Probably this was more the result of Councils' policy in allocating houses than anything else.

Also there was considerable re-migration to home settlements in Slovakia where conditions began to improve dramatically as migrants invested their earnings in new, brick-built family houses.

Meanwhile an estimated 6,000[25] nomadic Olach Roms (who regarded themselves and were regarded by other Roms as ethnically distinct) still travelled the Republic with horses, carts and tents.

The migration was viewed officially with mixed feelings. On the one hand it was acknowledged that it was partially a positive response to

24. Šmerglová, op. cit., p. 80.
25. 1958 estimate.

new opportunities "which they made use of ... by taking regular
employment and settling permanently" [26], but on the other hand there
were fears that concentration of Roms, both in their home settlements
and in towns, would "perpetuate the backward Gypsy way of life."

Eventually it was decided in 1958 to mount a massive national
campaign to raise the socio-economic level of the Roms by assimilating
them into wider Czechoslovak society. To accelerate this process a
policy aim of maximum dispersal was adopted. However, this could
only be achieved by adequate control of migration and for this reason
most major measures thereafter related directly to population movement.

The timing of the campaign can be explained partly by the fact that
the government was previously pre-occupied with more important
problems, partly by the fact that in the late 1950's Czechoslovakia was
preparing for the transition from a People's Republic to a Socialist
Republic (declared in 1960), which entailed, among other things, a
cultural revolution. Yet "we would not be able to talk of achieving a
cultural revolution . . . , if we left the group of our Gypsy citizens with
low cultural and living standards." [27]

To make matters more embarrassing, Roms were becoming increasingly visible largely as a result of migration but also because of their
rapid population growth. In 1966 the first really reliable census of Roms
showed 221,526 (1.55 per cent of the whole population). Another
census in the following year showed an annual increase of Third World
proportions in the Rom population of between 2.6 and 2.8 per cent in
contrast to the overall national rate of 0.4 per cent, itself one of the
lowest rates in the world. Stated another way, in 1967 every eleventh
baby born in Czechoslovakia was a Rom.

The campaign started with "Law 74/1958 on the permanent settlement of nomads". Although this appeared nominally to be aimed at the
6,000 nomadic Olach Roms, a register of nomads compiled in 1959 also
included those non-Olach Roms judged by local authorities to be "semi-
nomads" as well as a few non-Roms. Paragraph one of the law stated
that:

> local authorities shall provide comprehensive assistance to persons
> who lead a nomadic life to enable them to adopt a settled way of life;
> in particular they are obliged to help such persons in finding suitable
> employment and accommodation and by educational means to aim at
> making them orderly working citizens.

26. *Práce mezi cikánským obyvatelstvem*, ÚPV, Prague, 1959. Referred to in future references as "Handbook".
27. Op. cit., p. 5.

This was clearly different from the 1927 law where Roms' livelihoods were often removed at a stroke without any alternative being offered.

Registered "nomads", who numbered between 20,000 and 27,000 had their identity cards stamped and were to be refused employment in any place other than where registered, unless by mutual agreement between local authorities. If they moved without permission therefore, they were liable to up to three years imprisonment as parasites.

The elimination of Olach nomadism appears to have been remarkably effective, although some officials were unprepared for the quick-witted Roms. "What do the comrades from Nitra report?" asked a handbook for local authorities. Nitra reported:

> In solving how to settle nomads, we came up against the question of horses. Horses enabled Gypsies to move easily from place to place. We bought them but soon . . . (the Gypsies) used this money to acquire new horses from agricultural co-operatives that had a surplus as a result of increased mechanisation and were selling them off cheaply. We learnt a lesson from this.[28]

In a few years however, it was obvious that Law 74 was singularly ineffective in controlling the movement of "semi-nomads". This was because employers needing labour usually turned a blind eye to the regulations but more importantly because non-registered Roms migrated too. Local authorities were usually unwilling to use their powers to register them, since this involved supervising them and providing them with jobs and accommodation. It was simpler to ignore them.

Post-war Rom Population Movement: Nomadism or Migration?

"The Gypsy is primarily and above all else a nomad," we are told. Clébert's view appears to have been shared by many Czechoslovak administrators, although since the key terms "nomadic" and "wandering" were used without any precise discussion of their meaning,[29] it is difficult to impute any firm theory underlying their use.

The 1958 classification of Roms into "nomadic", "semi-nomadic" and "sedentary" suggests a historical, evolutionary model—a set of progressive stages through which sections of Rom society passed on their road to "ultimate assimilation". Yet the study of Rom history in Slovakia suggests that many Roms settled as long ago as the fourteenth and fifteenth centuries. In any case, most Roms appear to have been

28. "Handbook", p. 12.

29. Law 74's definition is little help here: "§2. A nomadic life is led by someone who, whether in a group or individually, wanders from place to place and avoids honest work or makes his living in some disreputable way . . ."

settled by the time of Maria Theresa and the 1893 census showed less than two per cent of Slovakia's 36,000 Roms to be in any way nomadic—and this at a time when nearly a quarter of all Slovaks were emigrating to the United States!

Given this historical development it is absurd to need to discuss "Rom nomadism" any further, but official and popular beliefs about Roms as incorrigible nomads linger on, despite historical evidence to the contrary. It is true that after 1965 government and ministry documents replaced the term "nomadic" by "migrating" and one major 1965 Government Committee report clearly recognized Rom population movement as rural to urban migration.[30] However, this frank treatment was exceptional and as recently as 1971 a Federal Ministry of Labour report explained Rom population movement by the "historically-rooted proneness to nomadism in Gypsies."

Local government documents are often little better, although a firm grasp of local history might have been expected. Some list Rom settlements in Slovakia allegedly founded in the 1930's yet which local informants, both Rom and non-Rom, remember as already long-established in the 1890's and which parish records show to be at least 150 years old. There they are in the records; the same Rom family names as nowadays. As for the Roms themselves—you ask them: "When did you first settle here?" Shrugs and puzzled looks. "I don't know—we've always been here."

When—after how many years of being settled—do you cease to be "sedentary" and just become "normal?" If you are a Rom, the answer seems to be—Never!

A leading sociologist of migration wrote:

> A social group at rest, or a social group in motion (e.g., nomads) tends to remain so unless impelled to change; for with any viable pattern of life a value system is developed to support that pattern. To analyse the migration of Gypsies, for example, in terms of push and pull is entirely inadequate—no better, in fact, than to explain modern western migration, as Herbert Spencer did, in terms of "the restlessness inherited from ancestral nomads".[31]

Accepting Petersen's point, if it can be shown that certain Roms have been settled for a long period, the positions are reversed and it is as inadequate to explain their subsequent movement as "ancestral nomadism" as it is to explain anyone else's.

---

30. "The departure of the Rom population to industrial centres is an objective process".
31. Petersen, W. (1970) *In* Jansen, C. (Ed.), *Readings in The Sociology of Migration*, p. 52, Pergamon, Oxford.

In addition to the historical evidence, data from field-work strongly supports the idea that post-war Rom population movement in Czechoslovakia is a fairly typical case of rural-to-urban migration rather than any resurgence of nomadism.

Particularly relevant is the prominent feature of chain migration, although official documents (and popular opinions) sometimes give the impression that Rom population movement is an aimless swirling over the face of Czechoslovakia, where any destination is as good as any other. This is well illustrated in a joke told about Roms.

Gypsy (buying train tickets)	"Two to Bohemia"
Booking Office clerk	"To where?"
Gypsy	"To Bohemia!"
Clerk (now irritated)	"Yes—but to where exactly?"
Gypsy (turning resignedly to wife)	"You see how stupid these Slovaks are—they haven't even heard of Bohemia!"

In a recent study of Rom migrants in a Czech city[32] it was clearly demonstrated that certain areas in East Slovakia were heavily over-represented. Similarly, field-work in Rom settlements in Slovakia revealed that for each village there were only two or three main destination areas and that outmigrants originally migrated with kinsmen and later usually to destinations where kinsmen were already established

In fact there is nothing unique about such migrations and to give one example of this point, much of an account of the migration of Kentucky mountaineers (in no sense nomads) is equally true of Czechoslovak Roms. In both cases there was chain migration of kinsmen and considerable movement between source and destination areas.

> Many . . . families facilitate and encourage migration and provide in crises "havens of safety". Furthermore "branch families" in the new communities provide a socio-psychological "cushion" for the migrant during the transitional phase.[33]

Other comparable factors are that:

(i) The pattern of extended families in the home area is related to the social isolation of these people from wider society.

(ii) Migrants travel direct to industrial centres, avoiding intervening farming areas, and perform unskilled labour.

(iii) Although not a pariah group to the same extent as Roms, Kentucky mountaineers are denigrated as ignorant rural primitives beset with social problems (e.g., drunkenness, illiteracy).

32. Davidová, E. (1970). Cikánské (Romské) etnikum v Ostravě, VÚVA, Prague.
33. Brown, J., et al. (1970) In Jansen, C., (Ed.), Readings in The Sociology of Migration, p. 116, Pergamon, Oxford.

(iv) This continued although lessened social isolation in towns has tended to broaden bonds amongst these migrants, gradually replacing extended family networks by wider regional-based ones.

If this categorization of Rom population movement is correct, the implications are profound, for characteristically the main motive for such migration has been the desire for improved economic and social status. Here emphasis must be placed on the migrants' comprehension of their previous poor conditions, their perception of the possibility of changing them and their desire to better themselves, all concretely expressed in the fact of migration. Petersen explained the puzzling paradox that in certain periods few migrants to the United States came from those European countries where conditions were objectively the worst by stressing that poor conditions, in themselves, are insufficient to trigger-off migration. Also necessary is some improvement in conditions in the source country to awaken hope in the would-be migrant of something better.[34]

As has been indicated, the history of Roms in Slovakia shows them not so much as nomadic tribes fiercely defending their independence and "tradition", as settled immigrants seeking a securer place in wider society. What happened in Czechoslovakia then, to change the objective conditions and to raise the hopes of Roms?

The simple answer is the post-war dominance of the Communist Party. This is not theoretic speculation, it is what many Roms have said—and it makes good sense. In 1927 the Party had opposed the law on nomads and already recruited Rom members during the First Republic. Later Roms fought with Communist partisans and the arrival of the Red Army is still remembered with affection—the open friendliness of the soldiers towards them and especially their children. These things are important—the Slovak Hlinka guards had beaten them. A Rom woman expressed it all charmingly: "In the castle nearby lived a miserly lord who treated Roms badly. So God sent the Russian army to punish him and drive him out. I think he lives in Vienna now with his rich relatives."

The 1944 Košice government programme proclaimed that there would be no more discrimination and while the Roms still preserved their deep suspicion, they felt it was worth taking a chance. When Gottwald (the first Communist president) took power in 1948, the main Rom settlement studied in Slovakia almost emptied as migrating families set off for the Czech lands and a new life.

34. Petersen, W., "Migration" In *International Encyclopedia of The Social Sciences*, ed. Seligman, E., p. 287.

The 1965 "Dispersal and Transfer" Scheme and its Aftermath

In 1965 a new "Dispersal and Transfer" scheme was introduced to speed up the stagnant dispersal of what were termed "undesirable Gypsy concentrations". The aim was to replace the continuing "natural migration" by a system of planned population transfers from Rom settlements in Slovakia to parts of the Czech lands with a low density of Roms, i.e., to spread them as thinly as possible throughout the Republic. To co-ordinate the whole operation and Rom affairs in general, a special Government Committee was established, although it had no powers to control local authorities, only to report to the government on the basis of information supplied to it by local authorities.

Quotas were agreed and transfers began. As a Rom spokesman later expressed it: "They plan how many there should be in each village: horses, cows and Gypsies"[35] In practice the plan proved difficult to operate and ground to a virtual standstill by the end of 1968. In 1966 the transfer plan was 85 per cent fulfilled, in 1967 51 per cent, and in 1958 only 20 per cent. In all only 494 Gypsy families were transferred from Slovakia to the Czech lands in the period 1966–1968. Meanwhile control of natural migration had again proved inadequate for in the same period, 1,096 unplanned family migrations took place. (Czech Ministry of Labour Report, 2nd December, 1969.)

There had been an attempt to modify Law 74 to make unplanned migration virtually illegal but the Parliamentary Committee for Constitutional Law had decided: "the proposed solution of restricting the movement of the Gypsy population in fact limits their freedom of residence and therefore is not in harmony with article 31 of the Constitution."[36]

Despite this hostile ruling, the Government Committee's 1966 "Principles for Organising Dispersal and Transfer" instructed local authorities that "every unplanned, unorganised, unconfirmed transfer of a Gypsy person or family should be considered as undesirable migration of Gypsy persons and consequently refused. The person or county who arranged the transfer should be charged the costs of returning the Gypsy person or family to the original place of residence."[37] Or in other words, if you were a Rom and not among those 494 families transferred as part of planned quotas, you could not move at all between the Czech lands and Slovakia—in theory anyway.

35. Quoted in Hübschmannová, M. (1968). "cikáni = Cikáni?" In Reportérova ročenka, Prague.
36. Quoted in Davidová, op. cit., p. 306.
37. Op. cit., p. 296.

Little more than a year later, the same Government Committee reported critically that "local authorities protect themselves . . . by refusing to register these citizens [i.e., Rom migrants] as permanent residents. However the Home Office directive on law 54/1949 Sb. about population registration specifically states that registration as a permanent resident may not be made dependent on any other conditions, especially accommodation, economic, financial, etc."[38] Yet these local authorities were only following Government Committee instructions in refusing unplanned migrants; the Committee seemed unaware that it was its own "Principles for Organising Dispersal and Transfer" which were in conflict with the Home Office directive.

The collapse of the "Dispersal and Transfer" scheme is difficult to explain—not because of the lack of causes but rather their abundance. However, comparison with the previous Habsburg assimilation attempt is instructive for then, as now, the main opposition probably came not from the Roms but from local authorities.

Many Roms were eager to exchange their overcrowded wooden houses in Slovakia for houses and flats in the Czech lands. Although they wanted to move to an industrial centre where they had kinsmen, and not to some bureaucratically decided agricultural area where they knew no-one, these Rom misgivings were not the determining factor. Crucial to the scheme were the Czech local authorities for they were to provide accommodation for the incoming Roms. Usually sceptical to begin with and soon further discouraged by the cynical way in which some Slovak local authorities unloaded their most troublesome Roms onto them, these authorities began to refuse transfers, pleading lack of adequate accommodation. They often had some justification, for the overall transfer plan had been prepared with little regard for the national building programme, but in any case the Government Committee, like its Habsburg predecessor, did not have the resources to evaluate independently such reports or the power to control the reporting local authorities.

With the ending of transfers in 1968, the Government Committee was disbanded and the whole policy towards Roms reconsidered. As a result permission was given for Roms to form their own socio-cultural associations and organize economic co-operatives. This was a complete reversal of the 1958 position that socio-economic equality could only be achieved by assimilating Roms and instead "recognised Romani national consciousness as a valid motivation for self-help along the new socialist path".[39] For a time Roms were treated virtually as a national

38. Quoted in Davidová, op. cit., p. 295.
39. Puxon, G., op. cit., p. 13.

minority, although never formally recognized as such, but the experiment was short-lived and in April 1973 all Rom mass organizations were dissolved.

Rom Identity and the "Gypsy Way of Life"

From 1958 onwards official documents frequently referred to "the Gypsy way of life" as a mixture of undesirable remnants of previous social orders, including such elements as nomadism, tribalism, animism and blood-feuds. The 1959 handbook for local authorities declared: "Over the majority of our Gypsy citizens yet stretches as a black cloud the burdensome heritage of the past," or more prosaically:

> As a result of oppression and persecution by the ruling classes, Gypsies were stamped with characteristic features of a way of life and psychological nature which are nowadays an anachronism and must be removed by a process of socialist education.

The argument was that the "Gypsy way of life" (embodying traditions, value-systems and attitudes) which had been formed, or rather deformed, by bitter historical experience, had been carried over into a period and form of society where it had no relevance. Resistance to change was perpetuated merely by the fact that Gypsies usually lived with other Gypsies in "undesirable concentrations". The "Gypsy way of life" was no more than a contagious disease and the remedy was isolation from other sufferers.

Looking at Roms in this way, the authorities naturally saw little point in preserving a separate identity for these people. In any case it was felt to be in their own best interests to assimilate for:

> experience shows that all forms, which revive Gypsy national [sic]! consciousness, their own special organisation and autonomy, preserve the present isolation and separation of Gypsies from the remainder of the population, prevent the penetration of everything progressive from our environment to the life of Gypsies and help conserve the old primitive Gypsy way of life with all its bad habits.[40]

This was the rationale behind the dispersal policy. Yet a theoretical justification was also necessary, for what sort of group were these people?

How Roms should be characterized is a basic problem that faces all administrators and researchers concerned with them. The former tend to describe them as a social rather than an ethnic group as this gives them a freer hand with policy—they are less likely to be accused of

40. "Handbook", p. 28.

discrimination.[41] In this they are aided by the theoretical confusion of the latter, especially social anthropologists who have pursued an inconclusive search for definitive objective criteria of the ethnic group. Fredrik Barth has recently attacked this whole approach, arguing that the ascriptive aspect is logically prior to any objective characteristics of the ethnic group which, for him, consists in "a membership which identifies itself, and is identified by others, as constituting a category distinguishable from other categories of the same order."[42]

To some extent the drafting of Law 74 on nomadism could be interpreted as such an administrative attempt to define Czechoslovak Roms (or at least those who migrated) as a social group, for great care was taken to specify a way of life and avoid mentioning the word "Gypsy" (see above). However, the associated Ministry Directives on implementing the law were not so oblique and soon a solution was found to the problem of designating Roms without referring to them directly in the general adoption of the formula "citizen of Gypsy origin", which enshrined the contradiction in the official attitude towards them. While Rom or Gypsy was no longer to exist as a valid identity, nevertheless a series of measures were enacted directed specifically at Roms.

However, little was at stake in conceding Roms ethnic group status, the real problem was whether they could be seen as a national minority, thus qualifying for guaranteed group rights under Marxist–Leninist theory.

Writing of Roms in 1961, a Czech theorist explained that:

> the assimilation of ethnic communities is one of the pre-conditions which hasten the elimination of class society. . . . Marxism still recognises at present the necessary existence of the most developed ethnic units—nations . . . Marxism–Leninism recognises as correct those actions which consciously accelerate the naturally continuing assimilation process.[43]

Sus claimed that since Roms lacked one or more of Stalin's four defining characteristics of a nation—common language, territory, economic life and psychological make-up manifested in a common culture—Roms were not a nationality but only an ethnic group and should therefore be assimilated. In any case, he argued, they were assimilating naturally.

Although claiming the full authority of Marxism–Leninism, Sus did

41. For example, in English law Gypsies are defined as a social group, whereas researchers see them as an ethnic group.

42. Barth, F. (1970). *Ethnic Groups and Boundaries*, George Allen and Unwin, London.

43. Sus, J. (1961). *Cikánská otázka v ČSSR*, p. 98, SNPL, Prague.

not give a single quotation or reference from any of the Marxist–Leninist classics to corroborate his analysis. A more important omission was his failure to point out that Stalin differentiated between nation and national minority, the second being a far more flexible category not requiring all four defining characteristics. Nor did he mention the awkward fact that Roms had long been considered a nationality in the Soviet Union, or consider the arguments of Soviet theorists such as Dzunusov whose position is close to that of Barth.

Not surprisingly some Roms in Czechoslovakia remained unconvinced by Sus-type reasoning.

> If the Gypsies have not been recognised yet as a nationality, the main cause has been fears of the results of granting various rights to the Gypsies as a nationality. Arguments—like the lack of several characteristics (territory, etc.)—which were employed according to the precepts valid until now, were only a means to prevent recognition of the Gypsies as a nationality.[44]

Their membership in Rom associations was in itself a refutation of Sus for these Roms were often officially regarded as "assimilated", the successes of the policy. Yet rather than seek to conceal their origin, they believed that the best way to solve the social problems of Roms was to strengthen the positive aspects of Rom identity by what amounted to a "Black is Beautiful" campaign, led by their own socialist-inspired organizations.

The need for such a campaign may puzzle some people for it is commonly believed that the Rom is unequivocally proud of his identity. In *Stigma*, Goffman accepts that while it is difficult for minorities to maintain positive self-evaluations in the face of denigratory judgements of them by dominant majorities, the Rom might be "protected by identity beliefs of his own, he feels that he is a full-fledged normal human being and that we are the ones who are not quite human".[45]

Field-work amongst Roms in Czechoslovakia does not confirm this; rather one encounters the same deep ambivalence towards their identity that Fanon chronicled for blacks and Sartre for Jews. Roms are at the same time proud *and* ashamed of being Roms. Proud of their music and dancing into which they pour their pain and joy; ashamed of their drinking and fighting—other ways of coping with the same feelings and the situations that arouse them.

Righteously angry at the hostile stereotype others hold of them:

"We're not the only ones who drink! The council chairman used to lie drunk in the street, pissing in his pants."

44. *Programme of the Founding Congress of the Czech Gypsy-Rom Association.* 1969.
45. Goffman, E. (1968). *Stigma*, Penguin, Harmondsworth.

"They say we're always in prison but we read the papers. We see what terrible crimes other people do. Gypsies don't do anything like that."

Unable to resist accepting this stereotype:

"She's so white and beautiful you'd never think she was a Gypsy."

"We're not going to tell lies like Gypsies, are we?"[46]

"I'm not drunk you understand—just in a good mood" (said by a Rom after collapsing into a snowdrift on his way home from a wedding). As Sartre put it:

> They have allowed themselves to be poisoned by the stereotype that others have of them, and they live in fear that their acts will correspond to this stereotype. . . . We may say that their conduct is perpetually overdetermined from the inside.[47]

These ambivalent attitudes of pride and self-hatred are the theme of many of their songs.

> You were born, my brothers,
> Of a black mother.
> What are you ashamed of?
> Perhaps that you're not white?
>
> You play at being gorgios,
> Your own blood isn't good enough.
> Couldn't pride grow then
> In a Gypsy heart?
>
> People don't treat people
> Just by what they're called.
> The blood of blacks and whites
> Is red just the same.[48]

Understanding Rom Social Organization

The Rom population in Czechoslovakia is known to differ from non-Roms in many ways. Some of these differences have been studied in detail (e.g., anthropologically, Štampach, Lesný and Suchý; historically and ethnographically, Horváthová; linguistically, Lípa), but no account has yet given of Rom social organization and its relation to their historical experience on the territory of Czechoslovakia.

This short section is not an account of Rom social organization but an example of the misunderstanding that can occur if Roms are simply

---

46. The colloquial verb "to tell lies" in Slovak is *cigániť* (literally "to Gypsy").
47. Quoted in, Fanon, F. (1970). *Black Skin White Masks*, p. 82, Paladin, London.
48. Quoted in, Hübschmannová, M. (1960). *Cikánské písně*, p. 65, Mladá Fronta, Prague.

seen as a closed community, whose social isolation has led to the pres-
ervation of a static, "traditional" social organization. In fact this is
usually how they have been seen and also how I thought of them when
starting my field-work. The plan was to look first at a Rom community
and see how it functioned as a whole, then look at an associated non-Rom
community and finally ask: what are the relations between the two?
How are they connected?

The first thing to look for was the formal power structure, having
read about Rom chiefs (*Vajda* in Slovak and *čibalo* in Romani). Yet
things didn't seem to work that way at all and questions to Roms met
with puzzled looks. Eventually someone remembered:

> Oh yes, the Slovaks chose a *vajda* during the war. They sat him on a
> ladder, put a red sash around him and we had to carry him round the
> settlement.

Not too promising, but perhaps there would be better luck with
tribalism and blood-feuds. They were there all right!

The main settlement studied in Slovakia was split into two hostile
lineage groups—their houses mostly faced each other across the track
which served as a main street and the Roms talked of "our side" and
"their side". Why was there this hostility?—"We've always hated
each other".

An old Slovak told with relish of an incident soon after the war, when
the balance of power was upset by migration. The lineage temporarily
in the majority attacked their enemies, breaking someone's arm. Immediately a telegram was sent to the Czech lands and next day the trans-
Republic express disgorged returning kinsmen of the defeated lineage—
enough to fill two "war-taxis". The Slovak villagers knew what was
coming but they didn't tell the police—they were looking forward to it.
The battle raged all night and next day ambulances were eventually
sent in to pick up the casualties.

So after reading *Tribes without Leaders* by Middleton and Tait, I
wrote the following:

> Preliminary findings indicate that in formal organisation the Roms
> have something resembling a segmentary political system: that is,
> "lacking ranked and specialised holders of political authority the
> relations of local groups to one another are seen as a balance of
> power maintained by competition between them".[49] This has im-
> portant consequences for understanding certain aspects of Rom
> behaviour, currently defined as social problems. For example, the
> prevalence of fights among Roms could be seen as an integral feature

49. Middleton, J. and Tait, D., *Tribes Without Leaders*, p. 6, Routledge and Kegan Paul,
London.

of social systems where violence is a form of self-help and indeed may be "the recognized means of maintaining law in default of a superior judicial authority".[50] Although fighting is often between individuals, it appears from local accounts that conflicts can often escalate into group warfare, where the original participants can call on kinsmen to support them. Detailed study of such conflicts should provide revealing evidence of Rom social organisation.

All that was needed to complete the picture was a leopard-skin chief.

Yet despite the similarities between Rom social organization and leaderless political systems, the crucial point was that the studies in Africa had been made of "indigenous systems, unaffected by European contact".[51] Roms however have never been known as anything other than a pariah minority, so perhaps this should be the starting-point, not something to be considered later. As Mick Lineton put it, writing of Travellers:

> "Being a Traveller" does not consist simply in having been brought up and living among Travellers, but also in a relationship to settled people. . . . An approach which began with an ethnography of Travellers as a minority group and then related the internal workings and conceptions of the minority group to the outside world would miss the way in which those very "internal" workings and conceptions and the "outside" were part of a *single* situation, interpenetrating in many ways, as mutual reactions, reflections and relationships. Yet many studies of minority groups do start as if they were dealing with cultural or social entities instead of relationships, and while there may be areas in which the context of the total situation can be ignored or added afterwards . . . the situation of Travellers is [not] one that permits such an approach without loss and distortion. We would therefore shift the focus from the minority as such to the point of articulation between the minority and others.

Looking at things from this vantage point, it is clear that these initial explanations artificially limited the total situation of the Roms as they perceived it. So what about chiefs, tribalism and feuds, bearing in mind the Roms' actual historical experience in Slovakia as a dominated minority?

Horváthová suggests that while an elected *vajda* was important among nomadic Roms, this institution took a changed form among settled Roms. "The vajda of a Gypsy settlement . . . was above all an assistant to the village authorities in matters of local Gypsies".[52] The non-Roms needed someone through whom to exercise control.

50. Op. cit., pp. 20–21.
51. Op. cit., p. 1.
52. Horváthová, E., op. cit., p. 239.

Tribalism must be discussed on two levels. Ethnographically Czecho-slovak Roms are usually divided into four groups (*Slovak* (Slovak),[53] Olach (nomadic), Sinti (German) and Hungarian), each having its own dialect of Romani.[54] While these groups see themselves as distinct this differentiation seems closely linked to the various non-Rom majority groups amongst whom they lived. This is true of other countries, e.g., Britain.

"Tribal" settlements in Slovakia, where perhaps 300 Roms share a handful of family names, are far more obviously the direct product of their historical situation rather than an age-old Rom tradition. A 1781 census in the region studied, showed only one or two Rom families settled near each Slovak village, the men generally working as smiths, the women and children as servants. As described in the historical section above, both Roms and non-Roms would have usually dis-couraged any influx of new Rom families, and so numbers grew by natural population alone to present levels. It is ironic that these artifici-ally highly immobile communities should later have been characterized as inherently nomadic.

Even today in Slovakia the situation has similarities to that of Maria Theresa's time. For example, it is extremely difficult for a Rom to move from one settlement to another unless by marriage, and the reasons are more or less the same.

> *Rural Council Official*: "There are lots of empty Gypsy houses here but if we were to start accepting Gypsies that aren't ours, we'd soon be swamped."
> *A Rom*: "We don't want any 'foreign' Gypsies here, it would only make things worse. It's better when there are less of us."

The Slovak villagers don't want too many Roms (a painful fact of which the Roms are well aware), although some are useful for odd jobs —shovelling coal or house-cleaning. Patron–client relationships still exist as they did formerly, although progressively weakening as the continuing industrialization of Slovakia makes alternative employment available, especially for Rom women.

Feuds possibly arose from competition between families for the desperately scarce resources doled out by their employers. The "colonial" experience of the Roms in Slovakia however, suggests that such conflicts should not be interpreted as an institutionalized "means of maintaining law" but as expressions of frustration in an unbearable

---

53. The vast majority and the subject of this essay.
54. Davidová, E. (1970). "The Gypsies in Czechoslovakia", *Journal of The Gypsy Lore Society*, Vol. XLIX, Parts 3–4.

yet insoluble situation. "In a colonial society all violence is turned inward; the natives kill each other rather than the settlers".[55]

This approach is also relevant to contemporary disputes where previous direct exploitation has been replaced by subtler forms of discrimination, justified by hostile stereotyping. Roms often see this quite clearly. They don't need to read sociology books to understand how stereotyping works; they have more direct ways of learning.

> *Rom member of Rural Council*: I've been round the village making a register (of cattle, etc.,) and some of those outlying Slovak cabins— you should have smelt them! But the whites keep quiet about their own bad examples—yet if any Gypsy is dirty, they point to him and say to us: "That's what you're like, you Gypsies!"

Understanding doesn't seem to help much though; not if you can't do anything effective to change things. So what you do is silly things, despairing things—and the whites laugh at you all the more. The same man took part in a Rom petition to demand the removal from the settlement of the three families the Roms were most ashamed of. It was senseless of course; who else would have them? The outcome was predictable— a fight—two Roms got six months in jail and the families still live in the same settlement. And the stereotype was confirmed once more.

While this approach sees the "Gypsy way of life" as a product of their past experience, it also throws some doubt on the claim that in a socialist society like Czechoslovakia this way of life is nowadays entirely an anachronism.

In 1958 there were predictions of a speedy assimilation of Roms but when these hopes were disappointed the "Gypsy problem" was reported to need several generations for its solution. The slow rate of progress was attributed simply to a cultural time-lag, an undynamic view of how traditions, value-systems, etc., are transmitted. However, as with class-consciousness, young people do not automatically adopt patterns simply because they are their parents', but also because they find the patterns of their parents relevant to their own experience, they realize their own situation is comparable to that of their parents.

The possibility must therefore be faced that within the socialist framework, which undoubtedly offers better opportunities for Rom integration than have ever been known, there nevertheless may be features which serve to perpetuate the Roms' deep-rooted hostility towards and suspicion and fear of non-Roms.

On a local level Roms sometimes encountered severe difficulties in trying to realize their ambitions to buy flats in town or build new family houses, as Sus frankly admitted.

55. Geismar, P. (1971). *Fanon*, p. 191, The Dial Press, New York.

Frequently either entire local authorities or their individual members . . . try to prevent Gypsy families from moving into empty flats amongst non-Gypsies. By means of bureaucratic methods they make it difficult for Gypsies to build a family house outside of the Gypsy settlement . . . and often make it impossible for them to obtain a building plot.[56]

Although many complaints were made of such flagrant violations of the official policy, little was done to punish offenders.

More seriously, despite the good intentions of its formulators, certain aspects of the 1958 policy were unwittingly discriminatory. While Roms welcomed the possibility of better houses, they resented the restrictions on their movements. When a recent national census of the whole population was made, the immediate assumption of the Roms in the settlement studied was that it was another "nomads' register" aimed at controlling them. As the Gypsy-Rom Associations pointed out, decisions were made about Roms but never by them.

Similarly the outright rejection of Rom identity as completely worthless can have done little to help these people to resolve their identity crisis, but served to undermine further their self-respect.

The situation in Czechoslovakia today is consequently a paradox. In some important respect the aim of socio-economic equality has almost been achieved. In 1970 the male employment rate for Roms in the Czech lands equalled the national rate and since, as heavy manual workers in a socialist state their wages are generally above-average, a recent study showed them to be one of the wealthier ethnic groups in Czechoslovakia.[57] Yet at the same time their rate of criminal convictions was four times the national average [1967 figures] and their alcoholism was comparable.

Roms still sing about their experiences—new songs as well as traditional ones—migrant and prison blues to comfort themselves, not for customers. Perhaps they say more than statistics.

> I don't beg for bread
> Even though I'm hungry.
> Just give the Gypsy
> A little respect.[58]

56. Sus, J., op. cit., p. 111.
57. Machonin, P., et al. (1969). Československá společnost, p. 537, Epocha, Bratislava.
58. Quoted in, Hübschmannová, M. (1960). Cikánské písně, Mladá fronta, Prague.

CHAPTER NINE

Irish Travelling People

Bettina Barnes

When we speak of Irish Travellers, we are referring to a social minority of over 1,036 families (*June 1961 Census*), consisting of approximately 5,800 people. Today, it is estimated the latter figure would have doubled. The "official" definition describes Travellers, or "itinerants", as social reformers would call them, as those wandering from place to place with no fixed abode but excluding travelling people.[1] In this essay, the term "Traveller" will be used throughout as it has less derogatory status than "Tinker". Membership within the travelling group is determined by strict rules and certainly members count on having one or both parents of traveller origin who "bred, bore and reared them on the road". Since, in recent times, travellers have begun to settle down, this distinction may have lost relevance, but, in fact, the persistence of an endogamous marriage pattern continues to define membership and reinforces a system of strong family alliances. Among the number of families mentioned above, only forty share surnames. Outsiders in the settled community are referred to as "quality folk", "gentry", or "countrymen", even if they come into the Travellers' circle through marriage. There is usually one such marriage in every parish, although the outsider spouse will not be considered a full member of either the the settled or the rural community.

The distinction between Travellers and Romanies appears when we explore the various theories of origin. Whilst it has been fairly well

---

1. Commission on Itineracy, *Report of the Commission*, Dublin, Ireland, The Stationery Office, August, 1963, p. 12.

established that Gypsies hail from India, Irish Travellers are thought to be of strictly Celtic origin. Unlike the Gypsies who spread over rather a wide area, Irish Travellers are limited to the British Isles and America.[2] In addition, Gypsies speak Romany and Irish Travellers Shelte, a language of Celtic origin. The greatest difficulty lies in trying to place Travellers in a credible historical context. Eoin MacNeill[3] suggests that Travellers are descendants of the *semonrige* (rivet-makers), members of a pre-Christian minority caste, who, while their service was unquestionably valuable to ancient warriors, were later relegated to inferior status by invading Gaels. The advantage of this theory is two-fold. First, it helps to explain the present prejudice of settled rural people to the Travellers, and second, it gives historical continuity to the existence up to almost a decade ago of the rural caste-like system of crafts in Ireland. Since the origin of Celts, however, is a difficult problem involving many ethnic groups such as Firbolgs, Danaans, Sythians, we are actually no nearer to solving the problem of the origin of Travellers.

Modern scholars have suggested that Travellers are descendants of the dispossessed of the Famine, of the evictions, or of the vestiges of defeated armies of the Battles of Antrim and of the Boyne. This type of explanation links the Traveller with MacNeill's conjecture concerning *semonrige*, but the pride with which Travellers refer to participation in the Boer War, or the World Wars, is scarcely evidence to bear out one theory of origin over another.

The "displaced lord" theory is alluded to by historians as well as by Travellers, some of whom refer to themselves as "knights of the road". It is more likely, though, that the medieval practice of vassals adopting the name of their lord, would produce the large number of "genteel" surnames the Travellers claim today: for example, Joyce, McDonagh, Sherlock. And if, indeed, the Travellers can claim a connection with such ancient lineages, there still exists the difficulty in explaining the displacement of such names from traditional areas where certain families were known. That is, the counties within which Travellers wander today are not necessarily the ones that originally were associated with their same names.

While Gypsies have a cycle of myths concerning birth, death and creation, the "displaced lord" theory, with all its refinements, is typical of the fantasy of Travellers. It has the advantage of myth, since it gives the Traveller a *raison d'être*, inverts the nature of the relationship to the settled community, and tests the flexibility of the individual powers of the imagination. It is possible, however, that some of the Traveller

2. See *The New York Times*, October 14, 1970. p. 49.
3. MacNeill, Eoin (1968). *Phases of Irish History*, Gill and Son, Dublin and Sydney.

families may have contained a lord or two. For example, the nineteenth-century historian, John O'Donovan, refers to a Captain Hart, the previous owner of many lands, who through misfortune had been reduced to a wandering way of life with a pack of hounds. Certain Traveller informants insisted that they once owned lands stretching from one half of the country to the other, that such and such a castle was once truly theirs and only through a great battle had been wrested from their hands. Others referred to Cromwell's campaign: "He said to Hell or to Connacht and our forefathers said they would think it over." All informants were consistent, however, in failing to refer back to more than five generations, but this may be due to the nature of the extended family system rather than due to a faulty historical memory.

When investigating the nature of Shelte, which is called *minklers thari, ceannt, gammon, Irish, caird,* and a host of other misleading names, we encounter new historical interpretations. Leland became convinced that Shelte was the language of the Picts, inhabitants of beehive-shaped clachauns, or subterranean dwellings. Estyn Evans[4] admits that the clachauns might well have been used as hiding places by outlaws, poteen-makers, and wandering outcasts. Scholars such as Kuno Meyer, Sampson, and MacAllister, all became convinced of the ancient nature of Shelte, and made extensive research into its structure. MacAllister[5] felt that the language was so cleverly constructed it could only have been the work of clerics forced into a nomadic way of life during the dissolution of the monasteries under Henry VIII. These clerics would have joined the existing schools of druidic bards who, after the Christian times, were considered the lowest order among five branches of freemen. That Shelte cannot be spoken continuously without reverting to English, can be explained by the fact that English on its own would have been comprehensible to outsiders, but mixed with other cant words, it provided a good cover and tended to hide the existence of a secret language. When, in 1953, a questionnaire was submitted to inhabitants of rural areas, many settled folk had no idea Shelte existed.[6] Informants among Travellers were very unwilling to "give out" Shelte words saying that it was a sin to "knock the talk" out of a man. Travellers believe this language is inherited alongside the craftsman's ability at tinsmithing. On the other hand, when the researcher used words of Shelte here and there, the Travellers seemed extremely pleased. At

4. Evans, Estyn (1967). *Irish Folk Ways,* Routledge Kegan and Paul, London.
5. MacAllister, Stewart (1937). *The Secret Languages of Ireland,* Cambridge University Press, Cambridge.
6. *Tinkers,* a postal questionnaire submitted by the Irish Folklore Commission, February, 1952.

times they held intellectual discussions on the various shades of meaning applied to certain Shelte words and how meanings might differ from region to region. If Shelte is connected to the craftsman's speech of the Travellers, one would expect there to be some corresponding development among sedentary metal-workers and blacksmiths, but this raises additional questions as to the adaptation of such trades to the road, which we cannot explore here.

Travellers also have a written language called "patrin", which affords them an easy device for communication. Rags, sticks and embers are left in a highly particularized manner so that "readers" will immediately know news concerning the direction a family may have taken on the road, the favourability of locals shown to beggars, the arrival of a colt, the death of kindred. This language of signs however is not particularly distinctive and is shared with other vagrants, wanderers, and Gypsies who also use it in embroidery on cloth and on metal decorations.

Census recordings of 1961 indicated that in the winter, Galway claimed over 800 Travellers, Cork 574, and Mayo 478. Over sixty per cent of Travellers were thought to travel in short circuits involving about two or three counties. Certain areas became associated with particular families. For example, Sherlocks, Donaghues and McDonaghs were known to Clare; Joyces, Wards, Mangans, McDonaghs to Connacht; Donovan and Cashes to Wexford. Indications are that travelling was once done over a far wider circuit even though the means of mobility were limited.

References to the Poor Law Reports (1856) revealed that Travellers used to sleep under haystacks, in disused sheds, and occasionally sympathetic cottage-dwellers would take in whole families even when there was the risk of disease. Asses were brought from Spain in the eighteenth century and during Wellington's campaign, the horse. Subsequent to the Boer War the pony and cart was adapted as a means of conveyance by the travellers, who slept under the carts on mounds of straw. Tents were brought in after the First World War. Travellers said that they borrowed the "way of the tent" from the English Gypsies: Tom McDonagh was the first. With the adoption of the tent and later the caravan, a somewhat conscious imitation of the Gypsies begins which seems rather strange when we consider statements such as "we don't want nothing to do with those pagans" and the fact that intermarriage is supposedly rare between Travellers and Gypsies.

Originally, the salt-box type of caravan was used with metal wheels; gradually, the shift was made to wooden-wheels and to the barrel-shaped caravan. Undoubtedly a study of the modifications in the style of cart, caravan, and horse "tackles" would be of infinite interest to the folklorist and would reveal just how much Travellers were influenced by Gypsies. Here, we have space to describe the tent briefly and to mention that today there is a definite trend towards the adoption of the motor-type caravan in preference to the horse-drawn caravan of the past. This is partly due to the fact that government authorized sites for the settlement of Travellers has provided a means of instant status. Also, the "flash" or "long" Travellers of the wealthier class have adopted the motor-type caravan as it affords greater mobility for the collection of scrap, which is the one occupation which is a stable substitute for the declining tinsmithing trade.

In general, the tent is used for daytime accommodation and the caravan, whenever possible, is kept spotless and used only as sleeping quarters. Few gateleg tents are used, the more usual type being the bow, bender, or humpie tent. This is constructed along a central set of supporting withies which are changed every six months or so and created by steaming continuously over a strong hearth. Tarpaulin or canvas is thrown over the withy frame and rocks thrown around the edge to secure the tent against the wind. Various flaps may be opened in either side whenever necessary and in summer the entire tarpaulin may be thrown back for ventilation. In winter the problem of smoke can be intense, the only refinement being a makeshift stove consisting of an overturned oildrum and stove pipe fitting through a hole in the centre of the roof; an iron stove is almost never used inside the tent and often smoke is left to circulate freely before reaching the top. The hearth will be in the centre of the tent. Stakes are driven into a bit of soft ground and the kettle thrown on to the hook; a set of cast iron pots are seen around the hearth, a set of tin cups, and often a candlestick. (Possessions are limited to a few cooking utensils and the minimum of furniture.) Oil drums are used for seats and occasionally old car springs. Clothes are placed in plastic bags or in hessian sacks with straw and used for mattresses. In the case of large families, additional tents are placed as "spare rooms" on either side of the tent and used for sleeping quarters for the boys and unattached males. Almost every family is proud of the wooden chest used to keep food from rats, of the big stove which will be placed outside the tent to be used as a "cooler" for the milk in summer months, and of the baby carriage used to transport food and clothes to and from town. Beside the radio, the most important single item belongs to the woman of the family, this being the pocket book containing the baptism certificates, the insurance cards, and family photographs, and usually several letters from friends—dictated to someone who

can write—as well as medals from neighbouring convents and monasteries.

The organization of each camp site varies considerably according to
the temporary social climate of the road, and the fluid status of Travellers. Those who choose to remain on the road often camp on sites that
have been traditionally set out by ancestors and dictated by the calendar of
annual fairs, births, deaths, and marriages. These sites are often named
for events that took place nearby, such as the birth of a foal, the death of
a patriarch, the presence of a peculiar-shaped thorn-tree, or the proximity
of a site to a religious pattern (*purdon*), or holy well. Sites will be near
water and usually the practice is to camp in a line of caravans along a
stone wall on a side road or boreen that is not yet tarmaced. Clothes
may often be spread on the trees to "air" and to keep "bogies out of
your hair"; straw may be scattered for hens and cocks. Goats may be
found among trees, pups and dogs nearby, and horses in adjacent fields.
With the introduction of the scrap trade, the neighbouring field will
more often be used as a refuse tip for non-saleable scrap. This will
create problems of rubbish and waste far more acute than the camp site
of traditional times even with its non-existent latrines. There is only
one unvarying pattern in the nature of all these sites and that is that
today most of them are located three miles outside the town centre.
This is due to the fact that one Traveller in County Limerick won her
case in court against the corporation which unsuccessfully tried to have
her evicted from her "cut", "spike" or "halt". Otherwise there is a
large number of authorized sites for the Travellers which have evoked
a sort of military uniformity of standard with only the occasional
provision for horses or for scrap-storage.

The physical appearance of Travellers sets them apart from the
rest of Irish rural folk, particularly the women, who are immediately
noticeable by their stalwart gait and ruddy complexion. Women wear
plaid skirts usually covered by a black muslin embroidered apron. A
number of cardigans are usually covered by a black or plaid shawl
under which provisions and children can be placed. Wellington boots
are worn by all children whenever possible but men and women
prefer leather boots. In urban areas, women are beginning to depart
from traditional dress and wear heels and miniskirts but such costume
is usually covered by a leather coat. This has become adopted to such
an extent that it has become associated with the wealthier Traveller
women. Men are less easily distinguishable from the rest of the
working-class population. They sport the navvy jacket of the Irish
labourer and the paddy's cap, or alternatively the country and western
style of dress that has become associated with the celluloid cowboy hero.

At times, men dress up in suit and tie and go for a drink at the "local" where they will not be identified as Travellers. On many occasions, informants related that they had duped many a poor country girl into believing they were members of the "gentry" and had married. Children are warmly dressed, the only distinguishing feature being that the young boys are often dressed in girls' clothing to protect them from being "carried off".

The kinship structure of the Irish Travellers differs in no way from rural Irish folk except perhaps in the preponderance of first and double cousin marriages. We have noted that among a thousand families are shared out only forty different family surnames. Irish Travellers continue a bilateral patrilineal system under the extensive authority of the local parish priest who is constantly on call to obtain a "letter to separate our blood".

Dispensations are relatively easily obtained and are required for second and even third cousin marriages; evidence shows that dispensations were once also obtained for marriages between uncles and nieces, though at present this type of marriage is rare or non-existent. One interesting aspect of the extended family is that when a marriage takes place, the bride is given equal status with the groom. Her relatives are referred to as "my wife's friends", whereas the groom's relatives will be referred to as "my husband's friends". The Irish term for relatives also brings out the importance of the affinal links. For example, an uncle is referred to as "my father's brother", daughter-in-law is reckoned as "son's wife". Father's father's brother is called grandfather's brother. The importance of extending kinship to siblings of the third cousins to include fourth and fifth cousins, is that it lends the Travellers a great sense of strength should the need arise in faction disputes. In fact peripheral relatives may enjoy the reciprocal relationship within the extended family which normally is counted to third cousin.

There is the mistaken belief that Irish Traveller families comprise clans, but this has proven not to be the case. Limitations are not so strictly defined as the individual cannot expand or contract the number of relatives aside from those in the restricted family of which he is a member. Arensberg describes the Irish extended family in the following manner:

> ... extended families present a picture of a series of interlocking pyramids in which each individual is assigned a definite place, but in which no two individuals (unless siblings) occupy quite the same place. It is a group of kindred reckoning common bilateral descent, and linking as equals all individuals occupying the same step within

that descent to the number of five such as step and including the corresponding group of spouse's kindred.[7]

Since many families share a common patronym, often we encounter Travellers living side by side bearing the same name but who claim they are not of the same family. The distance between them is, in fact, emphasized. On one such occasion, a group of McDonaghs explained their neighbours were not relatives, "They are MacDonaghs but not of the same family, they are not friends". Distant friends will be said to be distant cousins. Whenever the researcher brought a person to meet the Travellers the question was always asked: "is that your cousin?". The predilection of Travellers for marriages between "close friends", as for example between first and second cousins, brings with it a certain flexibility in the extended family, but, while it usually doesn't admit of outsiders, when it does, the consequences of "bad blood" often leads to "spleen" between kindred. Before we investigate this, let us examine two types of marriages that are prevalent today.

Traveller marriages take place at what is considered to be an early age by settled country folk. According to the Commission Report,[8] forty per cent of the girls were under eighteen, seventy-five per cent of the boys under twenty-five. Young girls are under pressure from their parents to marry young, for if they refuse too many partners they run the risk of being called "dirty". Some girls, however, hold out against the wishes of their parents. In instances where it is suspected a girl may be barren, she will not be forced to marry.

Marriages can often be arranged within a matter of hours. One girl had been working in Dublin for two years. Upon receiving a telegram that her mother was ill, she returned home only to find herself married next morning. Informants reported other cases where girls were "kidnapped" by members of the settled community. One such girl was known to the researcher. Unwilling to face what she considered an undesirable union, she prevailed upon a sympathetic member of the parish to get her a ticket to Dublin. When the family discovered she was missing, she was mourned as if dead, and her parents said they would call the police. They never did call the police, and after a week her name was never mentioned again either because it would evoke too much sorrow or because the girl by "opting out" of the family circle was no longer recognized.

7. Arensberg, Conrad, H., and Kimball, Solon, T. (1968). *Family and Community in Ireland*, (8th ed.), p. 90. Harvard University Press, Cambridge, Mass.

8. Commission on Itinerancy, *Report of the Commission*, Dublin, Ireland, The Stationery Office (Government Publications) August, 1963.

The traditional type of marriage will be arranged by a matchmaker, a respected person in the Traveller community. Such a man might often be the bride's uncle, or a man renowned for his ability at fashioning a bargain. Though marriage is essentially a bargain for the perpetuation of close family ties, the dowry does not play an important part in the proceedings. Rather the attributes of the boy and girl are discussed at length. Persons who are called on to represent the prospective couple are called "spree-makers", literally "dowry makers". These are often siblings of the prospective couple who can be trusted to "stand in" for their wishes. The two spree-makers with the matchmaker will talk in some place away from the couple, where the bride cannot hear. I saw one instance where the bride remained inside the tent and could hear all that was taking place, yet, to the outsider, she appeared as if all were proceeding naturally and completely unconcerned about what was taking place just outside the tent. After a lengthy discussion lasting several hours, she was approached by her brother who asked: "Are you quite satisfied with . . . ?". This question was put to her three times and each time the reply was a very soft-spoken "yes" to show that she was not too eager. Afterwards, a meal was prepared by the girl for the company. During the meal her eyes were never directed at her intended for this would also show a lack of modesty. The same girl explained that even once she was married, she must never even "nod" to her husband in town, unless he approached her first.

We have mentioned that dowries do not play a big part in the bargaining process. In the Poor Law Reports[9] there was mentioned the case of a family patriarch who was well able to afford seven horses as a dowry for each of his seven daughters. Today, usually what is involved is no more than a horse and cart and if the bride's family cannot afford it, they can call on others to help. When the match is drawn up and a meal taken, occasionally parents will allow the couple to "walk the field". It is interesting this term is used as the same term is employed among rural farmers, but in a different context. (In that case, it is the girl's father who walks the land of the prospective groom to determine the worth of the dowry which in some way compensates him for the loss of a daughter.)

In urban areas, Traveller courtship patterns are changing. Couples will sneak off to the cinema or to dog races before their parents discover and insist on their marriage. Even in rural areas, the pattern can change. On one occasion the researcher was brought into the role of chaperon.

9. Parliamentary Poor Law Report, *Ninth Annual Report of the Commissioners for Administering the Laws for Relief of the Poor in Ireland* (Poor Law Inquiry Board) (1856). Vol. XXVIII (Jan. 31–July 29), Edward Eyre and Willis Spottiswoode, London.

A young girl said she wished to visit her "brother" in a neighbouring camp and could she be driven there. When she reached the camp she asked her beau to return to her own camp so she could announce to her mother that a marriage must take place. When her mother was asked, she did not seem upset or surprised. She later explained that the match had been drawn up "by letters which brought the lad back from England and it was a good thing too." Informants explained that it was a question of whether a couple were "seen together" but not whether they had pre-marital relations. One couple who participated in a local parish play were forced to get married, for example, because they *had been seen rehearsing* together. *The play* incidentally was on the theme of marriage: J. M. Synge's *The Tinkers Wedding*.

This brings us to another form of marriage. In even the most rigid form of kinship patterns, there is often an "escape chute" for the exception that invariably arises. In the second type of union, the couple "decamp" together and return as married; later, the ceremony is solemnized in church. If the union is looked upon as unfavourable, there may be family ructions, but to "save face" usually the couple will be married in a church. In other cases, the couple will be no longer recognized and they will be treated like the girl who wanted to avoid marriage within the Traveller circle. Unfriendly marriages are often the cause of "spleen" between families. If unions were not solemnized in the church, occasionally Travellers evinced a disdain and referred to such couples as "worse than Tinkers . . . as bad as settled people". In other instances, when Travellers married settled members of the population, whether in church or not, the Travelling family might refer to their son as having married "worse than a family of Tinkers". In rare instances, even in the case where a couple has absconded and intends to present themselves as married to the parents, the parents can refuse. One case revealed that the union was so distasteful to parents of the bride, the father hung himself. Another case was reported where the father of the bride brought to court a man whom he accused of having "kidnapped" his daughter.

Unfortunately, there are no figures comparing the number of traditional marriages performed in church with the "runaway" type of match. Originally, there existed a certain amount of folkloric references to the subject. In order to marry Travellers were said to "jump the budget", the smith's set of tools. Country folk stated that the head of the Travelling family stood between two shafts of the cart and presided over some "pagan" ceremony. Those who made reports to the Poor Law Inquiry Board suggested that Travellers never married in churches; certainly, parish records have failed to turn up evidence of a high incidence of

Traveller marriages, but we cannot discount the fact that Travellers may have lied concerning what they might have considered their "humble" background. At present, it does appear that the number of church weddings performed among Travellers is on the increase. Travellers referred with pride to daughters who dressed in a white dress "like the quality" and whose marriages attracted the attention of local, settled people. The fact that the parish priest, the alderman, solicitor, and even the local sergeant "shook my hand" provided a kind of community sanction for the Travellers. Perhaps, the most important reason behind the increase of church weddings, beside community sanction, is the fact that certificates will be required for the receipt of government benefits. We can associate the number of church weddings with a pattern in which the Traveller seeks to identify himself with a parish church because it affords him a status which sees to the education of the children to catechism stage and includes the rituals which the Traveller looks upon with favour: baptism, communion, churching, last rites, etc. When we examine the attitude of the Travellers towards religion in general, this point will become clearer.

Following the wedding ceremony, couples celebrate in the local parking lot. Here, there will be rounds of drink and much dancing. Again, when locals join in, it often adds to the total impact of the ceremony. During the rounds of drink and general frivolity, the bride may express the wish to escape and may actually try and get one of her sisters to assist her in hiding somewhere. This is to show her "purity" and her unwillingness at being removed from her family if even for a short period. Occasionally, at such festivities the best man will be called to have a wrestle with the groom to prove the latter's virility.

The honeymoon period may often be as brief as a week. This period is followed by the return of the couple to the bride's parents where they often remain for the winter, travelling in summer to "his parents". Residence does not immediately become an "issue" until children are born. During this honeymoon period, the bride may return to her parents encampment and try to persuade them to keep her. Separations continue throughout marriage for short periods, usually involving the bride returning to her parents to beg for their mercy at having got such a "cruel beating man" for her. Again statistics are not available on the number of separations which are long term, but the pattern follows that of the rural Irish with the husband absconding to England for a protracted period on the pretext that work is available there and perhaps never returning except briefly for the wake of one of his own relatives.

The flexibility of the extended family becomes clear when we examine the adaptive patterns that come into play when there are children. Children born out of wedlock, or as products of incestuous unions (of which there is some evidence), are given equal footing with others in the family. They are "assigned" to grandmothers or aunts (usually maternal) who raise them: "this one was a little mistake but she got the baptism the same as any other one of them would do". In the case of children abandoned by a mother, or who have been left with a single parent, they will be on long-term loan to sisters of the mother, or in some cases the grandmother and even in rarer instances the paternal grandmother, or uncle. In the case of parents who agree to separate, girls remain with mothers, elder boys go with fathers. Even in cases where there is nothing "out of order", the eldest married child in a family often takes charge of younger sisters or brothers until they reach the age of puberty when the latter are then returned to their natural parents. The explanation for this may be that parents are ageing and unable to look after them or that the elder married daughters need help with household chores. In many instances, children are shared among families for begging. Such co-operation appears reminiscent of the *meitheal*;[10] similarly, there is a link with the rural tradition in the general *cooring*[11] that takes place when families pool their efforts together to pay tribute to the major scrap-dealer, or otherwise try to extend the credit system to enable a relative to receive bail, or in a dowry.

In early childhood, household chores of the sexes are similar. Young boys and girls participate equally in fetching messages from town, in learning how to hitch up the pony and cart, and both beg for their parents on demand. At puberty, a dramatic change takes place when girls are relegated to chores at the camp site and boys are allowed to go on scrap runs with the men folk. Although the girls will be allowed to beg almost up to the time of marriage, they are expected to adopt a shy demeanour with the boys and to do their bidding at the camp site. They prepare the meals for their parents and try to please their brothers as the latter will often act as interlocutors for the marriage spree. If girls have been "on loan" to elder married sisters, when the time for marriage approaches, they are returned to their parents. The deferential and secondary role the young girl takes on in the family setting changes upon her marriage when she becomes a potential matriarch at the camp site.

In the past, co-operation between the sexes was far greater. The

10. See Arensberg and Kimball, op. cit., pp. 255–256. (*Meitheal* is a group of men banding together in a co-operative task such as at harvest time.)
11. Ibid. (*Cooring* is a type of reciprocal exchange of goods and services.)

woman hawked the tins that her husband made at the encampment. It is only today that the hawking role has assumed greater importance because the men rarely stay at home making tins. Since little time is spent at the camp site, roles of men and women one might imagine have become equalized, but this is scarcely the case. Although boys are welcomed into the family, girls are the main source of income through begging and many Travellers boast that seven daughters are better than seven sons. Often the amounts of government allowance paid for large numbers of children are greater than the steady unemployment benefit, so again the woman has a greater economic sphere. It is left to the male to dominate the woman with occasional shows of brute force and "rough language"; many female informants confided that they could always "hide the money" from the men and "put them out of work". In the case where the male has a regular income obtained from a steady involvement in scrap-dealing, the roles are more or less compartmentalized; men dominate in town in the public eye, and only at home do women achieve a subtle type of psychological superiority based on a close relationship to the children and her disdain for the rough "drinking ways" of the men.

The average number of children born to a family is six or seven. The 1961 census indicated among Travellers infant mortality is extremely high: 113 per thousand which is higher than the rate among the settled folk (60 per thousand of lower income group). Most children are born in hospitals, today over sixty-five per cent. Much folklore exists on the ways a midwife was "kidnapped" so to attend to a birth in time. One such instance revealed how a midwife was driven fifty miles in the blinding rain to a place she knew not where. After she had attended to the birth, it was announced she would be the god-parent and was paid fifty gold sovereigns. A large family is a great source of pride among Travellers and when a couple are first married they are told: "I wish you the wealth of joy" which has come to mean: "May you be very lucky and have many children". Childlessness is a great source of embarrassment to a couple and in such cases the bride will attend many "priests" who will give her cures for barrenness. Orphans are equally pitied.

Before the birth of a child a mother must not weave or attend to heavy chores; usually she will write away to many religious organizations asking for special medals to be sent to assure her "an easy time". She will take special herbs and follow instructions given by the religious who guide her. After the birth of a child, a woman must be "churched" or cleansed, and she must not serve any meals until this time, which is usually a week after birth. It is at such times that the eldest girl in the family will act as a mother to the rest of the family, a role which is commonly assumed even when her mother goes on begging rounds with the younger children.

A typical day involves the family waking up at a late hour around eleven or twelve. The male family head "dresses' the horses and goes into town with the older boys. They may stay in town all day either on a scrap round or at the local pub or just "messing", returning home only occasionally for an afternoon tea of bread and butter. Otherwise, they return home at five and expect a large meal prepared by the women. Families when camped together usually dine in individual tents, but later a kind of community meeting takes place with as many as seventy in one tent recounting the day's adventures, telling stories or singing. During meals, families listen intently to the radio or stare at comic books, but they seldom speak. The day is spent with the eldest daughter in the camp minding the children and playing such games as "drunken tinker", "rip off", when all possessions are strewn about the yard, or "pony and car". Younger children will go with the mother into town to "my women", house-dwellers who have agreed to let her pay a weekly visit to collect clothes and provisions. Similarly, the children will accompany their mother on the round of her "stores" where certain shopkeepers have agreed to give her extensive credit, or to give her extra food. Only at the pub will children be left outside to sit in the van or in the cart usually unattended except by one of the older boys who happens to be in town. On Saturdays the entire family rise early and get "dressed up" for town. In town, Travellers from the surrounding countryside will assemble in individual parking lots which have become "family cuts". Often women sit in a circle with bottles and have a smoke and a chat whilst children are sent into shops and alleys to beg. Stall-holders in the market are approached as well as certain shopkeepers who are known to be sympathetic. The one pub in the town where Travellers are welcome (there is always one such pub in every town) is visited and there news is exchanged, the local publican reads letters, and packages are left to be picked up. Sunday is the day when the entire family are found at home on the camp site. There one meal is taken in the afternoon, often a large stew with cabbage.

Despite initiation into every area of adult life, children are not taught the facts of life. The real knowledge that is acquired from journeys to the pictures must be hidden. Morality is a subject which is sacred: the name of a prostitute is enough to make a child cry or run away in certain settings. Yet, with the birth of an infant son, there will be much joking often of a sexual nature concerning his potential virility. A newly married couple may often be mockingly called the "rollers". But children, though they may use language that might be considered to be vulgar, and are encouraged to put long strings of oaths together as a sign of "virility" and power, must never hint they understand exactly what it is they are saying. One amusing situation occurred when two women were speaking of the more intimate side of their life before a teenage daughter who "pretended not to listen" while in fact she could hear every word.

Infidelity in marriage could lead to *spleen* and it appeared, almost as a stopgap against this, that certain families were fond of "rough-housing". In these sessions, young children took part even though it appeared to be a ritual consisting of mock rape where every available female down to the age of five years was "roughed" up by a male and pretended to scream. Often men boasted among themselves that certain children were more virile than others and compared them to relatives known to have large families. Even though children were often the centre of sexual discussion, their involvement in the rough-house sessions was the one "letting down" of sexual mores, and this of course was only based on fantasy and was a form of entertainment which obviously served some kind of social function whilst relieving social tensions. Problems sometimes arose when wild sessions provoked locals to call the police and the latter could not distinguish between what may have been a row and a friendly "rough house". Similar to the pattern of mock rape, there are also mock sprees where families seemingly appear to indulge in all the preparations for a marriage match, only for it to be called off at the last moment.

Reviewing the ambivalent nature of these rituals, it is not surprising that we find rows and feuds breaking out even among closely-knit families. The pattern that such rows take are traditional. In the past at fairs, Travellers used to engage in mock boxing contests or jousting matches with ash-wands; but apart from this, the individual family feuds seem to be more bitter in nature and based on one event which arises and gains impact outside of time and space. For example, two brothers may not get along and one day they begin insulting one another. They come to blows, uncles join in, sisters, and other relatives. If this happens on the camp site where only a few family members are present, the chances are it will not amount to very much, but if at a wake, a fair, or in town, where there are fourth and fifth cousins to be called in on the spleen, then it will snowball. At times, rural towns have come to a complete standstill when two families engage in a street battle. In these the two families will line up on either side of the street with women and children joining in. One or more on either side will take the lead in bringing the rest to blows. Bottles will be thrown, bricks, anything within reach. At a certain point, one side suggests that the other give in, often a woman will do this and appeal to both sides. The truce is achieved with the swapping of horses, carts, or an agreement to let so and so "try a match" with the family concerned. Police rarely intervene in such battles because they have a superstitious fear of the "row" with the Traveller, or because they believe "it can be settled between themselves and they'll have it all forgotten in a few days".

To return to the more individual type of row. One man procures a Bible and asks someone to swear that so and so is an evil man and not decent to travel the road because he has molested a woman or acted "out of the way". Witnesses once procured, as many as possible, the person making the accusations challenges the accused to produce a similar number of witnesses. The person who wishes to defend such an accusation may hop off in a lorry to a neighbouring camp and fetch in a number of supporters who will vouch for him and swear on the mass book that he is a "decent man". It is important that an individual can count on his relatives not only for marriage ties but to defend "assaults upon his decency".

A man is "big" if he has a large number of relatives. Rows can develop in a variety of ways. A child may accidentally speak to a member of a forbidden family, that is, one which is thought of as a threat to his own; one family may accidentally camp in a "cut" when an alien family is in the area; injury can befall a horse belonging to such a family. Events which bring members of opposing families to blows is often unimportant and forgotten when the row reaches large proportions. What is of interest is that the machinery to deal with spleen, though it often appears to be completely absent, does exist, once the capacity for verbal insult has been exhausted. Brawls and disputes, though often involving physical violence, are taken as instances where the "word can be proven" and the character of a family can be adjusted in a tight stratification system. The intensity of quarrels in no way affects the alacrity with which the particular dispute will be forgotten until the "next time".

Wake games have been the subject of much research. The part Travellers played in these, as well as in the traditional ceremonies involving "straw boys", "wren boys", as well as their part in country patterns and festivals, could form a separate topic for research. Here, I shall give a brief description of wakes and of the burial ceremony.

These do not differ particularly from the traditional rural counterpart except in certain anachronistic aspects: the large number of relatives in attendance, the amount of drink consumed, the stylized manner of keening with writhing gestures, the practice of cutting nails and letting hair fly loose, of cutting hair, of splashing paint on clothes, of smearing ashes over the face. It is sometimes the practice of Travellers to come home from funerals with their clothes torn in shreds and to remain in mourning for a week. When a Traveller dies he is dressed up in his best "rig" or "tackles" and placed on a table in the tent or caravan. If in a caravan, all the doors are left wide open so he can pass notice and heed on all that passes down the "long acre of Widow Green". If in a tent, flaps are thrown back so all can be seen. For a week families parade down the road to pay respects. After a traditional Requiem in church, a large number of vans, caravans, and carts in the cortege may make its way to the family plot which may have been rented at considerable expense from a local farmer. Certain family plots become known as the "tinker's hole", "McDonagh's hole" or "the tankyard". Sometimes Travellers are buried with a favourite horse-whip, bridle, or tinsmith's tools. When a family cannot afford a plot, they bury him by the side of the road and erect a small white cross. The practice of burying the favourite possessions of the Traveller with him is a Gypsy imitation as is the practice of burning the clothes and occasionally the caravan of the deceased. Caravans, in any case, must be sold to a non-Traveller or else malevolent spirits may hover about. Yearly, usually at Easter or Christmas, or the anniversary of the departed, crosses and horseshoe wreaths will be placed on the graves. This again is a great occasion for mourning and heavy drinking.

Concerning funerals, Travellers are innately superstitious and will take three steps backward when seeing an approaching cortege. Also they put the blinds down in the caravan, or will throw down the tent flaps. At times of bereavement, women often take pledges not to visit a church for a certain amount of time, men take the pledge not to drink, and some sort of fasting promise is made in memory of the beloved relative. A child's funeral is an occasion of great sorrow. On one occasion when a Traveller woman was left alone with the child and the kin folk having gone to a fair, local settled townsmen were said to have turned out three hundred strong to pay last respects.

The concern with death as indeed with all the *rites de passage* is characteristic of the Travellers, but emphasis is placed on the "visual" comportment and the external nature of the ceremony, rather than the actual import attached to the religious content. All Irish Travellers are Catholics and see to the education of their children up to primary school age including Catechism and First Communion. The association with a certain church, or personality of a priest leads to certain "personality cults"; certain priests will become renowned for their ability to procure dispensations, to procure alms, to promote peace among disputing factions, or for the way of curing an ailment, or in solving a financial problem. Few Travellers in fact attend Mass regularly, saying that this would be impossible because of children, or because the locals wouldn't sit next to "the likes of us". The Church is a vehicle for interpreting the actions of the Travellers as it provides a link with the settled community; a sympathetic priest may intercede on the Travellers' behalf to let them remain in a certain area. On the other hand, members of the church can be viewed with intense disdain and meanness, become the butt of jokes, and even of obscene humour.

There is a second link with the religious context. This concerns the area of religious patterns (pardons). The identification of Travellers with the Holy Family, with individual saints and with the wandering aspect in particular, is fostered by the attendance at various local religious festivals, for example, the Whitsun Festival at Ballyvourney, County Cork, in honour of Saint Gobnait; Croagh Patrick in County Mayo; the patterns of the seven churches around Athenry, patterns at Clonmacnoise, at Glendalough and at Lough Derg. Often Travellers relate that at such and such a pattern they were nearly raped, or evil nearly befell a member of their family, or refer to the terrible rows which erupted as the result of attendance. Some saints are luckier than others. The identification with Saint Christopher is obvious, and with Saint Clement, and Saint Dunstan. The Travellers believe they were condemned to wander because they forged the fourth nail of the Crucifixion.

Whilst the attendance of large numbers of Travellers at many patterns appears to be religious in nature, it is clear that the exigencies of social function demand occasion where the Travellers can assemble in large numbers: the economic function of these festivals is such that many Travellers sell religious medals and other gew-gaws and gain a good begging pitch. A whole realm of folklore involving the Travellers' involvement in these patterns exists such as the discovery of a coffin with a travelling mother and child beneath one of the sacred springs where water never boils. This, however, appears to be a rationalization of calendar events which have distinct meaning in the context of rural Irish life.

Superstitions shared by the Travellers appear no different from those of the Irish rural folk, except that certain superstitions have been "adapted to the road". For example, asses see ghosts quicker than horses because of the cross on their backs; a Traveller once blinded the devil and on this account will never go to hell; never peg stones at a grey horse or at a crane as they might be the ancestors; a weasel is not lucky; never leave a comb in the road or the banshee will comb her hair with it; the banshee cries two times for Joyces, three times for Mc-Donaghs indicating death is near; Traveller women are so fond of fighting they neither go to Hell nor to Heaven; Travellers are free to take anything that isn't nailed down; you cannot meet a luckier thing than a Traveller with a clean apron hawking tins first thing in the morning.

The area in which the religious aspect assumes the greatest ambivalence is in language. Many have remarked upon Travellers' ability to curse and bless themselves in the same breath: "Bless me Father, for I have sinned . . . Let God strike me dead if I have told a lie . . . I swear by the letters of the Holy Mass Book." Despite the seeming flexibility of the language, a curse showered upon the shoulders of someone is thought to bring that person immediate bad luck. There is an apparent acquiescence to Travellers' power of speech, for, if in no other way, the locals will revere Travellers for their ability to make prayers, curses, and blessings. There was even a court case where a Garda was called upon to weigh the indiscretion of a curse against the strength behind a blessing. The case was decided in favour of the blessing and charges were dropped.

The link between Travellers and settled folk could be said to revolve around occupation. Areas where locals accord the Traveller a status included graves where they might be called upon to recite prayers, at patterns, at wakes, and also at fairs. The role Travellers have traditionally played at fairs is charged with an ambivalence. At fairs, such as those at Ballinasloe, County Galway, at Killorglin, County Kerry, or at the Cahirimee Horse Fair at County Cork, Travellers are either hawkers of wares, managers of certain stalls and booths, or act as "go-between" in bargaining between local buyers and sellers. It was linguistic ability and flair at "painting up" horses, that afforded Travellers a certain status. If good at making the bargain, Travellers expected to get "boot" money, that is, a portion of the money the seller returned to the buyer as "luck money". Otherwise, the farmer might count upon the Traveller as a supplier of cheap livestock; at the same time, he admired his ability to fashion a bargain. Other links with the farmer included the use of Travellers at harvest time for beet-thinning, turnip-picking, and during the potato season. With the introduction of farm machinery, however, the occupational context was reduced. Now with the gradual disappearance of some of the fairs, Travellers are losing status as horse-dealers. Plastic has reduced the need for tin and copperware, and so the value of the Traveller as a hawker again has been undermined. The position of the farmer himself has declined with the refinements of urban living, and a host of crafts which at one time existed side by side with those of the tinsmith and blacksmith and other metal-workers, have similarly declined. Whilst there were recorded 4,000 tinsmiths in an Ordnance Survey in Wolfhaven, County Donegal in 1835, in 1961, the Census recorded only 533 tinsmiths in the entire country.

The relationship between the Traveller and the settled community as evoked by the varying hawking roles could be made the subject of a separate study. Here, in summary, we can say that the subsidiary hawking arts have gradually diminished, leaving the Traveller to adopt new crafts, or other means of earning a living.

A review of the "Economic Classification"[12] will reveal that with the adjustment to new trades and occupations, there has emerged a stratification of the travellers based on three distinct classes. Members of each class can be identified by possessions and occupations, and by the particular Shelte dialect. At the same time, it would be wise to remember that wealth is fluid and a Traveller millionaire might rarely be in possession of all his wealth at one time. Rather it will be "on loan" among the members of other lower classes. In the wealthiest category we find 40–60 families, in the second 200–300, and in the third and fourth categories some 850 families. The third group is composed of those whose travel is confined to a small area. Those in the first two categories, whether possessing motor trailers or horse caravans, travel extensively. The ability to travel is connected with a higher status. Among Travellers of all social categories, an artificial élite is being formed by the creation of caravan sites with a higher standard of living.

Those who find themselves in the higher classes will be scrap dealers, collectors of feathers, antique-dealers, or horse-dealers; only the poorer families consider themselves tinsmiths or small scale scrap-dealers. Achieved stratification of Travellers is brought about by the control of the lower classes by the patriarchs in the élitist scrap-dealing class. The major scrap-dealers often form alliances across traditional family lines based on economics rather than social affiliation, with the result that lower-class families, across the board, are in constant attendance to the "overlords". For example, if money is needed for a wedding, for a wake, for a prison offence, or if horses are needed or caravans, etc., Travellers have a ready source. The economic independence of individual families is completely undermined by control from the top. Since scrap-dealers act as bankers, Travellers have access to an

TABLE 1   Chart showing economic classification

	These groups travel a wide circuit		These groups travel a small circuit	
	(1) Major élite. Motor trailer caravan owners	(2) Horse-drawn caravan owners. Horse dealers	(3a) Have horse-drawn caravans and tents	(3b) Tent-dwellers only
Number of families	40/60 families	300/400 families	350/450 families	300/400 families
Occupation	Dealers in lino, scrap, horses, antiques etc.	Dealers in scrap, horses, etc., some seasonal agricultural work	Small dealers in scrap, includes many tin-smiths. Do harvest work	Small dealers in scrap, mostly unemployed
Level of income	Sometimes includes millionaires. "Flash" travellers do not beg	£10–16 income including social benefits. Women and children beg	£6–10 a week income. Women and children beg	Income of family below subsistence level. Most income derived from begging
Property ownership	Own vans, caravans, horses and lend these out to members of other groups, but camp site does not necessarily distinguish them from those in other groups. Often rent or own houses where they settle for winter	New caravans owned by these sell at between £130–£180 and between £60–£100 secondhand, horses sell £50, asses £15, but much of group's property hired at high rates of interest from those in first group	Horse and caravan are "on loan" from those in (1) or (2)	Own flat cart, pony, or ass, and tent. These are "on loan" from groups (1) or (2)

(Figures quoted from "Economic Classification of Itinerant Families", pp. 79–83 in *The Commission Report*, August, 1963.)

accommodative mechanism which minimizes the necessity for contact with the settled community. In fact, it is only the wealthier travellers who pool scrap from others, and who deliver it to the agent who sells it to a merchant. The decline of the hawker and the small scale crafts has meant the decline of contact of Travellers with the settled community in the occupational context. Research into the position of scrap-dealers and tinsmiths indicated the current mobility of scrap-dealers who control large areas of "scrap" territory and have undermined the ritual patron–client relationship. As a result of long-distance travelling of family heads engaged in this business, wives and children have become isolated social units, promoting the disintegration of traditional kinship ties, contributing to the growth in the divorce rate, the number of abandoned children and a general laxity of kinship ties. The rise of scrap-dealers has ensured the insularity of Travellers as a group, yet has widened the gap between rich and poor and has placed the lower class Travellers into what Lewis has described as the *subculture of poverty*. This is characterized by complete family disorganization, low wages, chronic unemployment, shortage of cash, absence of savings, lack of property ownership.[13] There is further evidence that the patriarchs of families who would have been normally revered for feats of strength, and who relied on ascribed status within the concentric circles of the extended family, have attuned their standards to achieved status demanded by the major scrap-dealers. Some families in Connacht appear to be holding out against the major scrap-dealers and this has resulted in a major power struggle.

Despite the traditional association with craft, Travellers appear to adhere to scrap-dealing, but when an alternative craft scheme was presented to poorer families in Galway in 1969, over thirty families participated and appeared to welcome the change from begging and the former dependence on the wealthier scrap-dealers.

Aside from the occupational context, the relationship of Travellers to the outsider has become increasingly defined by legal machinery. Roads are being tarmaced, land use is becoming more complex and the problem of trespass is more acute. According to the Commission Report in 1963, 239 cases of retaliation by local folk were reported in 39 districts where Travellers were considered to be trespassing. Informants related that frequently they had been run out of their encampment, their tents set on fire, and their women threatened. Perhaps this was an exaggeration; others related that horses were maimed, shots fired, and property seized. It appears that the pattern was to

13. See Oscar Lewis (1968). *La Vida*, p. 51, Panther Modern Society, London.

leave the Travellers in their winter encampments, but in summer to "tidy up" for the tourists. Travellers explained that not all members of the settled society were against them, but certain families who had known their relatives and bore certain grudges for an act of "accidental trespass" that occurred years before. Hence, they tended to view outsiders as purveyors of particularly hostile acts based on an anachronistic appreciation of history, which the latter promulgated through the internecine quarrels with Traveller families. When confronted by people who wish to "move them on", Travellers rarely put up any kind of resistance; however, one instance in Connacht where this did occur brought instant action from a local committee and resulted in the acquisition of authorized camping sites.[14]

As mentioned with regard to family disputes among the Travellers, police rarely intervene. But there has been an increase in contact between Travellers and police due to trespass and begging offences. As most of the laws related to begging, for example, Section 3 of The Vagrancy (Ireland) Act of 1847 has not been amended, Travellers are often able to escape sentences and fines. Informants related with considerable pride how whenever their cases came up, they knew whether or not to plead guilty or not as they knew the various personalities of the judges. If their cases were coming up at an inopportune time, they could "hop it" off to another county thereby escaping sentence. Occasionally, instances were observed where local police had an understanding with locals, that only Travellers not native to the district would be prosecuted and those associated with certain districts as "local characters" would be left to their own devices. In Connacht, the general opinion revealed that most locals feared that if they did not respond to the plea for an act of charity, i.e., giving Travellers alms, some misfortune would befall his family. Accordingly Travellers time begging visits with the birth of a child, the death of a relative, or a marriage engagement.

Settlement in authorized sites does not always give Travellers instant status in the eyes of locals, especially farmers. Once settled in these sites, the Travellers may be more isolated than ever as they have little or no contact with settled folk. Sites are often located in districts which are away from the town centre and on land not used for farming. An interesting development has been that in Connacht, though settlement programmes have moved very quickly, Travellers have been allowed to settle in areas as long as they were unknown previously in a district. This bears out the almost "feuding" pattern of the relationship

14. See *The Connacht Sentinel*, August 26, 1969, leading article.

between certain travelling families with certain groups of locals in given districts.

The education of Traveller children has not become as great an issue as settlement, but the official position infers that settlement must come first, followed by education and work opportunities. Section 58b of The Children's Act of 1908 which requires offenders to be placed in industrial schools has rarely been enforced as it is considered too cruel by authorities to separate children from parents. Travellers often escape sentences by travelling away from an area where cases may be pending.

We have mentioned that most Travellers see that children are given primary schooling to the time of confirmation. Schooling rarely continues to secondary school age because of the insistence on early marriage and the economic needs of the family group. On the other hand, literacy is prized (the 1961 Census showed 783 out of 4,809 claimed literacy) and is important as the Traveller who can read will read out newspaper articles relating to Travellers, reports, comics, and can keep the rest of the family informed. Letters can be dictated to him; he will become a communications centre. Many informants who claimed they could read were only able to write their name and spot certain letters in the newspaper. This is typical surface literacy claimed by the Travellers. Those among them agree a person can read if he is able to obtain a driving licence and to read road signs. Women seem particularly afraid the new generation will become educated and "leave the decent life on the road"; some elder women confided their belief that education would bring down the morals of their children as much as the cinema. Another instance was given where an elder woman was glad her child could read a book "over a hundred years old". Informants related times when they felt a child had "gone bad on them" because he or she was able to read. One woman said her literate child associated with settled children and forgot the ways "she was reared to mind her parents". It is evident that education brings about a gap between the new generation and the older, but the latter often say they want their children to be educated and to settle down and acquire a house but only for the winter months.

There are certain indications that Travellers have learned to pay "lip service" to what they believe the local authorities and committees want. For example, the Census of 1961 showed that 211 out of 238 Travellers indicated they left housing because living indoors brought poor health, or they were unable to find suitable employment, or the rent was too high. One particular problem noted by the researcher was that often a Traveller family would refuse to settle in a house or site because members of "feuding families" were neighbours. The tendency of settled folk to lump the Travellers together as a group to be housed, clothed, and educated *en masse* does promote certain problems, as each extended family group is exceedingly particular about proximity to hostile factions. In urban areas such as Dublin, perhaps the largest number of families has been settled (near a hundred) and with fewer problems, since family disputes tend to flare up in the "closed society" of the rural setting.

Recent application of the subcultural models of Lewis, Miller, and Gans, to the Travellers, resulted in the creation of a new model based on the "compensatory folk culture". The latter 'was described as a means of projecting alternative concerns which when manipulated in the rural setting produced a faulty imitation of some of the lower-class folk idioms, a confusion of hierarchical roles, and a pseudo-functionalism based on the "travelling mystique". The bipolar outlook of the Travellers has been noted by many; psychologists could better interpret the ultimate impact of such dichotomies and a seeming ambivalence towards all facets of life. For example, this is seen in the dependence on films and on mass media versus the dependence on the folk patriarch and the denigratory aspect versus the fictitious mobile status caused by the acquisition of houses and education. Other aspects of the "compensatory folk" included the personal particularized relationship between patron and client versus the impersonal dealings with scrap dealers, the tinsmith as a hero and as a farcical outcast or persecuted "tinker".

Results of research led to the obvious need for an investigation of the rural settled counterpart of lower-class Irish, the methods by which Travellers perpetuate the folk idiom, the probable outcome of education and settlement programmes. Recommendations were made concerning alternative types of education which might be coupled with settlement yet based around craft which would appear to refer to a traditional means of acquiring a livelihood. It is apparent that Travellers have no wish to be absorbed into the parent society and want to maintain a separate identity albeit within the frame of industrial society.[15]

15. See *The New York Times*, September 11, 1972, p. 2.

References

* The author also acknowledges reference to the following works:

Arensberg, Conrad H., and Kimball, Solon T. (1968). *Family and Community in Ireland* (8th edition), Harvard University Press, Cambridge.
Cresswell, Robert (1969). *Une Communauté Rurale d'Irlande* (Travaux et Memoires de l'Institute d'Ethnologie), Vol. LXXIV, Université de Paris, Paris.
Danaher, Kevin (1965). *Irish Country People*, The Mercier Press, Cork.

Leacock, Eleanor Burke (Ed.) (1971). *The Culture of Poverty: A Critique*, Simon and Schuster, New York.

MacRitchie, David (1890). *The Testimony of Tradition*, Kegan Paul Trubner and Company, London.

Rehfisch, F. (1958). *The Tinkers of Perthshire and Aberdeenshire*. Unpublished manuscript in the Library of the School of Scottish Studies, Edinburgh.

Schuster, I. L. (1971). *The Gypsy Caravan in Britain: A Functional Example of its Significance in Traditional Gypsy Society*. Unpublished manuscript in the Library of Dialect and Folk Life Studies, School of English, University of Leeds.

CHAPTER TEN

The Effects of Economic Change on Irish Traveller Sex Roles and Marriage Patterns

George Gmelch

INTRODUCTION

The purpose of this essay is: (1) to examine economic changes which have taken place among Irish Travellers,[1] and (2) to examine some of the effects of these changes on family sex roles and marriage patterns. Field research was carried out from July 1971 to August 1972 in a large Traveller camp, referred to here as Rathfarnham, on the outskirts of Dublin.[2]

Today in Ireland there are approximately 7,800 Travellers or Travelling People (commonly called Tinkers and more recently, Itinerants by the settled community).[3] Like many other European itinerant groups they traditionally followed a nomadic lifestyle similar to Gypsies. But unlike Gypsies who came originally from India, Travellers are indigenous to Ireland. Most Travellers descend from

---

1. An earlier version of this paper was presented at the annual meeting of the *American Anthropological Association* in New Orleans, December, 1973.

2. I wish to thank the Institute of Social and Economic Research of Memorial University of Newfoundland which supported the research on which this paper is based. I also want to thank Patricia McCarthy and Eithne Russell for their assistance and valuable insights.

3. A census conducted by the Department of Local Government recorded 1,302 families amd 7,778 individuals in January 1971. This represents a 15 per cent increase in population over the 1960 census figures.

poor Irish peasants who were driven from their lands by conflict (notably Cromwell's conquest of Ireland in 1652), famine, and personal misfortune. Dispossessed of their property they took to the road where they adopted itinerant trades and begged for a living. After generations of social isolation those who remained on the road developed an ethnic identity separate from the surrounding settled Irish population. Travellers speak a secret argot known as "Gammin" or "Cant" which is unintelligible to the settled community and which is used mainly to disguise what is being said from outsiders.[4] (see also Harper and Hudson, 1973).[5] Travellers are treated as outcasts by settled society and are generally considered dirty, shiftless, and indolent.

TRADITIONAL ECONOMIC AND SOCIAL PATTERNS

Traditionally, the Travellers' economic relationship with the settled community was symbiotic. Travellers performed various jobs and services, notably tinsmithing, horse dealing, peddling, and chimney sweeping. Generally these were jobs settled people either lacked the skills to do or did not wish to do. In exchange for these services, Travellers received their subsistence—food, clothing, and less often, cash. Travellers were strictly a rural people. They travelled regular circuits through the countryside, stopping in each village several times a year. Most travelled on horse-drawn carts or in barrel-top wagons. The poorest walked.[6] They camped on the roadside usually on the outskirts of town. They slept under hedges, their upturned carts, or crude "shelter tents" made of burlap sacks and canvas. They stayed only as long as there was work, from a few days to two weeks. Disliked by settled people because of the damage their horses did to farmers' fields and suspected of petty pilfering of farm produce, they were

---

4. Most Gammin or Cant words descend from an argot called Shelta, which was based on Irish Gaelic. The morphology and syntax of Gammin, however, is English. The structure of Gammin is such that "an eavesdropper does not necessarily become suspicious, because when a conversation in Cant [Gammin] is overheard, it gives the impression of being ordinary English with a few garbled words". Harper, Jared and Hudson, Charles (1971). "Irish Traveller Cant", *Journal of English Linguistics*, **5**, 78–86. All Irish Travellers are able to communicate in Gammin, although the size of the vocabulary is declining with the younger generation.

5. Harper, J. and Hudson, C. (1973). "Irish Traveller Cant in its Social Setting", *Southern Folklore Quarterly*, **37**(2), 101–114.

6. Until the late 1800's most Travellers walked their circuits, transporting their belongings in push-carts or on their backs. Horse or donkey-drawn carts became common in the early 1900's, after some Travellers had been introduced to them while fighting in the Boer War. Barrel-top wagons were introduced by Romany Gypsies after the First World War when many Gypsies fleeing conscription in England came to Ireland. MacGreine, Padraig (1931). "Irish Tinkers or Travellers", *Bealoideas* (Journal of the Folklore Society of Ireland) **3**(2), 171–177.

encouraged to leave the area once their work was completed; if they failed to move on the gardai (police) often forced them out.

The residence and travelling unit usually consisted of several patri-lineally related nuclear families and was typically three generations deep (i.e., consisting of parents, male siblings and their families). Traveller groups, however, were fluid; the composition and size of the group were subject to frequent change. Conflict and disagreement was a common cause for one or more families to leave, at least temporarily. As an economically dependent population, Travellers lived dispersed much of the year. Local groups had to be small since the settled Irish population in any one area could only support a limited number of Travellers. The size of the group usually increased during the winter when Travellers were much less mobile. In winter there were fewer work opportunities (e.g., no demand for work horses, no chimneys to sweep, no farm jobs to assist with) and travelling itself was more of a hardship.

Traveller family organization was strongly patriarchal.[7] Men were authoritarian and wielded considerable power over their wives and families. The ideal of male dominance was accepted by both sexes; men were believed to be superior to women. Wife beating was not un-common. Men made the major decisions affecting the entire family; when and where to travel, what families to travel with, what kind of work the family would engage in, and so forth. The following account typifies the traditional, male dominated conjugal relationship. A Traveller woman who had been beaten by her husband was ordered to appear in court to testify against him; on the witness stand, however, she pleaded with the magistrate, "Leave him alone your worship. Who has a better right to beat me than me own husband?"[8]

In the economic sphere the roles of husbands and wives were comple-mentary. The man, sometimes with the assistance of his wife, made tinware, wooden clothes pegs, reed baskets, and other wares. The woman peddled these wares from house to house. The husband, how-ever, controlled the purse strings; any cash the woman earned was turned over to him. One old woman recalled with exaggeration:

> The woman would be afeared to hide a hay-penny (half-penny) for herself, because if the man heard it rattlin' in her pocket she might get killed over it.

Traveller conjugal role relationships tended to be joint rather than segregated, unlike the pattern that has been described for many lower

7. Irish Folklore Commission (1951). Tinker Survey. Unpublished material in the library of the *Irish Folklore Commission*, Dublin. Vols. 1255–1256.
8. Op. cit., Vol. 1255, p. 212.

class groups where strong male dominance is the norm.[9] That is, in both work and play there was not a sharp differentiation between the roles of husband and wife. Husbands and wives worked as a unit and also spent most of their leisure time together, usually around the camp-fire or if cash was available, drinking. On the surface this appears paradoxical since power (in this case extreme male dominance) generally decreases joint activities and companionship because it creates "psychological distance" between the partners.[10] To a large degree, however, the Travellers' joint conjugal roles were prescribed by the conditions of itinerant life: a small number of families camped close together in isolation from the settled community and its activities. Simply, there was no place for men and women to pursue separate pastimes; they were thrown back on one another's company.

ECONOMIC CHANGE

In the first two decades following the Second World War the Travellers' rural, nomadic way of life was destroyed, forcing them to seek new subsistence patterns. Rapid economic expansion, which transformed Ireland from a predominantly rural and agricultural nation into a rapidly urbanizing and industrializing one, introduced new goods and machinery which made many of the Travellers' traditional trades obsolete. Plastic containers and enamelware, which did not rust and were relatively inexpensive, eliminated the demand for the tinker's handmade tinware. Today only a few families are still tinsmithing, once the Travellers' major source of income. As many farms mechanized, horse dealing became the next victim of modernization. Tractors and farm machinery not only eliminated the need for the Travellers' plow and draft horses which were once swapped and sold to the farmers, but also many seasonal agricultural jobs. Travellers can no longer supple-ment their small incomes by pulling sugar beets or digging potatoes. Many of Ireland's former subsistence farmers have with machinery and new techniques turned to cash cropping. Most now send all of their produce to market and no longer have the odd bag of potatoes or extra slab of butter to give to the Travellers who come to their doors.

Improved roads, the private automobile, and efficient bus service have contributed to the demise of peddling. The country woman, who once purchased small household wares from the baskets of Traveller

9. Rainwater, Lee (1964). "Marital Sexuality in Four Cultures of Poverty", *In Family Roles and Interaction: An Anthology*, Jerold Heiss (Ed.), Rand McNally, Chicago.
10. Blood, Robert and Wolfe, Donald (1960). *Husbands and Wives: The Dynamics of Married Living*, p. 164, The Free Press, New York.

women and linoleum, Delft, and larger goods from Traveller men, is no longer isolated and is able to travel to provincial towns to do her shopping.

A New Adaptation

Travellers survived the breakdown of their former economic niche by finding new sources of income. Most importantly, the men turned to collecting scrap metal and the women, exclusively to begging, without the pretense of offering wares for sale. While these new jobs allow the same mobility and autonomy as the traditional ones, they are most successfully pursued in towns and cities. Here construction yards, factories, and private homes provide an abundance of scrap metal. Furthermore, in the 1950's Traveller men became eligible for the "dole" (Unemployment Assistance) which was distributed from labour exchanges located in the larger towns and cities. And begging, soon to become the most important source of income, was easier and more profitable where the population was concentrated. Just the fact that houses are close together in the city and town enabled the female beggars to cover many more homes each day. Moreover, urbanites tended to be more sympathetic towards the beggars and also had more to give.

During the 1960's a mass exodus of Travellers leaving the countryside for the population centres took place. Cork, Galway City, and Limerick all experienced a heavy influx of Travellers. The heaviest migration, however, was into the capital city of Dublin. By 1971, 248 of Ireland's 1,300 Traveller families were living on the outskirts of Dublin. Less than twenty years earlier there had been fewer than ten families in the city.[11] During this same period hundreds of families also emigrated to England mainly in search of scrap metal.[12]

CHANGE IN SEX ROLES

A New Division of Labour

One major effect of this new adaptation has been a shift of economic responsibilities in Traveller families from husband to wife. In short,

11. Commission Report (1963). *Report of the Commission on Itinerancy*, p. 115, The Stationery Office, Dublin.

12. Most Travellers who migrate to England stay only a few months collecting scrap metal, dealing in second-hand furniture, or laying tarmacadam. Some families settle for varying periods of time in slum areas of large industrial cities such as Birmingham and Manchester; here they sometimes take factory employment or construction jobs. Higher State Assistance benefits (unemployment, Children's Allowance) in England also attract Travellers. When a family has earned enough money they return.

men are no longer the major breadwinners. Initially, they were able to obtain a relatively good income from scrap collecting. Prices for scrap metal, especially copper and lead, were high and there was an abundant supply since few people had collected "scrap" before. As more Travellers arrived in the towns and cities, however, competition for scrap metal became stiff. Many factory owners and tradesmen (e.g., plumbers) also became aware of the value of their waste metal and began to sell it directly to metal merchants or else demanded Travellers to pay for it. Scrap metal was no longer given free to Travellers.

While the husband's earnings dwindled, what Traveller women earned through begging greatly increased. In the 1960's a nationwide voluntary movement, the Itinerant Settlement Movement, was organized to help Travellers settle and to raise their standard of living. Leaders of the movement conducted an effective publicity campaign in the news media, to heighten the settled community's awareness of the poverty and destitution of the Travelling community. Frequent appeals were made asking the settled community to exercise Christian charity, sympathy, and understanding towards their "less fortunate countrymen", the pariah Travellers. Since then begging has become even more profitable. Traveller women who beg on the streets of central Dublin can now bring home £2 to £3 ($5.00–$7.50) a day. Others go door-to-door through the suburbs where they receive more than enough food and clothing to meet the needs of their large families. In fact, many collect so much clothing that they in turn sell most of it at a weekly outdoor market for the poor. A number of charity organizations have also increased their assistance to Travellers. And the women now receive a Children's Allowance check from the government each month. In the majority of cases, Traveller women now satisfy most of the economic needs of the family, and conversely, men are contributing less to support their families.

In other ways the roles of husband and father have diminished in importance. As many families settle in the serviced camp sites provided by local authorities and as others become semi-sedentary, changing camp only a few times each year, the important male role of caring for the family's means of transport—wagons, carts, and horses—and directing the movement of the family, has been greatly reduced. Men once played an equally important role as protectors of the family in encounters with hostile settled people and with rival Traveller factions. This role has diminished as factionalism has declined between different groups and many settled people have developed more humane attitudes towards Travellers. The man's role as disciplinarian may have also declined. Travellers claim that both parents punished the children in the past; today it is almost always the mother. Men have lost not only their economic independence, but also the satisfaction and rewards which come with fulfilling many of these other roles in the family. In many contemporary Traveller families the men do little more than gather wood and keep the family campfire going.

Power Relationships

The shift in familial economic responsibility to women raises the question: what effect has this change had on the power structure of the traditionally patriarchal family? By power, I refer to "who dominates, who submits; who makes the family decisions—husband, wife, or both jointly; who gets his or her way in case of disagreements and who commands and who obeys".[13] Has the balance of power shifted to the side of the partner who contributes the greater economic resources to the family, as Blood (1960)[14], Levine (1966)[15], Hamasy (1957)[16] and others have found?

Although certain trends are apparent, it is not possible to provide a definitive answer to this question. First, the time that has elapsed since Traveller women assumed economic responsibility for the family has not been long. There is bound to be some lag before social relationships adjust to the new economic realities, if they do at all. Secondly, Traveller society is still undergoing a tremendous amount of change, and even in relatively stable situations, power relationships are not always clear cut. As Stephens points out, power relationships are "not neatly summarized into cultural rules" and "they tend to vary a great deal within the same society".[17] Furthermore, in Traveller society as in many poverty groups, physical force is a strong sanction not infrequently used to get ones' way. Power, therefore, depends to a degree on the size and strength of the spouse. With these limitations in mind, I will describe some changes in conjugal roles which indicate that Traveller women are gaining power and authority while men are losing it.

Today family finances are increasingly controlled by the women. Not only do most wives now keep what money they earn instead of turning it over to their husbands as they did traditionally, but many now insist

13. Stephens, William (1963). *The Family in Cross Cultural Perspective*, p. 296. Holt, Rinehart and Winston, New York.

14. Op. cit.

15. Levine, Robert (1966). "Sex Roles and Economic Change in Africa", *Ethnology*, **5**, 186–193.

16. Hamasy, Sheila (1957). "The Role of Women in a Changing Society", *American Anthropologist*, **59**, 101–111.

17. Op. cit., p. 296.

that their husbands give them part of the dole. Formerly, the dole was strictly the man's spending money,[18] and although men still keep most of the dole for their own pleasure, usually spending it at the pub, the fact that they are now obliged to give part of it to their wives is significant. One woman at Rathfarnham refused to prepare meals for her husband until he gave her a share of his dole. This caused an elderly woman in camp to comment:

> Women aren't so foolish as they used to be. Years ago the woman was soft and too honest. But now they've gone clever and they're more the bosses. They're able for the men . . . they ain't scared of the men no longer.

Many Traveller men now find themselves in the position of having to beg their wives for a loan after spending all their money at the pubs and still craving more drink.

In daily household decisions there probably has not been much change. Today women make most of these decisions and to a certain extent they probably always have, if not by right then by default. Most household decisions are of little interest to Traveller men. But in the more important decisions which affect the entire family—as in deciding to shift to a new camp, determining the location of the family's shelter vis-à-vis other families within camp, swapping or selling the family shelter, and so forth—women now play a much larger role. It is not a case of the wife unilaterally making these decisions, rather she is consulted and her opinions are heeded as they never were before.

Today women are more assertive and less tolerant of abuses from their husbands. A strong sanction against men who neglect to listen to their wive's views and demands is the threat of desertion. In the earlier rural setting in which Traveller groups were dispersed and the exact location of one's kinsmen was not always known it was difficult for women to run off. They had no place to go. Today, however, because Travellers are more sedentary and many are concentrated in urban areas, the likelihood of having kinsmen nearby is greater and it is easier for wives to temporarily abandon their husbands and return to their kinsmen. Frequently deserting wives leave their children behind for their husbands to care for as an added penalty.

Another indication of the women's assertiveness and increased power is the rising frequency of matrilocal residence for part of the year. This generally results from a young wife's insistence that the family spend some time each year camping with her parents and the patrilineage she

18. McCarthy, Patricia (1971). "Itinerancy and Poverty: A Study in the Subculture of Poverty." Unpublished M.S.S. thesis, University College, Dublin.

left upon marriage. With patrilocal residence (still statistically the norm), the young married woman has to live closely and interact almost exclusively with her husband's relatives who never fully embrace her as one of their own. Furthermore, she must respect the authority of her possessive mother-in-law, who is often competing with her for her husband's attention and loyalties. This situation frequently gives rise to conflict between spouses and between the wife and her mother-in-law. Traditionally, young wives had no recourse, except perhaps to seek solace in the knowledge that some day they would have authority over their own sons' wives. Today, however, a wife may force her husband to take leave of his kin group, at least for a while, by deserting him and returning to her kinsmen. Generally within a month her lonely husband will join her.

A factor external to the Traveller community which may be accelerating the readjustment in family power relationships is the influence of begging patronesses. In recent years as Travellers have become more sedentary and as some members of the settled community have become more charitable towards them, many Traveller women have developed patroness-client relationships with settled women.[19] Essentially this is a relationship in which a settled housewife selects one beggar to look after. The housewife no longer gives to any Traveller who begs at her door, but saves food and used clothing for a particular woman who calls on her regularly, usually once every two weeks. Some Traveller women have a number of patronesses. As the housewife becomes better acquainted with the Traveller woman she may invite her in, usually for a chat over tea and biscuits. In this setting Traveller women become aware of an alternative model of conjugal relations, that of settled society, usually middle or upper class. Here women are not treated as inferiors (at least not quite so much), are rarely beaten, and decision-making is more equitably distributed between the spouses. These differences are either observed in the patroness' home or verbally communicated to the Traveller woman by her patroness.

Because most settled people blame the "evils" of itinerant life (e.g., trespass, wandering horses, litter, petty thievery) on Traveller men, they generally view the women and children as helpless victims. The settled community negatively stereotypes Traveller men as indolent drunkards who force their wives to beg. Such negative attitudes are transmitted to Traveller women in their encounters with their

19. According to a recent survey, 76·8 per cent of the settled Irish polled, claimed to "usually" or "always" give to Travellers who came to their door begging. Of these, 39 per cent claimed to give regularly to one individual. Bohn Gmelch, Sharon (1973). "Settled Irish attitudes towards Travellers." Unpublished questionnaire results.

patronesses. Thus housewives bolster the Traveller woman's courage
to stand up to her husband. Mick Doran complained about his wife's
patronesses:

> I don't know what those ladies in the houses are telling her, but I
> don't like it. Everything is fine when she goes out (begging) but
> when she comes back she's pure vexed with me for nothin'... I
> haven't done nothin'.

NEW MARRIAGE PATTERNS

Age at Marriage

In the past decade there has been a sharp decline in the age at which
Travellers marry. In a demographic survey data was compiled on 59
marriages that occurred before 1960.[20] The mean age at marriage for
this sample, nearly all of whom married in rural areas under traditional
conditions, was 21.6 for males and 18.2 for females. Today the mean
age at marriage is approximately two years earlier for both sexes, and
it is not uncommon for Traveller parents in Dublin to make a "match"
(arranged marriage) for their 14 or 15 year old daughters and 16 year
old sons. Once a match is "drawn" or "thrown down" the wedding
ceremony usually follows within a week or two.

Why are Travellers marrying at a younger age than ever before?
Perhaps the major explanation lies in the inability of parents today,
particularly in the city, to control their adolescent children. Travellers
place a high value on premarital chastity; public knowledge that a girl
has had an affair would ruin her reputation and make it difficult to find
her a suitable match. An illegitimate birth would "scandalize" the
entire family.

Traditionally the activities of single girls were sharply circumscribed;
they were never permitted to be alone in the company of boys.

> Travelling girls was not allowed to see no boys. If they seen boys
> down the road they daren't pull up, they'd have to pass right on...
> Their mothers was always with them... always watchin' and not let-
> tin' them go nowhere. A good mother kept her daughters under her
> skirt.

Close supervision was possible in the traditional, rural setting because
camps were small and isolated from nearby villages or towns as well as
from other Travellers. And if parents discovered or suspected that their

20. Crawford, Michael and Gmelch, George (1973). "The Demography and Genetics
of Irish Tinkers", *Social Biology* (In press).

daughter was secretly seeing a boy in camp they simply split off from the group.

Today it is difficult for parents to keep a close watch on their teenage children. Many camps and sites are large, accommodating numerous families with many unattached adolescents. In these camps, especially in the city, there are many opportunities for undetected meetings between the sexes. Moreover, young girls who are permitted to leave camp with their female peers to beg or to see a movie may secretly meet their boyfriends. Some parents still leave the camp if they suspect their daughters are courting. One family left Rathfarnham after finding a charm bracelet that had been given to their 14 year old daughter by a boy in camp. Unless the family chooses to live alone, however, this rarely solves the problem. Powerless to prevent illicit courtship and thus protect their daughter's chastity and the reputation of both the girl and her family, parents are making matches for their daughters at an earlier age. One mother explained:

> Years ago the girls would be 18 before they was married, but now they're gettin' married at 14 and 15. I think the parents do be glad to get rid of them. The little girls is goin' out of control, against their mothers and fathers. They're off to the pictures and meeting up with boys . . . The parents is glad to get them married young, then they're off the parents' hands and they can't give you no scandal.

Because it is increasingly easy for teenage Traveller boys to get involved in petty crime (especially theft) in the city, many parents are equally glad to marry their sons off in the hopes of settling them down by giving them the responsibility of a wife and family.

The dramatic increase in early teenage marriages has so alarmed the Dublin Itinerant Settlement Committee that the co-operation of the clergy has been sought to establish procedures to stop, or at least postpone, "juvenile" marriages. Traveller couples wishing to be married, for example, are now asked to wait a minimum of six weeks until the banns are called in Church. The Committee and clergy hope that many prospective marriages, which are normally matched one week and carried out the next will dissolve before the six weeks are up.

Preferential Cousin Marriage

A second change in marriage patterns has been the increase in marriages between first and second cousins. Of the 37 couples who camped at Rathfarnham at one time or another during 1971–72, five were first cousins and six were second cousins. All but two of these were married within the past ten years.[21]

Traditionally, consanguineous marriages especially between first cousins were rare among most Travellers.

> Years ago you wouldn't hear tell of it (marrying a first cousin). It was a scandalous way of goin' on and you'd nearly be put in the newspapers. Everybody'd be talkin', sayin' you couldn't get no other body so you married your cousin.

Yet, in the past five years, the women who made this statement has matched two of her sons with her brothers' daughters and a third son with a second cousin.

An important factor behind the increase in preferential cousin marriage has been the break-up of former "marriage groups" (i.e., lineages who travelled and worked the same areas and who exchanged mates). One recent study found that 77 per cent of all Traveller, marriages were contracted between persons born in the same county and all but 7 per cent from within the same province.[22] The Wexford Connors, for example, once drew their matches from the ranks of the O'Briens, Dorans, and Flynns, lineages which worked roughly the same areas in Southeast Ireland. Today these lineages are widely dispersed. Many families now share a camp with Travellers they have never known before, especially in Dublin. Knowing very little about the background of these "strangers"—whether they steal, drink too much, beat their wives, or are in frequent trouble with the law—parents prefer to draw a match for their sons and daughters with kinsmen they know and trust.

One parent in a large Dublin camp explains:

> You've got Travellers from all parts of Ireland mixing up here (in Dublin). Those from the East don't know the background of the people belonging to the West—some of them do be very rough. And those from the West don't know them from the East. Travelling people are afeared to get in which strangers . . . But if you marry a cousin you know what you're getting into.

Furthermore, in the face of rapid social change and uncertainty which Travellers are now experiencing, close-kin marriages help strengthen existing kin ties and promote family solidarity.

The frequency of quarreling between spouses, which Travellers claim is on the rise, may be another contributing factor to the increase in

---

21. (Masterson, J. G. (1971). "Consanguinity in Ireland", *Human Heredity*, **21**, 1–12.) This study of all Catholic marriages in Ireland between 1957 and 1968 revealed that only 1 in 625 marriages were contracted between first cousins. He believes that Travellers have contributed substantially to this figure.

22. Crawford and Gmelch (1973). Op. cit.

marriages between cousins which is widely believed in the Traveller community to be a stronger union than one between non-kin, and therefore involves less likelihood of conflict.

> Travelling People believe that cousins will have more nature for one another and they won't use no violence on each other . . . The boy won't kick up the woman so bad if she is his cousin . . . If they aren't happy together they may stick on just for the sake of bein' so near a relation.

Maggie McDonagh mentions another advantage:

> And if the wife runs off, the boy has no trouble gettin' her back, because she's goin' to go back to her family. And her family is the boy's aunt and uncle. They're all the one people . . . they're all the one blood. But if you marry a stranger, if she's gone, well that's it . . . she could be gone.

SUMMARY

It was shown that the Travellers' traditional, rural way of life based on itinerant trades was disrupted in a modernizing Ireland. The forced adaptation to new occupations led to a mass migration of Travellers into cities and towns and transformed the Travellers' relationship with the settled population from symbiosis to parasitism. Travellers have now become more dependent on charity from the settled community, both through formal channels such as the dole and Children's Allowance and informal channels, such as begging on the streets and door-to-door. The women are the major beneficiaries of these hand-outs which has resulted in a new division of labour in the family. It was shown that the new economic position of the woman as breadwinner has led to changes in other spheres of family life. Women have gained power in the sense that they now control family finances and play a greater role in decision-making. Patroness-client relationships were shown to be one contributing factor in this shift of power to females. Lastly, two changes in marriage patterns were described: first, a decline in the age at marriage and secondly, an increase in the frequency of cousin marriages. Both changes are linked to factors extant in the new environment of towns and cities.

CHAPTER ELEVEN

Scottish Travellers or Tinkers

A. and F. Rehfisch

The aim of this essay is to describe some aspects of the culture and social organization of the Scottish Travellers as well as how they survived in spite of centuries of persecution and contact with a conflicting value system. The term "Traveller" is used here because the more common "Tinker" is resented by the group and is believed to be pejorative, as indeed it usually is. However it is quite impossible to treat this group in isolation. One must see them as a part of, even though relatively isolated, the larger society. Like any despised minority their behaviour patterns, values and attitudes are coloured to a considerable degree by the attitude of outsiders towards them and vice versa. Important in this respect is the necessity to maintain their own self-respect, if not to say feeling of superiority. Further it will be seen that this is done by valuing those characteristics in which they excel and downgrading those in which they do not.

In the context of this essay the meaning of the term Traveller will be that given to it by the people themselves. A person is a member of the group if he has had one or more Traveller parent and associates himself with the sub-culture. He may be nomadic, semi-nomadic or sedentary. There are nomads in Scotland who may associate with Travellers but are not granted full membership since they have no genealogical claim. Equally, children of Travellers can opt out by settling and breaking their social ties with the members, and changing the connection. No data are available to indicate the numbers who leave the group. While there have been a number of estimates as to the sizes of the group, I am not satisfied that any are accurate enough to reproduce here.

HISTORY OF THE TRAVELLERS

Literally gallons of ink have been utilized developing theories as to the origin of these people. It would seem to me to be an exercise in futility to review all of these and even more to attempt to justify any of them. Their origin is lost in the far past and can hardly be reconstructed. For many centuries references exist mentioning the presence of nomadic bands wandering through the length and breadth of Scotland and occupying the economic niche, to a greater or lesser degree, that the Travellers do today. In spite of draconian measures to get rid of them, from the time of James VI of Scotland, the group has survived. The civic authorities ordered that Travellers when caught be branded, whipped, executed or expulsed from the country but to no avail. It should be noted here that Gypsies in the British Isles and Europe fared similar threats but equally they have survived. Doubtless this part of their history helps to explain the attitude of Travellers to outsiders, but as we shall see the way that they are treated today by the mass society is not one to encourage confidence in the latter group by Travellers.

TRAVELLER–GYPSY RELATIONS

Very little is known of the relations between Travellers and Gypsies in the past. Confusion on this score is compounded by the fact that many of the early writers on the Scots nomads referred to them as Gypsies or sometimes Tinkers or Tinker-Gypsies. A careful survey of the literature has led me to the belief that little is likely to be gleaned on this subject.

However, present day evidence suggests that at some time in the past there must have been considerable contact. The most conclusive is that quite a large proportion of Cant (Travellers' secret language) is of Romany origin. Most of these are very commonly used words. But it should be noted that in the case of their adopting Romany words there is, or are, a word or words in the Cant of other origins. This might well mean that the Travellers' dialect existed before contact with Romany, hence there existed a community of Travellers before the first contact with Romanys. This would, however, be a very speculative conclusion.

A further suggestion that Travellers and Gypsies probably have enjoyed fairly intimate contact at one time is that they share some of the same taboos. For example, both agree that it is prohibited to wash clothes and dishes in the same basin. Equally, dishes should never be dried by means of a hand towel. One informant smashed up a complete tea-service when she discovered that this had happened.

However, an important question remains. Why is it that the Gypsies occupy the nomadic ecological niche in Wales and England, but not in

Scotland or Ireland where Travellers prevail? Considerable historical evidence exists to show that when the Gypsies first came to the British Isles there were already a large number of nomadic bands roaming throughout Scotland and equally I believe in Ireland. Hence the new group found little possibility of exploiting the area and hence did not establish themselves there. Equally they may have been driven out by the occupiers.

Today there are very few Gypsies in Scotland, except perhaps in the Border region. Informants have told me that the two peoples have little if any contact with each other. Our only experience with Gypsies was when a very small group came to Blairgowrie for a few days. They neither visited nor were visited by any Traveller.

The Travellers' World View

The Traveller group is a despised minority and is well aware of this fact. In this part of the essay will be discussed the attitude of the group towards the outside world and vice-versa.

Not surprisingly Travellers are extremely suspicious of "Flatties" (the term used to include all outsiders). For this they have very good grounds. The nomadic sector are constantly being harassed by the authorities. Once settled on a waste bit of land it is not unusual for the police or other agents of the local authority to arrive and order them to move. One example of this constant recurring phenomenon will exemplify the situation. Shortly before the raspberry picking season was to begin in Blairgowrie, two couples with children arrived, sought permission from a landowner to camp on his unused field and this was granted. The next day the police arrived and told them to leave. In spite of having had permission they were forced to do so. Having found a less desirable site, slightly water-logged, a camp was set up. The next day again the police came. In desperation the latter were asked where the group might go and the police showed them a site. The site was muddy and virtually waterlogged and extremely insanitary, but they had to accept it. Many are the tales we were told of similar situations throughout the recent history of the group.

Informants told us that whenever there was a theft in the area in which they might be camped, the first action of the police was to come to their camp to search for the stolen goods. In view of the fact that the popular image of the Travellers is that they are almost all thieves, this is not surprising. This is, of course, an incorrect assumption. As in any other category of persons there are a small minority who steal; the vast majority are honest. This does not mean that an occasional rabbit or salmon may not be poached, but further than that few will go.

The Travellers are for the most part convinced that outsiders would like to see the last of them and not a few have said that if possible the government would set up extermination camps for them and thus achieve "the final solution".

The settled Travellers are equally aware of the fact that they are persecuted. This does seem to be true and two of our experiences will serve as an indication of the attitude of the majority group and their actions. When we first settled in Blairgowrie the local population were very friendly. After a few days of associating publicly with Travellers no townsmen, with two exceptions, would speak to us. A more serious example of persecution follows. A Traveller who had been settled in Blairgowrie for several decades and owned a berry field for some time, had made several attempts to establish social relations with the local population. His attempts were rebuffed and he told me that the only Flattie ever to enter his house was the local policeman. At berry-picking time about thirty travellers camped on his field, as was customary, in preparation for the picking to start. Equally a researcher for the School of Scottish Studies and my wife and myself set up our tents on the spot. After about two days of picking, the health authorities came and inspected the site. They told all the campers to go, stating that there were not adequate facilities on the site, meaning too few water taps and toilets. The campers were given forty-eight hours to go. The owner was frantic, for if his labour supply left his crop would go to ruin. Hence he agreed that if the campers were fined for disobeying the order he would pay. In two days the authorities returned and issued summonses to all on the site except to the other researcher and myself, in spite of my making our presence very obvious and indeed asking for a summons. In the interim period I had toured several other fields, owned by Flatties of course, and found that many if not most, had less facilities than this one. The owner and myself contacted other berry field owners, trying to enlist their support, but of course to no avail. The result was that the owner was forced to obtain the services of a barrister, at great expense, who with no difficulty had the summonses quashed. I should perhaps mention here that the landowners of Blairgowrie had established a protective association but Travellers were not invited to join.

It may be said that the examples given above may be unique or very rare. I believe this not to be the case, but even were this so they nonetheless reinforce the belief among Travellers that they are persecuted if they remain nomadic and especially if they settle and attempt to compete with Flatties in their own sphere of activities.

I believe that this kind of persecution is more common in smaller villages and towns than in the larger anonymous cities. However, many informants in Aberdeen said that if they were to maintain reasonable relations with their neighbours they must keep their identity a secret. Several schoolchildren said if their affiliation with the group became known they would be shunned by all of their fellows. Examples were given to justify this claim.

Travellers' relations with church and school are definitely coloured by this prejudice. Some of our Blairgowrie informants told us that they would like to send their children to Sunday School but that the other children made it very uncomfortable for them. This was corroborated. I mentioned it to the priest in charge. He checked on the matter and found it to be true. The next week he preached a sermon on the subject of Christian brotherhood, specifically mentioning the matter above and admitted to seeing many shame-faced parishioners. Within the school context we were told of the social isolation of Traveller children, of physical aggression against them and perhaps worst of all, teacher prejudice being manifested quite openly. Is it then any wonder that members of the group rebuffed by the administrative authorities, the general public and institutions such as church and school, are ultra suspicious of outsiders?

Being made well aware of their status as a despised group it might be thought that members would accept the majority view and assume a very humble posture and equally a low evaluation of themselves. This is only partly true. The following will explain the above statement.

If a Traveller camp is visited by a Flattie, the campers will assume a very humble posture. Obsequiousness is often to be seen. The visitors will often be treated with great respect and constant reference will be made to the poverty and wickedness of the campers' lives. Their action and conversation would indicate that they accept the values of the majority as well as the status accorded them by the latter group. However, this is largely a performance which they have learned to play in order to gain sympathy as well as gifts of money and kind which are frequently forthcoming.

The reality of their self-evaluation is somewhat different. They believe firmly that Travellers are more intelligent and able than most Flatties. The justification for this stems from a number of factors. The first that they are not limited to one activity in order to earn a living. The Flattie is seen as knowing how to perform one task in order to make money and if this is not available he is in hopeless straits. The Traveller sees himself as having many strings to his bow, he can deal in scrap metal, rags, beg, do farm work, peddle, etc., etc.

Equally, Flatties are seen to be employees of others, during all their working lives being under another's authority. Members of the group are averse to giving up their independence and will rarely, except for very short periods if absolutely essential, assume such a subservient role. They value their freedom and independence and are satisfied that their achieving of this is a sign of their superiority.

An example of how two segments of one society can hold quite contradictory views on an activity is readily seen if we examine attitudes towards begging. The majority look upon begging as demeaning and shameful. Few would resort to it except in extremely dire circumstances. This is not the case among Travellers who consider it merely one of many possible means to earn a living. Indeed it is one of the more valued ways as it is concrete proof that as a group they are cleverer than the Flatties since they are able with considerable ease to wheedle hard-earned money or goods from the latter with little or no difficulty. One of many possible examples is cited here.

A friend who was quite well-off, owning several berry fields, dealing in used cars and having other interests, is used as a case in point. Having been made aware of his absence from Blairgowrie for several days, I was anxious to discover where he had been and what doing. Upon his return he informed me that he had been on a begging tour. He explained that it was essential that one keeps "one's hand in" this activity and also, while not expressed in these terms, why not, it proves one's superiority over the Flatties.

Perhaps a more concrete example of conflicting views between the two segments of the society is that relating to clothes. Few but the very poorest Flatties do not have at least one outfit which is reserved for special occasions such as going to church, weddings and other like occasions. This is rarely the case among Travellers. Ceremonial garb is virtually unknown and unwanted. Perhaps this is due to their attitude towards work and play. There is no strict dichotomy between the two. Should a person be on his way to a celebration of any kind and sees an opportunity to obtain scrap-metal, old clothes, rags or beg, he will not hesitate to do so. Here is another opportunity to prove one's superiority and there is no reason why one should not take advantage of it. Here it is important to note that the research on which this is based was carried out in the late 1950's. In Aberdeen, especially, there were signs that some of the younger members were beginning to assimilate some of the Flattie values. A few had accepted regular employment and were interacting more intimately with outsiders. This still required that their origins be kept a secret. I have no doubt this development will continue. A factor speeding up this development will surely be the widespread popularity of television, especially among the settled and semi-nomadic segment of the population.

Their attitude towards steady employment is coloured by a number of factors. The first is that employment would almost invariably put them in a position of inferiority *vis-à-vis* members of the Flattie group. Secondly, few Travellers have very much formal education, hence one is eligible only for menial jobs. In competition with Flatties they would not show to advantage, hence their self-imagery would be challenged. Then as has been mentioned, the absence of need for steady employment is taken as evidence that members of the group are cleverer than others, hence to take a job is an admission of failure.

The group is loath to enter into competition with Flatties. This I believe colours their attitude to clothes, i.e., showing no concern at all to dress well. Equally they are not interested in amassing much in the way of material goods. Those who are housed for the most part are satisfied with relatively little furniture and that not of very high quality: this is true even of relatively well-off Travellers.

One of our informants in Aberdeen had a relatively high income and was renowned for his generosity towards poor down-and-out Travellers. Yet if one were to judge his economic status by the housing he occupied, the furniture therein, and of course his clothes, one would classify him as being very poor.

Their general attitude towards material objects, differing considerably from that of the mass society, stems in part from the fact that hospitality and generosity are highly valued. This is especially true among the men. Many informants have told me that on certain occasions they have acquired quite substantial sums of money, mainly through the scrap trade. But it quickly melts away. Money to many of them is a means of conforming to the ideal pattern of being able to offer generous entertainment to their mates and to help others in need. Unfortunately there are always a large number of these. Several of the men who had acquired berry fields in Blairgowrie have told me that the means utilized in acquiring the necessary capital was to give their money to their wives for safe-keeping. Women appear to be less concerned with the status competition indulged in by the men.

In the hazardous situation in which Travellers have found themselves for generations, the value placed on mutual help has played a significant role in maintaining the viability of the society. Equally, of course, since until relatively recently the overwhelming majority were nomadic, the acquisition of many material objects would have more of a hindrance than an advantage.

It may seem surprising that two societies who have lived together for so many centuries, indeed share the same origin, can differ so completely in their cultural values. This can, I believe, be explained only by the fact that, while social interaction between the two groups has continued, it existed and indeed exists only at a very superficial level. Travelling women often have clients whom they have visited for many years, in some cases decades, yet the relationship is one where both, especially the Traveller woman, plays a strictly defined role. Wheedling, humility and in some cases an amount of verbal aggression, when the client does not conform by generous behaviour, are what is expected of her and she conforms.

One very interesting common belief about Travelling women is their association with the supernatural. Women encourage this belief among Flattie women and often are able to earn money by fortune-telling, selling magical potions, etc. Not only do these beliefs yield an income but also help to protect the Travelling women. Outsiders are afraid of interfering with them for fear that the latter will attack them through supernatural means.

The Travellers' World

Travellers do not in any sense form a corporate group. They have no all-encompassing political organization. The literature is replete with mentions of kings and queens, but these do not and probably never have existed. Informants explained how tales of such nobility proliferated. If an old man or woman died it was believed to be a good opportunity for obtaining money from the Flatties. The news was circulated that the king or queen of the group had died and there was to be a large funeral. Since all relatives of the deceased are expected, if possible, to attend the funeral, an aged person was likely to draw a large attendance. Local people attracted by the ascription of nobility to the dead and expecting esoteric rites came in large numbers. A collection was taken; individual begging was indulged in, and considerable cash was obtained. Equally it opened the way for another sham ceremony, the coronation of the heir, which again opened the way for financial gain in the same way.

The majority of travellers have a relatively limited area which they cover. This is not because territories are allocated to various groups and trespassers keep out, but rather, in order to make a living in an area, one must know it quite well. It is essential to know the sources of scrap metal, old cars, rags and old clothes as well as from whom it is likely to be best to beg. Equally it is extremely useful to know of those sites where neither the owner nor the police are likely to trouble one. Finally in view of the hazardous nature of the Traveller way of life it is often essential to have friends and relatives nearby in case of difficulties. Hence the Travellers' knowledge of the country as a whole is rather limited. For reasons which I do not know, several of our informants had travelled in Ireland. Some of the men had served in the army during the two World Wars and therefore had some experience of living overseas. To the best of my knowledge none had voluntarily crossed the Channel. A very few had relatives or friends in Canada and the USA, and sometimes considered the possibility of emigrating themselves. One of our informants has moved to Canada I am told.

The world view of the group then is limited for the most part. Equally it is a threatening one, where one must be constantly on the alert or the majority will destroy one; alert also to take advantage of any opportunity to reap rewards when they are offered. Children are very early taught of the dangers of the outside world. One is really safe when among relatives, friends or fellow members of the group. On the rare occasion when a stranger attempts to develop social relations, outside of the purely economic sphere, extreme care is necessary and usually results in a polite rebuff. Several times during field-work if stranger Travellers were encountered and an attempt was made to chat with them the result was silence. Only after displaying our credentials, knowledge of Cant and friendship with their relatives or friends was the barrier broken down.

The belief that body-snatchers, who killed the unwary and sold their bodies to the various medical schools in Scotland, was widely held. Tales relating the activity of "Burkers", as the body-snatchers are called, are a large part of the Travellers' folk lore. These stories express in concrete terms the view that the outside world is hostile and one must be wary of it. When challenged to provide evidence for the existence of Burkers informants would cite the missing person column in the *News of the World*, or tell of occasions when they had been chased by strangers who of course were Burkers. Further they talked much of a Traveller living in Aberdeen, who claimed to work for the Medical School thus supplying them with bodies. Whenever he arrived in a camp site, all the children were warned to be very careful and were closely watched by the resident adults.

Even today, we were told, men in tall dark hats toured the countryside in coaches and four, their horses being shoed with rubber horseshoes to ensure silence, and fell upon individuals and isolated couples, killed them and sold their bodies. This belief is important as it has the effect of keeping bands together. Rare indeed were cases of couples camping alone.

When we moved to Aberdeen several informants warned us not to go near the Aberdeen Medical School or Hospitals after dark.

Belief in fairies, goblins and other such supernatural spirits are also common though these are said to be much more common in Ireland. One informant told us that she had found a tiny casket with a fairy's body inside it. She kept it for some time and one day it mysteriously disappeared.

KINSHIP AND THE FAMILY

The Traveller family is founded, as in the majority of known societies, when a couple are wed. In spite of much that has been written, weddings are not circumscribed by ceremonies. A young man and girl who wish to marry either simply move in together into a tent, usually of their own, or if they expect opposition from one or both sets of parents or kin they elope together. While I have no statistics to prove this, it would appear that there is no particular preference for varilocal or uxorilocal settlement. Quite often the two set up on their own away from both sets of parents. In the case of an elopement, the young couple will return after a short period from a week to a month and the parents accept the union as a *fait accompli*.

Nowadays church and registry marriages are quite common, largely for the advantages to be obtained through the Social Welfare and Social Security agencies of having a legal, valid marriage. In the past, church marriages were often staged in order to collect money and gifts from impressed Flatties, but these were not taken seriously by the community. Equally peculiar rites were performed on the site for the edification of onlooking Flatties, for the same purpose, but these also had no real meaning.

A man may choose any girl for his spouse on condition that she is not a lineal ascendant or descendant. Cousins are often chosen and indeed marriages between double cousin, cousinage from both mother's and father's side, are far from being rare.

I have not met or heard of any celibate Traveller, though doubtless a few may exist. It is assumed in the community that all youngsters will marry. The age at marriage is usually quite young. Girls of twenty are almost certainly married as are boys of twenty-two or thereabouts.

With marriage, the couples traditionally become independent of their parents. They are given or otherwise acquire a tent, caravan or other residence of their own, as well as becoming an independent economic unit. Depending upon their choice of residence pattern, men may cooperate with the fathers and brothers in economic pursuits or daughters with their mothers and sisters. In some cases in-laws may co-operate, but whatever the practice followed, each family holds its own purse and is free to come and go at will. More will be said about the economic structure of the family below.

Contrary to practice in the larger society, the independence of the newly married family seems to be lessening among certain groups. Quite a number of our informants have moved into flats and/or houses. Rents are high and accommodation scarce, especially for Travellers, many landlords refusing to let to them. The result is that many newly-weds move into either the bride's or the groom's parental residence and hence lose their economic independence. Three generation family units are not uncommon among those with settled domiciles. In these cases they will act as an economic unit, that is the males will work together as will the women.

The division of labour within the family unit is marked. Domestic chores are exclusively the preserve of women though on some occasions men will buy the provisions. Men are in charge of the means of transport whether this be the horses, lorries or motor-cars. Both contribute to the family purse. Men earn money in many different ways but the most common are by dealing in scrap metal, bagpipe playing, second-hand and discarded furniture and other goods, farm labour and dealing in used cars. Horse-dealing which in the past was very important is now very rare as are many of the traditional jobs such as making articles in the home, clothes pegs, etc.

Women make their financial contribution by begging, collecting old clothes, rags and hawking. Wives go out as often as possible with baskets under their arms holding goods such as button-cards, combs, bits of lace and other small articles. The basket has two important functions. The first to contain articles to be sold, the second as a passport to gain contact with housewives. The woman knocks on a door and begins by attempting to sell one or more knick-knacks. She will then ask whether any old clothes or other articles to be discarded can be given to her. If this fails she may then beg for money or for food. Women hawkers prefer to have one or two small children with them in order to solicit sympathy from the house-dweller. A certain amount of child-borrowing within kinship groups is common. Needless to say while doing this work a wife will keep her eyes open for available scrap-metal or other large items, the existence of which will be reported back to her husband.

Children are very much desired and are very well treated. If food is scarce the children will be fed first and what is left, if anything, will be eaten by the adults. Most parents are very permissive.

Most infants are baptized at birth. This ceremony is seen to protect the newly born against health hazards. Few children attend church or Sunday school, partly as mentioned previously due to the attitude of the Flattie parishioners.

The majority of Travellers are anxious to have their children learn to read, write and do basic arithmetic. The rest of the school syllabus is said to be worthless. Equally they see no value in schooling over and above a rudimentary knowledge of the three above-mentioned subjects. Only one of our informants had attended school past the legal school-leaving age. This rejection of advanced education stems from a number of factors. The first is that the children are often mistreated in schools by both their peers and the teachers. Equally, the children of nomadic families were allowed by law to attend school for only half of the period required for children of sedentary people. Since most Traveller families took advantage of this law, consequently the children are not academically equal to their age-mates. Many Travellers with settled homes leave to enjoy their nomadic existence in late spring, long before the end of the school term and return after it has started again. Equally, children at an early age are expected to contribute to the family exchequer, the boys going out with their fathers and girls with their mothers, and hence cannot attend school regularly. Also, education above the rudimentary level is not seen to be of any great value in the society, as indeed it is not. Far more useful is for the child to learn the ways and means whereby he will be earning a living. Boys learn to mend cars, the types and value of scrap metal, etc., etc. Girls at a very early age begin to learn the complex role that they are to play *vis-à-vis* the Flattie housewife. Finally, school confronts the Traveller with a competitive situation *vis-à-vis* Flattie children, and one where he is not at an advantage, hence he resists it.

The older generation are much respected. Even in advanced old age when their contribution to the group's well-being is either nominal or totally absent they will be looked after by their children. My impression is that sons are more likely to care for their aged parents, but this is merely a hypothesis, since so few cases of this kind were encountered. Again I have no statistics, but I believe that the life expectancy of Travellers is not very great.

On several occasions we were told that it was impossible to understand how Flatties could send their parents off to institutions when they became old. Except in the case of extreme illness they resist even temporary hospitalization for the old. This is equally true for handicapped children. We met with a very few cases of seriously mentally retarded children. The authorities had tried to convince the parents to place them in an institution, but their pleas were to no avail. These aspects are certainly related to the Traveller belief in Burkers and their attitude towards the mass society.

Disputes between members of bands are not infrequent, these may even arise between kinsmen, and if of a really serious nature will result in one of the disputants leaving the group and associating himself with another one. Normally the new group will include relatives of the husband or wife, but this is not necessarily always true. The fact that, as is the case in many nomadic societies, disputes can thus be resolved, is probably one reason why formal political organization has not developed among the Travellers.

CONCLUSION

Scots Travellers have existed in a very hostile environment for many centuries. They have maintained themselves primarily by holding tight to values and attitudes which are often in conflict with those of the mass society. Very simply, if they had not done so they would no longer exist and would have merged with the Flattie group. They are not unique in this, as other persecuted minorities have been put under great pressure but have not ceded. Jews in Europe are probably the best known example.

CHAPTER TWELVE

The Social Organization of a Pariah Group in Norway*

Fredrik Barth

The following is an attempt at illustrating the application of some social anthropological viewpoints to field data on the *Taters*,[1] a Gypsy-like section of the population of Eastern Norway. Previous studies of Scandinavian Taters (Etzler 1944, Flekstad 1949, Heymowski 1955)[2] have been mainly concerned with genealogical and historical problems, in the tradition of Eilert Sundt (1850–65),[3] and with a prime interest in discovering the genetic origins of Taters. The present problem is one of social organization—simply to map whatever features of organization might exist within the group, and to see this structure in relation to the specific requirements of the Tater mode of life—in relation to the types of problems it is designed to solve. For the purpose of collecting relevant material, various visits were made over a period of three years to different Taters in Eastern Norway; wherever possible, the information

---

* First published in *Norveg*, Oslo, 1955.

1. This group is variously called *Tater* ("Tartar"), *Fant*, *Omstreifer* ("wanderer"), or *Reisende* ("traveller") in Norway. Since its origins from true Gypsies is at best problematical, and since the above terms are without derogatory connotations in English, the commonly used ethnic name *Tater* will be utilized below.

2. Etzler, Allan (1944). *Zigenarna och deras avkomlingar i Sverige*, Uppsala and "Gypsies in Sweden" (1946). *Journal of Gypsy Lore Society*, Vol. XXV, Nos. 3–4. Flekstad, Kaspar (1949). *Omstreifere og sigøynere*, Oslo. Heymowski, Adam de (1955). *Om "Tattare" och "Resande"*, Uppsala (mimeographed).

3. Sundt, Eilert, *Beretning om Fante-eller Landstrygerfolket i Norge*. Christiania, 1850, 1859, 1862–1865.

gathered was checked against the files of Norsk Misjon blant Hjemløse —a special mission institution concerned with Taters. It must be emphasized that the quality of this "field work" is generally low—the visits I made have been brief, and it has proved extremely difficult to establish rapport with informants. Participation has so far been impossible, as constant police and mission surveillance has produced defensive barriers of suspicion and avoidance on the part of Taters.

Economic Niche

Economically, Taters may be regarded as a typical parasite group. Their livelihood is gleaned from a number of sources: they are tinkers and tinsmiths, they trade horses and watches and various worthless trifles, they beg and occasionally steal, and sometimes take temporary work in roadbuilding or in the winter with their horses they may work in the forests, while the women occasionally work as house-help on farms. They may temporarily gravitate to towns for the duration of special fairs and markets, but are found mostly in rural districts of fairly high population density. Most Taters are now semi-sedentary, in that they rent or even own a small hut where they spend the winter; in the summer, they travel widely, visiting each other or camping in the open. A recently introduced, crudely suppressive law banning horse-cart travel by Taters on public roads has modified the traditional mode of travel somewhat, and resulted in a greater use of bicycles and an acceleration of the tendency to acquire cars and trucks in the place of horses. In the areas where this change has taken place, the traditional interest in tinkering and watches is developed into a further specialty as makeshift mechanics.

Definition of Group

Taters thus form a despised group of very low economic standing—are indeed, a typical pariah section of the population. As such, the problem arises whether they constitute a true organized group within the larger Norwegian society, or whether the term Tater is merely a general label for a despised rural social status, sociologically comparable to "criminal" or "poor man". This problem is discussed by Heymowski[4] who points out the several, partly contradictory criteria for the ascription of individuals to the group—descent, mode of life, physical appearance—and draws attention to the great fluctuations between different census counts in the estimated number of Taters, based on ascription. Regardless of

4. Op. cit., pp. 4, 5.

such indefinite criteria for the ascriptive application of the term Tater, the question of the group's internal constitution is an empirical question, and must be seen from the Tater point of view. In fact, Taters themselves distinguish between members and outsiders; there is strong internal loyalty *vis-à-vis* the larger society; there is linguistic unity in that most Taters of E. Norway speak a (debased) Romani as home language;[5] and the group is able to persist and hold together in the face of considerable pressures, which, under the direction of the mission organization, have at times reached the magnitude of large-scale forced separation of children from parents, schooling and settlement centres for whole families, etc.

Problem

The problem of how such a group can persist, as reflected in how it is organized, becomes a question of some theoretical interest. Certain practical requirements must be satisfied: as an economic parasite group, the Tater population must be dispersed over a large area, as small local groups within an infinitely larger host population. Or, from the point of view of the individual Tater: in view of his manner of exploiting the environment, localization should be temporary and relatively exclusive, and he should have a wide net of potential contacts over a large territory. At the same time, to ensure the persistence of the group, one would expect features of organization regulating: (1) the recruiting of subgroups, (2) the organization of co-operating individuals—i.e., the internal organization and distribution of authority in corporate groups, and (3) the rights to utilize territories. These multiple requirements might seem difficult to satisfy, particularly since, in the presence of the established rural police system of the host population, no organized body can utilize force to maintain internal discipline. In fact, the organizing principles which are utilized, are mainly derived from relations of kinship, and are thus of a type frequently analysed by social anthropologists in numerous societies—the specific combination of factors is none the less uncommon.

PRINCIPLES OF FORMAL ORGANIZATION

The formal criterion for Tater status is descent from a known member of the category. This descent requirement is ideally patrilineal. But as there is no all-inclusive genealogical charter for the whole group, the

5. Words given in the text are, however, the Norwegian terms utilized by informants.

criterion of ancestral status as Tater must be the ancestor's remembered mode of life, and assimilation is thus possible: if a member of the sedentary population adopts the Tater way of life, he will always be known as an outsider; but his *descendants* of the second or third generation can point to a line of ancestors who lived like Taters, and thus validate their own membership in the group. Many Tater families trace descent from a farmer. On the contemporary level, none the less, Tater status is transferred patrilineally from one generation to the next.

Lineages

The principle of patrilineal succession is elaborated through remembered genealogies to define subgroups among Taters. Such subgroups are called *stamme* (tribe), *slekt* (family), *folk* (people), and consist ideally of all the known patrilineal descendants of a named common ancestor or ancestress, i.e., they constitute what are known as patrilineal lineages.[6] These lineages have proper names, often related to the name or some other characteristic of the apical ancestor. Storjohan-folket, the descendants of Stor-Johan, Lysgårdsfolket, descended from a son from the farm Lysgård, Nystufolket, descended from a woman who cleared land for a cottage ("Nystue") by the highway in N. Norway, etc. Lineages are the largest units that ever act as corporate groups. They are also the only persisting social groups in Tater social organization. They vary in depth, i.e., in the number of generations intervening between the common ancestor and the present adult generation, but are usually shallow, on the order of 3–4 generations. Some lineages may count as much as several hundred living members, others are quite small.

Bilateral Kinship

Each individual Tater also occupies a position in a net of formally recognized dyadic kinship relations. Taters invariably emphasize their deep emotional dependence and attachment ("warmth") towards all kin; this identification, with its constituting rights and obligations, is bilateral, and varies in intensity depending on the degree of relationship, not on whether such relationship is traced through women or men. Thus the inner circle of parents, siblings, and children form the central focus; but the field extends out to second and even third cousins. A necessary requirement for maintaining such extensive relations is the knowledge of widely ramifying genealogies; and indeed, no subject is more readily discussed with informants, nor given with a greater wealth of detail, than are genealogical charters.

6. Evans-Pritchard, E. E. (1940). *The Nuer*, London.

Affinal Relations

The importance of relationships established by marriage is not at all clear, though of considerable importance in this connection. Marriages established sets of relations between groups which might conceivably be utilized in organizing these groups, somewhat in the manner of bilateral kinship. However, this does not seem to be the case among Taters. The marriage tie between spouses, though rarely blessed in church, is ideally a permanent and lasting tie (*Når vi har slite ut den vi har teie, lyt vi vere fornøgd*—"When we have worn out the one we chose, we should be satisfied") However, this tie appears to remain an individual, dyadic tie between spouses, and does not involve other persons. I thus found no examples of persons coresiding by virtue of affinal relations through a person not present, nor did I hear of cases where individuals made visits to each other on such basis. A strong tendency towards near-family endogamy, which will be returned to later, may be related to tensions and the low degree of identification between otherwise unrelated affines.

Combination of Principles

It would seem from direct discussion with informants, and from the analysis of the various types of data collected, that the two formal principles: lineage, and bilateral kinship, are the only ones utilized in Tater organization. One might question the validity of conceptually distinguishing and speaking of lineage *and* bilateral kinship, as if the relations of lineage were not a subclass of the larger category of bilateral kinship relations. From the point of view of the type of framework they offer for the organization of a social group, they are however different. Patrilineal descent, as expressed in lineages, defines an invariant system of groups and segments, independent of the genealogical position of an "ego", as Evans-Pritchard has so lucidly shown. Bilateral kinship relations as a whole, on the other hand, constitute a net of dyadic relations, different for each sibling group. Though these two "principles" are derived from the single body of kinship relations, they give two different types of framework, which, as features of organization, may be conceptually separate, and may also be combined to produce a more complex social organization. When Taters identify groups made up of the patrilineal descendants of an ancestor as "tribes", they utilize the lineage principle to define social units with absolute limits and a pattern of internal segmentation. This framework is utilized in the relations of authority between persons, and in ordering the rights to exploit territories. When Taters simultaneously feel "warmth" and obligations towards all relatives, they utilize also the bilateral principle. In respect to territorial rights, both principles may be combined: a local lineage segment, with wives, recognizes the obligations of its component members to others by virtue of ties of bilateral kinship, and extends the rights to utilize the territory also to them according to that principle. Thus, by distinguishing between persons eligible and non-eligible to local group membership, bilateral kinship becomes an organizing principle added to, or combined with, that of lineage affiliation.

Territorial Groups

Lineages define permanent subgroups in the Tater population, and give, through their organizing genealogies, a pattern for authority distribution and internal segmentation. Bilateral kinship defines for each person a field, declining in intensity towards the borders, within which are found partners in dyadic relations of obligations and privilege. Through this combination, certain fluid, localized co-operating groups appear to be recruited and organized. These groups are (1) households, functioning as economic units, (2) wandering bands, temporarily camping together and co-operating on the road, (3) hamlets or local sections, sharing the temporary right to exploit a territory, and (4) localized tribes.

Households

Households vary in size from 2 to 12–15 individuals. Most Taters of E. Norway are semi-sedentary; they are stationary a major part of the year, when the members of a household live together in a usually one-room cottage. However, households persist as units also in periods of travelling and roaming in the summertime; they are independent of the physical structure of a house, and persist by virtue of a joint economy and commensality. Membership may be transferred from one household to another; there are no invariant and unbreakable affiliations, and members may be related to each other in various ways. However, small children almost invariably live with their mother, while persons unrelated by kinship or marriage very rarely coreside. In almost all cases where a census was taken, all members belonged to one extended family; but each household represented only a selection of the existing members of such a family. The two examples A and B (Fig. 1) illustrate most of the relations between members of a household, and how each is based on a combination of the formal principles of lineage and bilateral kinship. A, is a nearly pure lineage segment; B, represents a more

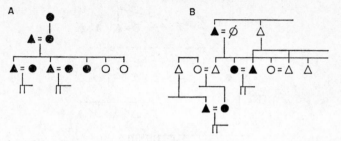

FIG. 1   A and B: Examples of households: triangles—males, circles—females, black—present in group. Horizontal lines continue where sibling group is incomplete.

complex combination of both criteria. Affinal relations, other than the marriage tie itself, never seems to play an independent role in building up the group.

Visiting

More secondary groupings are formed by the extensive Tater pattern of visiting, whereby the members of two or even more households temporarily fuse. Such visits take place at any time of the year, though not as frequently in the winter, and are of variable duration, sometimes leading to a more permanent grouping in a hamlet or local section. Visiting may take place between categories of relatives of nearly any kind, each bringing his or her whole household into the group. Most visits, however, take place between parents and children, siblings, and to less extent uncle/aunt and nephew/niece or between first cousins. Where unrelated persons are brought together by such visits, the chances of brawls and knife-fights occurring are considerable.

Bands

A similar, nowadays even more ephemeral and loosely structured grouping develops where two or more households meet on the road and temporarily join, forming a larger migrating band (*følgje*). These groups form for the sake of company, or for co-operation in begging, pilfering, or creating situations desirable for bartering and cheating. There may well be no kinship ties between the constituting households.

Hamlets or Local Sections

A single household of Taters does not generally have the exclusive right to utilize an area; such rights are temporarily vested in larger groups, and relate to moderately large areas. Within this area—usually a

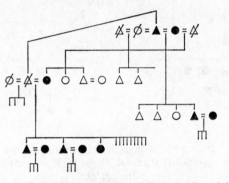

Fig. 2   A local section. The male in the upper right is leader of the group. Though they still reside close to each other, there is beginning fission. The widow and her sons (left) hesitate to recognize the authority of the leader. They have moved just across the border to a different rural police area (*lensmannsdistrikt*); the widow is strongly religious and trying to "pass". Some of her twelve children work and reside in Oslo.

naturally defined, heavily populated rural district—one finds a hamlet or a locally dispersed group of huts or cottages normally occupied by Taters. Two such groups are shown, in terms of their kinship composition, in Figs 2 and 3. Such colonies seem to develop through time by accretion around a single household or lineage core, as suggested in connection with the pattern of visiting. The order of appearance (by immigration) representing the growth of one such section over a period of twenty years, is indicated in Fig. 3. The implicit fluidity should be emphasized: it is easy to see how this group might, through further accretions and possible departures, shift from a centre of organization in the lineage 1–2–3–6 to being organized around the lineage represented by 4–4.

Each such local section has a formal leader, who, if the colony is large enough, is sometimes referred to as "king". The section is regarded by other Taters as a segment of the lineage to which its core belongs; no matter what the lineage membership of its other component members might be, it carries the name of the tribe of its lineage core. In the composition of such local groups, one may thus recognize the same organizing principles—lineage, and bilateral kinship—that were relevant to the composition of households. As noted above, affinal relations, other than the marriage tie between spouses, do not seem to play an independent role in building up the group. Persons are brought in by virtue of their kinship relation to one or the other of the central spouses, and purely affinal relationships, present in the Figs 1B and 2, are not made use of.

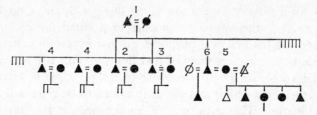

Fig. 3   A local section. Order of appearance by immigration is indicated by numbers. 1 started spending the winter in the area 30 years ago. 2 arrived nearly 20 years ago. 3 first arrived 13 years ago, bought a house nine years ago. 2 and 3 are working to become assimilated. 4, two households, arrived some years ago, rent a house for the winters. 5 left her husband's area when she became a widow, and spent about six months, partly in the neighbouring rural police area, before she became engaged to 6, about a year ago.

As in the case of households, it should also be noted here that only a fraction of the persons qualifying by the principles of lineage and bilateral kinship are in fact present in the group—nearly all members have full siblings living in other places.

Local sections defend their rights to utilize an area, and attempt to hold other Taters away. Since such rights are not legally recognized, the group can dispose only of informal sanctions, threats, and pressures. Where the districts of unrelated groups adjoin, there is usually an armed peace whereby neither group trespasses on the other's territory. Such arrangements are explicit: "If they cross the bridge, we will throw them in the river." When travelling, the central foci of unrelated groups are avoided.

Larger Regions

There is a further tendency for some major Tater lineages to concentrate each in its own region of Eastern Norway. Thus, the Stor-Johan lineage is found mostly in the lower valleys of E. Norway, Lysgårdsfolket travel in the upper valleys, Fredriksen-slekten lives mainly in the south-east, etc. Larger regions may be roughly on the order of 50 by 100 miles. Other lineages, however, have no such major localization, and appear sporadically in hamlets all over Eastern Norway and Trøndelag, or even all over the country.

Within larger areas controlled by a single lineage, fragments of other lineages are also often present. If these are small and unimportant groups, the pattern usually called matrilateral grafting (Evans-Pritchard 1940) is adopted: these non-lineage members remain in, or alternatively can enter, the area only through marriage with women of the dominant lineage; and they and their descendants come in time to be regarded as members of that lineage, though there is no fusing of genealogies. In other words, members of a small foreign patrilineal lineage become for practical purposes grafted on the dominant lineage by their descent from a woman of that lineage. This is a special case of persons added to the group according to the principle of bilateral kinship, and then converting this tie so it comes to be regarded as one of lineage affiliation. This pattern is of importance for the internal authority relations within the area. The small intrusive lineage in Fig. 1B, which forms a part of a local settlement of a large dominant lineage, is an example of one such grafted lineage.

It should be emphasized that this hierarchical classification of territorial groupings represents an idealization. Households grade into hamlets—it is difficult for the outsider to discover to what extent relatives, living in one-room cottages ten feet apart, have a joint economy. Further, local sections grade into larger lineage cores, with accretions, controlling larger regions. None the less, the outlines of a territorial system like that sketched above, are usually visible.

Functional Adaptations

A lineage system might be thought too rigid to give the fluidity that is functionally required in the Tater mode of life; their organization must give scope for much individual movement and a scattering of contacts. We have seen how these requirements are in part satisfied by the combination of the lineage principle with the principle of bilateral kinship, to organize the accretion of other persons around a lineage core. A purely demographic feature enters to make this all the more effective in multiplying the number of alternative group affiliations of each individual, and thus solving the problem of fluidity. Tater sibling groups are strikingly large; one documented partial genealogy, spectacular, but not unusual, is given in Fig. 4. Twenty-one carefully checked sibling groups give an average count of 6.8 individuals reaching maturity. As an economic parasite population, however, Taters must live dispersed— the local groups must be small, and the large sibling groups are thus forced to scatter. A married couple should on an average dispose of more than ten live siblings; only a fraction of these can, for purely practical reasons, live in the couple's own local group. There is thus a

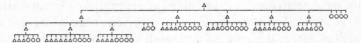
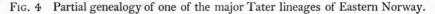

FIG. 4 Partial genealogy of one of the major Tater lineages of Eastern Norway.

necessary dispersal of immediate kin, giving contacts in numerous other small local groups. An elastic and fluid type of organization is essential for Taters. None the less, it can be satisfied within a lineage framework, due to this unusual disproportion between the size of sibling groups and the size of local groups. Each local group constitutes essentially a lineage core with accretions through matrilateral grafting and other bilateral kin ties. But, as emphasized in the discussion of territorial groups, each such group is made up, at any time, only of a *small fraction* of the individuals *potentially* eligible by those criteria. The average Tater couple will have siblings in more than ten different extended family households, and probably in nearly as many hamlets or local sections. Even strictly patrilineally, the minimal lineage segment of the husband will probably form the core in several different local groups. And proceeding to uncles, aunts, and cousins, the spread of contacts becomes tremendous. Within a semi-sedentary and formal framework, Taters can thus remain floating and mobile: households may form and dissolve and change, local sections may grow and shift, larger areas may maintain their unity and change their borders, while other large groups maintain a structure without any territorial localization—all within an organizing framework conbining the two principles of lineage affiliation, and affiliation through ties of bilateral kinship, with the demographic factor of large sibling groups.

Persistence

Certain aspects of the persistence of these groups have as yet not been discussed, mainly the distribution and transfer of authority, the system of marriage, and finally a demographic requirement leading on to the problem of mobility to and from the whole status group Tater.

Authority

To co-ordinate the actions of members of these social groups, one would expect established rules governing the distribution of authority within them. The ideal pattern, agreed on by all informants, is very simple and specific: the qualifications to leadership are male sex and seniority in the lineage by generation and by relative position in the sibling group. In view of the pressures Taters are subject to as a pariah group, the formal rigidity of this rule is probably highly functional. With the genealogical knowledge of Taters, it leaves no room for competing pretenders and factionalism—external police interference prevents co-ordination within the group by means of force, at the same time various institutions and groups in the sedentary population are ready to take advantage of any internal conflicts within Tater groups, to the detriment of both conflicting parties. Factional conflicts within the fluid Tater organization are thus solved by migration rather than power struggle, and *de facto* authority distribution can remain in full congruence with the ideal pattern. Thus, if a son no longer recognizes the authority of his father, he leaves the local group of his father, and attaches himself to another group with a more congenial leader; similarly, a younger brother who cannot accept the authority of his senior brother, will depart to another group, and maybe seek or establish a local section where he, by virtue of his relative seniority, holds authority.

The only problem arises in the case of seniority over whole lineages, with claims to authority beyond that of a local group. Characteristically, such status as leader or "king" of a tribe is more talked about by sedentary romantics than by Taters, and seems to be an ineffectual and usually bogus affair. Whole lineages normally come together only at funerals of some importance, and very rarely co-ordinate for example economic activities. In the known cases where a "king" has been able to control a dispersed lineage with any degree of effectiveness, he has in fact been the apical ancestor of that lineage—the authority of lineal, generational seniority is much stronger than that of lateral seniority between brothers. Thus, the lineages segment as effective "political" groups at the death of the common apical ancestor; though nominal kingship may be transferred to his eldest son at the funeral, the whole lineage ceases to function as a corporate unit.

In summary: the authority instrumental in co-ordinating the actions of members of local groups is regulated by lineage seniority between males; this ideal rule is maintained through the departure from the local group of persons not recognizing such authority. Wider authority beyond such local limits is rare, and depends on the continued respect of sons for their fathers—these patterns of authority are clearly related to the pariah status of the group, that is, its economic and social position in the host population.

Marriage Patterns

In a semi extended-family organization like that of Taters, any marriage has consequences for a large group of persons, and one might expect organized patterns serving to regularize a set of inter-group relations. The only pattern that has so far emerged from my material and analysis, is one of close kin endogamy: parallel cousins, cross cousins—marriage with *any* close relative outside the elementary family. Heymowski,[7] on

7. Op. cit., especially Appendix 4 and 5.

a statistical material far larger than mine, utilizes a genetic coefficient of inbreeding and arrives at striking figures for the Taters of Sweden. Of greater sociological importance would be statistical manipulations of this material to discover specific preferential patterns. The informants emphasize the importance of equality between spouses: that the one should not regard his or her status and family as being more distinguished, richer, more important than that of the other. Structurally, one might see endogamous choices as a defence against the multiple potential demands of bilateral relatives of the spouse—people who, if the spouse is not a relative, are complete strangers to ego and his group, while they would, if the spouse is a relative, be those with which ego is himself already reciprocally identified. A further clarification of such and other factors is required.

Social Mobility

A study of some of the problems connected with the demography of the Tater population would require vast material spanning a considerable time depth. None the less, certain crucial features are self-evident. The lineage growth illustrated in Fig. 4, indicates a very high rate of self-reproduction for the group. According to the estimates of Norsk Misjon blant Hjemløse, the number of Taters in Norway is declining. In Sweden, on the other hand, there is some (questionable) evidence that the Tater population is growing (cf., Heymowski, pp. 4–6); but nowhere is there a question of it growing by a factor of 3.4 (half of the average adult sibling group) pr. generation. Unless this reproductive rate is a recent phenomenon—and deeper genealogies give no evidence of this—population pressure within the Tater group must be relieved, and the high rate of reproduction balanced, by social mobility. In other words, in every generation a large number of Taters are assimilated in the host population.

The problem of "passing"—becoming assimilated in the sedentary population—are of major concern to a considerable fraction of the Taters I interviewed. Psychologically, in terms of the ambivalent attitudes which contribute to the motivation in each case, the problems of passing are indeed complex. A purely structural description of the elements in the process is however deceptively simple: the mechanism is essentially one of non-participation in Tater life, centering around the non-fulfilment of kinship duties. There are no complicating barriers of physical appearance or language. For the sedentary Tater in a rural district, the conflict and dilemma is one of family pressures and identification—close relatives who come to visit, who settle in the community and try to utilize you as a local contact—vs. the pressures exerted by sedentary neighbours, and the desire to become accepted by them. Passing here seems to be preceded and accompanied by the adoption of a fiercely puritan and"bourgeois" explicit code of propriety. Failures in the attempt revert to Tater life. A maybe simpler avenue of mobility is urbanization and assimilation into the ranks of unskilled or semi-skilled labour. In the urban setting, family pressures are reduced, though the technical problems of a new milieu are greater. Failures in these attempts are lost in the marginal urban world of bums, alcoholics, prostitutes, and criminals. The summing-up is strikingly unanimous, and is given both by those who are in the process of becoming assimilated, and those who dare not embark on the attempt: "The difficulty with settling down is you are on your own, you have to stand on your own two feet—no one to help you, no kin to fall back on."

Summary

The present paper summarizes some results derived from the attempted application of social anthropological viewpoints to the study of *Taters*— a Gypsy-like vagabond population in Eastern Norway. The primary attention centred around the social organization of this pariah group. Taters maintain themselves as an economic parasite group within the larger host population. They thus form a thinly dispersed, floating population; their organization must be elastic and adaptable, and offer the wide net of contacts desirable in a roaming mode of life. The basic framework of organization is the patrilineal lineage. Local groups— households, hamlets, local sections, and local tribes—are structured around a lineage core, but form by accretion along lines of bilateral kinship. Thus both patrilineal lineage, and bilateral kinship, serve as organizing principles in regulating group membership. The functionally required elasticity of the system depends on the unusual discrepancy between the size of sibling groups and local groups—sibling groups are very large, and are forced to disperse because of the small economically optimal size of Tater local groups. Each local group consists thus of only a small *fraction* of the persons eligible to group membership by the two principles of organization; each person thus has a number of alternative groups to which he may belong. Territorial localization is temporary, and the many contacts are maintained by a pattern of visiting, and knowledge of widely ramifying genealogies. The organization thus defines a framework with the required high degree of elasticity, by means of these simple principles. Within this framework, authority can further be regulated by the simple rules of lineage seniority, since conflicts may be solved by separation rather than competition. Factional struggles within local groups, destructive to a pariah group under constant police pressure, are thus to some extent avoided.

Several other problems, among them the high incidence of close family endogamy, and the necessity for, and mechanisms of, social mobility, spring more clearly into focus on the background of such viewpoints. The scope for more detailed and penetrating study should be considerable.

GLOSSARY and INDEX

Ardener, S., 62
Ayers, G., 5

Baro (Big Man), 49
Báro Devel (Great God), 144, 145, 149, 155–166, 169–170
Barth, F., 60, 63, 222
Baxt (Theme of ritual and doctrine, also good luck), 47
Beng (The Devil), 147, 148
Bengalimata (Lit. Drink with the Devil–Epilepsy), 148
Boyash (Rumanian Gypsies), 5
Bridewealth, 27, 239
Bujo (switching the bag), 17
Burkers (body snatchers), 279–280

Caravan Site Act, 1968, 58
Clébert, J. P., 21, 46, 202, 205, 206
Cotten, G. R. M., 1, 2, 12, 21, 53

Death and Funerals, 18, 116–118, 156–160, 176–177, 247
Debleskri-Daj (The Virgin Mary), 146
Definition of Membership, 61, 231, 271, 286–287, 287–288
Didikois (given a variety of meanings. By outsiders used to refer to half-breeds or "bad" Gypsies. The Gypsies use the term with a pejorative implication to refer to their enemies or rivals), 59, 60
Diwano (Discussions held to solve problems or the group that takes part in the discussion), 3, 53
Dji (Heart-Spirit), 143

Douglas, M., 41
Dubled, H., 140

Economic Activities, 6, 16–18, 21–39, 45, 65–68, 72–75, 86, 88–91, 125, 126, 133, 177–180, 188–189, 207, 242–243, 249–252, 258–263, 265–266, 269, 275, 276, 278, 281–282, 286
Education, 77–78, 254, 292
Eliade, M., 21
Ellis, W., 57
Evans, E., 233

Falgje (Norwegian Tutare band), 291
Family and Kinship, 75–77, 99–107, 109, 134–138, 171, 280–283, 287–291
Familiyi or *Familia* (extended Family), 3, 52, 78–81, 176, 180–188
Fanon, F., 203
Flatties (used by Scots Tinkers to refer to all outsiders), 273, 274, 275, 276, 277

Gaje or *Gorgio* (Non-Gypsy), (includes Gajo-Gypsy relations), 1, 20–22, 45–48, 50, 57–59, 62, 63–66, 82–83, 95, 107–109, 124, 127, 139, 166, 190–192, 211–212, 249, 271, 273–280, 295, 297–298
Gammin (Irish Travellers' language), see also Shelte, 258
Gitanos (Spanish Gypsies), 169
Genealogies, 11, 12, 288, 291, 292, 293, 294
Gossip, 50
Gurkwe (Gypsy Kin group), 7, 10

Harper, J., 258
Harvey, D. E., 86
Heusch, Luc van de, 140
Housing and Local Govt., Ministry of,
    Circular 6/62, 58
Hoyland, J., 58, 59, 69
Hudson, C., 258

Jones, G., 29

Kalderash (A Tribe or Nation of Rom),
    22, 53, 125, 140
Kashtare (Gypsy Kin group), 8, 9, 10
Kenrick, D., 124, 212
Kidemos (collections for needy), 23–25
Kornblum, W., 124
Kris Romani (Gypsy tribunal), 2–3, 18,
    51, 53, 149
Kumpania (economic and spacial group-
    ing), 1, 2, 3, 4, 5, 18, 20, 23, 24, 28
    functions of, 3
Kuneshti (Gypsy kin group), 7, 9, 10

Lachi or Lache (Spanish, see Shame)
Lāj (Shame), 154–156
Lee, R., f.n. 1, 2, 3, 22, 23
Legal system, 113
Lameshti (Gypsy kin group), 10
Lavoro (division of a collection), 27
Leland, C. G., 233
Life cycle rituals, 3
Lineages, 288, 292, 293, 294, 295
Lowara (a tribe or nation), 3

MacAlister, S., 233
Machawaya or Machvaia (a tribe or
    nation of the Gypsies), 5, 8, 9, 10,
    29, 53
MacNeil, E., 232
Mānuš (Alsatian and Rhineland Gyp-
    sies), 139
Marime (rejected, defilement, or pollu-
    tion), 19, 27, 28, 41–57
Marriage and Sex Roles
    American Gypsies, 3, 10, 44
    Spanish, 176, 180–186
    Irish Travellers, 231, 237, 238–241,
        259–260, 261–269
    Scots Travellers, 280–281, 281–283
    Norwegian Travellers, 296–297
Marriage, with outsiders, 59–60
Maximoff, M., 140
Meker, K., 233

Mikailesti or Micheleshti (a Gypsy kin
    group), 6, 10
Miller, Barbara, 4, 5
Mineshti (A Gypsy kin group), 16
Ministry of Local Govt., Gypsies and
    Other Travellers, 68, 74, 86, 87, 101
Mulo (ghosts), 158–159, 161, 162–166
Murin, S., 12

O'Donovan, J., 233
O Fisa (fortune telling premises), 26
Okely, J., 61, 62, 66

Patrin (signs left on the road to give
    information to those following),
    234
Payo (Spanish G. Non-Gypsy), see
    Gajo
Phurotem (the elders), 44
Physical appearance and clothing of
    Irish Travellers, 236–237
Police, relations with, 6, 7, 21, 95,
    107–109
Pomana (death feast), 8, 12, 18, 24, 48
Population, 68, 69, 231, 257
Postarni Ko (people obsessed by the
    need for a particular food), 49
Puri dai (old mother or grandmother),
    143
Purity and Impurity, 42–54, 62–63,
    149–157, 156–158, 162
Puxton, G., 124, 202, 212

Rehfisch, F., 61
Relation of Scots Travellers with
    Gypsies, 272–273
Religion and Supernatural Beliefs, 115,
    142–154, 157, 243–244, 247–249,
    280
Renisch (A marginal population of un-
    known origin, many found in
    Alsace), 139
Rom (Husband or adult Gypsy male), 1
Romania (Gypsy law and ceremonial
    behaviour), 3
Romanitchal (a Gypsy kin group), 10

Sampson, J., 233
Saville, J., 87
Scandal, 50
Settlement pattern, and Housing Con-
    ditions, 5–12, 97–99, 128, 141,
    208, 254–255

Shame, 154–156, 194–197

Shelte or *Shelta* (Irish Travellers' language), 233–234

Sinté (see *Mānuš*), 139

Slava (Saint's day Feast), 18, 21, 24, 48

Spree makers (Marriage makers), 239

Socialization, 77–78, 244–245

Tater (A Gypsy-like group in Norway), 285

Television, 120, 121, 277

Thompson, E. P., 202

Tinkers, Irish, 59

Tomkins, J., 7, 25, 26, 28, 39

Travelling, 11–20, 55–57, 70–75, 87 (f.n.), 87–97, 109–110, 125, 132– 133, 134, 141–142, 177–180, 215– 221

Tsera (tents or households), 3

Tserha (category of kin), 2

Vesey-Fitzgerald, B., 68

Vitsa (category of kin), 2

Ward-Jackson, C. H., 86

Welfare, 5, 29–38, 38–39, 170

Weybright, V., 12

World View, Scots Travellers, 273–278

Worfacha (partners), 1, 3, 22, 23, 27

Yoors, J., 2, 51